The Oxford I
Malayalam Dalit Writing

'The sun of our land used to set there.'
—S. Kalesh

'Words that blossomed from the fury of lowly ones, swirled like a cyclone within the stone walls of the church on the hill. Were the walls shaking?'
—Paul Chirakkarode

'The grass has its own grievances and so do the plants. ... The birds, the squirrels, the hedgehogs, the thieving owls ... let them eat. ... It is they who really own the land.'
—P.A. Uthaman

'How can we assemble? We sweat blood to grow rice, coconut and other crops. Yet if we are not allowed to walk on that soil, to assemble somewhere or to form an organization. ...
Every day after college work was over, Karuppan master would arrive on the lake in a small boat. Pulayas and others from all the nearby stretches of land assembled in little boats. The boats were bound together to form a platform. Seated in them, they discussed their future plans. The main goal of these discussions was to create a Pulaya organization.
—T.K.C. Vaduthala

On a Sabbath day
when God was on holiday.
Out of their settlements were they
driven out, dispossessed.
—Kaviyoor Murali

The Oxford India Anthology of
Malayalam Dalit Writing

edited by

M. Dasan
V. Pratibha
Pradeepan Pampirikunnu
C.S. Chandrika

OXFORD
UNIVERSITY PRESS

OXFORD
UNIVERSITY PRESS

Oxford University Press is a department of the University of Oxford.
It furthers the University's objective of excellence in research, scholarship, and education by publishing worldwide. Oxford is a registered trademark of Oxford University Press in the UK and in certain other countries

Published in India by
Oxford University Press
YMCA Library Building, 1 Jai Singh Road, New Delhi 110 001, India

© Oxford University Press 2012

The moral rights of the author have been asserted

First Edition published in 2012

All rights reserved. No part of this publication may be reproduced, stored in a retrieval system, or transmitted, in any form or by any means, without the prior permission in writing of Oxford University Press, or as expressly permitted by law, by licence, or under terms agreed with the appropriate reprographics rights organization. Enquiries concerning reproduction outside the scope of the above should be sent to the Rights Department, Oxford University Press, at the address above

You must not circulate this book in any other form
and you must impose this same condition on any acquirer

ISBN-13: 978-0-19-807940-8
ISBN-10: 0-19-807940-0

Typeset in Adobe Garamond Pro 10.5/12.5
by Sai Graphic Design, New Delhi 110 055
Printed in India at Artxel, New Delhi 110 020

Contents

Editors' Note   ix

General Introduction   xiii

POETRY

POIKAYIL APPACHAN
Songs by Poikayil Appachan   5

K.K. GOVINDAN
The Killing Field   6

KAVIYOOR MURALI
The Gospel for Dalits   7

K.K.S. DAS
My Soil   14
The Black Dance   15

RAGHAVAN ATHOLI
Justice Cooked   17
Where Hunger is Sold   19

SUNNY KAVIKKAD
An Uncharted Map   21

G. SASI MADHURAVELI
With Love   22
Mother   23

S. JOSEPH
Group Photo   24
Some Dark Spaces   25

SIVADAS PURAMERI
Some Types of Fingers   27
A Leaky Room   29

M.R. RENUKUMAR
The Silent Beast 30
The Poison Fruit 32

M.B. MANOJ
Survey of India 33
Mothers 35
O Ant, O Paddystalk 36

VIJILA
A Place for Me 37
I Can't Grow My Nails 38
The Autobiography of a Bitch 39

BINU M. PALLIPPAD
Six Philosophers Unite to Exclude Amavasi from the Play 40

S. KALESH
Hairpin Bend 43
Siren 44
Not because She Felt Like Weeping 46

SHORT FICTION

T.K.C. VADUTHALA
Sweet-offering at Chankranthy 53

PAUL CHIRAKKARODE
Nostalgia 61

C. AYYAPPAN
Madness 68

P.A. UTHAMAN
The Story of a Sickle 71

P.K. PRAKASH
Luminous White 80

M.K. MADHUKUMAR
Paalakkunnan's Journey 81

EXCERPTS FROM NOVELS

T.K.C. VADUTHALA
When Shackles Break 91

D. RAJAN
   The Festival at Muthan Kavu   105

PAUL CHIRAKKARODE
   The Pulaya Ghetto   122

P.A. UTHAMAN
   The Death Wail   139

RAGHAVAN ATHOLI
   Legacy of Blood   148

DRAMA

A. SANTHAKUMAR
   Dreamhunt   169

LIFE WRITINGS: AUTOBIOGRAPHY AND BIOGRAPHY

KALLEN POKKUDAN
   My Life (Excerpts)   185

VELAYUDHAN PANIKKASSERI
   Excerpts from Ayyankali   197

K.T. REJIKUMAR
   Poikayil Sreekumara Guru—A Historical Record
   (Excerpts)   212

T.H.P. CHENTHARASSERI
   Pampadi John Joseph (Excerpts)   218

ELIKULAM JAYAKUMAR
   Kallara Sukumaran   222

TAHA MADAYI
   Adiyar Teacher   230

CRITICAL INTERVENTIONS

KAVIYOOR MURALI
   The Uncompromising Dalit Language   243

K.K. KOCHU
   Language and People   248

A. SOMAN
The Return of the *Thampurans*   256

SUNNY M. KAPIKKAD
The Dalit Presence in Malayalam Literature   259

SANAL MOHAN
Caste and Accumulation of Capital   267

K.K. BABURAJ
Identity, Alienation, Expression: Dalit Writing in Kerala   277

PRADEEPAN PAMPIRIKUNNU
What did Literary Histories Say to You?   280

LOVELY STEPHEN
The Issue of Self-liberation   284

REKHA RAJ
Dalit Women and Political Empowerment   290

Glossary   295

Note on Authors   301

Note on Translators   311

Copyright Statement   317

Editors' Note

This anthology has its origin in our friendship with Mini Krishnan of Oxford University Press (OUP) who drew our attention to the distinct lack of anthologies in this particular area. Unlike most anthologies compiled and edited to serve a preconceived set of expectations, this is a collection of voices that had hardly been heard so far and that have been missing from the readers' understanding of Kerala society and Malayalam literature. We went through a long process of discovery, listing people who could make significant contributions as well as locating efficient translators who could do justice to the source texts and more importantly to the ideology central to Dalit experiences of life and thus to their art. At least half of them were Mini's friends who soon became our friends as well. Our circle expanded with every such link.

Today, Dalit literature which draws its energy from engaging with a deeply embedded anti-caste sentiment and approach has become an inevitable part of Kerala's socio-scape. It could also be said to have played its own role in the democratizing process of a national-linguistic culture and in diversifying the very concept of a conventional aesthetics. Traditional standards of literary excellence in no way prepares a reader for the complexities of responses the writings included here will evoke. Readers will discover the limitations of their reading practices as they encounter the emotional, intellectual, and aesthetic demands of this collection and might feel uncomfortable at the challenge it poses as they realize their complicity with the status quo. These selections will also bring the mainstream critics and reviewers face to face with their own prejudices, who, insufficiently equipped to understand or accept the truth of Dalit experiences and perspectives, often label this body of writings 'bitter', 'biased', 'militant', 'angry', etc., and, might, therefore, have dismissed it as not serious 'literary' writing. Most Indian publishers, also influenced by such views, have also always controlled what was published. It is in this context that the significance of this venture by OUP becomes clear. It will enable and facilitate the historical process of bringing forth these long silenced and neglected voices from the fringes of Kerala society into the worldwide literary firmament.

We have tried our best to trace the trajectory of Dalit writings in Kerala right from its beginning to its current diverse state. We have also taken care to incorporate and integrate its historical evolution and the multifarious discourses reflected in them, marking the spread and vibrancy of this growing body of literature. Varied literary genres and approaches have also been explored which demonstrate a wide range of values, attitudes, experiences, and perspectives. While we cast the net ambitiously we were also in a position to include a large number of writers from disparate sources, so that no single reader is likely to have read them all; we hope that everyone will find something new in this collection.

Diversity is at the heart of this anthology. But it is interesting that this range is showcased in the service of a unifying concept of cultural recuperation and rediscovery of indigenous traditions. No reader will fail to recognize the deeply-held commitment to Dalit heritage, culture, and tradition of our anthology. It reiterates that there is no monolithic Dalit literature. The compilation of individual works into an interesting and varied anthology, we feel, is much more than the sum of its parts.

Today there are innumerable Dalit writers in Malayalam who are surging forward with different linguistic techniques and strategies not to mention specificities associated with their castes and sub-castes. We feel some satisfaction that we were able to represent most of these polyphonies in this anthology. True, some writers and pieces had to be left out; even so, we believe we have been able to accommodate the essence of even these missing writers, and their inner turmoils and conflicts. When we began work in January 2010 we were confronted with chaos—missing texts, elusive books, writers without addresses—but chaos was a source of vitality in the preparation of this book. The work of compiling and editing this book has been very exciting because of the people we met, the friends we have made, the joy of teamwork, and also because of the intrinsic value of the collection. As a team of editors, our talents complemented one another's and by the grace of the spirit of our ancestors, we have been able to channel it all into the making of this anthology. In this creative process we found a power of integration which went beyond our caste identities.

We would like to share our appreciation and gratitude to the generous financial support from Government of Kerala, to A.K. Balan, former Minister for Scheduled Caste/Scheduled Tribe and Other Backward Communities Welfare; M.A. Baby, former Minister for Education and Culture; and Paul Antony (IAS), former Secretary, SC/ST Development

Department. We are particularly grateful to Mini Krishnan for the faith she showed in us and for inviting us to edit the anthology, for being the master brain behind this project, for her constructive criticism and patience, and for her 24×7 commitment, and obsession with the work amidst all her other projects. Our thanks are also due to Kerala Sahitya Akademi, Thrissur, for helping us to access numerous obscure texts, and to the solidarity of many Dalit writers, critics, and activists who encouraged us, listened to us, and offered invaluable critical advice. We would also like to record our appreciation of P.V. Anil Kumar, Assistant Professor, Government Arts College, Thrissur, for his unending support, help, and extraordinary commitment to Dalit causes; K.S. Madhavan, Assistant Professor, Department of History, University of Calicut, for sharing his insights about the Dalit world around us; and Anitha, who helped shape many parts of this anthology so impeccably from the almost indecipherable scripts we gave her. We also remember Isabel Fernandes, who was always there, a ready reckoner when it came to authors, details, and dates, and many others who were a source of inspiration to us.

With immense pleasure we present the English-reading public worldwide with this selection of Malayalam Dalit literary expressions which reflects the truth of the Dalit as an individual as well as the truth about his/her entire community.

M. DASAN
V. PRATIBHA
PRADEEPAN PAMPIRIKUNNU
C.S. CHANDRIKA

General Introduction

'For darkness to write history, I offer my eyes'*

The Oxford India Anthology of Malayalam Dalit Writing in English translation was planned to demonstrate to English readers worldwide the political and aesthetic difference between this Other writing which has not received its due attention and Kerala mainstream writing which has already been widely translated. This anthology attempts to chart a history and sensibility which has remained unrepresented in the canonical tradition of Malayalam literary discourse. The editorial team has compiled a selection of creative and critical interventions representing diverse genres, themes, styles, and aesthetic and ideological positions.

What I intend here is to offer a highly compressed historical, cultural, and social context of Malayalam Dalit writing hoping that it will provide the reader the logical and conceptual framework of the selections and help him/her gain a better understanding of this hitherto marginalized discourse.

Dalit Discourse: Breaking the Silence

Even though the word 'Dalit' in the sense in which it is used in this anthology was prevalent in other parts of India, especially Maharashtra, as early as the 1920s as part of the movements spearheaded by Jyotiba Phule and Bhim Rao Ambedkar, it appeared in the socio-cultural milieu of Kerala only in the late 1970s. The late appearance of the term in Kerala has much to do with the particular trajectory of 'Renaissance' that the state underwent which succeeded in camouflaging and silencing many discourses besides the marginalized. Whenever such attempts at silencing failed, the hegemonic/casteist discourse would appropriate the marginalized voices in a form acceptable to the hegemonizer. The proof of this brutal silencing and appropriation is reflected in the works

---

* Sunny Kavikkad, 'An Unchartred Map', translated by Catherine Thankamma.

of none other than Amartya Sen, who, unaware of its hidden caste-conflicts, theorized the politics of Kerala praising the 'Kerala experience' because its human development indices matched that of developed countries despite its poor per capita income.

The 1980s were the years when Dalits in Kerala started realizing that they had been the perennial victims and outsiders of the developmental and welfare discourses controlled intermittently by the Right and Left camps, both of which have international promoters. So the question that arises naturally is: What prevented Dalits from realizing that they were excluded from the Kerala dream of a liberated, classless society? This dream created a mirage that once a classless society was realized and established, it would end all other exploitative and dominating social structures. This 'Kerala-Renaissance' dream had the power to lure Dalits and they took it for granted that the struggle for liberation had only one form: the struggle against class exploitation.

If we trace Kerala's socio-cultural history to the 19th century, we are presented with a double face. While, at the turn of the 20th century, it helped the consolidation of community identity and modernization of the upper caste and the cream of the OBCs (Other Backward Communities), especially the Ezhavas, it precluded the same in the case of the lower castes. When many similar caste collectives with different caste names grouped under the umbrella terms Nair and Ezhava and consolidated their power, Dalits remained fragmented as castes and sub-castes. At a later stage in Kerala's history, the elite communities and castes which had earlier consolidated their position through identity politics, transformed their accumulated energies into nation-building politics and class politics. In 1891, a mass petition known as the Malayali Memorial submitted a memorandum to the Maharaja of Travancore. It admitted a representation of all native Malayali populations and was signed by more than 10,000 Namboodiris, Nairs, Thiyas, Syrian and native Christians, East Indian, Eurasian landlords, merchants, and officials. It called for reservation for Malayalis in various government positions. It did not mention either Dalits or tribals. Were they not Malayalis? This exclusion enabled the elite classes to promote their own material and cultural bias, an empowerment they saw as their birthright. In this altered social discursive space, talking about one's caste was tantamount to being reactionary because it was seen as divisive (that is, against the spirit of the unified nation with only one interest) and retrogressive. It was fashionable to say that one did not practise casteism. Caste was a non-issue, class and class enmities were the main issues.

Thus, by masking caste in the public realm through a 'progressive' discourse based on class, the upper castes made sure that the cultural, symbolic, and social capitals which their elite caste status had conferred upon them were not visible.

How do we explain this politics of double standards of the upper-caste reformers, of their being progressive within the community and reactionary outside it, especially in matters of caste relations? We need to understand the attempt of the elite upper castes to overcome the anxiety created by the wave of colonial modernity which stirred in them insecurities and fears that they would lose the privileges they had taken for granted. Just as the colonizer needed the colonized to maintain the former's sense of enlightened superiority, so too the upper castes needed the inferior castes to shore up their own sense of worth. They never accepted and addressed conventions and superstitions as the problem of society as a whole. For them, it was just a community problem. So the dream of emancipation was limited to internal reforms.

Early Dalit Movements

In contrast to this, the Dalit politics of the period took a different form with a different vision of emancipation. One of the prominent movements of the lower caste was the Sadhujana Paripalana Sangam (Organization for the Welfare of the Marginalized). Instituted in 1907, this movement captures some of the ecstatic moments of the Dalit vision. Whereas the Bhakti movement conceptualized equality as 'equality before God', the foundation here was the physical and raw agony of caste life. An equal political space within the emerging liberal scenario of colonial modernity was what was envisioned. Starting from the material and caste circumstances of Travancore, this movement developed into a form where modern citizenship became inevitable. The political struggles focused on the right to education. There was also a stress on 'cleanliness', which was denied to the Dalits by social edicts that prevented Dalits from attaining the means to this same state: clean clothes and water to wash in.

Even before Ambedkar, Ayyankali, the leader of the Sadhujana movement, realized that the essence of social justice was freedom. He challenged the casteist embargo on Dalits using public roads by travelling in a 'villuvandi' along the prohibited road. He conceptualized freedom in a radically new way: it was not through mercy, he said, but through action that freedom is created. The fashioning of the Dalit body itself was an action. In contrast to the Dalit body formulated discursively by the elite community, where it was marked by subservient postures to every form of feudal lordship, Ayyankali acted out the posture of the *thampuran**. He wore clean, white clothes, a turban—the symbol of aristocracy—and sat cross-legged and erect in the bullock-cart he rode. He rebelled openly. With these gestures he subverted the bodily lexis constructed by the dominant discourse, showing a remarkable understanding on his part of the statement that 'the personal is political'. The Dalit understanding of everyday politics and the urge for liberation through action could also be located in the 'Kallumala Struggle', where Dalit women refused to be the mute objects of history. They broke the *kallumala*† in public, chains they had been forced to wear to signal their caste status. They did this with a firm pledge that they would never wear such chains again.

Ayyankali's politics was about the emancipation of all the oppressed people and a radical transformation of the whole of society. The 'Sadhujanams', as formulated by Ayyankali, was the conceptualization of the broken people (Dalits), locating them as the agents of history, as the producers of material wealth. In other words, the labour or workpower and oppressed/depressed identity of the 'Sadhujanam' became a negotiating signifier. And herein lies one of the significant treacheries of the elitist reality and historiography. This radical agitator, who dreamed of the emancipation of the oppressed, was labelled the 'Pulaya King' and not a Malayali hero, by none other than Mahatma Gandhi, a term which instantly distanced Ayyankali from the Dalit communities he was seeking to emancipate.

The most interesting fact about Kerala's official historiography which was framed in tune with Marxist positivism is that it failed to historicize the dichotomy of reform and renaissance and instead wrote the national past of the upper castes as the history of 'colonial modernity' and 'social reform' of Kerala as a whole. This is why Ayyankali, who fought for a casteless society, is still regarded as a 'community reformer' whereas community reformers like V.T. Bhattathiripad and Mannath Padmanabhan, who spent most of their energy in consolidating and

---

* *Thampuran*: Term of reference or address denoting upper-caste landlord or aristocrat.

† *Kallumala*: Dalit women were not permitted to cover their upper body. Instead they were forced to wear several chains of shells and stones; the number of beads/stones in the chains was a sign of the woman's age.

modernizing their respective communities, are hailed as major progressive figures of Kerala. Ayyankali never visited the Sri Padmanabha temple after it was open to Dalits through the 'Temple-Entry Proclamation', (1936) despite it being near his residence, proving that in Ayyankali's vision of Dalit emancipation, temple entry was not a paramount issue. The contemporary Dalit reading of the Temple-Entry Proclamation regards it as an attempt by the rulers and the national leadership to prevent Dalits from embracing other religions and to contain them in the Hindu-fold. In mainstream Kerala historiography's elite politics, rooted in the fear of a possible loss of prestige, this proclamation is hailed as one of the supreme moments of the region's 'renaissance'. Whereas the spirit of western renaissance lay in its opposition to papacy, priesthood and the authority of the established religion, the renaissance spirit hailed by Malayali historians is quite the opposite: what it celebrated was no renaissance at all for Dalits. They continued to be trapped in priesthood and upper-caste superstitions. This could be the reason for the ambivalence shown by the post-renaissance Dalit identity in Kerala in its inability to even imagine a self-liberated Dalitness freeing itself from the deep shadow of Hindutva.

It was because of Ayyankali's anti-caste approach that the Sadhujana Paripalana Sangam could not become a decisive force in the post-Independence parliamentary politics. Distance from that time makes it clear that Ayyankali denied himself the power he might have gained had he collaborated with upper-caste politicians. The caste reforms, anti-landlordism, and community consolidation that began in the second half of the 19th century in Kerala is today known as progressive and liberal politics. One of the other significant political events in the history of the Dalit struggle, which is conveniently ignored and silenced by elitist historiography, is the struggle Ayyankali led in 1907 for the right to education. Though illiterate, Ayyankali realized the radical potential of education. In his scheme of things, education was understood as the means through which social and cultural capitals could be attained and Dalit liberation be realized. What is fascinating about Ayyankali's struggle for education is that when he took two Dalits to school for the first time, they were girls, the politics of which was modern by any standards.

When his demand for education for a people who had been blocked from formal learning for centuries was denied by the caste system, he called for an agrarian strike, the kind of which is unique in world history and has been taken up many times in later political struggles of the region. In this novel struggle, he reversed the usual strategy of the feudal lords punishing the lower caste bonded agricultural 'slaves'. Previously, whenever there was a conflict, the landlords would starve their landless labourers by denying them work in paddy fields. In Ayyankali's plan, Dalits risked starvation and voluntarily stayed away from field-work till their demand for education was met. This year-long refusal to work eventually led to the emptying of the landlords' granaries. Thus, this illiterate, who could not have heard of Marx, not only taught the feudal landowners what labour was and what it meant, but also defined it critically and used it to engage with colonial modernity to attain citizenship in the emerging democratic social space.

A Dalit reading of dominant historiography would also reveal a series of other erasures: Poikayil Appachan's PRDS (Prathyaksha Raksha Daiva Sabha), Pampadi John Joseph's ATCS (Akhila Thiruvithamkur Cheramar Sangham), and K.P. Vallon's KPM (Kochi Pulaya Mahasabha), SEEDIAN (Socially, Economically, Educationally Depressed Indian Ancient Natives), Janakeeya Vimochana Viswa Prasthanam, and Adasthitha Navodhana Munnani are telling instances. Of these, SEEDIAN was a radical Dalit movement formed in the 1970s in response to the failure of the Indian Left to address the issue of caste within the analytical framework of classical Marxism. Breaking away from the Left, this intellectual collective began to theorize Indian social reality drawing on both Ambedkarism and Marxism. Their method was to rewrite dominant history and retrieve Dalit cultural life and past. In fact, SEEDIAN was the first attempt in the history of modern Kerala in which a concerted move to build up a theoretical basis for Dalit liberation was taken up. Simultaneously, there were parallel moves within the extreme Left also. They formed small radical collectives with an aim to address issues that were left unaddressed by the extreme Left. One could even trace the spirit of the beginning of latter-day Dalit/ tribal struggles in Muthanaga or Chengara[*] to these radical breaks with classical/parliamentary Marxism and Maoism. But the mainstream historiography and politics avoided these issues for years till the landless Tribals and Dalits raised their voices in Muthanga and Chengara, threatening the parliamentary comfort of the ruling elite.

---

[*] Chengara and Muthanga: Sites of Adivasi/Dalit struggles for land rights.

Nair Consolidation and the Socio-cultural Scape of Kerala

Unlike other states, where caste realities could be construed through the paradigm of *chaturvarna**, Kerala again presents a unique picture which is evident in the practice of untouchablity and unseeability that existed well into the 20th century, and which shocked Vivekananda into remarking that Kerala was a 'lunatic asylum'. What this Hindu reformer saw in Kerala was a form of caste exploitation he had not seen elsewhere in India where upper-caste Hindus and Dalits lived in two different villages. Due to Kerala's geographic features and the division of labour that was in operation, both Dalits and upper-caste Hindus were obliged to live in the same village, making frequent social interactions unavoidable. This led to the Brahminic upper castes imposing a brutal and inhuman distancing strategy which precluded the untouchable castes from achieving social, cultural, and economic breakthrough and kept them as the 'untouchable other'. In that sense, one could say that Vivekananda was partly right and partly wrong. Right because he sensed something specific about the nature of caste domination in Kerala. Wrong because he thought that caste domination in other parts of India was not as powerful as it was in Kerala.

If we try to translate this into the chaturvarna paradigm within the political and social matrix of Kerala, it is the Nairs, a caste group that did not belong to any of the three powerful varnas—Brahmin, Kshatriya, or Vaishya—who emerged as a decisive force in the 20th century. The history of Nair emergence is beyond the scope of this introduction. Suffice it to say that this passage of Nairs into colonial modernity and beyond is the story of their appropriating the Brahminic and Ambalavasi culture and transforming the imagined nation into their own culture. To shorten a long story, I would only focus on a few issues in connection with the emergence of Nair subjectivity. A cursory look at Kerala society will reveal that it is Nair subjectivity and its epistemological programming that constitute what is known as the Malayali sensibility.

First, the much celebrated matrilineal system of lineage, where wealth in the form of land/property is transferred through mothers to their daughters. Coupled with this was a form of conjugal relationship

---

* *Chaturvarna*: A theoretical caste-structure of Hindu society; source, Rig Veda, 10:90.

known as *sambandham**, where a Nair woman could have more than one (simultaneous) relationship with Brahmins or other upper-caste Hindus. This is projected as an emancipatory form of female sexuality in certain quarters of contemporary feminist discourse. But at the same time one cannot be blind to the fact that this celebrated sexual freedom was not a choice of free will, but was restricted and controlled by the patriarchal Brahminic order and was actually an instrument which promoted the same. That is, a Nair woman was not free to choose a Dalit, Muslim, or Christian as her man without the risk of social excommunication.

In a sambandham family structure, the father's significance was markedly lower than his pre-eminent role in a patriarchal social formation. The child is known to belong to the mother's household and family, the *tharavadu*†. The colonial value system, with its Christian privileging of the symbolic and material father-to-son transaction over the mother-to-daughter transference, was decisive in breaking the structure of the Nair matrilineal system. Within the altered landscape of colonial modernity, the Nair community underwent a change from their traditional matrilineal system to a patriarchal one and the father was made the locus of the newly-formed patriarchal exchange. With this, the Nair community broke with the age-old Namboodiri system and its sexual exploitation. This historic shift is well-documented in *Indulekha*, a novel written in 1889.

Another anxiety of the Nair community can be seen in C.V. Raman Pillai's text *Videshiyamedhavitvam* (*Foreign Domination*, 1921). This text supplies all the ambiguities and contradictions that a postcolonial text can offer. The main surprise it has in store for us is the term 'foreign' and 'foreigner'. The 'foreigner' in this text is not an Englishman who ruled the then not-yet-imagined India but the Tamil Brahmin who controlled the administrative system of Travancore State. The political battle against 'foreign domination' by the Nairs ended in the latter's victory through job reservations and other such affirmative actions. Here too one might locate a Malayali irony: when Dalits and other marginalized groups are derided for being the beneficiaries of job reservations and

---

* *Sambandham*: Literally, a 'relationship' unmarked by sacred rituals prevailing in Nair homesteads and accepted socially. Namboodiri men formed liasion with Nair women and visited them in their homes. In the Nair matrilineal system neither the Nair woman (wife) nor her children left their home as they were entitled to the property.

† *Tharavadu*: Nair homestead which belongs collectively to all the members descended from the women of the family.

accused of compromising merit and excellence, what is forgotten is the fact that every other community in Kerala is already the beneficiary of an affirmative system and always has been.

The subtle political dynamics of the Nairs who outwardly mimicked colonial modernity and packed away lower castes as the 'Other', resulted in defining the nature of public space in Kerala. If we look closely at the above-cited examples, we can see that Brahminic hegemony in both its Malayali and Tamilian varieties is posited as the visible Other. But there is yet another that is completely absent: the Dalit. By appropriating the hegemonic systems of both colonial modernity and Brahminism and by erasing the Dalit other, the Nairs created a new space of Malayali nationalism. It is through the cultural capital of the Nairs that Kerala has been imagined and constructed. The very icons specific to the upper castes, especially the Nairs, have been projected as 'Keralaness' and 'Malayaliness'. In other words, what makes Keralaness distinct from other cultural formations is the upper-caste culture. This is how Kathakali and *kasavu mundu* (brocade-bordered cloth) have become the iconic markers of Kerala and being Malayali. Hence, being a Dalit or Muslim or Tamilian is tantamount to being excluded from the sites of Kerala. It is in this constructed space of Kerala and Malayaliness that all the emancipatory histrionics of Kerala have been enacted. Naturally, this society's emancipatory dreams have no place for Dalit emancipation or anti-caste politics.

The Blindspots in Progressive Kerala

What is hailed as the 'Kerala experience' is this glittering surface of the liberal and democratic politics that conceals the dark underside of intense communal feelings. This is evident from the fact that the various political measures undertaken in the name of development in Kerala and hailed as progressive by 'Malayalis' are anti-Dalit and anti-Adivasi. The Land Reform Bill (1969) which was envisaged to give land to the tillers, actually turned the Dalits into landless agricultural labourers and did not change their class position. Those communities that had been cultivating leased lands were given ownership and the landless Dalits who had actually tilled the land were pushed to the periphery. Besides, the various governments that ruled the State forced the Dalits into ghettos called colonies—devoid of even bare necessities like drinking water—restricting their social mobility. These policies modelled on colonial governments placed the Dalits continuously at the mercy of welfare measures, a large part of which never reached those it was earmarked for.

The Education Bill, a so-called landmark bill that aimed at liberating educational institutions from the control of private managements, became yet another means of ensuring the continuation of status quo. After six decades, private managements still enjoy absolute control over the policies of colleges, including the appointment of their teachers, though the salary of teachers in the 'aided colleges' is drawn from the general treasury. This system precludes the possibility of educated Dalits or Adivasis or other marginalized persons from being recruited in private/aided educational institutions. As a consequence, instead of being institutions of democratic diversity and plurality, these centres are reduced to institutions functioning within the management's ideological framework. The ratio of private educational institutions to government schools in Kerala would explain the situation. In such an authoritarian educational scenario, there is no space for Dalit literature or knowledge.

So what was supposedly 'progressive' about Kerala was old wine in a new bottle. With Maoist politics there was an attempt to break with the Leftist progressive politics in parliamentary garb. In the Naxalite Movement of the 1970s, there was an intense awareness of the feudal social structure of society that was linked to a colonial bureaucratic machinery. But the tragedy is that this awareness, when transformed into political praxis, could not overcome the very structure of thought that it found detrimental to Indian society. Maoist leadership in Kerala was in the hands of urban, educated upper-caste intellectuals who fought the feudal form of material and labour reproduction ignorant of the way they themselves reproduced the same social relations at the organizational level. Their political praxis, with the bloody killing of petty local landlords in the most backward parts of Kerala, alienated a large chunk of the middle class from their zeal and convictions and has had terrible consequences for latter-day Dalit politics in Kerala because when Dalits or Adivasis try to articulate their frustration, hopelessness, and aspirations through various modes of political struggle, most of the time, the media, peopled with middle-class intellectuals and catering to middle-class tastes conveniently labels them Maoist, which instantly gives the government a moral high-ground to use violence to silence such efforts.

With the death of Maoist resistance politics in the 1980s and the consolidation of the middle castes and middle class following the liberalization policies of the early 1990s, Kerala too shed its 'progressive' masks. This was further intensified by the fact that the 1990s was also the period when the Left in Kerala, like its international counterparts elsewhere, faced an immense identity crisis following the dissolution of the USSR. Moreover, China's emergence as an international superpower began to be perceived in Kerala with a sense of pain because of its market-friendly policies. Thus dream of a progressive, egalitarian society, a dream with which Dalits or other repressed communities could align, ended.

Birth of Dalit Identity

As cracks in the Kerala dream and international Socialist dream became increasingly obvious to the Dalits, their new cry was not for a radical overhauling of the entire social structure and system but directed towards gaining their legitimate share in the existing power structure.

This trajectory explains the difference between the Kerala Dalit experience and other Dalit experiences in India, with which I began this study. Unlike Dalits in other parts of India, Kerala Dalits were conditioned in a dream that was trans-national, anti-imperialist, and anti-bourgeoisie. They were also forced to believe in a Hegelian teleological vision of history, for which the grand-narrative known as Marxism supplied the vital political fuel. In this particular sense, the disillusionment that the Dalits in Kerala felt was also experienced by many when they were obliged to recognize that all meta-narratives had ended. The only one that survives is the one known as liberal democracy. Contemporary Dalit politics in Kerala is situated within this liberal space where Kerala Dalits have again taken up the issues of land, sharing of resources and power, democratic redistribution of wealth, exclusion, marginality, and so on. They have learned that if they want to survive, any bargaining must be done within the existing frames of reference of liberal democracy.

But that is not all. Dalit thought carries a radical vision, which is evident in the vision of the infinite and the absurd exemplified in some of the Dalit art forms performed in Kerala. Here it is not a tragic acceptance of liberal democracy and the subsequent bargaining, but an experience that cannot be conceptually reduced to rational thought or logic.

Only the future can tell whether Kerala Dalits will enter the emerging digitalized cyber-world successfully. Will they point to a new alternative to the whole of humanity itself or is that too much to expect?

The Genesis and Spread of Malayalam Literature

The Wor(l)d of the Mainstream

Malayalam, accepted by many scholars to have evolved from Tamil roughly in the 9th century, has a history of writing that dates back to the 12th century. The aesthetics of Malayalam literature have been overdetermined by the literary traditions of Sanskrit which include *sruthi* (cosmic, subliminal communication), *smrithi* ('remembered' literature, secondary texts), and epics and legends. The development of Malayalam literature is primarily through epics and legends ('Ithihasa-Purana tradition'). Beginning with *Ramacharitam* (14th century), said to be the first written poem in Malayalam, the process continued without much difference in perspective. In these works, 'Hindu spirituality' was embraced as the sole solution to the complexity of human existence, thereby ignoring a dynamic and productive life-world. It was the pain of this group on which the upper-caste Hindu world of leisure was based. The literature produced by upper-caste poets was the by-product of a lethargic lifestyle, far removed from the world of sweat and toil which supported it. Culturally and epistemologically focused on concepts like *moksha**, *nirvriti*, and *anubhooti* [spiritual liberation, fulfilment, and sensual ecstacy], it is easy to see that the dominant literary tradition of the period known as *Manipravalam*† had its focus solely on sexuality and self-indulgence and was in tune with the luxurious lifestyle of the upper castes of the time, in Kerala.

In the 16th century, a low-caste named Thunchath Ezhuthachan, wrote such memorable poetry that later history called him the 'Father of the Malayalam language'. Given his birth in a caste that is today categorized as OBC, this should be a matter of some astonishment. The reason for conferring this honour is interesting: he was instrumental in Sanskritizing Malayalam language and its tradition. What is even more striking about his work is the fact that it completely ignored the polyphony generated by a caste-ridden society and the regional topography. Instead, its whole preoccupation was, metaphorically speaking, with two avatars of Mahavishnu: Sri Rama and Sri Krishna.

---

* *Moksha*: Sanskrit, meaning liberation, merging with the Great Reality and the end of cycle birth and death.

† *Manipravalam*: Compositions made up of a mix of Malayalam and Sanskrit.

It is only in the 18th century, in the writings of Kunchan Nambiar, that characters started appearing with regional specificities. It was Nambiar who localized and regionalized the Sanskrit arts. At the same time, he not only created an art form known as Thullal*, improvising something that had originated from the untouchable communities like Parayan and Kaniyan, but also used the local languages and dialects that the elite Sanskritic tradition had not even glanced at. Thus, he created a carnivalesque literary space which is a hybrid of the crowd, combining a plurality of voices and different power centres. But one should not miss the ambivalence of his literary radicalism. There was a process of simultaneous acculturation by which he incorporated the farcical tradition of the untouchable communities and also the Sanskritic tradition to mock the hypocrisies of the dominant communities.

In *Kuchelavritham* by Ramapurathu Warrier, a writer of the same century, poverty is pictured not as the essential result of economic inequality and social injustice, but as a human situation that could only be solved by the divine intervention of Lord Krishna. Both *Attakathas*† and *Chamboos*‡ are the literature catering to the recreational needs of the elite. Their imaginative and meditative poetry were not reflections of the real state of social relations. They were, instead, attempts at idealized representations of nature and beauty. The man of poetry is a purely imagined creature, unrelated to any social reality. This body of poetry is conspicuous by the absence of regional, caste-specific, and everyday life experiences.

Not only literature but other Kerala art forms are also the products of an aesthetics that prioritizes pleasure over everything else. The life experience of the spectator of a *Kathakali* or *Kootiyattam* is not conditioned by the angst of survival. What classical arts focus on is *saadhakam* (mastery by repetition). Classical arts, similar to the neo-classical spirit of European literature, prioritize repetitions of received norms and patterns over an innovative break with past norms and patterns. The structural effect of this is that the classical arts became the exclusive domain of a consuming elite who had enough leisure to acquire the skills for repeating already perfected patterns. Artistic genius,

---

* Thullal: A folk performing art of Kerala comprising dance and song. Over the last two centuries the form has gradually evolved and assimilated into a classic art form.
† *Attakatha*: The literary component of Kathakali recitals.
‡ *Chamboo*: The literary component of the theatre of the Chakyar community. It might be a mix of prose and verse.

defined from the same paradigm, thus became the exclusive territory of the upper castes.

By rejecting the topology and the bio-world of the region, mainstream Malayalam literature has produced a world that is alien to the subaltern people. As Kancha Illaih has pointed out, it is by othering the material labour and its epistemology that the holy 'Indian' epistemology and its aesthetics was created. As a consequence, within the matrix of elite literature, Dalits have a space only as the 'others', as the uncouth and pathetic to be civilized and sympathized with. These representations and the 'innocence' that went into their making have to be deconstructed.

Dalit Literature: The Differential Paradigm

The politics of representation and exclusion described so far explains the invisibility of Dalits in early Malayalam literature despite its long literary tradition. Also, this invisibility is quite understandable given that Dalits in every region of the country have been denied education. However, this same invisibility in the written realm is strongly by-passed through a powerful tradition of Dalit orality that attests to the fact that education and literacy are distinct things. What is most interesting about the Dalit oral tradition is that it does not take into account the notion of an author. Rather, Dalit orality is pronouncedly concerned with an experience that is not individualistic but is always collective.

In Central and South Kerala, Dalits have had their own oral traditions with immense historiographical potential. *Chengannuradi*[*], *Idanadan Paattukal*[†], *Krishigeetha*[‡], and other folk-songs are instances. It addresses the formation of an agrarian society in which Dalit communities produced the subsistence and surplus and still remained subservient to the dominant political authorities. In North Malabar, there are more than 500 ritual performances known as Theyyam/Thira, the *thottam*[§] of which is a powerful reminder of the complexity and diversity of Dalit orality and its markedly different epistemological foundation.

---

[*] *Chengannuradi*: Traditional heroic ballads.

[†] *Idanadan Paattukal*: Songs of valour sung in Central Kerala (Kuttanad region) while sowing and reaping by Parayas and Pulayas; the protagonist of these songs is Idanadan.

[‡] *Krishigeetha*: songs sung at harvest time; *krishi* = farming.

[§] *Thottam*: In 'Theyyam' (deivam, meaning God) performances, ritual songs recited to invoke the spirit of the deity. Performers are drawn largely from Dalit/ tribal communities.

In the realm of music, since the Sangam Age, Dalits have been known for their earthy and instinctive music. In *Purananooru*[*], the Pulaya is described as 'the Pulaya who plays *thudi*[†]'. Parayan means the one who beats the *parai*[‡], the drum. Paanas are known for their musicality and skill in drumming the '*udukku*[§]'. Mannan has used *eezhara*[¶] as an instrument in *kalampaattu*[**]. The *chenda* is a subaltern musical instrument. Both *nanthurni*[††] and *pulluva veena*[‡‡] further enrich the ancient musical traditions of the untouchables. One of the perennial themes of Dalit epistemology as unfolded in this complex matrix of music, dance, and songs is the irrationality of the caste system. In Pottan Theyyam, evoking the historic moment at which Sri Sankara was questioned by an untouchable about his *Advaitha*[§§] philosophy, Pottan Pulayan asks the question:

Isn't it blood that oozes when you are wounded, Brahmin?
Isn't it blood that oozes when I am wounded, Brahmin?
Then why ask about my caste?

In an old folk-song the purity and elitism that a birth in upper-caste community guarantees is questioned:

To play the drum[¶¶] *in the temple, the cattle's hide is okay*
To pluck the flowers for worshiping in temple, Paraya's basket is okay
What is purity, Brahmin?
What is impurity, Brahmin?

---

[*] *Purananooru*: Sangam Tamil composition (AD 3rd century) of the singers, 16 are women.
[†] *Thudi*: Percussion instruments of Dalit origin and used by them.
[‡] *Parai*: Percussion instruments of Dalit origin and used by them.
[§] *Udukku*: Percussion instruments of Dalit origin and used by them.
[¶] *Eezhara*: Percussion instruments of Dalit origin and used by them.
[**] *Kalampaattu*: Song sung during the preparation of coloured drawings on the ground with rice-flour and turmeric.
[††] *Nanthurni*: A highly sophisticated two-stringed instrument used by the Vannan community.
[‡‡] *Pulluva veena*: An indigenous stringed instrument of tribal origin, used by the men of Puluva community.
[§§] *Advaitha*: The philosophy of monism which says that every living being is a form of Brahman or the Great Reality.
[¶¶] Drum: Made of the hide of cattle, it is used as the common percussion instrument in temples, where the Parayas who make the parai, are prohibited.

The problem of sexuality, caste, and social labour is addressed in a critical way in narratives like *Poomathai Ponnamma, Neeliyamma Thottam*, and so on. Even the genesis of Dalit feminism can be traced to *Poomathai Ponnamma*.

Another fundamental difference that Dalit epistemology has with the Brahminic one relates to the way in which knowledge is conceived. Dalit arts view knowledge as the product of material history. In Dalit life, what happens is not the accumulation of knowledge and its expansion in an abstract manner; rather, something oriented to life-praxis and material reproduction. It is concrete as opposed to the Brahminic knowledge system which concerns the abstract.

Dalit Cosmogony

The complex vision of Dalit cosmogony in Kerala is still not understood in all its subtleties. On the one hand, it evokes the realm of the transcendental with which human correspondence is impossible. On the other, this cosmic transcendental background, as in the case of some world religions like Judaism or Islam, is not absolute. Nor is its transcendence pronouncedly articulated. Rather, this works as an unconscious knowledge, as an unconscious background information that structures the narrative of faith. So, in Dalit cosmogony, God as the absolute Other is not a pronounced truth. Instead, the whole system of faith and belief operates within a different frame of immanence. As Sebastian Vattamattom observes, 'In Parayapuravritam, there is no conception of a God who rules over everything. But they see divinity in everything that they interact with; the rock on which they are going to sit; the coconut tree they are going to climb; the sword and armour, in the waist-thread; the self-disclosure of the One-beyond-words. They believe that the dead and the gone and the killed would visit them when needed.'

A striking and significant feature of modern Dalit resistance is their unconscious struggle towards a not-so-pronounced transcendental otherness. This is, it seems, a spontaneous reaction to the idols and idol-worshipping traditions of Hindu cosmogony within the matrix of the Advaita philosophy. Four significant Dalit resistances point to such an understanding. When Poikayil Yohannan (Poikayil Appachan), a Dalit convert to Christianity and a preacher, came to the conclusion that Christianity with its many churches could only reproduce the caste divisions of Hinduism, he took the extreme step of burning the Bible in public. He was shrewd enough to realize that the Church, with its visible human-divine, would reproduce all the human divisions within its body. The second instance is what is now known as the Malabar Rebellion, where a significant number of Dalit converts to Islam fought the feudal lords before whom they had earlier bowed respectfully. It was the profound ideological shift offered by Islam that surrender before the non-representable God freed its followers from earthly powers which gave the Dalit converts the courage to make such a radical onslaught on the feudal machinery. The third is Ayyankali's rather lukewarm reaction to the Temple-Entry Proclamation, which is still celebrated by elite historiography. The fourth would be the early Dalit fascination with Marxist atheism practised in Kerala.

In Sangam texts—Sangam Age being a socio-culture space to which Dalit life-world is traditionally linked—one hardly finds any reference to the immortality of the individual soul or the pervasiveness of *Brahman* and moksha. The difference is clear. Dalit thought is not concerned with the transmigration of souls or moksha, that is, liberation from the cycle of birth and death in a final union with the Brahman, the universal. Dalit thought is concerned with the immanent. Its spirituality is geared towards the well-being of the mental, ecological socio-scape.

In a beautiful moment in the life of Poikayil Kumaragurudevan, he explains why cattle should not be slaughtered: 'We should not kill cows and buffaloes. Not because they are sacred animals. But because during our slavery, the Parayas and Pulayas shared their pangs with these animals.' This marks the organic humanity of Dalit discourse. Therefore, in his writings we find evidence of a Dalit consciousness which is sceptical of upper-caste consciousness and historiography.

I do not see a single word about my people
I see the histories of many races
There was no one in the past to record the story of my race!

This absence of a narrator capable of recording the 'story of my race' is powerfully manifested in the history of Malayalam poetry from the Bhakti movement onwards. There are some marked differences between the Bhakti movement in Kerala and in other parts of India, where it has been known for its powerful anti-caste consciousness. The Bhakti poetic tradition in Malayalam represented by Ezhuthachan, Ramapurathu Warrier, and Poonthanam, from that paradigm, effects a difference from the general trends of the Indian Bhakti movement. The Malayali Bhakthi poets did not raise the question of equality before God as it was done in the writings of Kabir, Thukaram, Namdev, Tulsidas, Basaweswara, Chokamela. Instead they exaggerated the devotion to Krishna and Rama in fits of madness. They were not even ready to minimally address the issue of caste. Only later, during the 'Kerala renaissance', did caste became a topic of poetic imagination. This anti-caste poetic discourse that has its basis in Narayana Guru, Sahodaran Ayyappan, Kumaranasan, Ulloor S. Paramaeswara Iyer, and Vallathol Narayana Menon during the renaissance, has visible representatives in the post-renaissance period in the writings of Niranam M.P. Kesavan, S. Padmanabha Panicker, and Pallath Raman.

Though issues of caste and identity became popular themes for poetic composition, one could hardly discern an aesthetic sensibility that is rooted in Dalit or anti-caste consciousness. On the contrary, they were the manifestations of condescension and compassion. This artistic sympathy, even empathy, could not make any radical change in the structure of mainstream poetry. It remained what it had been, except that Dalits became a topic for serious study and there developed a fascination with the wretched of the earth. Poetry became more and more ornate and the Dalit experience became one more subject matter for poetic experiments and embellishment. That is probably the reason why Changampuzha Krishna Pillai could deal with platonic love in *Ramanan* and the Dalit experience in *Vazhakkula* in almost the same poetic structure as though they were a seamless continuity. Mainstream poets merely accommodated Dalit experiences in their poetic machine, obliging all themes and subjects to conform to the dominant aesthetic tradition.

Within this dominant aesthetic paradigm, the artistic forms that tried to evoke Dalit experience were categorized as inferior, uncouth, and, sometimes, condescendingly and quaintly folk. A popular Malayalam saying that reveals the thought process and world view of many Malayalis goes: 'Whatever forms/comes in the mouth is song for Kotha'. Here, 'Kotha' metonymically and metaphorically captures the Dalit life experience as it is perceived from without. What is interesting about this derogatory remark is that this very spontaneity that they deride in Dalit creative expression is hailed and admired at another level in European romantic expressions that prioritized spontaneity and regional and cultural specificity and otherness. So, in the elite scheme of things, poetry was not judged on the basis of its spirit, but rather was based on who framed the discourse. If it was the European colonizer, the Indian elite would admire and emulate it without being able to capture its spirit. In the margins of Kerala modernity, the oppressed were forced to conceal themselves and obliged to feel inferior.

Colonial Modernity and Imagi(N)ation

The novel has from its beginnings incorporated certain caste concerns that have been ignored by the poetic world. The reason could be traced to the genesis of the novel. Unlike poetry, the origin of the modern novel is easily located in Europe and European modernity. A novelist's imagination requires a leap in conceptual mode, in the way one perceives and organizes the world. So, framing a novel challenges the author to look at the world and organize it from a space which had not existed before colonization. This is why many of the concerns rooted in the modern concept of man gains an entry into the texture of the novel. In the novel we see the power of fantasy, narrative, and the build up of sentences and are invited to make moral judgements about the behaviour and choices of the characters. The writer reveals to us a universe into which we journey looking for meaning and truth. From its very beginning the Malayalam novel in one way or another has dealt with the issue of caste as a problematic field within the space of modernity. In *Indulekha**, supposed to be the first perfect novel in Malayalam, one sees the system of *sambandham*. If *Indulekha* reveals Nair anxieties triggered by the waves of modernity (it was a critique as also a descriptive narration of it for the British officials O. Chandu Menon worked with and for during the Marriage Act discussions), *Saraswatheevijayam* talks about a different caste experience. Here, for the first time, we encounter in written form the experience of a Dalit that is quite individualistic. This novel, although written in solidarity with the experience of the untouchable communities, in effect, becomes an apotheosis of both colonialism and Christian evangelism. The novelist Potheri Kunjambu envisages in colonial modernity and Christianity a cure for the plight of untouchable people. In this celebration, the novelist has resorted to an unusual structure. Its central theme is the experience of an untouchable. But the curious thing is that this untouchable figures

---

* *Indulekha*: A point of discussion might be the publication of well-structured novels in Kerala before *Indulekha* (1889) which is traditionally seen as the first novel in Malayalam. Mrs Richard Collins published *The Slayer Slain* (English, 1859) which appeared in Malayalam as *Ghathakavadam* (1878). Besides this, *Pulleri Kunju* (1882) was written by Archdeacon Koshy.

only in the beginning and at the end of the novel. In the first chapter we see him trampled deep into the mud by the village master and his steward. Along with the criminals, at this stage, we are forced to believe that the untouchable boy is dead. There follows the prolonged journey of the boy to escape the clutches of his oppressors. After many years, the village master and his steward are caught on the charge of the boy's murder and taken to the court, where Judge Yesudasan, a Christian convert, sets them free on the prima facie evidence that the boy was not killed because the judge identifies himself as the very person who was supposed to have been murdered.

This says a lot about the texture of the newly adopted artistic medium known as the novel in capturing the nuances of the local and the unheroic. The prolonged absence of the possible hero in the novel points to a lacuna—the lacuna of the epistemological violence that both colonialism and conversion forced upon the untouchable. It is as though the untouchable's journey to colonial office and recognition and Christianity is a smooth passage that involved no violence at all! The novel at that point in time was not rooted in a conceptual ground that was strong enough to visualize the world from a Dalit's point of view. Rather, in order to capture Indian reality, what was to be erased is precisely this subjective Dalit experience.

The next paradigm shift in Malayalam sensibility occurred with the modernist break with the past. In hindsight, the whole modernist revolution in Malayalam literature could be seen as a revolt against all forms of establishment. It was also triggered by an intense disillusionment with emancipatory dreams set off by the Bolshevik Revolution. This disillusionment was actively fought by embracing a Sartrean existentialist project where the individual, rather than the collective, finds his own existence in a fit of existential fury. One could say that the Malayalam modernist literary project is peopled with miniature versions of Sartre without Sartre's political 'commitment'.

Conclusion

Any movement away from the centre that the 'grand' is obliged to make, creates a space and platform for the birth of the 'little'.

From the 1990s onwards the Malayalam literary scenario has seen celebrations of the differing and plural voices of the historically marginalized, oppressed, and unrepresented. This not only includes the Dalit discourse but other silenced groups—feminists, environmentalists, and religious and sexual minorities. One of the characteristic features of emerged and emerging discourses is its tension with the national imagination. Hence, they seek alliances and constellations with the transnational, micro, and the local. Any new movement has to pass through three phases: ridicule, resistance, and acceptance. Dalit literature in Kerala has fast-forwarded to the third phase and is beginning to provide the colour and power that only people who live close to the earth can express.

The hope of the editors of this volume is that the reading of Malayalam Dalit writing in translation will facilitate the growth of an alternative perspective, and provide the English-reading public with the means to rethink the norms of what constitutes culture and literature.

2011 M. Dasan
Kannur

POETRY

Tracing the poetic tradition of Kerala Dalits is a delicate exercise because such a tradition challenges the framework and surpasses the limits set by our conventional understanding of poetry. In fact, Dalits before they began to write down their poetry, used to refer to their oral renderings as *paattu*, which literally means song. Broadly, three traditions of song-compositions are discernible among the Dalits of Kerala.

The first is associated with labour (*koythupaattu*). Like in other predominantly oral cultures, the composition of a particular song cannot be attributed to any particular individual. The song, thus, signals a very significant moment in indigenous history and there is no question of authorship and its concomitant idea of the creative individual. It points to a compositional practice that is collective and spontaneous. The space of the composition, one is forced to conjecture from the songs, is the space of labour. The collective composes the songs. Individuals may enter or leave the field of composition but the process of composition, rooted in life and labour, goes on undisturbed. The songs are replete with issues ranging from the philosophical to the mundane, without any apparent prioritization of the former over the latter. Everything around the composers is either deeply mysterious or farcical. Sometimes, the songs are even commentaries of the simultaneous events happening around, like a reference to the feudal master approaching to oversee the work. The songs thus, besides being collective therapeutic experience in a sea of pain, also become an inventory which reveals the complexities of pastoral and agrarian worlds.

In the second tradition of *paattu* the composer is recognized by his caste and not by his creative individuality. That is to say, singing for communities like Paanas and Malayas was a caste occupation and the singer was known by his community rather than by his name. Here, the singer's songs are inherited from his community and offer versions of history in the form of facts and figures. He improvises because that is what is expected of him. He is a messenger whose duty includes carrying news around in the form of songs. In short, he is an itinerant singer, a carrier of news and history, the present and the past. He is also a eulogizer of kings and lords. Yet he is his caste; he is the collective.

The third tradition is rooted in ritualistic practices. Most lower-caste rituals have songs built into their texture, which often are inherited by the members of the performing communities. Along with this, the performer produces something new, which is hardly remembered. The performer, when possessed, sings and talks to the people around in the ritual space. In certain cases, when the performer is possessed by the spirits and is in another time-space into which his audience cannot follow him, his is a sheer ecstasy of deconstruction in practice: the spirit is revered and simultaneously abused; there is prophetic vision; there is the shamanistic healing touch.

With Poikayil Yohannan* here was a definite rupture with these traditions of oral rendering. His was, as it were, the moment of the emergence of a Dalit song-composition that is quite individualistic. His songs were not composed as soothing experiences to overcome the drudgery and pain of forced labour. Nor were they the products of caste occupation. It was poetry in the modern sense—that is, an individualistic enterprise. He could rightly be credited with our present notion of 'genius' but his poetry differed from modern practices of the art. Its purpose was to educate and persuade the untouchables into action and also to contest the Hindu and the indigenous Christian world views. As in earlier traditions, in Yohannan too the complexities of Dalit life were captured, perhaps violently and passionately. But, unlike the earlier songs, his compositions had a deliberate mission: to change the world and not just to record it.

The beginning of Dalit poetry, like poetry everywhere else, was powerful: an unleashing of experiential pangs; an opening-up of concealed traumas and angsts; a reclamation of negated self; an assertion of identity. But then Malayalam mainstream poetry incorporated all these into its texture and made them an aesthetic experience to be consumed. Kumaran Asan in classical period (*Chandalabhikshuki*), Changampuzha Krishna Pillai in the transitional period (*Ramanan*), and Kadammanitta Ramakrishnan in the modern period (*Kurathi*), were the great stalwarts of Malayalam poetry who represented Dalits as though they were speaking for them. True to the teaching of the French philosopher Michel Foucault who taught us not to speak for others,

---

* Poikayil Appachan's name after conversion was Poikayil Yohannan. He is frequently referred to as Kumaragurudevan.

this speaking for Dalits was permeated with all the representational containment and distortions such an act entails. The tragedy is that many still consider these works to be genuine 'untouchable' experience!

Even though the above-mentioned poems, for a long time, overdetermined the Dalit experience from without, through the writings of K.K. Govindan, K.K.S. Das, Raghavan Atholi, Sivadas Purameri, G. Sasi Maduraveli, S. Joseph, M.R. Renukumar, M.B. Manoj, Vijila, S. Kalesh, and Binu M. Pallipad, Dalit poetry gradually made its presence felt in Kerala. Their poetry creates a field of the heterogeneous as these poets differ widely in their craftsmanship and ideological anchorage. While a poet like Raghavan Atholi writes poetry in a manner reminiscent of the possessed ritualistic performer, evoking forgotten memories, desires and language, the younger poets experiment in loose prosaic forms from a seemingly detached and alienated space. And, in Dalit poetry, there is this clash of ideological positions as well: different positions and visions unfold without offering a solution but encapsulating the difficulty of the situation one is trapped in.

The truly remarkable trait of Dalit poetry is that it not only challenges the savarna poetics in its creation of a different poetics, sensibility, language, consciousness, and cultural paradigm but also widens our visions of being and becoming: a new becoming for woman; a new becoming for humanity; a new becoming for nature. In that sense, it effects a new disclosure of the inside and the outside: a glimpse of the outside from the hut without a window, a search beyond the colour of the skin. Unseen places, untouched terrains, unsmelt fragrance, untasted foods, and thoughts not encountered in mainstream poetry.

Songs by Poikayil Appachan*

Poikayil Appachan†

About my race ...
I see no alphabet
about my race
I see histories
of many races.

The world's histories-
Think each one
as two races
I see no alphabet about my race.

Oh, that there was no one
in the ancient world
to write the story of my race!

When I think of it, regret begins
within me
let me add something
in my own melody ...

The story of how
a people who lived from times long ago
in Keralam
came to be lowly on earth.

I'm not ashamed
of the frailties of our castes

* Original title *Poikayil Appachante Paattukal.*
† Poikayil Appachan reportedly sang this song during the Sree Moolam Praja Sabha of 1921. The part that is included in the speech made on 1 March 1921, reads thus: 'They were the ancient race that made this land fertile. At one point they became the slaves of this region.' Race is an important construct in the ideology of the Prathyaksha Raksha Daiva Sabha. The word is ideologically linked to the signification of salvation. It has also been interpreted as a referent to the original inhabitants, marginalized by history. The word race exists on several planes of signification in the songs of the Church.

we are offspring, forever damned
to blabber this and that on earth

Everyone blames us without a qualm
How is it
that God, who gave shape to everything
today, allows everyone
to blame us in this manner
till earth and sky end?

—Translated by Catherine Thankamma

The Killing Field*

K.K. Govindan

You should know the truth
The thampurans† are going to kill me today
You should prove this truth
Even if age upon age passes after my death
Then he asked the executioners to kill him
They pulled back his arms
Tied his hands
They made him bow down and began to hack his head
But it wouldn't separate from his neck
And blood splashed on every face
Four or five of them tried
Repeatedly and in vain
They could not cut the head away
Finally the victim himself told the henchmen
To remove the copper talisman from his body
And to place it beneath the peepal tree
And *then* to cut off his head and go get the fee for it
Following what he said they chopped his head
It rolled away, reddening everything in its path
They presented themselves before the thampuran
Carrying the bloody knife they had killed the man with

* Original title *Arukolakandam*.
† Thampuran: Feudal overlord in the caste structure of Kerala.

They narrated the whole story to the lord
About the man and his talisman
That copper talisman still lies
Beneath the peepal tree
Even today, the thampuran's household
Believes the story of what happened
To have truly happened

—Translated by Ajay Sekher

The Gospel for Dalits*

Kaviyoor Murali

INTRODUCTION

1. I, Kaviyoor Murali,
   who, in his teens, revelled
   in yanking back by its tail
   the snake retreating into its hole,
   outsmarted friends in crunching
   deadly chillies and bitter neem leaves,
   pelting stones, no catapult,
   and hitting bull's-eye, targets from afar.
   Climbing steep rocks,
   sharp white pebbles in hand,
   on them his name to etch,
   behold, the Gospel according to him,
   for the Dalits of the world!
2. I have the right, I insist,
   to think for myself.
3. And the right, besides,
   to ponder about my parents,
   on the life of death they lived
4. The horoscope of the present
   is written, don't you think,
   in stones from the past?

* Original title *Dalitarkkezhuthiya Suvisesham*.

5. Darkness, as with my days past,
   encamps each day of my present.
6. Newer and newer spectres rise
   and around me do the death-dance.
7. My people they kill and consume
   like ants gnawing a dead fly
8. Kerosene they pour on
   our living bodies to set ablaze.
9. My sisters, coerced and pierced
   to rape they subject.
10. The prowling gang-rapists spare
    neither tottering women past sixty
    nor tender trembling girls under eleven.
11. Broken in body and mind,
    their cries strike the face of heaven.
12. These, the media, under wraps keep.
13. Media ethics become anachronistic rags.
14. Law and justice stand still like signposts.
15. Then my inner being begins to flare.
16. My ambience rains fire,
    my soul glows red-hot,
    like iron in a smith's forge.
    And thrashes about
    like fish out of water flung.
17. Oh, my people of sorrows!
    Will any heart melt in your tears?
18. And does anyone hasten to you in solidarity?
19. Your redemption: is it not your own duty?
20. To fight, hence, put on the whole armour.
21. He who resists wrongs
    and refuses to sanitize injustices
    blessed is such a man!
22. Generations will call him blessed!
23. I stood firm by this in the days of my youth.
24. Now? I am weak and altogether frail
25. Upon my vocal cords
    feeble words fumble and fall.
26. Less blood in my veins, am robust no more.
27. My nerves gone numb,
    my joints in chronic ache,

do you think I can stand up straight?
28. My arms, not yet paralyzed.
29. And my thoughts, not yet without light.
30. Therefore I write and record.
31. My works, the balm for the broken.
32. Oh, my people!
    This into your hearts receive,
    and share the sorrows of my heart.
33. Be not vexed
    when with you I share.
34. Tell me not you're too busy
    for this, I say, is only for you.

* * *

III

1. Man, a wanderer on the earth,
   mated the first woman he met.
2. And she, on her part, clung to him.
3. They, on pastures green, did pitch their huts,
4. Beside the still waters they settled.
5. Living as families,
   farms and orchards made.
6. They sang and danced
   revelled and rejoiced.
7. On a Sabbath day
   when God was on holiday.
8. Out of their settlements were they
   driven out, dispossessed.
9. Thistles and thorns their bodies ripped
   all along the way they fled.
10. Snakes, on the rocks and in the caves,
    slithered and crawled on them as they slept.
11. The roaring of wild beasts
    terrified their offspring.
12. Who grew up, even during the day,
    from the sun and light shut out
13. That vast, dark forest, remember,
    to them held no refuge.
14. Forest thieves and opium thugs plagued them.

15. God, holidaying, was not even then in charge.
16. Their vineyards and fig trees felled and despoiled
17. Their thatched houses pulled down.
18. Land and goods snatched away by force
19. The war-cries of predators in hot pursuit,
    the army of marchers and archers
    shouting and screaming:
20. Catch them.
    Blot them out.
    Butcher their children to extinction.
21. Even one among them, if spared will
    to the land lay claim and say,
    that it once belonged to them.
22. Raise a hue and cry claiming,
    they were, of everything, the source.
23. A time will come when try they will,
    to regain all they lost.
24. Spare not, hence, even their first-born.
25. Holidays over, God returned
    when the monsoons were in full fury
26. Flashes of lightning, the land illumined.
27. Those who escaped in its light
    took refuge among gigantic creeks,
    huge rocks and roomy caves.
28. Little had they to eat or drink.
29. For food they roasted rats and wild cats.
30. And their thirst they quenched
    with water dripping
    from broken stems of forest creepers.
31. They cried out in prayer
    to the ghosts of their ancestors dead.
32. Other gods they had none.
33. Offered in oblation to ancestors
    python fat and peacock oil
    lighting before them wild cotton wicks.
34. Among the women caught,
    those found to be attractive
    were degraded into keeps and chattel.
35. And the young men bound to bonded labour.
36. When the keeps conceived and delivered

clans and tribes commingled.
37. The clans covered the land.

* * *

XII

1. A treasure pot I retrieved
   from the depth of a smoke-shrouded history.
2. Opening it, I saw rubies neatly stacked
   in copper sheets all enwrapped.
3. Diamonds dazzling like morning stars,
   and sapphires rivalling lunar asterisms.
4. My mission, I must fulfil!
5. Since you too are joint-heirs
   to these precious things
   I put them out on a fresh sheet
   at the crossroads of history.
6. Take what you will!
7. Behold how beautiful were the jewels
   on the crowns of your ancestors!
8. Their splendour undimmed
   by the passage of centuries
9. And their value wholly undiminished.
10. My people, wear them upon your hearts,
    you, who have great men's purity of hearts!
11. Then on, a new life you'll receive,
12. And know then the truth
    Dalit you simply aren't.
13. Your mind will chant it to yourself.
14. The story, remember, of Vaamanan begging,
    for land mere three footfalls long,
    gaining for himself three worlds in the end.
15. It happened in the chasm of a stalemate:
    unspeakable betrayal, on the one side
    and ultimate of purity, on the other.
16. Into the self-same hiatus
    your fathers too had tumbled.
17. Yet weren't they degraded.
18. I tell you, hence, what to do,
    deem not yourself Dalit or untouchable.

19. The world, you know, will degrade
    those who devalue themselves.
20. Unless you're complicit,
    who can you ever degrade?
21. May your voice be bold, self-confident
22. And your glowing words spark fire.
23. Aren't you, the heir of a great tradition,
    imbued with innate worth?
24. A multitude of witnesses,
    bears it testimony.
25. The Aayira hills, you know, is home
    to cyclones that buffet and scatter
    the smoke screens of historians.
26. Ask the archaeologists
    why they mock not the mockers,
    of those who tell it again today.
27. Ask, why they at this are indignant
    when with pride they behold the stuff they fetch
    from the sea's depth and the earth's womb?
28. Remember your forefathers,
    who honoured poets,
    with bars of gold and swathes of land?
    Regain your pride!
29. Sing and celebrate
    the generosity of your ancestors
    who gifted elephants to *Eravalars*[*].
30. Forget not, they were
    of the Southern land the overlords
31. Their fame will endure forever.
32. The Panans and the *Parayas*,
    they were the pride of the land.
33. With what elan they danced and sang
    and made every accolade their birthright!
34. Thiruvalluvar, the awesome genius,
    remember!
35. Wasn't he the son of a Paraya woman?
36. Know this too, that it was
    a Kurathi woman who gave birth

* *Eravalar*: He who asked.

to Imayavaramban Nedumcheralathan!
37. Her with reverence hail and acknowledge.
38. For wasn't she Nallini*, the Chola princess?
39. Avvaiyyar and Elaveini,
    Vennikkuyathi and Kanni Kaamakanni†,
    doubtless they were *Paanathies*
    who, through poems, bewitched the world?
40. Ask, then, if branded they should be Dalit.
41. How did a poetic people forfeit their language?
42. Princes become hired planters of seedlings?
43. And geniuses deformed into idiots
44. All these, forget not,
    were by deceit wrought.
45. Abjure, at least now,
    ingrained allegiance to these fraudsters.
46. Heed the lessons of history.
47. Reckon your plight, Oh, how pitiable!
48. Like that of a baby elephant
    fallen into a deep ditch.
49. Elephantine bullies
    lug you to lairs of cruelty.
50. Prodded, kicked, whipped,
    your native instincts you lose.
51. Mounting on your back
    tamed and spirit-broken,
    those who trapped you in the ditch,
    ride in obscene pride
52. They, upon your heads,
    load their demons and deities.
53. And you? Not resist even once!
54. None can, if you stand firm,
    move you from where you are.
55. Their whip and spear
    will not over you prevail.
56. Can they stick it in your nether jaw?
57. The reach of your proboscis they have not.

* Nallini: Women poet of the Sangam Age.
† Avvaiyyar, Elaveini, Vennikkuyathi, and Kanni Kaamakanni: Woman poets of the Sangam Age.

58. Hear again the groan of the bamboo grove
and the dirge of the forest streams.
59. They are your mother, your provider.
60. To them do justice.
61. A new age beckons you.
62. And to the clamour of an epoch, pay heed!

—*Translated by Valson Thampu*

My Soil*

K.K.S. Das

Breaking the chest of hell
an ember,
the flowers of thorny plants
hurl my patrimony
over the head of dharmashastras.

Breaking the boundary-stones of generations
in the heart of my father land
I am born again.

Beyond Aryabharat's
Non-aryan clans'
unfinished house.

In the soil snatched from
the first tribes' makeshift
I stand firm.

With smiling skulls
and talking bones
I rush to the prisons of fellow tribes.

Wounds kiss wounds
the springtime of chain scars
in the old songs of the Paanan
in the field-songs of Pulayas

* Original title *Ende Mannu*.

in the sayings of Mahar.
Dancing in a group.

They who triumphed over time
devouring kaalakoodam
pouring poems of thunder and lightning.

One community
One clan
One nation.

* * *

O castes that are not castes!
O people without Vedas!
Death that doesn't succumb
to a culture of freedom

—*Translated by Lekshmy Rajeev*

The Black Dance*

K.K.S. Das

O black girl
you reap the paddy fields
you reap everything with your sickle
come along! O come along
come along with the wrath of Kali!

O black cubs
you shade the black soil
you cubs of lions and panthers
take the staff of the Vela
and the rope of the Kaala
come along striding like demons!

You became the manure in the soil
the colour of the river

* Original title *Karumaadi Nritham*.

you were pushed down alive
under the mud as slush
so many Pulaya heads were chopped
and the blood drained into the fields and farmlands

They come back with long hair and nails
with dangling tongues
they shake the hillock
uproot the palms
stir up the stream
the dark ones roar
we will pay them back for sure!
We will pay them back!
We sacrificed roosters
we fed the spirits
but now we have become the prey
we will break your back and bastion
we will avenge all this!
We will avenge you all for sure!

We are those black souls
scattered and dumped around your barns
today we shake the forest and the woods
today we shiver and shout at you

Blood for blood
for beheading us
for stripping and raping our women
for burning down our cottages
for making us flee
we will destroy your citadels and mansions
blood for blood!

As time opened its eyes
they razed the barns and reserves
they snuffed out the lights and lamps
they tore down the clothes and ornaments
as the slaves smile
the masters tremble
in the flames of the slave-smile
throbbed the heart of Kannaki

With the swords snatched from captivity
the blood of princes drained down
the royal stairs and citadels
Kali danced on
the sacrifice was on
the dark-dark ones danced too
until their minds had cooled somewhat

Let tormented arms be raised to avenge the wrong
let uprooted tongues flare into flames
let the oppressed rise to repay old debts.

—Translated by Ajay Sekher

Justice Cooked*

Raghavan Atholi

Somebody cleans up the blood
on the claws of the vultures
that fall upon
the half-burnt corpses
of the ant-paced wind's
mistimed reckonings
as it dared to cross the border
in a sudden flash of lightning
that cut through the ruthless downpour.
Do you think the swords have been blunted?
in the corridors of history
where outspoken tongues are crushed to death.
Children serve a banquet of justice
and go to their hungry death on the streets.

Pompous inanities scripting horoscopes
for lives worn out in cooking and serving justice.
Burned alive on caste's highways.
Waiting endlessly at the portals of knowledge.
Where enemies trade wisdom.

* Original title *Neethi Vevichu.*

We make wreaths out of plucked children
as the dead turn martyrs overnight.
Where the malicious
blow out all lights
and the coterie of big guns
distill the heady brew of agony.

The haughty palliatives
doctors never dreamed of
are sold across the counters.
The 'good' boys
who go on a rampaging spree on the streets
are only watching a good play.
In the theatre
old hags act without a hero.
Their heavy make-up
burns the stage.
As they make a windfall
selling old melodramatic wines
cloned in new bottles.

But somewhere someone's land is broken.
in some hovel
a livelihood is smashed to bits.
But the poetry of resilience
rises from the empty pots.

Come.
The mislaid offerings
of the past beckon.
In the racing streams of blood
which never look up to words
the surges of indomitable truth
crash like breakers:

The caverns of hell.
The long saga of suffering
they call human life.
Closing the doors
on the parade of resistance.

—Translated by K.M. Sherrif

Where Hunger is Sold*

Raghavan Atholi

In these burning boughs of hunger
Salt and chilli on the open wounds
Burning the law books of tears that
drink down the pool of justice
In the casinos of the new worlds
The diabolic rise of the other worldly
Flesh flavours of the concubines
Taboos and tags
The excess of education
Rocks of poesy and communicable fantasy
Fertile fields to sow the seeds
Maidens sacrificed as the virtue of rivers
The erotica of aberration and incest
Bombastic farces, speedboats.

Haunts and bullets
Reaped heads in ballet boxes
The brewery of the betrayer
The schools of reality
Vast estates, big shots
News and conversations
Painless death.

Dried up river and elusive tide
Menstruating goats
Rivers that never wash away the pollution
Boiled fish.

Crows piercing the eyes
Tiger dens, little sheep
Chatter of cheating silver
The rise of the Perar river in floppies
Sensual medley in CDs
Sexy columnists, virtues of Kovalan

* Original title *Visappu Vilkunnidam.*

Kannaki breeze in the country boat ashore
Attempts an etching of time
The three lions become a barking statue
The straight line an image
Ribs crushed by the turning wheel
White painting green with blood red
Mediating eunuch
World trade gang in the bar
Copulating buffaloes
What is left to sell
Organic wastes of consumption
Human resources, ballooning wombs
Brooding mercy and poetry.

Walking on fire, sleeping in waves
Nuclear arrogance in the burning river
Anonymous friendships, parades
Esteemed debts in perilous times
Blind drought in indebted eyes
Recurring justice meets
Lovesick and cancerous currencies fake
Wretchedness asks for boiled pots
Field asks for crops
Heart asks for burned poetry
Asks for bowed and bent minds
People expelled by Manu ask
Where are hearths and the power
That shaped the times
Where is the lamp that lighted up
The paths that were unseen
Where is the force that bore the brunt of
Untouchable theory
The tongue that ended the pain
Truth that is never sold out
Place and date where and when
Food is not begged for.

—*Translated by Ajay Sekher*

An Uncharted Map*

Sunny Kavikkad

Truth
dissolves in sighs.
For damp hair,
a flower of ingratitude.

Having struck with poisoned fangs
alphabets in the bowl of plenty,
a serpent slithers.

For darkness to write history
I offer my eyes.
Into the shadow of destiny I fell
pierced by an arrow.
The one who plucked out words
from my unsanctified mother,
that too, is me.

The uncharted map
of clod, swept away by the sea
is what the child draws, again.
Thunderbolt descends—
Kisses the green.
My love, a torso
that yields the taste of salt.

—*Translated by Catherine Thankamma*

* Original title *Kanakkukalillatha Bhoopadam.*

With Love*

G. Sasi Madhuraveli

Saumini,
Didn't you say that black is beautiful?
And haven't the poets sung so too?
How then were Blacks disgraced?
Not we the ones who drink and drain sweat and blood
We are the ones who melt
We are not caressed
By the blazing flames of the sun
Or the blistering red-hot earth.

Amme, we Blacks lack space
to hide under your wings
We are being shooed away

Mother Kali whose severed heads
form the garland round your neck?
Whose chest do you mount
to cool your rage
as you drink and drain blood

Saumini,
you'd better not merely say,
or merely sing,
that black is beautiful.

Black is the seed of self-rage
The mount of tumult
The shadow of endurance
The shade of love.

—Translated by Lekshmy Rajeev

---

* Original title *Pranayapoorvam*.

Mother*

G. Sasi Madhuraveli

Amma today, is
just a battered kanji-bowl
a few grains of rice
and many tears.
A hundred curses
two smallpox pustules
and the milk they oozed
all for the other.
Mother is a suckling mammal.
A burden on brother's head
unburdened ones,
abuses howled back and forth
for father, a creeping reptile,
Amma alone is sight, sound and light of wisdom
thus came many faces to Amma
Kannaki, Sheelavathi, slut ...
the deerskin and bark dress changed,
the puranas and proverbs failed
giving way to the age of kitchen stories
mother gave birth again and again
got dirt-smeared ...
got drenched in soot
thoroughly dishevelled
seated in an unknown corner
she plunged her head
into the dangers of hell.
In the end
like the unclaimed carcass of the cow
that yielded milk no more
Amma rots away.

—*Translated by Lekshmy Rajeev*

* Original title *Amma*.

Group Photo

S. Joseph

Tomorrow is the social and the group photo
Don't forget to turn up
I have paid the money
And let's stand close to each other,
says one girl.

Could've been at college
Could've been long back,
The readers may guess
You may think so too.

Had a life estranged
Some way or other from every one
So just went underground
Hiding in shelters available.

What do you think?
Think it's a complex?
How does a poor, low-caste fellow,
And dark at that—live in Kerala?
Have you any idea?

Yes, this is the experience of different people, in different places.
Including women.
Don't always read it as mine alone!

That's why I said
it doesn't have to be a college.
If it is,
we can strike work together,
study together
but, mind you, I will disappear once in a while:
Haven't you seen those who do?

She shows me the photo.
One who chased her
One of her own caste
Stands touching her.

It's because of this disease that
he chose to stand just there.
You can remove him
Copy–paste my picture there instead.
The times have changed.
So I leave it at that.

Do you know—
There is a cursed life
That some Malayalis lead
All by themselves.

—Translated by K. Satchidanandan

Some Dark Spaces[*]

S. Joseph

Even when the noonday sun
runs across the rubber groves
some dark spaces remain here and there.
Mostly birds like *uppan*[†] or *olenjaali*[‡]
arrive there.
Flying low and lower still.
Plot by plot,
tree by tree,
they fly close to one another.
Their cries light up
those dark spaces.
My appan sent me to find out
where their nests are.
By the time I set out
the rains came pouring down.

I flew up the hill like a dragonfly.
Watched the waterfalls gnawing
the insides of the hollowed rocks.

[*] Original title *Chila Irunda Idangal*.
[†] *Uppan*: Crow pheasant.
[‡] *Olenjaali*: Tree-pie.

In the bushes where leaves rotted,
while I leaned and listened
the crickets stuck to my shoulders.
As I wake up
under the tree,
fruits are falling.
One there, one here.
O, no! It is the jingling laughter
of a forest girl.
We built a house on the meadows
in a glade.
The herd of deer, turned into sunlight,
was looking for shade.
The herd of elephants, turned into darkness,
was looking for sunlight.
One day she showed me a cave
in the heart of the woods.
The sounds that go into it would come back
The lights that go into it would also come back.
It was full of water.
Do all birds and men come
from here, I asked.
O, I don't know,
I remember her saying.
Then one day,
lying in her lap I said,
the search for the birds' addresses took me nowhere.
I also remember her saying then:
there, both our children.
Appan called me
in a dream.
Hearing him call we left the woods.
By the time we reached the village,
The leaves were falling.

My house and my appan
lay covered with leaves.
Only now I realized
My house too was in a space
knotted with darkness.

The lights there had gone out long ago.
Now at noon, an *uppan* arrives there.
And in the afternoon, an *olenjaali* too.
Their cries light up
those dark spaces.
And then one day when the children could understand things,
I called them and said:
I went in search of the origins of these birds.
Failed to find out.
Now you should go and find out.
By the time you return
The leaves will be falling.

—*Translated by K. Satchidanandan*

Some Types of Fingers*

Sivadas Purameri

(On an Incomplete Album)

A severed thumb
as a foreword
Like the symbol
of the defeated
That's how one starts thinking
of an album of fingers.

One needn't search for long to find
the drops of blood
splashed on the forest green
One need not delve
into the *Mahabharata,*
cutting through the
commentaries and rewritings.
There is no need to traverse
Attapadi or Wayanad
It is enough to look

---

* Original title *Chilatharam Viralukal.*

at one's own palm
to discover an Ekalavya*.

Like the lizard's twitching tail,
Sliced fingers
that fell in the East India field
as layers of defence,
are seeds awaiting rain.

Thumbs that look alike
came together. Fingers
with the traits of traitors
drop down on their own.
Like the symbols
of the mortgaged,
they will remain
imprinted on contracts
as the victory of defeat.

Though the album is incomplete,
On each page
Stands out a thumb
Arched like a question mark
Straight like an answer
More fingers and still more.

The fingers cut will not recall
Their past vigour, arrows shot,
the writings of the forgotten.
The last finger smells
of the kitchen.
A woman's imprint on the contract of consent.
A sign at the bottom
of the page, unnoticed,
A thumbprint.

—*Translated by E.V. Ramakrishnan*

* Ekalavya: A brilliant low-caste student of archery in the Mahabharata. As an offering to his guru Drona, Ekalavya was obliged to slice off the thumb of his right hand.

A Leaky Room*

Sivadas Purameri

Finally, when the poisoned supper is served,
the rain pours from darkness in torrents.

When the rain descends upon my very being,
it is not a touching ballad or a lullaby.
Nor a nocturnal love song, nor the footsteps
of the dead that come crossing times past.
Soaked are the mattresses, clothing, bedsheets,
pillows, books, medicines, hearth, the firewood
kept to dry. The word is getting soaked,
so are the eyes and dreams.
You are scorched within, though it is bitter
cold outside; the last lesson of love!
'Let us share a few moments of love,
before we embrace death. Let us awaken
the children.' Your words, growing moist,
still have a lust for life.
On the pages of the book of life,
columns of debt alone stand
to account for mother's throbbing love.

As you wait callously,
before the poisoned rice,
to act out the final scene,
and as I wake the children,
sleeping like faded buds, fatigued—
Within me a torrent!

I shudder as the lights go out,
my mind covered in cinders.
In a couple of days, we would
be on the front page in putrid images.
Soon our deaths and the tale of
our cursed lives will be

* Original title *Chornnolikkunna Muri*.

drowned in some other news.
Even after the rains cease, this room will
stand for many a day,
like the shadowy figure,
of a man without hope!

Like a strand of grey hair,
light will filter in
making the roof look like
a pierced skull.
The floor ploughed by the rains,
the mud walls flaking, creeping with
ants, mites, insects and cobwebs—
pervading silence, pervading void.
The moth-eaten door will remain shut
like the laughter of an aged patient.

How terrible this monument to unnatural death!
No, I am incapable of
snuffing out the lights of life.

May I wash off all miseries into this rain,
that pours down from darkness,
along with bonds of debt, layers of grief,
memories of shame and
tonight's supper.

—*Translated by E.V. Ramakrishnan*

The Silent Beast*

M.R. Renukumar

Must wake up
before the crow lands.
Must clear the cattleshed
of cowdung before
the milking begins.

* Original title *Mindaprani*.

Must keep the milk pot
and the oil bottle ready.

Must not forget to mark
with a pencil in the calendar
the measure of the day's milk
the man took with him.

Must climb the loft and
draw out some hay
from the thinning haystack

Must collect the rice-water
from the backyard
of three neighbouring houses.
Must cross the singeing stares
of the anglers on the canal bank
while returning with
the earthen jar against the hip.

Must stir the rice-water well
when the cow delves for the
undissolved dregs of
the oil-cake in the bran.
Must crush at one stroke
the gadfly that sucks blood from its belly.
Must, with the same hand
that rolls one's rice and water,
stroke and scratch the cow's dewlaps
when it chews the cud,
its stomach full.

Must sharpen the sickle a bit
whetting it on the washing stone.
Must go to the Potti's place
to cut grass.
Must wait for the stray passenger
to help lift the grass-bundle.
Must take care not to slip and fall
while crossing the narrow bridge,
the trunk of a single coconut palm.

Must lie down, on one's side
all blank inside,
after one has drunk the gruel,
washed the bowl,
put out the lamp,
left arm for pillow,
no sheet for cover.
Must wake up
before the crow lands.

—*Translated by K. Satchidanandan*

The Poison Fruit*

M.R. Renukumar

Sitting under the othala tree, the poison-fruit tree
I saw:
My appan
and her appan
pour and drink
from the same bottle
in the shop.

My brother and
her brother
playing with the top
in someone's frontyard.
My sister and
her sister
playing *ittooli*†
just next door.

My appan's younger brother
going to the pond for his bath
exactly when

* Original title *Vishakkaya*.
† *Ittooli*: A game played by children. One throws a tiny object like a safety-pin and the others hunt for it.

her amma's younger sister
goes there to wash clothes.

While trying to find
the dust mote in her eyes
with my tongue,
I heard the small boat in which
my amma and her amma
go to cut grass, beat against the rock.
While my teeth were groping for
the fish-bone stuck in her thigh,
I heard my appan and her appan
throwing up in the coconut grove
on the mud-bank.

While rolling towards the stream
unconscious after many bites
of the poison-fruit,
I heard my amma and her amma
fall to the ground in the frontyard
and scream and wriggle
like centipedes.
While lying lip-locked
under a slimy blanket of mud,
I understood—
Fishes turn bodies
into their dwelling.

—Translated by K. Satchidanandan

Survey of India

M.B. Manoj

Who weighs more?
A cow or an outcaste?

The former eats grass,
the latter is eaten.

The cattle's gruel drinks,
is drunk.

Poster-paper, stumps of bidi and cigarette,
the skin of bananas,
eat and are eaten.

Can piss in public,
grand.
Can shit,
grander.

Is milked by holy hands,
children drink.

Is milked by unholy hands,
the udders get sucked empty and bitten

Milk, curd,
ghee, butter

earth, stone,
steel, cement

The former
can enter anywhere
the latter
can wander anywhere,
one who sleeps in ancient legends
and on an old mat.

Who weighs more,
An outcaste or a cow?
Don't be afraid:
A dead cow weighs
five times a live outcaste.
A live cow's weight equals
two hundred and fifty million outcastes.

—Translated by K. Satchidanandan

Mothers*

M.B. Manoj

I like a mother turned bad
more than
a father who is good.
She pulls us out
of a sold-out body
pats our back
until we cry and say:
breathe in, breathe out.

Your mothers were
as good as ours.
They made them toil
in the woods and hills and on roads
and asked them to tell their children
schools are bad.

If someone says
a mother is bad,
even if it's your father,
You'll simply have to rise up
and hit him.

Gazing at the ladles
with which they serve,
while making a rice-ball,
dipping it in the curry
chewing and then
devouring it.
Telling oneself,
'A stray fellow
polluted the passage
we had come by.'

—*Translated by K. Satchidanandan*

* Original title *Ammamar*.

O Ant, O Paddystalk*

M.B. Manoj

Will you give some land,
asks the ant.

Only if you can swim across
the river and reach here,
—comes the reply.

Shall we reach, dangling
swinging on the branch of a rubber tree,
a rope around our necks-(ant.) ?

Who do you think you are? Tarzan?
—the reply.

All the lotteries we sell
are to make your nest bigger

But there are no stalks
to weave the leaves into a nest
There are only the latrine pipes left
to dig the earth and build the walls

Are you the best citizen journalist,
pat comes the retort.

These plastic roofs burn
scald my skin.
Trees hide themselves
left with no clothes to change into.

Are you the chaste Sheelavathi[†]?
Or, who the heck do you think you are?
—the sarcastic reply.

O rice stalk
broken headless paddystalks,
can I take you home?

    * Original title *Erumbe, Kathire*.
    † Sheelavathi: A legendary character considered the ideal wife, utterly devoted to her husband and submissive to his slightest whim.

No, wait until the machine comes,
—the reply.

O Ant, O ant,
me too, like you stuck deep in this bog.
By the time the machine arrives,
all my heads will be ripped loose
and float away.
And my paddystalks will be
stillborn children.

Dear paddystalk,
I asked them
if you could be
given to me.

They say
they will soak both you and me in kerosene
and set us both on fire.

—Translated by K. Satchidanandan

A Place for Me*

Vijila

Remembering eternal friendships that
hide thoughts of death in forgetfulness,
stepping out, bag in hand, forgot
Father's stopped watch,
the tablecloth to be washed,
the blanket bought for the house
by the side of the field
resembling an island
on rainy days

The memory of the land
and the small house

* Original title *Idam*.

forfeited to creditors—
debts forever continue

For the plentiful bowl of relationships
never to be like the watch that stopped
for want of human touch.
Never ever forgetting to pick up
and carry the bag,
Drishya's gift
the dark blue diary
enriched by letters of the alphabet
unmarked by life-policy logos.

Maybe, never ever to remember
that I am all alone.

Not even six feet of land
crossing the land
that oozes mud
to which graveyard?

This is the afterword
of one unfit for life.

—*Translated by Lekshmy Rajeev*

I Can't Grow My Nails*

Vijila

Gazing at the long nail,
don't ever forget everything,
like the woman seated
before TV serials.

When teeth and nails
search for the woman who resists.
It's not pressing the mobile keypad
not surfing on the computer.

* Original title *Enikku Nakham Neettan Kazhiyilla.*

It's all being stunted with
wounds and calluses.

With the ups of the grinding stones
and the lows of the floor,
a graph rises on the nail.

Nail polish begins to flake
along with blackened vessels

When the nails break,
they could be completely trimmed
(the chores too perfected)

Do maintain the grown nail of at least one finger
like an iron nail
to pierce those
venomous fingers
that dare touch your body.

Complying with the poet's words,
there remains,
a nail half-broken,
to scratch, to rend.

—*Translated by Lekshmy Rajeev*

The Autobiography of a Bitch*

Vijila

We in the street
amidst garbage
hungry, hungry
smelling the chewing gum
someone chewed and spat out ...
Even while being blamed
for breeding incessantly, again and again
to divide up and carry off the sons
and drive away the daughters,
thousands come ...

* Original title *Oru Pennpattiyude Atmakatha*.

Before us
no human
appears to be great at all!
Not enough valour
to spot and bark strangers away
in the porches of their houses ...
Not enough beauty to
display either
or bargain.

In their markets,
we've neither milk, flesh
nor skin.
We're not offerings
for their gods either.

Oh world, world
our kind
hides in the backyards
eye fixed on leftovers
lies curled up in back-verandas
finds solace in darkness.

—*Translated by Lekshmy Rajeev*

Six Philosophers Unite to Exclude Amavasi from the Play*

Binu M. Pallippad

They sit in front of a thatched hut
at twilight.

Seen from a distance, they are seated
in five blue chairs, in the soaked,
bleached soil. At the kitchen door
one is talking to the housewife.

---

* Original title *Aaru Darshanikar Chernnu Amaavasiye Naatakathilninnu Purathakunnu.*

Six Philosophers Unite to Exclude Amavasi from the Play 41

Another rolls the big wooden grain pounder
and seats himself on it, with others.

The short dark man, the postmodernist,
(Vinod) decides that there will be
no actors in the play.

We have doubts about his rationale.

The second one, the Expressionist (Thundathil Rajappan)
volunteers to paint
the backdrop of the stage.

That the six consent,
as it appears from their expression.

The Social Realist who also represents the Sixth
Ward of the Panchayat (Puthuvalil Kumaran),
fond of lullabies as he is,
wants the music to be melodious.

Also shows the Expressionist
the sickle tucked
into the makeshift palm-leaf door.

Now, in the paddy waters before them,
a water snake with a half-swallowed frog in its mouth
is caught in the creepers of the water lily.
The fourth one, the Surrealist who owns
a catapult (Daveed—Converted), makes a mental
note of this, to use it in the play as an allegory.

The postmodernist rises and asks the post-Impressionist
(Chirayil Raveendran) who has been silent till now
to prepare the stage.

Five persons, in this order, are now
active in the discussion.

At this moment, the Neoclassic scheme
Sandalwood paste marking his forehead
(Thiruvanchan of the 'laksham veedu')[*]

---

[*] *Laksham veedu*: A state government project to provide housing for homeless people.

advances from the kitchen door
almanac in his calloused right hand
and sits among them.

The seventh one, Amavasi, the boy
of the last generation
rises from the chair, respectfully.

All of a sudden, Amavasi moves to the front
and with the left hand folded over his left ear,
and the right hand pointing afar,
his head tilted and the gaze lost in the distance,
breaks into a loud rendering of a Sanskrit quatrain,
'*snathamasvam gajam matham*'*,
like one of those boatmen singing
full-throated, a song from a popular film.

The panchayat member now insists on seven women
carrying seven headloads of hay
to walk the stage with their hips swaying to this rhythm.

Presently, we are glued to our seats, entranced,
rendered tongue-tied
engrossed as we are in this play by Sanskriti.
A make-believe authenticity envelops the scene.

Amavasi takes this opportunity
to talk of a laptop.

One of us springs to his feet
with a 'you-son-of-a-bitch' expression.

The six philosophers and Amavasi
return to the play, a little baffled.

Again, Amavasi comes before them
and angrily demands that his hut in the play
be thatched by a thousand amputated hands.

Neoclassic devoted to Manu and Vaastu,
wipes his face, leaving his sandalwood-paste mark intact

---

* Quotation according to which an educated sudra is likened to a wet horse, an elephant in musth, etc. Another version is that after a bath, a horse is as majestic as an elephant.

and says: you may use hands or any thing else
for the roof, but as per science, be it in drama or real life,
paddy banks are essential for a house
and as for roofing, perishable softwood is a must.

His eyes brim with contentment.
Amavasi rises, advances and slaps him across his
face. All ten fingers are imprinted on
Neoclassic's face. We raise slogans
asking for Amavasi's exclusion
from the play. Amavasi leaves, bent over.

Since Chathan was dead, the Social Realist
ceremonially presents Mala the waiting Dalit woman
With a sickle.

'Hell with the bourgeoisie, even your mother
will vote for communists' (set to the tune of
a romantic lyric): the panchayat member agrees
to raise this slogan over the microphone.

By now, Neoclassic with eyes reddened,
hastens out and returns with a drum, palm fronds
and a red scarf to fasten around the forehead.

The panchayat member turns up the hand,
and strikes a pose, forcing the muscles to stand out,
looking upward, a tune set in his mind.
Night deepens.

CURTAIN.

—Translated by E.V. Ramakrishnan

Hairpin Bend

S. Kalesh

Fixing hairpins in her hair
looking at the bends,
she leaves.
On the way even if anyone comments

on the growing heaviness of her tiny breasts
and the fine down on her limbs
like Arabic letters ready to be read.
She says nothing.
I know her house is on the last stop
of the line bus that goes up the hill.
Were you to dig a well there
even below the visible water-level
is where I stand.

Slowly spreading
the black legs of the hairpins
and tucking them into her hair ...
I haven't asked about these preparations.

Seated in the room with the large
misty windows
I can hear at night
the vehicles that go singing
climbing the hill in one breath.
At dawn
before anyone wakes
when I go to that bend
I might find something or the other there
hairpin legs apart or something ...

—*Translated by Shreekumar Varma*

Siren

S. Kalesh

She yearned for a life with him
and I with her.

The moment the distance between us grew
I decided to go to the city.

Must go to the city and see him
tell him

that he should give her back to me.
But
what if he doesn't agree?
what if his love for her is as unworldly
as mine?

My eyes welled up even as I imagined that moment.

I thought of her as I sat in the Express train to the city.
Crossing the bridge, I felt like jumping to my death.
Fear held me close to itself.
As I wailed in my mind,
the train dropped me in the city.

Children seated in the bus rotated their pin-wheels.
I walked around in circles, rotating.
Found the company where he worked.
It stood gazing at the sky, smoking.
In a corner of the yard cars and bikes stood in a huddle.
Seeing big buildings with their iron rods spreading like
the roots of huge trees, I was scared.
Rows of blue-uniformed workers kept coming and going.
Spotting someone who looked just like me
I asked his name.
He's in such-and-such block, so-and-so room.

Searching for that room, I climbed a winding staircase.
Metal doors that open beneath the earth
ejected me and quickly shut again.
Sharp glances, and many of them, came at me.
Even the sight of the whirring fan startled me.
Even the heights offered fear.

How much higher than the stream-bed back home
would this floor be?
Would it be as high as the coconut tree at the edge of the stream?
How far from there would this be?
Then, the distance and height if tied together,
I'm utterly helpless.
She must have climbed all that distance.
She wouldn't want to climb down again, would she?

I only know the answers to small questions ...

I leave aside the bigger ones.
And so
without searching in any of those rooms
that stare back, I returned.

Workers walk in, coming and going.
Cars and bikes were all preparing to leave.

As I passed the company gates
the siren hooted.
At first I was scared,
and then I was not.
I felt he stood on top of the multistoreyed
building with his companions,
and chased me away with their hooting.

—*Translated by Shreekumar Varma*

Not Because She Felt Like Weeping*

S. Kalesh

On the hillslope we had a lot of land
There the soil was the colour of soil itself
In the evenings
The sun of our land used to set there
From between two hilltops, a red light shows
I'd be there before that moment
One of the children taking the road below
To the distant school, while returning
Aimed a stone and scared me
Even below that, with the sound
Of a hurled stone falling in the water
That swirls around the rocks
The valley filled with friends and games

Here it's the canopied trees that have planted the shade
They are easy to climb

---

* Original title *Karachil Vannittonnum Aayirikkilla.*

Sitting there, straight across, through the hill
Covered with mist and smoke that we called Ooty
We can see a little of the solitude of the old woman
Walking with the logs she's gathered.
Then straight above our heads a plane rumbling
And its passengers see us
As they see the trees we're sitting on
Like we saw the old woman a while ago, perhaps
Howl out aloud, they may throw us something
Through these cross-games of vision we discovered
We'll not forget until death
The mathematical principle we studied in class
Once returning from school,
Grandmother said
Child, you needn't go back there ...
On what Achachan lost for a bottle of toddy
Even before the intoxication faded
Someone built a mansion
Sometimes to refresh our memory
When my friend and I went there
They scared us, letting the dogs loose.
Even before the mansion was completed, achachan's pyre burned down

Many days later, returning from the market and all,
On the foothills, I lost my ammamma trailing behind you.
Searching for her, I found she'd left the vegetables and fish
on the banks and was down in the stream washing her face.
Not because she felt like weeping.

—Translated by Shreekumar Varma

SHORT FICTION

As in the case of other Indian languages, in Malayalam as well, the transition from folktales to short stories came about in the mid-19th century. The year 1824 witnessed the publication of stories intended for children, translated from English. Thereafter, periodicals and journals published stories like 'Oru Kuttiyude Maranam' (The Death of a Child, 1848), 'Aanayeyum Thunnaneyum Kurichulla Katha' (The Story of an Elephant and the Tailor, 1849), 'Oru Kallan' (A Strong Man, 1881), and so on, all part of the evolution of the short story in Malayalam. It is generally believed that the genre of the short story in its specific form first appeared with the publication of the story 'Vasana Vikriti' (Prankster by Birth, 1891). Thus, through the pioneering author of this story, Vengayil Kunjiraman Nayanar, the Malayalam short story came into its own, passing various milestones of growth and development.

The early stories in Malayalam did not focus on serious issues of social realities. In general, they were mere entertainment, meant for the reading pleasure of upper-class and upper-caste readers. And hence the major themes such stories addressed were love, glorious deeds, social blunders, crime detection, hunting, litigations, etc.

In the second stage of development of short stories in the period otherwise known as the 'Kerala Renaissance', we cannot fail to notice the emerging significance of the zeal for social reformation. Yet another main focus of the stories of this period was class exploitation. Dalits came within the thematic framework of short stories only as part of these trends. Thus, Thakazhi's 'Vellapokkathil' (Floods, 1935) is a story that portrays a Dalit family. Again, his other stories like 'Velutha Kunju', 'Maanchuvattil', 'Swathukaarude Nattil', etc. also portray the Dalits. Yet another story of the same period 'Neeli' (1935) authored by M. Narayana Kurup is also noteworthy for its portrayal of its protagonist, a Dalit woman. So also we can see Dalit representations in Kesava Dev's stories like 'Red Volunteer', 'Nikshepam', 'Aalapuzhakku', 'Ghoshayatra'; in Ponkunnam Varkey's stories 'Chaathante Makal' and in S.K. Pottekkad's stories 'Viplava Beejam', 'Vallikaadevi', 'Braanthan Naaya', etc.

We also get sympathetic portrayals of Dalit life in Kaarur Neelakanta Pillai's stories 'Thekkupattu', 'Annathe Kooli', 'Oru Pidi Mannu', 'Kuttikal Ethra'; in Uroob's 'Koombedukkunna Mannu'; in Pulimana Parameswaran Pillai's 'Kadathukaran'; in Lalithambika Antharjanam's 'Maanikkan', 'Churanna Mula', 'Kaattupoovu'; in G. Vivekanandan's 'Kurutham Ketta Kukkirippara', etc. Following this, Kovilan, Madhavikutty, Anand, and M. Sukumaran started writing stories representing Dalit life. So did M.T. Vasudevan Nair, M.P. Narayana Pillai, M. Mukundan, C.V. Sreeraman, Sarah Joseph, K.P. Ramanunni, Asokan Cheruvil ... a list continuing up to Santhosh Echikkanam. But none of these stories made attempts to enquire into either the aesthetics or the epistemology pertaining to community life of Pulayas, Parayas, and others. On the other hand, they shared the aesthetics of romantic realism and Renaissance egalitarianism, inherent in the general reading sensibility. Hence, a critique of mainstream savarna values became almost impossible in it. They did not accept the Dalit perspective nor did they accept any identity other than class identity.

As different from the case of mainstream and stereotypical approaches to conventional class identity, it was in the stories by the Dalit writer T.K.C. Vaduthala during the same period, that the focus shifted to caste identity. He not only took interest in reforming the existing customs and rituals of the untouchables, but also tried to explicate the very essence of caste/community identity. While others looked at caste from the outside, the self-reflexive Vaduthala chose to create a self from within. The majority of his stories are about Pulayas. 'Jaatheeyatha' (1964), 'Chankranthi Ada' (1959), 'Randu Thalamura' (1950), etc. were a few of his anthologies of stories; through which he brought out the internal conflicts in the Dalit's life. His stories sprawl across nine collections. The mainstream critics did not recognize these caste specific experiences, nor did they bother to understand the alternate epistemology the untouchable castes projected, through these stories about Pulayas. The Renaissance generation in general entertained an aesthetics of universal paradigm. In the story 'Chankranthi Ada' itself, we find intermingled, the general discourse of caste reformation of the Renaissance period and the search for a Pulaya identity. It seems that those who criticize him for adopting a savarna perspective, failed to foresee the validity of the expression of 'otherness' we find in Vaduthala's stories. The ideological and aesthetic position that he maintained was a sort of resistance to savarna ideology. His stories are primarily manifestos of the conflicts that a Dalit of the period experienced by way of binaries like civilized/

uncivilized. Hence one has to formulate an alternative aesthetic criteria to evaluate them.

There are lots of other writers in the post-Vaduthala generation who wrote focusing on Dalit life. The most prominent among them is Paul Chirakkarode. We find a commitment and dedication in his works, focusing on Dalit conversion to Christianity. Resistance of savarnatha is its chief characteristic and it is moulded in the kiln of realism. The collection of stories like 'Olichupokunna Mankoonakal' and 'Nananja Bhoomi' representing the imaginative world of Paul Chirakkarode, have made a significant mark in the Dalit literary scenario. Most of his works talk of the experiential conflict of the Dalit Christian—the identity crisis of dual existence. The story 'Grihathurathwam' clearly portrays this and was not something that mainstream modernism had accepted and recognized.

Following Vaduthala and Chirakkarode, the one who became an icon in Malayalam Dalit short stories is C. Ayyappan. In the modernist period, short stories in general were engulfed in the problems of a search for identity and the issues of urbanization. Anand, Vijayan, Sethu, Zackaria, Mukundan, Kakkanadan, and others share the general sensibility of the period. But Ayyappan chose to be different and initiated a dialogue between the discourses of modernity and the Dalit perspectives of writing.

Ayyappan, who is conscious of his Dalit identity, was far ahead of his times in the neat blending of his unique craft and sharp intellect. Ayyappan constructed a Dalitness beyond and above mainstream aesthetics through his characters. By the skilful use of narrative strategies based on the likes of lunacy, possessed self, and soliloquy, he creates a counter-discourse of the downtrodden. He was able to rupture the sensibility of mainstream writing by creating an element of magical realism in his writings. Ayyappan enriched Malayalam short stories through his collections like *Njandukal, Uchayurakkathinte Swapnam,* and *C. Ayyappante Kathakal.* He filtered out the superficial attitudes of romanticism and realism and made visible Dalit life in all its intensity in his stories. No doubt, through Ayyappan, Dalit stories underwent a transition from its position as the reflection of multifarious lived experiences to an expression of identity and a deconstruction of established cultural norms. The distance from early writer Vaduthala to Ayyappan can be measured as the distance from mere recording of objective reality out there to a critiquing of subjectivity.

Yet another major issue raised in Malayalam Dalit short stories is Dalit elitism. As a result of the social changes created by anti-feudal struggles and Reservation policies, there emerged a new kind of elitism among Dalits. We can see this portrayed in two different ways in the writings of non-Dalits. One is that it embraces savarnatha and the other that it establishes new elites from among the downtrodden. The best examples of this trend are C.V. Sreeraman's story 'Duravastha Pinneyum Vannappol', and Sarah Joseph's 'Viyarppadayalangal'. Both these stories are clear indications that the general aesthetic sensibility of the Malayalis is still with savarnatha. But today the fact is that Dalit writers as well as the general public have recognized this and become critical of it. Even a book *Dalit Paathakal* (2006) had been published on this issue.

In the post-Ayyappan phase the Malayalam Dalit short story changes direction. In this context P.A. Uthaman's stories become noteworthy. Uthaman who authored story collections like *Sundarapurushanmaar* and *Kavaadangalkkarikil* won the Kerala Sahitya Academy Award for his novel *Chavoli*. His stories skilfully express caste-specific dialect and culture of the marginalized group and attempt to reclaim them. These are the narrations of Dalit orality during the period of internal emergency. Uthaman throws light on the hitherto invisible and silenced experiential world of the Dalits. His fiction infuses avarna Dalit language and its consciousness into the savarna world view.

If modernity came to its conclusion with a resurrection of fringe dwellers, what followed was a large scale production of non-Brahminic Dalit systems of knowledge. The stories authored by P.K. Prakash and M.K. Madhukumar are essentially attempts to explore these possibilities. They bring to discussion binaries like black/white, mainstream/ marginalized, and modern/feudal in the light of Dalit consciousness. In these new-generation stories the characters of the realistic stories are absent. Rather these stories project lived experiences or interpretations of constructs/contexts. These stories do not concern themselves with detailed character delineation or characterization.

It is not possible for the non-Dalit to create and portray the experiential world of Dalits, as reflected in the stories written by Dalits themselves. Dalit stories are heading off along a different trajectory, distancing themselves from the empathetic portrayal of Dalits as seen in the works of Thakazhi and the writers who followed. They link themselves to and are a continuation of all kinds of widespread intellectual debates and deliberations of the contemporary period.

Sweet-offering at Chankranthy*†

T.K.C. Vaduthala

Thimthimi—thimthimi—thimthimittaaraa—thai thaara—
Thimthimi—thimthimi—thimthimittaaraa—thai thaara

Hear me, hear me—Chengannuramme, my mother
I must journey—Chengannuramme, my mother! (thim)
Whereto, whereto, my dear son, O golden one!
To Kunnumaamdesham, oh mother mine (thim)
Is not Kunnumaamppennu my wedded bride, oh mother?
Had cast her off there in the marriage bower (thim)
Want to see Kunnumaampennu, I want to see
Give me a little gruel, early at morn (thim)

The waves of music rising up from the breast of the rice fields, so vast that the eye could not reach their end, so expansive that the voice could not reach the ear beyond, billowed in the breeze. That *njaatu*-song which had sprung from the sweet, tender, beautiful voice of some rustic girl—divine, mellifluous notes in clear timbre—rippled simultaneously through many such throats, equally gifted. What unearthly rapture! The toilers in the field immerse the whole universe in music.

The replanting has begun in the *virippu* fields. This is the season of *nirathu*—'to lay out in rows'.

They stood in rows amidst the thick, lush growth of rice saplings; Pulaya women, young and old, knee-deep in the mud. They were a large number of them. Surging forward like a troop of soldiers. But their war is creative, not destructive. Ahead of the female army, leading them, were a few men too. They were plucking the saplings for the paddy planters. Pulling the saplings up by hand would hurt them. The clods

---

* Original title *Chankranthy Ada*.
† Chankranthy (see glossary). Dalit version of Sankranti—the date which marks the transit of the Sun, a day in which ritual offerings are made to the souls of the dead.

of earth holding the saplings should be loosened so that they would not be hurt—that is the work of menfolk. They too were moving forward quickly, digging up the saplings with their roots intact with the shovel of twenty-eight *palams*. Isn't it shameful if the saplings aren't dug up, ready for the nimble rice planters? That's why the men are hurrying so. Are they so stupid as to fall beneath the womenfolk? Indeed!

Thittannam thaittannam thaaro—thimi
Thittannam thaittannam thaaro
Thinthimi thinnaayi thaaro—thimi
Thinthimi thinnaayi thaaro ...

A spry one among the womenfolk started off a new song. The beats were changing as the work speeded up and spirits rose; others would take up the refrain.

The cloud, it rained, it poured forth—little
fields, they filled, they brimmed over
Tilled them, readied, then called out—little
saplings were tossed in the bunches (thittannam)

The workers, toiling and weary are advancing, swaying back and forth to the rhythm music. They had forgotten that they were people sunk knee-deep in the mud. Nor did they think about the masters who climbed up on their shoulders to eat their ears. They had surrendered themselves to the seductive powers of the Music Goddess who pushed all sorrow into oblivion.

All except Kochukarumbi, that is. She was planting and climbing up like a machine, barely aware of anything happening around her. Not even a faint glimmer of the joy and verve that could be seen on the faces of the others on her face.

She had been here in the same field last year for the replanting. It was Tevan who had loosened the saplings for her. How eager she had been then, to move ahead planting the saplings he dug up for her! That scene was still fresh in the mind's eye. She still remembered how the other women had sung a *kuthu*[*]-song full of hints about her and Tevan. It began like this:

In the pouring of the downpour
In the rumbling of the thunder

---

[*] *Kuthu*: Critical, sarcastic not to be confused with *koothu*.

Did you see the bridegroom come
A fine mundu on his shoulder?

At that time the song had made her bashful. But remembering it today, sorrow flowed unchecked.

A beautiful head of curly hair. Eyes, long, dreamy, red-rimmed, as if drunk on wine. The broad chest covered with luxuriant dark down. Limbs, as if they had been finely carved. So handsome, that even the dark-skinned god Krishna would have been put to shame. There was not a single Pulaya maid around there who did not long to be Tevan's spouse. But, somehow, this fortune fell to Kochukarumbi's lot.

She entered Tevan's little hut bearing flower-baskets of hope. But it was not long-lived. They did not have a child together. The honeymoon had hardly ended. The play of light and dark in home life had not progressed much. The boat of life had not moved very far, buffeted back and forth by the rocks of joy and sorrow. Before long, the captain was thrown overboard. He disappeared forever into the fathomless depth of the undercurrents in the sea of life.

Kochukarumbi and her stilled dreams remained. She now passes her days racked with pain.

It took but a single night for Tevan's illness to begin on a slow note and reach a crescendo. It began as a chest pain and breathlessness. The *cheramallan*[*] got him in the fields, said the neighbours. There was a blue scar right across his chest, they said! As if he had been beaten with a stick! This was revealed by those who had bathed his body for the funeral. She did not see it. How could she? Had she not been unconscious for two days and two nights after his death?

Around then, many had said, Tevan should be summoned into the 'light'. She agreed. But how? It was not as easy as it sounded. How expensive it was! The ritual could go on and on, for one, two, or three days, even. So many materials were needed for the *poojas*. Toddy, rice-flour, and all that was needed for the *kalam*s. The exorcist and the chorus would have to be paid in cash. Where was she to find all these? How was she to bear it all by herself ...

Thaatakkita tanthaare...
Thaanappam thakkita tanthaare!
Thittaka theyyaka theyyaka thakkida
Theyyaka thakkida thantaare!

---

[*] *Cheramallan*: A supernatural entity, harmful to humans.

The womenfolk are still singing the *njaatu*-song with great gusto. Kockukarumbi was oblivious of it. She is moving forward, carrying out her tasks like a machine. Others have got ahead of her in the planting.

Thekkenthiri thiri kothambele
Why have you been so late, so late, edi?

To Kochukarumbi, who had fallen back in her row planting the rice, the older woman's *kuthu*-song was like a stab. She quickened her pace and caught up with the others.

Nature's face had changed since morning. The rain ceased. The wind calmed down somewhat. The sun began to extend its scorching arms towards the denizens of the earth, pummelling their foreheads. That's what all those who have been able to climb on the heads of other human beings have done till now—that is what they do now, and what they will do tomorrow.

The backs of the womenfolk crouching over the field standing knee-deep in the muck were like the scorching desert.

It did not bother Kochukarumbi. Her inner feelings were far more searing than the heat on her back.

She did not even realize that the labourers had reached the other end of the field; her mind was so buffeted in many directions by the torrent of thought. Poor thing, so many sighs, so many times! She collected her wages and headed towards her hut.

The universe was drifting away from the hectic world; at first towards the dark, then to solitude, and finally, to rapture. Kochukarumbi reached her hut, harried. She had never felt so exhausted. It was pitch dark inside. She felt as though the fire and the smoke that had leapt out of her mind were lingering there. The dark stifled her. Her life had been smothered, crushed. Her desires had lost their wings even before they had spread and taken to the sky.

The stone in the yard to the south of her hut was put up there the day Tevan's body was buried. A block of granite, moved here from somewhere. From that day, without fail, she lit a small lamp there every day.

She believed that Tevan's soul resided in that stone; not only she, but so did all the other Pulayas. Go to any Pulaya hut—the stones in which the dead have been sealed up are lined up in the south-side yard. The dead do not leave their clan and family. Some of them also appear, entering the bodies of their descendents. If they are not properly worshipped, the family will face trouble after trouble. So the living do not shirk that duty. That worship does not end with the lighting of a lamp. Once a year, *kalamvaippu* must be held; sacrifice must be performed. Goats, roosters, are sacrificed. Most often, a crushing expense.

Kochukarumbi could not afford the ritual drawings (*kalamvaippu*)* and the sacrifice. Every day, after dusk, she would light a wick on the stone. And then she would beat her breast and lament, relating her woes to the stone in which Tevan resided: 'I can't give, no *kalam*, no *kuruthi*, if I find a way, I'll do, *arinju cheytolam*. Pray don't sorrow. I too suffer, I'm in distress that I can't give a thing.'

That day too, as usual, she bathed and lit a lamp on the south-yard stone. The living should see light only after the dead have been given it. So she lit a lamp inside the hut only later.

She was sad that life was passing by fruitlessly. The cup had broken before the heady wine of the honeymoon could be fully enjoyed. Not that she was bereft of desire, but what could she do? It was forbidden fruit to her. She was bound by the promise they had made to each other, that the thought of a third person would not cross their hearts as long as a wisp of breath bound their bodies and souls together. She could not betray herself. She is preserving her repressed emotions and desires, shrouding them with the white sheet of sincerity.

Kochukarumbi lives by herself. Her kith and kin live close by and so she lives without fear. But the loneliness of the night was unbearable. She needed someone for company in the evening, with whom she could 'talk and say'. She did not have even that. A life without a man in the home, without a pillar for the roof!

Vallon did interrupt her lonely existence. He had long loved her. Kochukarumbi, too, did have a hint about it. But her mind had fixed itself on Tevan. Not that Vallon was a bad one. The local folk did not think very well of him. Both the rich local grandees and his own penniless people feared and disliked him. That was because the rays of a new light had penetrated his mind. He challenged the old ways of thinking and doing, set since the times of the *Paranki*†. He said that the Pulayas ought to stand together firm and surely oppose those who unleashed violence on them and squeezed out their very lives. He worked tirelessly for this cause, too. Vallon was the first in that place to have learned English, cut his hair in the new style and kept it combed and neat, sported a curving mustache, worn a silk shirt with a collar sewed

* *Kalamvaippu* is the corruption of *kalamvarappu*.
† *Paranki*: Feringhee—foreigner, that is, the Portugese.

on, walked about in a neatly starched, bleached, ironed double-mundu. Before long, all the young men lined up behind him. They followed him and copied his ways. He became an eyesore to the grandees—the *tamirutamprakal*—who considered the Pulayas to be nothing but beasts of burden. He became a thorn in the flesh of those two-legged cattle— like Kandankoran—who happily put their heads under the yokes of the grandees. This is the history of the general fear and dislike towards Vallon. No surprise that Kochukarumbi, who did not know very much of the world, disliked this impertinent fellow, but the old-fashioned and hardworking Tevan! She used to say sometimes, 'Those who didn't care for the departed folk, the respected ones, and the elders, won't ever come to any good.'

Vallon did not hesitate to declare his love after Tevan's death. Being idealistic and true to his feelings, he could not turn to another woman. He lived on, loving Kochukarumbi and declaring his feelings for her. But she passed the days remembering Tevan and holding fast to their mutual pledge. Those who move on parallel lines can never meet!

Like on many earlier occasions, that night too, the hut witnessed Vallon's presence.

It must have been past nine. Kochukarumbi had not yet gone to bed; she had just finished dinner. She was sitting opposite the tin lamp, lost in thought. She heard the sound of someone clearing his throat outside. She called out, in a harsh voice:

'Who's there—*aaraneeyedaake?*'
'It's me.'
'*Ethu*—Who, "me"?'
'Didn't make out?'
'No!'
'Open the door.'
'What for—*ennathinnanee?*'
'Will speak up inside!'

She guessed who it was. Let him go away if he would, that was what she wanted. These questions were all to that end. But the visitor is not the sort who would. In the end she had to open the door. He entered. Sounding vexed, she asked:

'Why have you come—*enthinaanee vanthekkanathu?*'
'*Chummaa*—just like that.'

'Just like that—in this *anthippaathira,* midnight hour?'
'There's no time at all in the day!'
'*Enthe?*' why?
'Have other work.'
'*Paranjechu po*—Say what you have to and leave!'
'Must I say it?'
'How else—*allandu* ... ?'
'Kochukarumbi, you are my love ...,' his voice faltered.
She cut in: '*Athu pandalle*—wasn't that long ago?'
'No, even now.'
'What about it?'
'Why do we live like this?'
'We can't die, can we—*chaakaan pachva?*'
'I beg you, for the last time.'
'*Ennatha?*'
'Let us live together for the rest of our lives.'

Kochukarumbi turned her face away. Moments throbbed, taut with emotion. Vallon lingered there. It was a heart-rending wail that he received in reply.

It was the *Chankranthy* day in the month of Karkatakam. There is no day more sacred than this for the Pulayas. It is on this day that all those who had departed were offered *taakam.* They would be taken care of, even if that meant that the living had to starve. Not even the most penniless fellow would fail to offer a *thondu*-full of toddy, flour and other items, placing them before the stones on the south side.

Kochukarumbi too did not forget this. She had kept apart a little from the wages she got each day. This was the first Chankranthy after Tevan's death. She wanted to prepare something so that his soul could rid itself of its thirst.

By dusk, all the preparations were done. When all the other necessary items were bought, she had just enough money left for a *thondu* of toddy. She cooked the *ada* stuffed with jaggery and coconut shavings. Ground the rice and winnowed the flour, put it all on a fresh-cut plantain leaf and placed the *thondu* of toddy next to it. She lit a wick first on the south-side stone and then put before it the plantain leaf full of offerings. She bowed low, folded her palms in salutation, and withdrew into the hut. The offering could be made inside the hut, too. If so, a pedestal should be readied on the southern side of the hut on which a lamp should be lit. The toddy and other foods could be offered opposite the pedestal. But Kochukarumbi felt that she should make the offering on the stone outside.

After all, wasn't that where Tevan really was?

The living should eat only the leftovers of the offerings to the dead! Whatever was cooked should be left on the plantain leaf for the departed. After some time, these could be eaten by the living. The departed would have soaked the essence and juice of the offerings. But the materials in the leaf and the *thondu* would remain.

After a few minutes, Kochukarumbi returned to the south-side yard. The wick lit there still cast a faint light around. The leaf and the *thondu* were intact. She realized it only when she stooped to pick up the leaf. The leaf and the *thondu* were bare, dry. Not a bit of the sweetmeat, not a drop of the toddy remained. How sad! Kochukarumbi's heart was shattered. How could it not? She beat her breast and wept aloud:

'*Ente Taive*! My God! *Ittaram porinchaanu* ... so famished ... *aen arinjchillalla*, I didn't know! Would've borrowed and got something more ... *kado velemedicchu enthenkilum konduvanthu tanthaanella*!' She could say no more. She returned to her hut, heartbroken.

She lay down on the mat, but could not sleep. She tossed and turned; if she shut her eyes, Tevan appeared up close. She did not feel strong enough to look at that face, wan with hunger and thirst. How could she? Did he not spend the whole of last year burning with hunger, and was she not the cause of it? If only she had had kept offering something in between, he would not have been so starved! Poor Kochukarumbi! She pressed her face in her palms and wept, lying face down on the mat.

She got up later than usual the next day. Her eyes and face were swollen. The incident of the previous day gushed back into her mind again and again. Uncontrollable sadness and guilt rolled up inside her.

She was thus standing at the door, leaning on a pillar. Vallon passed by just then. She disliked the way he smiled at her lightly. She asked him, angry, 'What is there to laugh—*enthaneeyedake*?'

'Nothing,' he said.

'*Onnumillengippinna*, then what?'

'The Chankranthy *ada* was very tasty.'

'Oho, so what?' Her lips trembled.

The words emerged through gritted teeth.

'Nothing at all,' he began to speak slowly. 'Better you realize it is no use waiting with *ada* for the dead.' He walked on, not waiting for her to respond.

Her face turned pale. As if she had blundered badly. All over, her skin, turned a sweaty pallid shade of the young coconut palm frond. Not knowing what to say, she stood stunned, staring at Vallon walking away into the distance.

—*Translated by J. Devika*

Nostalgia*

Paul Chirakkarode

Employment as a clerk in the Secretariat was not one that Ramachandran enjoyed, at least not initially. In the ardour of youth he had had more ambitious dreams. Finally, as he realized that he was growing older, the wings fell away from the desires of his heart and he sat down in the clerk's chair. 'To dream sky-high was foolish. If he had to be a clerk, then clerk he would be.'

Mother was happy. Daniel preacher returned with the joy of transforming sinners for Christ, put down the Bible carefully, and asked, 'Is there any letter from our son?'

'Here.'

Through his spectacles Daniel read his son's mind in the town far away. There were many such letters!

'Praise the Lord!'

No change came over the small hut near the bund. The seasons changed. Daniel preacher regularly set out with the Holy Bible, girding himself with his faith, to return six or seven days later.

'Praise the Lord. A hundred people confessed their sins and accepted the faith. The world is lighter of sin.'

Baby, his son would sit in the dark corner of the mud hut, reading. The dim light from the flickering wick of the tin can lamp fell before him. Through the letters, the world of knowledge spread, as endless amazement, within him. Daniel preacher prayed for everyone. He never asked for anything for himself.

But Daniel preacher prayed for his son everyday.

'God, give my son the intelligence to study. Grant him health.'

With the arrival of harvest time, festivities began in the nearby colony.

---

* Original title *Grihathurathvam*.

There was hectic work, night and day. Heaps of hay, freshly reaped grain in woven bags, the scent of new rice cooking, the sound of rice being beaten to flakes. Daniel preacher would have gone out in search of men, into the valley where the strong stench of sin spread. Baby would go to the Pulaya homes. There was nowhere else to go.

'Here, eat ... eat till you've had enough.' The Pulaya women placed beaten rice and a slice of coconut in front of him, and stood to a side.

'What to do? The preacher goes away to preach. Does the preacher know to cut and dig?'

The Gospel was the speech of spirituality, a tongue of flame. After such knowledge can a person go out to chop and to dig?

There was poverty in the house. When he returned Daniel preacher would talk about the human beings he had saved. Finally he slid his hand into his shirt pocket, and gave a handful of coins to Amma.

'Here. This is all.'

The son grew. He grew in knowledge and strength. 'Son, it is my wish that you should go out of the village like me and spread the word of God, the Good News to all people', said Daniel preacher.

For the first time Amma opposed Appa.

'For what? So that he might starve like you?'

Then the son knew how intense his mother's suffering and frustration had been. Baby wanted to get out of the mud heap. Become a great man. If he walked along the length of the land, preaching the Good News, would there be anyone to hear the holy word from a Dalit? Only a few Dalit Christians. When he returned to the discontent of the mud house after a week's preaching, all that had gathered in his shirt pocket would be a few coins.

'You should not force me, Appa. I can't.'

'Then what will you do?'

'I'll look for a job in some college.'

It was the time when many new colleges were coming up. Universities were gaining extensions.

One day the parish priest sent for him. Baby climbed the hill, cut across *vayattadi* field, rested under the *mazhavadi* tree, and reached the mission bungalow. He saw the priest's smiling face as he climbed the bungalow steps.

'Sit down.'

The priest spoke in a low voice. 'I'll give you a letter addressed to the revered bishop.'

The next Monday, he boarded the bus with the letter, his heart filled with anxiety. He passed Chetty Hill. By the time he reached the old building the white missionaries had built in Chetty Street, he felt his helplessness spread like the sea within him.

The bishop read the letter and looked at him intently for some time, like one performing a surgery. The destitute's sense of abandonment is great. He felt words in the form of pleadings, compete within him. In the growing silence between the bishop and himself, did the words resound like drums?

Finally, the bishop asked in a mild voice, 'You are Daniel preacher's son?'

'Yes.'

'Daniel preacher is a fervent believer of God, I know.'

Again silence.

'Wait. Pray to God. Haven't you read the Gospel? "If you have as much faith as a mustard seed, you can order this hill to go into the sea, and it will move to the sea." You hear me? "If you have as much faith as a mustard seed ...."'

He returned ... to the desolation of the village, the discontent of the mud house, the rupturing of dreams.

He trudged along the red mud roads of the village and sat for a long time on the cracked edge of the culvert beside Erappan canal. The canal had dried up some time ago. Where were the golden fish that used to swish their tails in the water? Where were the Brahminy kites that hid among the branches of the coconut tree waiting to snatch them?

This summer will scorch and destroy the land.

He stared at the cracked clods, the barrenness of vayattadi field. The harvest was over. Charal Hill stood tall on the northeastern side. He did not think anymore. His feet felt heavy, lethargic. He walked wearily, across Chuvattu rock and Mulakkal stream, passed Paruthi corner ... passed dark rock, and reached the top of Charal Hill.

Was climbing the hill a symbol of success in life?

Was it connected to the leaps of the heart?

Cashew trees spread along the ground. He sat down firmly on one of the branches. Fine, light breeze. Sunlight filled the deep valleys.

On east a glimpse of the Pamba river. In the flame of the summer sun, it shone like a drawn sword, as it flowed along the edge of the valley.

'All right? How did it go?'

A question by his ear. Warm breath. He saw Rosamma, a look of uncontrollable grief—like an elegy, on her otherwise vivid face.

'What else? I realized that there are many more doors to knock on.'
'You should not lose heart like this.'
'Then what should I do?'
'Pray. I too am praying.'
One more to pray for him! Are not hopes like fading flowers? They cannot spread fragrance and bloom forever. They wither, fall, disappear. If the flowers of hope also wither, what could one do?'

Another day, they met on the ridge in vayattadi field. Rosamma said, 'You must forgive me.'

'For what?'

'My wedding has been fixed—next month.'

He moved to the edge of the ridge, to let her pass. He turned back to hear a sob die down.

His youthful desires had glowed this long, like the noon sun. Only to fade. Now their colour would dim and they would disappear. He prayed for courage to stand alone in the dreamless empty desert.

One day in the reading room, the secretary advised him. 'Can you not change your name?'

The Dalit Christian is a strange creature. He is not a true Christian. He is depressed. Does he get the reservation granted to the Dalit? No, he is denied that too. He is a social amphibian. Baby smiled. A social hybrid.

He felt he had reached a tower of light.

He did not waste time thinking. He should get out of the world of the wounded. The situation of being an amphibian was an unbearable burden. It was not the salvation Daniel preacher spoke of, he had to create an address in society, a new identity.

* * *

He changed his name. Ramachandran. It was like changing his face. He was utterly bewildered. Gradually, that changed. As he sat in his chair in the Secretariat, the air from the slow whirling fan, cooled him somewhat.

Saudamini sat in the chair next to him. She was all dazzling movement, and dynamism. As the sentences lengthened, they became revelations of naked souls. Finally, marriage.

Daniel preacher did not attend the wedding.

'My son moved away from the true faith, for worldly comforts.'

He took Saudamini to his village. The land where dreams lay like old torn rags. He went to the Dalit colony.

'When did you come, saar?'

'Saar! Am I not one of you?'

Severe famine in the colony. There were no heaps of hay. No cattle lay in the sheds, chewing cud. Giant water weeds filled large parts of the uncultivated paddy fields. The taste of newly harvested grain was just a memory. Dalits who smelt of slush were a rarity.

He saw red flags aflutter in the colony.

As the sun set, he climbed the hill to the graveyard on the southern side of the church. Wild shrubs grew in the corner. Bats hung down from the branches of the jackfruit tree. Ramachandran's gaze roamed, searching everywhere. Where was Daniel preacher's grave? The man who had tied faith around his waist like a girdle, saved sinners, wandered about preaching the Good News ... that man's grave was being swept away by the sky's tears. Finally he found the place.

'Ende Apppaa—!' A cry tore out of Ramachandran's throat.

Try as he might, he could not locate his mother's grave. Once again he gazed at the eroding mounds of mud, then walked out.

They boarded the bus to town in the morning. They reached their room in the concrete building. Pictures of gods and goddesses lined one wall. The lamp Saudamini had lit stood on the floor, burning.

Ramachandran said, 'Oh all the gods are here.'

'Aren't they the ones who bless us?'

The next day Ramachandran brought a framed picture of Ambedkar.

'What is this?' Saudamini asked.

'This is the man who blessed me. If you ask me whether he is God ...'

He pulled the table and climbed on to it. He hammered a nail into the wall securely, and hung Ambedkar's picture.

He got down and stood gazing at the picture for a while. He looked at Saudamini's bewildered face and said: 'Do you know, if this man had not sculpted the Constitution, you and I would be crawling in the village clay.'

The afternoon heat grew less intense.

Ramachandran stood up.

Roads lay like black streams. They met, cut across, moved parallel at times; at times drifted apart. That was the blessing of towns. There were any number of roads to walk on. One need not fear the road would come to an end after four paces.

As Ramachandran walked, yellow light, like spikes of corn, coloured the sky above him.

Suddenly he stopped walking. At the corner of the street, above the clamour of people in the market, bloated with greed for profit, he heard another piercing voice, 'Children of the serpent, move away from the approaching fury. Now is the dawn. Now is the day of salvation.'

A couple wearing expensive clothes commented contemptuously, as they walked by, 'Listen to that Pulayan preacher!'

Loudly, like an echoing gong, the dark man began to sing.

For me it is song and praise
The divine lamb
and his Cross!

Was this man his father's reflection? Was not he too a Daniel preacher? Bushy crop of hair. Dark body. Dwarfish. Would not his pocket too contain some small change?

This man who preached salvation; would his son too have lost the girl he loved? Had he walked troubled, along the loveless desert? Had that son put on a mask for a job, for food? Had he changed his name?

The questions intertwined within him. Whom should he ask? Ramachandran walked on quickly. He realized he had reached the big church, in the centre of the town.

He looked up. He could not see the huge cross above the church. Where was the sky? He had thought the sky to be an intense blue expanse. Even after he read the books of Eddington, James Jeans, and Stephen Hawking, this poetic image remained. He could see nothing. Like a cloak of mourning, unfastened and thrown down, the night flowed as darkness over the town.

Buses plied the roads with their three-eyed lights. Place names on their lighted brows. All those places teemed with people. The slush-like Dalits lived on the margins. Would the Dalits whose bodies smelt of the soil, become a rarity? In a land where agriculture was becoming alien—without cutting and hoeing and digging deep into the soil, without the Pulayan's sweat to irrigate its breast, sighing heavily like the sigh of a virgin who has lost her fantasies—the Pulayan was losing the scent of the shrub-covered earth.

Ramachandran left the town's main road and turned left. The horizon was now behind him. The crimson of the setting sun had faded. Since he walked with his back to it, he was not certain if any vestige remained.

When he turned a corner, a thousand glimmering dots of light from the row of single-storied houses on the brows of the eastern hills met his eyes. Ramachandran recalled that one of these dots was his own house.

The government employees' colony, which environmentalists mockingly called the concrete jungle. There his son sat, his head bent over his book; there his daughter sat mournfully, because she could not watch TV; there Ambedkar's photograph hung on the smiling whitewashed wall. Nylon curtains swung playfully on the windows.

Was this growth?

Was he growing into a master?

A bestial nostalgia seized Ramachandran. An intense obsession. He wanted to smell slush; the slush in the paddy fields. In childhood he had smelt slush as he tasted the freshly harvested rice. Where were the mud pots? The smell of slush? What he had lost was so many experiences.

City buses, with place names in the third eye on their foreheads, came, stopped, then sped off, panting. Finally, he got into the bus that went to his colony and sat down at the back. His fellow passengers enthusiastically discussed the next Pay Commission.

Immediately, the song of the Dalit preacher began to echo in his heart.

For me it is song and praise
The divine lamb
And his Cross!

The song fell like waves on his heart even after he got down from the bus. He walked towards the employees' colony, listening to the song. A thousand lights, a thousand windows. He knocked on the door of number 141. Saudamini opened the door.

'Shall I serve dinner?'

'After a while.'

His son raised his head from the book he held.

His daughter sat before the TV, her face a thundercloud.

Routine sights.

Ramachandran sank into a chair.

That song. It was being sung by none other than his father, Daniel preacher. That musical voice that had so often called out to him, '*Mone*, son!' Ramachandran returned to the past, the past that had gravel hills, the lower Chuvattu rock, and vayattadi fields. With the ears of his soul he hearkened to the song. He closed his eyes and lay in an intoxication of oblivion.

—Translated by Catherine Thankamma

Madness*

C. Ayyappan

A couple of days ago, you—my childhood friend and neighbour—had dropped in at my staff quarters. You couldn't possibly have forgotten what happened then, could you? But then, any incident has to be witnessed by no less than two people with their own eyes (or at least eyeglasses) to grasp even a speck of its sense, so you must listen to my version of what happened as well.

It was in the morning that you landed at my doorstep with your cronies that day. When I answered the door, you and your gang began talking all at once, like a floodgate thrown open. I was somewhat taken aback at first but could make out two things from all your drivel—that my sister's illness had taken a turn for the worse, and that I must help get her admitted to the nearest mental asylum.

I remember my response quite well. You suppose you know more about my sister's illness than I do, I had said; but I am certain that it is not her but the lot of you—who ran from pillar to post, pooling money and turning up here, car and all—that has gone mad.

That was when you pointed to my sister in the car parked outside, screaming for her chains to be unshackled. I insisted—I don't see a thing. And although your next question, pained and incredulous one that it was, made me turn a shade paler, I slammed the door shut rather dramatically and managed to save my skin.

This lone incident has turned all your notions and ideas about me upside-down, hasn't it? No doubt you believe that my behaviour that day was sheer savagery. You may even allege that I'd forgotten my origins, what with a decent job under my belt and a good-looking, well-employed wife. Right now, I have no comment to make on that.

Truth be told, even I couldn't understand why I behaved the way I had at first. But when I did, I was rather in awe of my smartness and could not help congratulating myself. You don't get it, do you?

Have you ever thought of what would have happened to me if I had done your bidding, dear friend?

Suppose I had come with you to the mental asylum, which, by the way, isn't very far from the quarters where I stay—there's more than

---

* Original title *Branthu*.

a fair chance that the residents here would have got wind of it. If not anyone else, that writer—the one who always lifts whole chunks from award-winning works into his own stories—is sure to sniff it out in no time at all. That is enough for the entire neighbourhood to buzz: 'Krishnan maash's sister has gone mad!'

You may think this is no big deal, but can't you see what would happen then? When the news gets around, several of the quarters' residents would gather at the hospital, and at least a few among them are sure to notice the sharp difference between me and my folks. Forget the madwoman; the problem is with those who tend to her. Their clothes and mine would be endlessly compared. And then my neighbours from the quarters would add, almost unwittingly: 'Krishnan may have become a teacher by chance, but his kith and kin are still low-caste, aren't they?'

Needless to say, this is a matter of deep shame for me, and I am prepared to put up with it too. But that's when the embers of another problem emerge, eyes glowing.

Now that my sister has been admitted in a hospital here, anyone would suppose that my wife ought to visit her. I shouldn't think otherwise either—but then my wife absolutely despises all the riffraff that are her husband's relatives. It may sound unpleasant, but I think her predicament is natural, especially for one you'd never suspect is herself a low-caste. Given her fair skin and her good looks, her aversion to people descended from those that lived on the beef of dead cows cannot seem so odd, can it?

Well, it is still possible to silence her somehow and get her to the hospital. If I suffer her long tirades about my 'uncultured' folks like a deaf-mute, I know she will tire. Thereafter, I can manage her. But that brings me to another problem from which I see no escape...

It is our only daughter who opens the door to it. She is a peculiar character. You could say that both in looks and outlook, she is a perfect miniature of her mother. Do you know what hurt and humiliation my own mother had to suffer when she had come over to see her? You don't? Let me tell you.

It happened long ago, about half-a-dozen years into our stay here at the quarters, when our daughter was six years old. Amma had come all agog to meet her son's daughter with a small parcel of *pappadavadas* from the local tea shop. Despite her repeated calls (and my silent fuming), our daughter refused to go anywhere near her grandmother. Slamming the door shut and without a second glance, the girl fled to a friend's quarters nearby—only to return when she was certain my mother had left. I had not said anything then. Wasn't she a mere child? And then I thought my mother was also partly to blame. Perhaps it wasn't a big deal that my daughter was seeing my mother for the first time, but surely Amma could have worn a cleaner, whiter mundu-blouse? Especially when she isn't all that fair-skinned in the first place. You see, black is not a colour my daughter is familiar with—even her friends have the same complexion as those angelic mannequins you see in front of the textile shops in town!

I must add here that both my wife and daughter are nothing if not good-natured—it is just that they despise my folks with all their heart. Born of well-employed, fairly well-off parents and not really having known any hardship, my wife's understanding of the world is meagre at best. As for our daughter, she is being brought up in these upper middle-class quarters where the only dark-skinned and shabbily clad people she has seen are the Tamil coolies and beggars. Just my bad luck that my people happen to share the colour of their skin.

Even if my wife and daughter refuse to come along, why can't I go ahead and visit my ailing sister? That is a good question. To which my counter-question would be—how come my state of helplessness has not yet touched your hardened hearts?

If I take charge of my sister, a family quarrel is sure to break out. Trust me, my wife and daughter are not a pretty sight when they get angry. Even if I decide to put up with it somehow, it is of no avail. How will I escape the jeers of my associates who always see me through scorn-tinted lenses! To be recognized in public as the brother of the one who was admitted to mental hospital by the many kindnesses of the townsfolk! As it were, I slouch around, limping and dragging my feet, riddled by an inferiority complex. If this, too, were added to it ....

No, there is nothing wrong in what I have done. There is but one more question, and let me be the one that ask that too: All said and done, is it not the duty of a brother to visit an ailing sister in hospital at least once?

I have no qualms in endorsing that the visiting of a patient by the latter's near and dear is an admirable exercise. I truly believe that the earthen lamps of human kindness and culture are kept aglow with practices such as these. But I do not intend doing the same just yet. Do not assume it is because I am a heartless man. You see, there is no point in my meeting a sister who is not of sound mind and who cannot recognize me, to begin with. When my visit itself would mean nothing to her, what is the good of bending over backwards to indulge in that pointless exercise? Seems a no-brainer to me. Seems, too, that you're as unwilling as ever to admit I have some brains after all. Else why would you, my childhood friend, ask me with such anguish, even as I looked at my screaming sister in the car and claimed I didn't see a thing: 'Krishnankutty, have you gone mad as well?'

Well at least now, you know that there's absolutely nothing the matter with me, don't you?

—*Translated by Abhirami Sriram*

The Story of a Sickle*

P.A. Uthaman

I was standing near the washing-stone by the well, to wash our baby's soiled swaddle-clothes, our elder son's shorts and shirts, and a couple of underskirts. 'There's nothing shameful about him washing the underskirts that he undoes every night,' my wife gloats to her friends. She washes my clothes, after all, so it is a fair exchange, although something in me demurs from washing a sari or blouse. And no qualms about the title 'henpecked'. The lot of one who lives in his wife's house! And I am not saying anything about my own house either ....

Kurumba Muthukki†, the old one, arrived just as I began washing the clothes. The silent laughter that would bubble up in me when I had heard that name first, is now missing.

'Appee, my boy, aren't these clothes to be washed by women?' she asked.

After watching me for some time, she continued, 'Son, will you write out a letter for me today?'

Her left leg and hand did not flex freely, and she struggled to move her left leg forward and pull herself along. Manodattan, my son, had nicknamed her 'Tableau Granny'. The stillness in her movement had fascinated him.

I was hard-pressed for time ....

'I will write it for you when I am less busy.'

---

* Original title *Oru Pullaruppothiyude Katha*.
† Muthukki: An old woman.

She smiled, opening her toothless mouth and smacking her lips. 'Ah, so you don't have time, son.' And turned and hobbled slowly away.

There was a sickle tucked away at her back. When she removed the towel wrapped around her head, you could see her closely cropped hair. After a futile attempt at wiping her face with the towel, she wrapped it around her head again in a peculiar rhythm.

My wife who brought tea, stood looking at the flakes of the baby's faeces swimming in the water in the basin like fingerlings. 'Oh, *you* ...' she muttered angrily under her breath as she went back to the kitchen.

A week passed. On one of those early morning walks undertaken with all the enthusiasm of someone new to the neighbourhood, I saw Kurumba Muthukki outside her little thatched hut, lovingly tending the courtyard. The tidy courtyard was fringed by a hedge of hibiscus. A *mandaaram* tree stood in full bloom next to shrubs of *pavizhamalli*. Not a dry leaf left unattended anywhere in the small plot. Pepper vines spread at the foot of trees. The ground around the coconut trees had been hoed and manure-beds prepared. A whole new world within four or five cents of land.

'Did someone write out the letter for you, Muthukki?'

She squinted into the alleyway, trying to make out who it was. The moment she recognized me, she said, 'Didn't you say you will do it when you are free, son? Then why ask anyone else?'

'What to write?' I stepped down into the courtyard.

She entered the hut. A room, veranda, and the kitchen.

On one of the rafters of the hut hung a couple of old reed baskets, one covered with the other and fastened together.

'Let me untie the round-box,' she said, and took out an Inland Letter Card and a pencil stub from the reed basket.

The letter was to her daughter, son-in-law, and children, living in some far-off place. It is not easy to reproduce her words verbatim. Hence my version in neutral language:

You didn't come for Deepavali. Nor for the Karkkidakam New Moon. Neither for the Festival at Paaranada. You stayed for just a day on Onam. Our neighbour Mayamma's cow Nandini has delivered. All six kittens of the black cat are female. Kuttan the dog went rabid. People clubbed him to death. He had not bitten anyone. Neeli's daughter eloped with the man who came to teach in the Sanghappura. After a month, she came back alone. It's three months now since her last menstrual bath.

That was the end of the letter.

Half in jest, I asked the old woman to sign. She plucked a mandaaram flower, pressed it on the paper with a rigid finger and said, 'This'll do.'

When she plucked the flower, the tiny birds perched on the shrubs rose in riotous clamour. A cluster of butterflies hovered over the hedges.

She showed me a piece of paper on which her daughter's address was written. Then she asked me, 'Read what you have written, son.'

Straightaway she made me correct a word that she had not dictated, and add three words which I had omitted. She said she would post the letter.

'You don't need to walk to the post office, Muthukki. I'll post it,' I offered.

She would have none of it. Folding up the Inland, Muthukki kept it in the round-box.

'Son, if I don't walk about, I may curl up somewhere soon,' she said, laughing.

'What shall I give you in return for writing this letter, son?' Pointing to the coconut tree that had grown to a man's height, she said, 'Pluck two tender coconuts for yourself.'

Muthukki's hut became one of the halts on my early morning walks. If she was found outside, I'd stop by briefly and chat with her.

And then one day there was no sign of her. By and by, the courtyard and the compound were covered with dry leaves and overgrown with weeds. Birds and butterflies were about to desert the place.

After two months, on a holiday, she came to my house. It was about noon. She refused to eat the lunch that we offered.

'Where were you?'

No reply.

She said that I must write her story. She showed me a photograph of herself with the sickle held close to her cheek, like a question mark. Her eyes were brimming over.

'What is this for?' I asked, laughing.

'I don't want to live anymore. Before I die, I want to write a letter to my grandchildren.'

'If I die, don't cremate me. It will cause a terrible, unbearable stench. Bury me instead. Each particle of my body should crumble and be absorbed by the soil. And all the while, my sickle should be in my hand.'

But how to die?

'Can't climb a tree, make a noose and hang myself. If I am to drown myself in a well, I have to climb onto its parapet wall. What if my head strikes awkwardly somewhere when I plunge into the well? Besides, people won't be able to drink water from that well anymore. If I were to take poison, what if someone found me out and saved me?'

All the same, she had resolved to die.

Said Kurumba Muthukki (I am trying to record what she said in her own style as faithfully as possible):

When I got this sickle to cut grass, I was all of six. Ever since, that's been my only support. When my father died, there were three children younger to me. And mother. Took them all on my shoulders. Cut grass along with mother. Mother fell ill after long years of working in the fields. Of the three children, God snatched the hand of one. The other two grew up to earn government salaries. I was the one who was hated. Then too, I had only this sickle.

Mother was gone. So were the siblings. Who was there for me?

And then my elder sister, my maternal aunt's daughter, died, leaving behind five children. Five boys. Their father took me on to support them as a mother. He put a thread around my neck, and I became the mother of those five. As days went by, he developed a relationship with his own niece, behind my back. But I found out.

Who was there to support me, though I was acting as the mother of someone else's five children? I too wanted a child, of my own flesh and blood.

One midnight, he slunk away from me and the children to his niece's place. I followed him there, dragged him back to our house, put him in a room and closed the door. That was how my daughter, my own blood, was born.

He eloped with his niece shortly after. But he came back home one day, alone. (Got to know later that she had left him and eloped with someone else.) My brother caught him and tied him to the coconut tree. When the ant-nest burst and red neeru* ants covered him all over, biting him, I said, 'Untie him, Sankaran.' Sankaran obeyed me, but was totally cross with me afterwards and hated the child growing in my womb as well.

When I was pregnant with my daughter, I had this craving to eat roasted plantains. Leaning a bamboo ladder on the tree, I climbed and plucked two plantains from the bunch that grew on the tree in the courtyard. When the plantains roasted in the fireplace, its aroma spread all over the place. Just then, Sankaran came up to the courtyard and stood under the plantain tree. The sap from the raw bunch from where the plantains had been plucked, dripped on to his head. 'Who's it that plucked plantains from my tree?' he roared.

'It's me da,' I retorted.

'You found only the plantain-bunch on *my* tree to feed your craving?' he asked.

Pulling out a machet, he cut down the tree and hacked it into pieces. 'Getting knocked up by someone, don't you dare climb my plantain tree again!' he said.

---

* *Neeru*: A species of red ants that are found in clusters on trees.

Raising all the five children with care, and seeing them doing well, I left them to their father. I was left in the street, all on my own, along with my daughter.

When my little one was able to walk about, I once went to see her father, just to stop the child's tantrum of wanting to see him. He bought a piece of puttu and kadala and tea for her; and just stroked her hair once. That was all. I haven't seen him ever after; neither has my daughter.

How we suffered! I was bedridden, paralysed in one leg and one arm. Was there anyone to take care of my child? She looked after me, working and studying. I recovered, like a hen who got a second life.

'The ammyar* who once got her fields ploughed, rice-saplings planted, the fields weeded and finally harvested only after consulting me, suddenly didn't want the grass I cut, and wouldn't give me any work in her fields. The other labourers who used to work with me hung their heads whenever they saw me. A time when people were making it impossible to live. Who then in Puthiyakaavu market would take the grass I cut! And how many miles away Puthiyakaavu was! I would take a break every now and then, setting the bundle down on the wayside milestones. If not, my neck would have broken. Walking all the way to the market, I'd wait for people to buy the grass. Nobody would pick it up. Couldn't throw it by the wayside either. Wasn't it the fruit of my struggle? How could I throw it away? I would return, the child by my side. The distance would seem twice as long on the return trip. The child would be hungry, I knew. But what could I give her? In the moonlight, a bundle of grass on my head, and the child.

When the road came to an end, the paddy fields came to view. The endless fields that stretched beyond the distance I had already walked! The paddy fields were full of ripe paddy. I was the one who'd gather the labourers together for harvesting. I got them together to work in the fields. Today there was no one to call me for work. They wouldn't even acknowledge my presence.

When we had passed about half the way through the fields, the child took the sickle from my waist and asked me: 'Mother, how much do paddy we need to make kanji?' Just as I answered, she cut the paddy-ears. Collecting the cut paddy-ears, and with the bundle of grass on my head, I ran. Going past the mud-dykes in the paddy fields, we climbed the hill. If some straying eyes happened to fall on me or my child in the moonlight ...

I told only Kumaran Master.

'Kurumba, you must cut that ammyar's head like you cut the paddy-ears,' laughed Kumaran Master. 'Your daughter is smart.'

I had to bring up the daughter. And also fight with the landlord! Kumaran Master said, 'Far to the east, near Parassala, there is an ammyar's matham. Put

---

* Ammyar: Tamil Brahmin housewife.

your daughter there. She will take care of her expenses. The child can study as well.'

Master gave us the money for the bus-fare. When we reached there, it was already dusk. It started raining. Wherever we looked, there were palmyra trees. Those eastern palmyra trees that let out a kind of howling laughter. Where would we go in the dark? A man who came that way showed us the ammyar matham. He said the ammyar wouldn't let anyone in at night. He said, 'Try your luck. If she doesn't let you in, that house nearby, where you see the light, is mine. Come over, you can stay for the night in my house.' The kindness of that man born to a good mother! Otherwise, where could I have gone with my youthful daughter?

Standing in the courtyard of ammyar matham in the rain, I called out to her a number of times. An ammyar opened the door and asked what the matter was. When I told her, she said, 'Come tomorrow morning. We don't take in anyone here at night.' 'Where will I go with this child?' I pleaded in tears, describing my predicament.

Finally she gave us a place to sleep, a lean-to in which so many things were stored. Bless her. At night, when I wanted to go out to pee, I found that the door was locked from the outside. Me and my child passed urine there itself. Our clothes were all wet ...

In the morning, she opened the door ...

'I locked you in because you were strangers ...,' she explained.

Let at least my child be saved ....

But my daughter told me of her sufferings only later ...

After all of us were given plots of land in the landlord's compound and we settled down, when she began to go to college, and worked as a daily labourer ... returning home, she would tell me little by little ....

Kurumba Muthukki grew silent for some time, her eyes were brimming. Suddenly she resumed:

During the struggle with the landlord, I had shouted 'Zindabad' throughout, holding aloft the red flag. Once, AKG* put a garland of red thread around my neck. Another time, when Namboodiri* came, he held my hand and said something, which I didn't understand. Then, how many more people! Wherever 'Zindabad' was to be shouted, Kurumba should be there in front! Also Kurumba's daughter! Shouting the slogan, thus ....

The young leaders of these days do not know me or my daughter. They won't even wait to listen to us. But, Kumaran Master, he was different ....

Even now, when I see the red glimmer at the top of poles in people's hands, fluttering, these legs and hands of mine make me really restless ....

---

* A.K. Gopalan and E.M.S. Namboodirpad: Political and social leaders and reformers.

Of late, even my eyes have begun to fail me. The red of the flag is not as red as it used to be in the olden days. When I go to see my daughter and family, I must tell them to do something for my eyesight ....

Comrade Sukumaran Nair brags, 'Can a woman fight a landlord singly who has as much landed property as an entire panchayat? A Kurathi, at that! Comrade Kumaran Master, former President of Kunnummal Panchayat, is a good man, but a simpleton too. If he so much as sees someone's tears, then that's it .... All his ways are that of truth. I talked to the landlord, as Kumaran Master was too busy .... I took over the supervision of the cases of Kurumba Kurathi, and of a few more like her. When Kurumba said, 'I must get a stay on the case on the land', I hinted to her, 'if someone advises you to get a stay, it is to hoodwink you. Don't go in for a case or quarrel. I will see that you get the right of a homestead on the land you are occupying.' I kept telling Kumaran Master that all was well. I also told the landlord that I would ensure that the tenants would somehow be evicted. That's how Kurumba's hovel was pulled down and burned with the assistance of the police, and she was put behind bars. I knew that if she could be subdued, all the other cowards would lie low.' Comrade Sukumaran Nair, the Member of the Panchayat ward, laughs.

Comrade Kumaran Master says, 'Kurumba's case is not hers alone. It's that of all the tenants of the old Kunnummal Panchayat. It was not as the President of the Panchayat that I got involved in this case. My relationship was that of the red of one's blood. Comrade Sukumaran Nair being the Ward Member I felt he could pay more attention to it. That's how I handed over to him the struggle that I had led so far. I got to know that he had been feeding me with wrong information, only when Kurumba's hut was set on fire and she was shut away in jail. The landlord had bribed Comrade Sukumaran Nair. He had also collected money from Kurumba and other tenants on the pretext of conducting the case.'

Those were ominous times, when the entire land was on fire. Emergency. Even then, our struggle was with the landlord, who owned two-hundred acres. On the path, they planted thorny shrubs. They mixed faeces into our drinking water. Faeces in the food cooked in the hut. They denied us work throughout that locality. They persecuted us endlessly.

One noon, I was cutting grass. Not yet enough for a bundle. It was then that a child came running, saying our hut was on fire. Leaving the chopped grass behind, I raced down, sickle in hand. When I reached my compound, the police and the henchmen of the landlord had pulled down my hut and set it on fire.

As I roared, 'Who burned down my hut?' and rushed forward, they caught me, threw me into the police jeep and drove away. They shut me away in jail.

They had planned to kill me that night. When they thought I was sleeping, one of the police officers opened the cell and stepped in: 'We must kill her with a single kick.' Even before he began, I sprang up and shouted. 'Kill me. But you must finish me off with one kick. If not, you'll have to eat me alive.' He turned around and walked away.

I said, 'Why are you keeping me here? Why don't you present me in the court? I want to tell the magistrate everything.' Those cowards. They didn't dare.

I was sitting thus, when Kumaran Master arrived. He got me out on bail. I was worried about my child. She got to know that the hut was set on fire when she was at school. A fire was raging in my child's heart. I touched her chest.

It was after this incident that I put my child in the ammyar matham to save her.

Kumaran Master made Sukumaran Nair accompany him to Thiruvananthapuram, to meet Gowri Amma, taking me and my child also along. We somehow reached her, after wandering about in that mansion with so many rooms.

Kumaran Master said certain things to Gowri Amma. She then told Sukumaran Nair, 'Depraved fellow! Couldn't you stop your betrayal at least after seeing the face of this child? Would you have betrayed her if she was your own daughter?'

She told me, 'Sister! This scoundrel has been cheating you. Taking the money you earned cutting grass, he was siding with the landlord, burning down your house and even trying to kill you.'

She told Sukumaran Nair, 'Away from my sight, you dog!'

The blaze that singed my heart then! What if my child had been in the hut, and they had burned her too! If I had the sickle with me, I would have hacked him to death then and there. Or I would have beheaded my daughter, cut my own throat and made him eat us.

I didn't wait. Holding my child's hand, I ran from there. The Thiruvananthapuram railway station was somewhere near there.

Running after her I could catch up with her only in front of the Secretariat. A mother and daughter, as if caught in a terrible storm. According to Kumaran Master).

The trouble I had, trying to turn her away from her resolve to die.

Finally, the struggle dragged on till the plot was registered in her name and a hut could be built near where her old hut stood.

It's about one who's dead and gone. One who tried to dig a hole to bury us alive. Panchayat Member Sukumaran Nair died, maggots crawling from his rotting body.

Kumaran Master, one who stands smiling below a fluttering red flag. How sharp and shining, the sickle on that flag!

Wiping away the sweat on her face, Kurumba Muthuki sighs. She continues, slowly:

A lapse on the part of my daughter and me. Some useless fellow fell at my feet and begged me. One who had been her classmate in college. Melting at his tears, I gave my daughter to him. He left her in a short time. And my child ….

From so many deadly situations, so many people saved my daughter. Then pillar to post, court, case … till she was freed of him.

She grew silent. After sitting like that for some time, she left.

A month later, I met Kurumba Muthukki during my morning walk.

'Where are you going?'

'To my son-in-law's house. To see my grandchildren.'

'Where is your sickle, Muthukki?' I asked.

'Oh, I gave the sickle to my son-in-law, when I went there the last time. What else to give him, who gave a second life to my daughter, without seeing anything, without asking anything.'

On another day, when Kurumba Muthukki appears before her house with a sickle, I ask, 'Didn't you give the sickle to your son-in-law?'

'Yes, I gave it to him. This is another one I bought.'

'Can't you live quietly with your children, Muthukki …?'

'Only if I die on this soil, will my soul find its peace. Till then, with this sickle ….'

Kurumba Muthukki begins to laugh.

(The details of such a struggle as the above-mentioned one would never be found in Panchayat records. All of this would have been formed in the muddled head of Kurumba Muthukki. I even stopped my early morning walks along that route.)

—Translated by A.J. Thomas

Luminous White[*]

P.K. Prakash

1

Curiosity transformed into character.

2

Once, not so long ago and yet not so recently, was born a certain Curiosity, in the tiny space on earth called Keralam, in a state of parallelism. The scents of the soil, the misty cold, the stony caresses. Overwhelmed, curiosity's eyes turned red.

3

Curiosity sits gazing at the sky. It is now of the age they call 'youth'. This one, too, like all other youngsters, is mere husk. If this Curiosity looks like it is going to weep tonight it's because your vision and mine have focused and merged. And what is Curiosity looking for, all alone and uncaring of the romantic shades of night the whisper of leaves in the moonlight?

4

Over to the mindscape of Curiosity.

Above, the vast expanse of the sky. Real fun to watch the grey clouds break and shift. A kaitha appears on the cloud-mat. Avoiding romantic cowardice, there stands the kaitha in full bloom. Nebulae fill up. Galaxies break open. If the illusions of the Milky Way are so enormous, what about the universe? My! O Light that began its journey tens of thousands of years ago, how could you shine through these eyes even today? Know this: if there is a race, it is yours. Light, the root cause beyond tens of thousands of years, you touch us like chains and split us into rows.

5

Curiosity pales at the thought of race. It gets so distortingly close to old age. In *Del Age*, Simon de Beauvoir stated categorically that old

---

[*] Original title *Veluppu*.

age is not an ugly state. Now, extreme old age is being distorted. In the clarity of youth, sometimes old age and at other times youth, become undercurrents. Polluting components are created. Race becomes chained bondage.

And therefore proletarianism ripples away, creating an emotional sensation. The illusion that the reality that society is oppressed, is employed. At the close encounter of its alienated lower and higher levels, Curiosity vomits. Now it can stand on its feet like an ecstatic lover after love-making.

With no accusations, with no complaints, absorbing struggle and oppression from spaces personal and otherwise, Curiosity becomes as still as a tree stump.

6

Now Curiosity expands the parallelism and melts away into nothingness. You and I cannot see it afterwards because it is invisible to man.

'Man'—what a limited word!

—*Translated by Shirley M. Joseph*

Paalakkunnan's Journey*

M.K. Madhukumar

Putting his foot down on the exuberant voices of Onam and sending them to the netherworld, Paalakkunnan left. The eyes that had once sketched the glories of the new dawn were pouring torrents now. Paalakkunnu—the village on the hill on which the ancient paala tree stood—was now dead. The paala that towered into the sky and threw its green canopy in a wide circle let its hair down and split the sky into shards. Paalakkunnu clung to the roots of the tree and slept fretfully. Held by roots that had grown across the cycle of innumerable births and deaths, the last fount of its nourishment yet to dry up, the giant tree held its breath, smothering the pulses of generations.

Paalakkunnu's slumber was broken by human voices. Pathways were thrown open to it. Its history unfolded into a grand spectacle. The

---

* Original title *Paalakkunnande Yaatra*.

visitors hugged one another and wept, like long lost friends. Their tears flowed in an unending stream—like the vast ocean of the past leaking through a hole in the seabed. Paalakkunnan had arrived from the shores of the distant past—a time before Paalakkunnu's history began. Nobody knew when. Wearing the mystery of his origin like a halo, he smiled triumphantly. He then set out on his furious campaign that spanned ages. Squatting under the paala on the hill, stretching his legs, he chewed betel-and-nut dressed with lime and tobacco and spat out the red concoction ceremoniously. He spent sleepless nights listening to the agonizing voices in the valley. The anthills on the hill waged a desperate battle, bleeding themselves to white death. New gods were consecrated on the hill with ringing bells and spinning conches.* Death possessed the oracles who screamed and split their foreheads with long swords. But the gods were frozen in their silence. The new gods in their gorgeous mansions laughed and danced over their overflowing barns.

Paalakkunnan was still listening.

The call of the kingdom of heaven resounded in the valley. It coiled itself into a trumpet and climbed on to the crest of the hill. It shuttled between heaven and hell. It intoxicated many. Some swooned. Some rose to challenge it. But the trumpeting voices crushed them ruthlessly. Finally, on a night when everything that was suppressed exploded into a blaze, Paalakkunnan flung the trumpet into the valley and went back up the hill.

Miseries piled up in a heap around Paalakkunnan. Seated in their midst he writhed. The cycle of birth and death hibernated in the roots of the paala. Paalakkunnan lay back on his own roots.

The ancient kings with their sceptres and crowns...

As ages passed like murmurs on Paalakkunnan's lips, the eyes of the hill clouded.

'Do not send the generations that sprung from you on to wander in a maze.'

Generations squatted under the paala and the harrowing tale of the journey from royal splendour to captivity stagnated in Paalakkunnan like a pool of muddy water. The long line of generations that descended from him scooped it up in their begging bowls. The god that held the heavenly bodies in the palm of his hand descended on the boughs of the paala. Hope bloomed. Storms that were unleashed from all directions

---

* Conches: Rituals associated with both consecration and magic.

swept the hill. They brushed against the corpses floating on the flood waters. Corpses sprang to life on the rocks of terror and screamed before locking themselves in an eerie embrace.

Paalakkunnan continued to live on the hill, linking generation to generation. Nobody came to find out how life pulsated on the hill. All those who came were marauders who ravaged the hill. There were others who merely wandered in the valley, adrift. Never leaving his seat under the paala, Paalakkunnan drove his dream-chariots of the golden ages of the past into Paalakkunnu. The roots of the paala reached down to the valley and kissed the sprouting springs. But the wanderers in the valley mercilessly chopped off the new sprouts. Blood oozed from its groping fingertips. Paalakkunnan held the young generation close to him and whispered the message of his heart in their ears. Beyond Paalakkunnu, the world was in turmoil. Roars and battlecries were heard in the distance. Paalakkunnan pressed our tiny fingertips on a patch of sand under the paala and taught us to write. Along with the letters, Paalakkunnan's benign smile and the tears it hid imprinted themselves on our minds. The flickering flames of knowledge sprouted to life in the dark caverns of history.

As the flames sprang to life we saw Guru's face with a shudder.

'Once ...' Guru tuned history in the strings of his voice.

'Once ...'

'Once upon a time ...'

We huddled closer and listened with rapt attention. A breeze stirred the paala's canopy. Guru nodded, paying obeisance to the murmur of the leaves.

Guru passed on the tale of Lord Maveli to the young tongues of Paalakkunnu.

'He was the progenitor of us all, mighty and righteous, the embodiment of justice ...'

'But Vaamana sent him to the netherworld!' we children chimed.

'That is what Vaamana and his cohorts will always say.' The flash of rage in Guru's eyes disturbed us. Then, turning to the recesses of his soul for a moment, he added: 'No Vaamana can ever send Truth to the netherword.'

A storm lashed Paalakkunnu. The wanderers in the valley lost their steps. They trained their guns on the storm. But the guns only pursed their lips and growled. Paalakkunnan heard the growls.

'My task is coming to an end.'

Paalakkunnan wept. Nobody saw the tears—his first and last. Pressing his lips to the bosom of the paala, Paalakkunnan wept copiously. 'Keep your great truths in abundance for all those who come here henceforth.'

As the paala swung the long strands of its hair, particles of life spilled on its roots and swayed in a wave of memories.

'Take unto you the conch the Black One sent spinning.'

A clap of thunder descended on the paala out of a clear sky.

'Keep his bell and skull safely.'

The call of the conch resounded on Paalakkunnu, on which the first rays of the Onam sun fell hesitantly. The blackbirds which roosted on the paala flew away, their wings making no sound as they vanished into the distance.

Nobody spoke.

A long sigh broke the silence.

Then everything was quiet again.

Paalakkunnan heard the call of eternity as he invoked the *Thiruvonams** of the distant past. The paala shook its hair. No, your roots will not allow you to fall.

O, Guru, we receive your seed unto our empty and barren wombs. There are only the unending, unbearable roars of our machines to watch over your stirring seed. Shall our machines fold it neatly, pack it into a colourful carton and deliver it?

—*Translated by K.M. Sherrif*

---

* *Thiruvonam*: The last and most important day of the harvest festival which falls on the lunar asterix of the star, Thiruvonam.

EXCERPTS FROM NOVELS

The novel in Malayalam had its beginnings in 1878 with *Ghathakavadham*, the translated version of Mrs Richard Collin's *The Slayer Slain* (1859). This novel portrays the continuing subservient status of Pulaya converts to Christianity. Yearning for relief from their inhuman conditions and in utter despair, there was a mass conversion of Pulayas as a protest against injustice. Most of them were agricultural workers in bonded labour to their upper-caste landlords in a highly exploitative and oppressive system. Squeezed at the bottom of the most repressive socio-religious structures known to man, conversion to Christianity was an escape from the suppressed feelings of revulsion at, and opposition to, the evils of landlordism. However, it did not turn out to be as liberating as promises had led them to expect. Though Dalit converts were to an extent protected from physical violence, the landlords with their tactics of intimidation and coercion continued to be oppressive. Moreover, people in general, irrespective of whether they belonged to a high or low class, subscribed to a feudal notion that manual agricultural labour was the life order and destiny of Dalits. This established casteist/feudalist notion was reinforced by the physical agility of the energetic Dalit labourer. In such a traditional social system, the control over Dalits was threatened when the converted Dalit demanded a weekly day-off on Sunday to worship their Saviour and ensure liberation for their souls.

'We are also humans. We also have a soul. We will work as hard as possible on six days of the week. But we need a holiday on Sunday to think about our souls and of the Lord above.' (*The Slayer Slain*)

This demand was considered against the norm and was strongly resented by the landlords.

Yet another novel of the same period *Pullerikunju* (1882) by Archdeacon Koshy depicts the brutal manhandling of Pulayas within Hindu society. Following this, *Sukumari* (1897) by Mooliyil Joseph and *Parishkaara Vijayam* (1906) by Chori Peter also depicted a Christian perspective on the prevailing Hindu caste system. All these novels were instrumental in presenting religious conversion as an emancipatory project, which turned out to be a myth.

In North Malabar, the Thiyyas/Ezhavas who had been educated in English were introduced to the concepts of modernity, which were western in spirit and nature. Potheri Kunjambu who belonged to the Avarna Thiyya community, wrote *Saraswathivijayam* (1892), which presented characters like Mathan, the educated Pulayan who rose to the position of a judge and Kuberan Namboodiri, the ex-landlord who as both accused and culprit had to pay obeisance to the Pulaya judge. Potheri Kunjambu was deeply inspired by liberal humanist concepts. *Saraswathivijayam* is the first exemplar of a socially committed novel of its kind written by an avarna. Also, the Malayalam novel right from its inception chose to move away from the prevailing self-indulgent romantic poetic tradition to focus on an explication and analysis of day-to-day life in Kerala.

Thakazhi Sivasankara Pillai's (who could be called Kerala's Mulk Raj Anand) *Randidangazhi* (1945) and *Thottiyude Makan* (1947), Nagavally R.S. Kurup's *Thotti* (1947), Kesava Dev's *Kannaadi* (1973), and *Ayalkkaar* (1963), etc. were novels focusing on the condition of the economically poor who had not even been considered worthy subjects for novelists. Thus in general, Kerala Renaissance novels described the hidden subaltern lives in a new perspective. They gave greater romantic aura to subaltern life. Thakazhi could be cited as the best example for this. Here is what Koran, a character in Thakazhi's *Randidangazhi* says:

'You know what? Nairs will abuse Christians and Christians Nairs too. But in fact there are only two castes: one who has and one who does not have money and paddy. So when it comes to a matter of money and paddy there is no caste or community.'

The Marxist position was that caste which is a superstructure would disappear with the change in the constitution of the base. This happens to be the dominant ideology of the period. T.K.C. Vaduthala was the first Dalit novelist who recognized the ebbing of political power from one's own community, in the wake of this new political equation. Through his novels like *Kattayum Koythum, Nanavulla Mannu,* and *Changalakal Nurungunnu,* Vaduthala raised pertinent questions regarding the low caste attaining social or cultural power. They problematize the common ideological stance of national politics. We get a clear indication of this through the character Kannappan of *Changalakal Nurungunnu,* who understands that in the existing social pattern only savarnas deserved national independence and that political power was for savarnas alone. This points to the fact that even in independent India Dalits/Adivasis were forced to fight another battle for freedom to attain equal status as human beings.

The novel *Kattayum Koythum* is about the formation of an agricultural labour union by the Dalits. This novel raises the point that political power would remain in the hands of the rich even when there is a change in the socio-political system. Namboodiris and Warriers become the leaders of the union. But in crucial situations these savarna leaders go underground abandoning their Dalit followers, to be beaten to pulp. This resulted in the low caste's internalization of the fact that in order to mould one's life in one's own terms, one needs to ascertain political power through the consolidation of one's community. Interrogating casteist slavery based on one's profession and trying to understand problems through class analysis, characters like Chothi embrace class politics itself as an ideology for liberation. The novel *Nanavulla Mannu* (Damp Soil) strongly supports the Communist world view. A major weakness of post-Renaissance Kerala Dalit identity was its inability to even imagine a self-liberated Dalitness, freeing itself from the deep shadow of Hindutva. This is reflected in Vaduthala's novels as well and is an indication of the fact that Kerala Dalits are not secular enough to denounce Hinduism as such but only the caste discriminations within it. Quite naturally, Dalit writing often tends to maintain a dialogical relationship with Communist ideology. As different from the general trend in Malayalam novels of the period to focus on class perspective, Vaduthala attempted to make visible the intrinsic conflicts arising out of a negated Pulaya identity.

The novel *Changalakal Nurungunnu* very strongly corroborates these words.

From among the novels of Paul Chirakkarode, Vaduthala's contemporary, almost nine deal with Dalit issues. *Pulayathara, Mathil, Nizhal, Nyayasana, Velicham* (three volumes), and many other novels were written by Chirakkarode. The underlying current in Chirakkarode's works is mainly the Christian life and world view. Through his novels he attempts problemetizing the caste-centred social order. He successfully portrays the complex identity crisis of converted Dalit Christians.

'A Pulayan always remains a Pulayan, even in churches—merely and only a Pulayan.' This internal conflict gains prominence in *Pulayathara*. Although Vaduthala and Chirakkarode follow the tracks of Kerala Renaissance novels in their empathetic portrayal of Dalits, they stand apart in their clear picturization of the experiential pangs of casteist conflicts. This self-consciousness brings them into proximity with Dalitness.

D. Rajan's novel *Mukkani* is a literary representation of Paraya life. It speaks of three generations and the conflicts in connection with the changes over time. *Mukkani* is bamboo with which Parayas make *kotta* (baskets) and *vatti* (trays), for their livelihood. Mukkani here becomes a symbol of Paraya life. This novel also throws light on the growing awareness that conversion to Christianity is not a remedy for the suppressed state of Dalits.

In *Mukkani* we find plenty of caste-specific vocabulary. As is the case with mainstream novels, it is used not just in the dialogue but is interwoven into the very narrative structure. '*Eda Kannam thirinja kayveri, hende vaakkum chelllum kekkathen chora peduthu chakum. Paravaathakalane ithu achattanu.*' [*You scoundrel, one who won't listen to my words and advice will surely vomit blood and die. Upon the spirits above I swear.*]

Thus he makes maximum use of the authentic Pulaya dialect. As far as Dalit novels of a later period are concerned, *Mukkani* influenced and made acceptable the intrinsic strength of caste specific language.

We can also see a stream of non-Dalit writers attempting to represent Dalit lives, beginning with *Pulleri Kunju* and *Ghathakavadham*, developing through Thakazhi, moving on to writers like Lalithambika Antharjanam, N.P. Muhammed, M.T. Vasudevan Nair, P. Valsala, V.K. Narayana Kurup, U.A. Khader, and others. A significant novel of this group is M. Sukumaran's *Sheshakriya*. It depicts the confrontation with caste/class prejudice and the ensuing identity crisis of a Dalit working in the media. This could also be seen as a non-Dalit reaction to the silenced casteist discourses in modern society. One of the reasons for this is the strong influence of Dalit literature which contested and continues to challenge the casteist social order through its writings.

We generally come across an objectification of Dalit representation in non-Dalit writings. Beginning with *Indulekha*, the shadowy figures— those with no form and language, who remain hidden and proselytized, and heard only through their shouts—continued to be invisible in modern novels as well.

It was at this juncture that C. Ayyappan through his short stories and P.A. Uthaman through his novels brought Dalit subjectivity into visibility. P.A. Uthaman's *Chaavoli* (2007) is a very poignant powerful novel which marks the internal vigour and beauty of Dalit life and its language. This novel which won the Kerala Sahitya Akademi Award is written in the local dialect spoken by the Kurava community of Nedumangad village in Thiruvananthapuram district. The Dalit past and present are conflated in the narrative, foregrounding the general trend in Dalit narratives to intermingle memory and the present. This novel also completely rejects elite language and constructs a Dalit life-world and discourse with all its inherent stress and conflicts. Raghuthaman, the protagonist simultaneously becomes a representation of Dalit life and mainstream life. An interesting aspect of this novel is the absence of a villainous Brahmin in the slot of the oppressor; instead it is the Nairs and Ezhavas who represent the Brahminic epistemology. *Kuppathuppa* (2010) is yet another novel by P.A. Uthaman published posthumously.

Raghavan Atholi's versatile creativity moves along and across poetry, novel, and sculpture. His novels attempt a portrayal of the specific myths and nobility of Dalit life in all its intensity. They actively relate to the indigenous and non-Hindu traditions and the concepts of clan and tribe and strongly project the novelist's notion that all low-caste people belong to the same lineage. The novel *Choraparisham* depicts the politics of permeation of kinship relations. It idealizes and valorizes labour, survival, past and history, modes of worship, and songs and dreams of Dalit life. Raghavan continues with his writing in the specific caste dialect of the Pulayas retaining all its originality and intrinsic worth. Thevan and Maatha are the representations of Pulaya life. Each character in the novel is in one way or other wounded at different sites of Dalit lifescapes.

The Malayalam novel which launched itself in 1878, through its different phases of development, portray Dalit experiences in dark colours of self-contempt and negation, resistance and self-esteem whereas contemporary Malayalam Dalit novels through various means have attained a new and specific identity and language consciousness in opposition to standardized Malayalam.

When Shackles Break[*]

T.K.C. Vaduthala

Kannappan sat at the stern, carelessly plying the paddle ... the tiny boat seemed to slip and slide over the chain of waves on the broad breast of the vast lake. When Kunjappan who stood in the middle of the boat spread the throw-net and flung it in a wide sweep, the boat would roll about a bit. When he began to pull at the rope securely knotted to his left wrist, it seemed as though the boat made a forward thrust, tilting sideways, obligingly.

Kannappan was now familiar with this technique. When Kunjappan was alone he fished only from the shores of the lake. It was when Kannappan joined him that he arranged to take the boat into the middle of the lake. One got only tiny prawns and small fish from the water close to the shores. But in the middle of the lake huge prawns and more sought-after varieties of fish got caught or entangled in the net in large numbers.

The blazing heat of the sun fell on the head and body all the time, like molten metal. The cap-umbrella could protect the head from getting scorched. But it could not prevent the body from getting sun burnt. This limited its use during the rains as well. So they just wrapped a towel around their heads.

'Fishing is a nice and free occupation, isn't it Kunjappa?' Kannappan asked, seated on the stern

'Oh that feeling of freedom ... you are free only so long as you are on the lake. Once your feet touch the shore it's all over,' Kunjappan replied.

'Aha, that's true. The thamiru (evil) masters will be there, after all.'

'There is freedom to work. But not when it comes to selling the fish you catch. It is the plunderers who have power.'

'Isn't there anyone to prevent all that?'

'Those designated to prevent do the same.'

'So it's not the Pulayar alone who have problems.'

---

[*] Original title *Changalakal Nurungunnu.*

'Everyone has them, big brother, everyone. I saw this with my eyes once. Koran Arayan and his children caught fish and drew near the landing. Varuthachan thampuran was waiting for them. He selected two or four of the biggest fish in the boat and began to walk away. Koran Arayan called out, reminding him to pay for the fish before leaving; the thampuran walked back and kicked him once or twice for that crime. No one's hand rose to resist the blows. Neither Koran Arayan's nor his children's. I felt my blood boil. But then upon thinking, I decided that this was none of my business.'

'The pain that slavery and humiliation create is the same for everyone. It's not right to differentiate between mine and theirs in that.'

'The ideals that you express are good to preach, big brother. But why should we feel the anger which his own children did not?'

'That is because they are not conscious of the feelings of freedom and self-respect. Those feelings should be planted in them.'

'Our people's situation is the same, isn't it?'

'Yes they too should be awakened and made conscious. Only a conscious people can resist the horrible practices.'

'Listening to your words makes it all seem so easy, big brother.'

'Nothing is easy. We need a lot of patience. Should be willing to make any sacrifice. Even then it will not be easy to change their minds from centuries-old belief-systems.'

'Why go looking for problems when you know all this?'

'Without moving through suffering one cannot reach the essence. Look at Achan's situation at home. Achan is determined to educate his son and make him respectable like other folk. But when he is told to resist Varuthachan's atrocities he cannot digest it. He believes that Pulayas are fated to endure the beatings of the thamiru lords.'

'Karthachan belongs to the old generation. They got used to that way of life.'

'That is true. We can place our hopes only on the younger generation. Kunjappan, finish your studies, we can plan an organized struggle.'

Kunjappan did not reply. There seemed to be something heavy in the net. He began to pull the rope carefully. Looking at his face at that time, it seemed pulling the rope was the most important occupation in the world.

'Like you catch fish in a net, organized strength can capture any aggressor. All one needs to know is how to handle the string of that organization.'

Kunjappan continued to be absorbed in pulling in the net.

When he reached home in the evening amma handed him a letter. A letter that bore the postage stamp with the King of Kochi's head on the seal. The postal peon had come into the compound on the eastern side and thrown it into the yard, she said.

He broke open the seal. When he finished reading a whole lot of emotions rushed into his heart. His eyes filled with tears of joy. His voice cracked and words failed him.

'Amme, I have got a job,' Kannappan said, hugging his mother.

That mother did not ask what job her son had got nor where it was. Filled with joy, the woman stared at her son, unblinkingly, as though at a strange wonderful creature.

To just stand watching him was as pleasurable as a dream. Her employed son getting dressed and going to work! Handing her the salary he got every month! She, his mother, gaining a new dignity among the other women. Saving money from the salary and renovating the house. Arranging a marriage for the son. Handing the responsibilities of the household to the beautiful and sophisticated bride, and settling down to a life of rest, playing with grandchildren. Such joyful dreams flashed through her mind.

It was at nightfall, when Achan came in, humming a tune—having gained peace by consuming a measure of toddy—that mother and son returned to the world of reality. Achan was overjoyed when he heard his son had got a job. At the same time he felt a great pang. His son must have good clothes. He must have a suitcase and a mattress. And some money for expenses. His pain came from his inability to collect so much money at once. That and even more than that can happen; let the day dawn. Kandari built a pillar of courage in his mind and asked, 'What job did you get?'

'School teacher.'

'That is, the job of teaching children?'

'Yes.'

'In which place?'

'The government school in Mangayi'.

'Mangayi is the land of the aristocratic upper castes.'

'Where will I stay Acha?'

'You must stay in Maradu or Kundanoor. We'll find a suitable house. When does the letter say you should join for work?'

'Within a week.'

'Aha, so there is time. Our Kalachamuriyile Kunjan chettan's son Mathavan is a teacher somewhere, isn't that so?'

'Yes.'

'Then my son, go there tomorrow. You can get to know everything by asking Mathavan.'

'I will. I'll take Kunjappan and go in a boat.'

'Yes do that. Keep this to have some coffee or tea.'

He took out a four-ana* coin from the small change tied to the end of his cloth and gave it to Kannappan.

As he lay down to sleep Kannappan heard Achan and Amma heaving sighs of relief. A big relief, as though a huge weight had been lifted off their heads ... yes, it must be such a feeling.

* * *

They tied the boat in the canal on the right side of the house where Nedukattil Ramanvappan, a younger brother of Achan's through family ties, lived. They climbed the shore, and placed the paddle facing the east. Kannappan and Kunjappan entered straight on to the veranda.

'Who is this, Kannappan, is it you?' Vappan came out, heart brimming with joy. He embraced Kannappan who stood respectfully palms together, and patted his back.

'Who is this with you?'

'Nittetharel Karthachan's son.'

'Name?'

'Kunjappan.'

'What do you do?'

'Studying, in the ninth class.'

'Father and mother are well?' Asking this mami too came out.

As they sat talking and exchanging news, steaming black coffee and stewed vegetable balls were placed before them. Mami was indeed blessed. How quickly she prepared all that! The coffee and stewed vegetable balls were so tasty.

Kallachamuri was at a nazhika walking distance from there. They stepped out. Vappan and mami accompanied them some distance.

'You must return here for lunch.'

'Aha, we will, we will.'

They began to walk. As they moved forward, Kannappan felt as though he was going through haloed ground. The prelude to the struggle

---

* Four-ana: Coin currency, a quarter of a rupee.

to put an end to the sufferings of his people had begun on that soil. He felt a thrill as he remembered it.

'This land has a history, do you know Kunjappa?'
'Every land has a history.'
'The history of our race's independence began here.'
'I did not know that.'
'It happened some ten-twenty years before we were all born.'
'Do you know, big brother?'
'I'll tell you the story I know.' Kannappan thought for a while, then spoke thus:

The Maharaja of Kochi, who abdicated his throne, was a man of modern ideas. He was eager to bring in many administrative reforms. It was the sixtieth birthday celebration of that king, and the whole kingdom was immersed in a string of festivities. The crowd was intoxicated with joy. Waves of joy, everywhere. Public meetings, concerts, dance and drama, all added to the thrilling atmosphere that enveloped the land. Even the blades of grass seemed to have acquired a new zest. Palace and hut were equal in their feelings of loyalty to the king. The people of those times believed that the king was the visible form of God.

That evening a group of Pulayas left the shores of their land, and moved towards Ernakulam town. They sang songs, called out greetings, played their instruments . . . their boat reached Husur jetty. By that time it was dark.

Maharajas College where a play was being enacted that night was not all that far from there. *Balakalesham*, the play that Karuppan master wrote, protesting against evil practices like the caste system and untouchability. Members of the royal family, aristocratic chieftains, and important citizens occupied the front rows of the audience. Do you want to know what question the playwright made the character Kochalu pulayan ask?

All ... in all the worlds are children of God. Can caste keep apart those created equal, God is watching, isn't he yogapenne?
Isn't caste an affrontery njanapenne?

Isn't caste an affrontery? The world heard the question with a start. It had the effect of a bomb going off in every mind.

Kannappan stopped his narration for a while to watch Kunjappan's face. Kunjappan was listening to it all gravely.

'None of the Pulayas had the good fortune of seeing that play. They weren't even allowed to enter the place. In those days they did not have right to walk on the roads. So they sat in the boat drawn near Husur jetty, and sang songs in praise of the king. Waves of the songs that arose from the parched throats of those helpless folk, reached the audience that sat watching the play.

With the permission of the organizers in the audience Karuppan master sent someone to bring them into the college grounds. He told them to sit quietly under a tree till the play was over.

The play ended. The audience left. The Pulayar continued to sit sad, silent and frozen in the mist covered darkness under the tree.

Suddenly they saw someone coming towards them carrying a large lamp. Behind it a majestic and handsome form—a symbol of manliness—wearing the headgear of authority and a black coat. A face that reminded one of the bright full moon smiling down from amidst clouds. To add a bit of poetry, a veritable symbol of manliness. That was Karuppan Master. The great poet K.P. Karuppan.

The leader of the Pulayas, Krishnadi ashaan, stood up and greeted Master. Seeing this, the others too greeted him. He greeted them in return; then asked Krishnadi ashaan, 'Why did all of you embark on this journey?'

'We cannot walk in the open. If we see any upper caste we have to take flight, and hide in some stream or along the shore. Or else a rain of stones will follow. They make the rowdies beat us. Ho! that sound jerks us awake, even from our sleep!'

'Caste is the terrible curse that is destroying the land. If you want to exorcise this ghost you must organize and fight it as one!'

'How can we assemble? We sweat blood to grow rice, coconut and other crops. Yet if we are not allowed to walk on that soil, to assemble somewhere or to form an organization.'

'What a huge lake lies ahead of us. If you are denied space on the soil you work on, come along with me to this lake, that is as vast and deep as the ocean. I'll create an organization for you, that even the waves cannot destroy.'

Krishnadi ashaan and his followers were rendered astonished immobilized. Their eyes filled with tears of joy. They looked at Master with gratitude. They were wondering whether this college teacher who stood before them was a human being or a messenger of God. What courage! What willingness to resist!

They returned home enthusiastically, like warriors who had decided on a new strategy of resistance.

Every day after college work was over, Karuppan master would arrive on the lake in a small boat. Pulayas and others from all the nearby stretches of land assembled in little boats. The boats were bound together to form a platform. Seated in them, they discussed their future plans. The main goal of these discussions was to create a Pulaya organization.

I do not think such a struggle for human rights has ever taken place in any part of the world. In the eyes of those who write the history of the struggle for human freedom, Karuppan master will spread light like a messenger of God.

Four long years went by in that manner. In those days, except the proselytizers of Christian brotherhood, no one granted Pulayas land to hold an assembly. Discussions that began in 1084 ended in 1088.* That is how Pulaya Mahasabha was formed in Kochi. Kannappan stopped his narration and looked at Kunjappan. He saw Kunjappan wipe his tears with the edge of his shoulder cloth.

'Why are you crying Kunjappa? Everyone is content as long as they embrace ignorance. It is easy to forget reality, lie immersed in a day dream. But is it possible for us? Rays of knowledge have entered the brain. How can we now sleep?'

'Keep awake, always stay awake. I am willing to stay awake for all time to awaken our community, now immersed in a deep sleep'.

'Karuppan master—who searched out those among us who had the power to stay awake and made them leaders—also ensured us representation in the legislative.' Kannappan stopped and let out a sigh.

'There is so much more distance to cover. It is not enough to stay awake. We must be willing to take part in the endless struggle against injustice.'

'I am willing for that too,' Kunjappan replied.

Kannappan raised his face and looked at him. Kunjappan's eyes were shining. They seemed aflame; their sparks flying in all four directions.

Those two thinkers followed the path of thought stepping out bravely.

* * *

A small hut with unplastered brick walls and a palm-leaf thatched roof; one of the better Pulaya houses in those days. The overhang on the southern side had been turned into a reading room.

Short, slightly dark, not hefty, but well-built body; the lips pressed close together as though to hide the jutting row of teeth made his face appear pointed, at one glance, and thereby look needlessly serious.

When Kannappan entered he was reading. As the first man in the community who had acquired a BA degree, Kannappan greeted him with due respect. Kunjappan behind him, repeated the greeting.

---

* AD 1872.

He looked at them enquiringly; straightened himself up in the chair. Kannappan said, 'We have come from the eastern shore.'

'Name?'

'My name is Kannappan. This is Kunjappan with me, my maternal uncle's son.'

'We've been hearing about you, Kannappan.'

'What?'

'You are doing something there, I heard.'

'Did not do enough to be talked about.'

'When a person lives among prohibitions even his sneeze counts as defiance of norms.'

'I believe that obsolete beliefs and the rules that justify them should be resisted.'

'Belief alone is not sufficient. You must bring it into action. But the isolated attempts of a few cannot bring about change.'

'That is true. But won't the isolated struggles create at least a slight flutter in the hearts of men?'

'An organization is the force that can draw strength from the isolated flutters.'

'We must all unite to strengthen the organization.'

'I think the same. Well, what do you do now, Kannappan?'

'I have finished my school final examination.'

'And Kunjappan?'

'Passed the ninth standard and now in the tenth.'

'Let more and more people get educated. Then we'll see what we can do!'

'I do not have the patience to wait till then. So I gave up the desire to go to college.'

'I do not think that was right.'

'I am not against your opinion, master. I want to get some kind of job and serve the community.'

'How long can you manage social service and employment together?'

'At the point I find I cannot manage them together, I'll throw away my job.'

Master did not reply. The young man's words were powerful! Every word whizzed out like a bullet. He looked at Kunjappan's face. Shadows of bewilderment played on his lowered face.

'What is your opinion of all that has been said, Kunjappan?'

'The situation and circumstances justify actions, that is what I believe.'

'That is what I too believe.'
'So we have arrived at the same opinion,' Kannappan quipped.
Everyone laughed, chuckling over the comment.
'Now I'll tell you something straight,' Kannappan said in a tone that gave rise to anxiety.
In truth, Madhavan master did indeed become anxious. He asked, 'What is it?'
'I have come here with an appointment letter.'
'What job?'
'Schoolteacher.'
'Where?'
'Primary school, Mangavu.'
'That land is full of caste rivalry.'
'Where does it not exist?'
'That too is correct. Want to hear my experience? I'll tell you. It happened four five years ago.'
'Things have not changed all that much even now.'
'For that very reason this story will be useful for you too, Kannappan,' Madhavan master began ...
'To get a job as you get your BA degree. That too, to get a job as a high school teacher, it is truly an experience isn't it! Yes a unique opportunity. Everyone was happy at home when they heard that I had got a job in Elamkunnapuzha High School. Just half an ana distance by ferry from home. I could have lunch in my ammavan's home that was near the school.'

I stepped out in the morning, wearing a new mundu, coat, and tie, carrying an umbrella. Not just to escape from sun and rain; in those days an umbrella was a status symbol.

On the way to school I went to ammavan's home. I had to get his blessings and good wishes after all! Nothing could have made ammavan and family happier. Ammavan felt proud when he thought that his nephew had been deputed to teach upper castes like Namboothiri and Nair students. Not only did he bless me, he accompanied me part of the way.

'Lunch at home,' he said, when we parted.
'Aha, I'll definitely come.'
The headmaster had chosen a room at the end of the school building for me. Maybe he wanted to spare the upper caste teachers the sin of passing in front of a Pulaya teacher's room. Wonder whether that

innocent of innocents headmaster, Raman Menon has thought that far ahead.

The students looked at me not as though I was a strange creature, but as one who had committed a grave sin. No point in blaming them for that. Those were the circumstances under which they had been raised. In such circumstances even the most logical person succumbs to emotions. What was the point of being educated? What was the point in the government's laws? A group of people—slaves of tradition, infested with hate for their fellow human beings, they were the ones seated before me. Therefore even as I taught I felt I was fighting for self-respect, the kind of battle Abhimanyu fought, entrapped in the chakravyuha.

When I returned after lunch in ammavan's home, I got a terrible shock. My blood boiled as never before. Were my eyes growing dim, were my muscles and nerves failing, or was I forgetting myself? I cannot explain my feelings at that moment.

Someone had placed a spade across my desk. Who? I looked at the faces of each child. Whom should I ask? Whom should I suspect? Whoever it was had to be one diseased by casteist feelings, an unmanly coward. If he dared to face me, I could slash his throat with that very spade.

But what could I do without knowing who it was? I sat down to calm my blazing emotions a bit. My mind could find no rest. The regret that I could not avenge the deep insult to my community still remains.

I beckoned to the peon. He was reluctant to approach me, as though obeying a Pulaya teacher was a matter of shame.

'Didn't I tell you to come here?' I think I shouted.

He came like a dog, tail between the legs. What humility!

'Take this and hand it over to the headmaster.' My words came out like a roar.

The peon took the spade. Did he give it to the headmaster, or did he hide it somewhere? I do not know even now, but no one talked about it afterwards.

Kannappan let out a sigh. Kunjappan dabbed his eyes. What insults one had to suffer till the end of one's life, for being born a Pulayan!

'Did you continue to work there, master?' Kunjappan asked that question.

'Of course. To continue there, became an obsession for me. The transfer came after the end-of-the-year examinations.'

As they said goodbye and left, the thought of whether he should accept the job or give it up and engage in the battle against every kind of injustice, plagued him. Finally to spare his aged parents' disappointment, he decided to accept the job.

* * *

He began his new job with total commitment. Students sat in disciplined focus, in front of their new teacher. No one had injected poison into the young minds. They obeyed Kannappan as they would every other teacher. They listened attentively to what he said, trying to take in what he taught.

During the noon break Kannappan went to the teacher's room. He thought he would get to know his fellow teachers. An unusual silence spread through the room; the shadow of sorrow played on each face! No one said a word. Everyone seemed to eye him like a criminal, Kannappan thought.

He asked himself what crime he had committed against them. He had gone there to work according to a government directive. He did not know whether he had committed any other mistake. If they were angry about his caste, should not their anger be towards the government that had appointed him, knowing his caste? But nobody had a grievance against *that*. If they had, this appointment would not have taken place, would it? There were no answers to these questions that Kannappan asked himself.

His fellow teachers treated him like an enemy. Without a single word, without a single pleasant glance in his direction giving no opportunity for close interaction, they isolated him. They detected mistakes and inadequacies in the way he taught and spread these opinions enthusiastically.

When he left the classroom in the evening, Kannappan heard older children behind and in front of him, call out:
'Pulayan Sir is coming, run!'
'Pulayan Sir is coming, run!'
Those who shouted were also running. They ran, clearing their throats and shouting.

* * *

Well, well ... didn't it begin grandly, Kannappan said to himself. His caste had reached the place even before he had. It also revealed itself to be a frightening thing. Under the circumstances there was no need for a game of pretence. Confront the challenge with courage, that was all.

By the time he crossed paddy fields and canals and reached the house in Kundanoor, where he stayed, he had taken that decision.

There was still time before nightfall. What should he do till then? He did not have acquaintances in Kundanoor. There was no man of his age in the house where he stayed. Just the middle-aged house owner, his wife, and two young children. What could he say to them? Ramakrishnan's place was nearby. He had written a letter to him before he left his place. But he had not seen him. If he could find him, he could talk about the day's experiences and lighten the burden in his mind.

'Kannappan mashe!'

As he changed his mundu and shirt and stepped out he heard the call from the door. He looked quickly; Ramakrishnan stood in front of him.

'What a surprise! I was thinking about you just now,' Kannappan said as he shook hands with him.

'I wanted to come to the school in the morning.'

'Why didn't you?'

'By that time another wonderful thing happened. I too have got an appointment in the same school.'

'Ha, how lucky!' Kannappan embraced his friend. Tears of joy rolled down his face.

Holding hands they walked along the broad ridge that bordered the paddy field and walked towards the coconut grove beyond.

He lay down to sleep, utterly at peace. When he woke up he felt a strange enthusiasm. The energy of becoming a new man. Though not great, he had got a job that gave him enough money to fend for himself. He should try to sail forward, holding on to it. That was Kannappan's desire just then.

By the time he returned from his bath in the lake, it was time to get ready for school. It was a long walk from there to the school, which was in the upper caste stronghold. He had to eat something from his place before he started the walk. Or else he would go hungry. But no food had been prepared in the house. Why was that? When he asked he understood that there was no water.

The pond in the next compound was beside an Ezhava home. Pulayas were not allowed to go down there and fetch water. If they placed their pot near the edge of the pond and waited at a distance, someone from the house would come along and draw water to fill the pot. But that someone should have the goodwill to do it. Sometimes it did not happen, even if one waited one or two hours. That was what had happened that day.

That was a new experience for Kannappan. In his village there were wells and ponds attached to large Christian houses who did not practice untouchability. Pulayar could draw as much water as they needed. But here you could not draw water from an Ezhavan's house? He felt ashamed when he thought about it, and an even greater sadness. Anger flared in his heart.

He reached school with a shattered heart and a starving belly. Intense hunger consumed him like fire, creating a burning sensation in his stomach. But he took class paying no heed to it. There were students in the group in front of him who too were starving like him. It was a place where co-sufferers in sorrow came together to be one. So he forgot the intensity of hunger.

During the noon break Ramakrishnan entered Kannappan's classroom. He had a packet with him.

'Don't you have lunch?'
'No, I did not bring anything.'
'Why?'
'Nothing could be prepared over there.'
'Didn't you have rice and provisions?'
'Everything was there.'
'Then why didn't you cook?'
'There was no water—water.'
'Water?'
'Water, to boil rice.'

Kannappan briefly described that day's incident. Ramakrishnan thought for a while then said, 'Well, come. We will share my food.'

'That won't be sufficient for two people. You eat, Ramakrishnan.'
'No, that is not possible.'
'I don't want to.'
'Then I too will not eat.'

They sat for a while, without talking. Finally, Kannappan gave in to the pressure. They shared the puttu and banana in Ramakrishnan's packet.

That was the only topic of conversation among the teachers that day. Ezhava Ramakrishnan and Pulaya Kannappan had shared a meal, that too from the same plate. They had not even heard about anything like that before.

Now Kannappan ceased to be alone in the teacher's room. Kannappan and Ramakrishnan sat together, talking. Their friendship made the others envious. They saw the wall of rejection they had built around Kannappan dissolving.

Kannappan had thought of going to his village during the weekend but decided not to.

That house was among one of the better Pulaya houses in Kundanoor region. The house owner and the people in that region rejoiced that Kannappan had decided to stay there. They were willing to do anything for his comfort.

As he thought of the difficulties of getting water Kannappan became aware of the intense caste prejudice that existed in that land. His first resolve was to find a solution for the problem.

From Saturday morning he visited every home, got introduced to people. Hardworking men and women. Healthy and able-bodied. Work till the bones crack, then eat a belly-full of food, was their slogan for life. They were not determined to build nice houses or wear good clothes. They were slaves to the unwritten rule that Pulayar should not desire these things.

Literate people were rare. The dominant groups would not allow them to study and uplift themselves. Education was not necessary to work in the paddy field. So none of them bothered to look towards the realm of education.

You could order the ignorant, make them obey, tell them to do slave labour. If he could break the wall of ignorance that surrounded them he could let the rays of self-respect into their hearts, so Kannappan felt. That was the thought that was uppermost in his mind as he visited each house. He said this to all those he could meet face to face.

Most of the Pulayar had tiny ponds near their homes, ponds where they could get good water. They used the water for their crops and for bathing. Why could they not dig and clean at least some of these? They could then draw water to drink at all times, without depending on anyone. What other way was there to spare themselves the shameful act of going to another's plot and stand waiting for a pot of water.

As he returned to his dwelling that evening, thoughts regarding this solution filled his mind.

—*Translated by Catherine Thankamma*

The Festival at Muthan Kavu[*]

D. Rajan

New moon of the Karkadakam month.
That's the day of the Muthan Kavu festival.
This is the national festival of the Parayas of Vembannur. On that day women who married from Vembannur and moved to other localities return with their husbands, children, relatives, and friends.

This is a special day they had, once a year, to be happy, to celebrate, and to renew memories. All those who had moved away from that land and lived elsewhere congregated on that day. That is customary.

A pomp-filled festival.
The grand festival of the people of Vembannur!
On that day, Muthan Kavu and its surroundings are mown and spruced up. There would be decorations everywhere, palm-leaf hangings and decorations and red silk. Muthan Kavu and its neighbourhood would scintillate in the blue light of petromax lamps. The locality becomes festive.

At dusk, the *chenda* would reverberate, mesmerizing drum roll. When people hear the sound of the chenda, they grow restless. With children, family, and paraphernalia, everyone in that land flows towards the festival ground.

Old women with rolled-up mats, and singing and dancing and gossiping, would amble and stagger towards the festival place. As darkness falls, small groups carrying sparkling palm-leaf torches course towards the festival grounds. Soon, Muthan Kavu would turn into a cacophonic human ocean.

The procession of kettivilakku is the main ritual.
People belonging to various regions and localities would bring the traditional lamps in ceremonial procession to Muthan Kavu. Traditional lamps of all sizes and shapes! Traditional lamps with illustrations and engravings and decorations! Palm-leaf horses were made, and children sat astride them, jumping and prancing, escorting the procession.

The procession of stud bulls was also an important ritual.
How magnificent is the sight of these people carrying traditional

---

[*] Original title *Mukkani*. Mukkani is the species of fine pliable bamboo used to weave baskets.

lamps on their heads to the festival ground, dancing to the rhythm of the drums and piped nadaswaram music and ululations!

Even before dusk the festival ground comes alive.

Surging humanity everywhere.

The tea-stall and paan-shop owners do good business. Rows of vendors of perfume, soaps, combs, chändhu colours, ribbons, bindis, bangles, and hand-mirrors fill the festival ground. Their business would prosper there.

On one side, the 'karakara' sound of the merry-go-round, on another side the 'kudukudu' sound of the motorcyclists in the 'well of death'. In another place, the sound of the gamblers' dice containers. Everywhere, there was noise and bustle!

After toiling for a year, whatever money remained was blown up in that festival ground. Vessels, cheap dress materials, children's clothing, odds and ends, bric-a-brac required for the house would be spread out for sale on the festival ground. Those who needed these things would select, bargain, and buy them.

It is on this ground that lovers buy and present love-gifts to their loved ones. As far as lovers are concerned, the festival is an unforgettable experience. Sweet sensations to remember all through life ....

Kakarishi Natakam is an important item of the festival. Manikkan Asan's, Kakarishi play is quite popular. The entrance song of Manikkan Asan, the rhythmic 'O—thaka—thaka—thaka—thakaa' chant and the consequent step-dance are greatly renowned. People would sit, watching with bated breath and wide-eyed wonder, Manikkan Asan's chants and final foot-beats that stretched on for hours.

Before the play began there was the children's piece. With golden crowns on their heads, two children from either side of the stage sang in obeisance to the audience.

'O Elders who live in Vembannur, the largest land in the world,

We, little children, offer our single-minded obeisance ...'

When the children's song and dance began, that big, humming sea of humanity would become silent. All eyes would turn to the stage. Wide-eyed and curious, they sat watching.

After the children's piece, the kakkathis would arrive. With unstitched cloth bags tied to their shoulders, two kakkathi women would appear.

Tha tham thakathee thaka thakathai ...
Theethom thakatheethaka kai thai ...
Seeing the Kakkan coming
The Kakkathi's eyes were mesmerised ....

Both kakkathis are elaborating on this song. They dance to the tune of the song to the particular rhythm. When the song and dance begin to intensify, the kakkan would arrive carrying a lighted torch.

And that entrance itself make the audience wonderstruck.

Torch in hand, a stick on the shoulder, at the end of the stick a small cloth bag, face completely smeared with soot; on that, little white dots.

He would roar at the top of his voice:

O ... thaka ... thaka ... thaka ... thakaa ...
O ... thaka ... thaka ... thaka ... thakaa ...

Roaring out like this, amidst the people, with a peculiar rhythm rising to a crescendo, and dancing with amazing body control, he steps on to the stage.

'Seeing the Kakkan coming
The Kakkathi's eyes were mesmerized ...'

Singing this song, the kakkathis who were standing there move to one side of the stage.

And the kakkan proceeds with his stage-breaking crescendo.

Keeping to the beat of those accompanying singers who lacked clarity of words, Manikkan Asan would maintain the rhythm and conduct the dance. Manikkan Asan's body control, the thumping beat and rhythm of his anklet-clad feet were a speciality indeed.

The human sea would melt in the beat and movement of that primitive ancient dance.

Following the Kakarishi play, Nanjan Moopan's kuruthi thullal (sacrificial trance-induced dance) would begin.

Wearing a silken waistband, and anklets on his feet, a lighted torch in his left hand and a shimmering sword in his right hand, dancing and swaying, this chavittu natakam would stretch on for a long while.

One chunkam's over ... ayyaa ...
Two chunkams are over ...
Three chunkams are over ... ayyaa ...
Four chunkams are over ...

In this manner, singing, dancing, stamping in rhythm, waving his sword to a peculiar beat, moving with flexibility, he would exhibit his prowess. Afterwards, the tempo of the song would be increased. The beat of the feet would quicken. The Paraya women would loosen and spread their hair, circling their necks with breakneck speed, keeping to the beat of this song. These Paraya women would sing away, invoking the blessings of their paradevatha (folk deities) for the coming year.

The pace of the music would quicken. Simultaneously, the beat of the feet. Finally, holding aloft a black hen by its neck, moving in rhythm, he would cut its neck. The patriarch would then drink the blood of that hen, sucking and sucking.

In that trance, the karanava (elder) would fall down unconscious. The sacrificial dance would end with that.

* * *

Climbing the Areca Pole

The Muthan Kavu festival that lasts two days. A variety of programmes, the stage-breaking Kakarishi theatre, Nanjan Karanavar's sacrificial trance-like dance! The final item is climbing the areca pole.

That is a kind of a sport, a competition. The Olympics of Vembannur.

This is a ritual that displays the sporting capabilities and talents of the Paraya youth of the land of Vembannur. It is here that the strongest youth of the year, the most expert youth, the shining example of sporting youth, are selected. As far as the youth were concerned, this was a fine competitive arena to exhibit their sporting potential. A stage to depict their physical prowess.

All youths without exception would be present, filing themselves in rows, their dhotis tucked up in typical fashion, to exhibit their capabilities and endowments. All young girls would wait to see that sight with amazement in their eyes and anxiety in their minds.

A sight that thrills the young girls!

A programme that intoxicates the people!

A ritual that ignite enthusiasm.

A feat that stop one's breath with anxiety!

A big areca tree is uprooted and brought to Muthan Kavu with song and ululation and ritualistic hoots. It is planted in the sacred ground of Muthan Kavu. On top of it would be tied a bunch of plantains and a brand new, jerry-lined dhoti. The areca tree, already trimmed and polished, would be rubbed with melted animal fat. And on that, a mixture of gingelly oil and beaten egg would be sprayed. That slippery areca pole would have to be climbed without even wearing a leg-grip, and the new dhoti tied on top retrieved. That is the contest. The one who takes it will be that year's most talented youth of Vembannur. Mr Vembannur!

The Paraya youth considered winning that spirited contest a matter of great pride. To achieve that, there would be a healthy competition among them.

The Vembannur Olympics, full of spirit and verve!

To intensify the excitement of these sports competitions, unmarried girls would clap their hands in rhythm and sing in tune:

Rarirararo ... Hendappa ... Rerirararo
Rarirararo ... Hendappa ... Rerirararo
Are there children to eat the tobacco from my Pouch?
Are there children to eat the betel leaf from my hand?
Are there dressed-up children to walk charmingly before me?
Are there dressed-up children to walk charmingly before me?

A meaningful song.

Who, who is the young man worthy enough to take the betel leaf from my hand and eat it?
Who, who is the young man who's free enough with me to take the tobacco from my pouch and chew it?
Which, which is the groom that should walk before me, full of dignity, head held high and chest spread out?

A song that shone with emotion.

When that song is over, the drumming begins. When the drum roll intensifies, keeping to its beat, one by one, the young men would come forward and meditate on the deities, pay their respects to the gathering, and climb the areca pole. When they've climbed a bit, their hands and legs lose their grip, and they slip and fall. Once again, they clutch hold of it and try climbing up. Once again, they slip and fall.

Finally, the climber with his debilitated hands retreats in defeat.

Each time someone retreats in defeat, the areca pole is again sprayed with animal fat and the egg and gingelly oil mixture.

Another person comes into the arena. He too retreats in defeat, his legs debilitated. Instantly, a third person appears.

The drum roll would intensify. With this the spirits of the young men soar. To keep up their spirit and verve, the young girls continue with their cheers and applause.

This sporting entertainment would continue for hours. Finally, one after the other, they all would retreat in defeat. Even when a majority of the competitors were losing piteously and withdrawing, disappointed, arms and legs exhausted and weakened, one or two others would be in the arena, enthusiastic and spirited. Finally, one of them, regardless of everything else, would cling on to the areca pole and reach the top.

And he is that year's champion of the Paraya community! The smart one who captured the respect of every Paraya! The spirited one who attracted the hearts of all the young girls! The strongest!

The Muthan Kavu festival has yet another significance. All youngsters without exception would assemble there. Along with that, all the young girls of that place. That festival ground is the venue for *pennukaanal*, a place to view future brides. Similarly, it was also the place for girls to meet their lovers exchange love-gifts. These young charmers have the talent for passing on love-gifts to their beloveds unseen by anyone else. Like they say, 'The bugs on the calf would be removed and so does the crow's hunger be appeased.'

One day, when she went to Mukkani, Painkili lovingly invited Chennan to the festival.

'You'll come to the Muthan Kavu festival?'
'And if I come, what will you give me?'
'What do you want?'
'I want everything ... you'll give?'

Chennan gazed at her full breasts and overflowing buttocks and spoke meaningfully.

She became shy. Her plump cheeks blushed.

'I'll give everything ... not, now, after marriage,' she said shyly, biting her nails.

'I'll come for the festival. Will you buy me groundnuts and sweetened areca?'

'I'll give, I've no problem in giving. Not at all difficult for me.'
'Then I'll certainly come. Let's see how smart and bold my lass is.'
So Chennan, accepting this early invitation, reached the festival.

This is the festival spot of the Venparaya folk. He was a Kolan. He had no business here. 'What business does the goat have in the marketplace?'

Everyone stared at the alien Kolan standing isolated in the festival ground.

Why is he here? Who invited him?

As though trying to drain out some deep secret, everyone focused on Chennan. He became the target of their eyes.

Painkili saw Chennan standing all alone in the midst of that human flow. Chennan too saw Painkili. But one look or one word, and all would be lost. Explosives all around. The feeling of standing in the midst of that, if one small spark were to fly up and fall—then everything would be over.

Painkili looked painfully at Chennan standing there, forlorn, with no one for company. Chennan had come because she had invited him. At that moment she felt she shouldn't have. Her mind couldn't focus on anything. A terrible confusion. An anxiety. Nervousness!

Painkili had in her hand a packet of groundnuts and sweetened areca that she'd bought. How was she going to reach that to Chennan? If only she got an opportunity; if those eyes were averted once ... then she could've thrown it over to Chennan.

She stood waiting for an opportunity.

The Kakarishi play got over. Nanjan Moopan's sacrificial dance was also over. The next programme, climbing the areca pole, had begun. All eyes are on the lads who, keeping to the beat of the drums, are clinging and climbing and then hitting the ground with a 'dum!' Everyone is immersed in that entertainment.

This is the moment; this is the opportunity.

Painkili moved slowly to where Chennan was standing and threw the groundnut package before him.

Some youngsters, who had been carefully watching the movements of Painkili and Chennan, spotted this.

They yelled and howled out .... Catch that Kolan.

'Kill that Kolan ... beat up that rascal ... catch him and tie him up.'

People started running. Agitated women and children scattered in various directions. The others, not knowing what was happening, stood stunned.

* * *

Gift of Tongues and the Arrival of Healing

Smash him.
Beat him.
Fist him.
Kick him.

The youngsters who had gathered in the festival ground surrounded Chennan and slapped and kicked and fisted and smashed him up.

'Ayyoo .... Don't kill him ...'

Painkili cried out painfully.

Many elders came running.

The youngsters who were hopping with rage were forcibly removed.

Chennan was lying motionless. Beaten and fisted and kicked, he had lost consciousness. Blood spurted from his mouth.

Must be dead.

Everyone decided.

Four old women caught hold of Painkili, dragged her away and forced her into her hut.

Drag Chennan and throw him in the Karunkolli river. That abandoned corpse will flow away and reach some other bank. The police will find and bury it. Or it will decay and rot and sink to the bottom.

They found relief in these thoughts.

Two or three hefty fellows dragged the inert body of Chennan to the river's edge. They swung him by his hands and feet and threw him into the river. They entered the river and washed their hands and feet and then went on their way.

They reassured themselves ...

'So that's the end of that Kolan.'

Chennan, who had crashed into the river with a 'potho-oo!', sound regained consciousness. Two gulps of water, and he realized where he was. Chennan was an expert in diving and swimming. But his hands and legs remained immobile. As though they were tied down by heavy stones. Sinking lower and lower into the depths, Chennan suddenly felt as if he was strengthened, and moved a little. Using all his strength, he came up. Once again he descended to the unfathomable depths of the undercurrent.

Call it luck.

At that time, 'Podi' Parayas from Mayiladi, who were cutting bamboo and fashioning them into rafts of logs and floating them downriver, noticed some movement. They peered closely.

Dawn was just breaking and blossoming.

Just a dim light.

In that dim light, they realised that it was a man. One of them jumped into the water. He grabbed the hair of Chennan who had sunk to the depths. He dragged Chennan to the top. Laid him down on the raft.

They raised the wick of the lantern. In that light they peered carefully at him.

Chennan! Chennan, whom they knew!

Mathias, the oldest of them, brought his ear close to Chennan's chest and concentrated.

Not dead. He could hear the heartbeats. A slight movement.

Prising open his mouth, they poured a little rice gruel. Wrapped his body in a blanket.

They rowed the raft at great speed. They reached the Mayiladi jetty. They took Chennan to Mathias's hut.

The Parayas of Mayiladi are Christians. They are people who have heard and known the good news of Jesus, the Lord. The saved ones. Ones who had attained God's grace. Those who knew hymn and prayer.

A class that had been chosen by God!

The pure, who had been called by God!

They have no faith in medicines or chants. Prayer—fasting and praying. They believed that God would hear if you prayed intensely. Knock—the door shall open, Search ... and you will find, Ask ... and you shall receive; they had learnt all this from the Bible.

There are forty-three Paraya huts in Mayiladi. They are all of the Pentecost faith. For generations they have believed in the Church and the Bible. They have accepted Jesus Christ as their saviour.

One of them is Mathias.

Chennan was brought to Mathias's hut. Mathias's wife Kunjeli is also a believer like her husband. They have two children—Yaramya and Israel.

The unconscious Chennan was laid down on a string rope cot. Lighting a fire in an earthen pot, pepper leaves were heated up in the fire, and boiled. The warmth spread through the arms and legs of Chennan who lay frozen.

The news of Chennan being brought to Mathias's house spread like wildfire. All those who heard it came to Mathias's home. Those who came looked at Chennan lying there unconscious.

'Oh Lord! Please bear this sinner's soul in your arms,' they prayed.

Even after hours, there was no movement whatsoever in Chennan. Only a faint breath. Life, hanging on a slender thread, could snap at any moment.

Those believers prayed to the Lord.

Hearing the news, the counsellor and his wife charged over to Mathias's home.

Counsellor Caleb is the servant of God with the arrival of healing and the gift of tongues. Only those who have attained the grace of God can speak in tongues. The Holy Spirit will merge with them in tongues of flame.

Centuries ago ...

After the heavenly ascent of Christ ...

Eleven disciples, including Peter the Apostle, Christ's mother and some more had congregated in a building near Olive Mountain in Jerusalem. They were a group of a hundred and twenty people. People who had come from different places. Among them were (Mesopotamians), Jews, Egyptians. and people from Crete. From different lands, speaking different languages. They joined in prayer.

Suddenly, from the skies there was the roar of a storm. They had visions of forked tongues like flames. Those tongues were branded on each one of them. Having attained the Holy Spirit, they began to speak in the other language.

Counsellor Caleb is one who is been blessed by that Holy Spirit.

Counsellor Caleb has the boon of healing. If he places his hand on the head and prays, any chronic illnesses will be cured. He has the experience of praying and curing thousands of sick people.

'The Lord Jesus Christ gave sight to the blind. Gave the dumb the power of speech. Gave the lame ones legs to jump and walk about. Cured the leper and gave life to the dead Lazarus. If you pray with faith, God will listen to your prayer. Hallelujah.'

This is Counsellor Caleb's counsel.

'If you believe, you can be saved,' Counsellor Caleb pronounced firmly.

Long ago. Centuries ago.

In Jerusalem, there was a pond by the name of Bethesda, also know as the Sheep Pool. It had five arches. By its banks lay in wait a large crowd of the blind, lame, dumb and deaf, lepers and other diseases. Once in a long while, an angel would get into the pond. Would stir the lakes. The one who got into the water immediately after this was rid of his sickness. The one who got into the water would be cured.

A test of fortune.

There was a lame man who had been waiting near that pond for thirty-eight years for an opportunity to test his fortune. He had never been able to enter the water as soon as the angel had stirred the water. For years, that seeker of fortune survived there, waiting for the moment when the angel would enter the water and stir it up. Finally he prayed to the Lord on bended knees, 'Oh Lord! Save me.' Christ told him to 'get up and take your bed and walk'.

He was lame no more.

Counsellor Caleb made non-stop speeches about the boon of healing.

Anyone who saw Counsellor Caleb once would never forget him. Dark and short. Shorn head. His white jubba descended below his knees, a leather bound Bible in his hand. Also a hymn book. Stifled voice.

There are very few people who don't know Counsellor Caleb and his dark, thin wife since he is at the market corner every evening delivering his Good News speeches.

In the evenings, after the Good News speech, the Counsellor and his wife would stand at one end of the market. People would be hurrying home to their huts after selling mats, muravu, vatti, and other baskets; and buying rice, tapioca, salt, and chilli for their dinner, the members of his 'congregation'. They would give Counsellor Caleb some offering or the other. Ten paise, quarter rupee, with this sort of offering the Counsellor and his wife would buy rice, salt and chilli and go to their home which was called Bethel.

The Counsellor would lecture to the congregation ...

'Look at the birds in the sky. They don't seed. They don't reap. Still, God gives them what is theirs. In the same way, the children of God will never starve.'

The Counsellor and his wife came to Mathias's house. The faithful who had crowded there rose respectfully and praised the Lord. Counsellor Caleb and his wife knelt at the head of the motionless Chennan. Clapping hands to the beat of the thambora, they sang. Praising the Lord, we are praising the Lord ...

'I am praising Jesus, my saviour.'

Counsellor Caleb said.

David from the choir is saying ... David, the psalm-singer says

'Praise Jehovah, praise Him with veena and kinera. Praise him with percussion and strings and pipes. Praise Him with high notes of clapping hands in rhythm.'

The tempo of the thambora intensified. The pace of clapping hands increased. The singing became louder.

They prayed in unison, 'Hallelujah.'

The sound reverberated. 'Praise, praise,' they shouted loudly.

Even after this, Chennan didn't open his eyes.

He still lay motionless.

* * *

The Association of Paraya Upliftment

Even after praying for a full day, there was no change in Chennan. Lay there like that. Lay there motionless. Just that strained breathing. Not opening his eyes. Not moving his tongue.

Counsellor Caleb, who had even cured cancer, knelt in prayer to god. Finally, Counsellor Caleb had a revelation.

Chennan is of an outside faith. A Hindu. He has not been saved. He hasn't been baptized. He has not accepted Christ as his own saviour. That's why he has not got any relief.

Still, they continued to pray.

It was at this time that the sadhu, P.G. Ilavattam Shastrikal, arrived there. He is the president of the All Travancore Hindu-Christian Paraya Upliftment Association. In order to uplift the downtrodden Paraya community, this society had been formed. Ilavattam Shastrikal is a man who works day and night for the upliftment of that community which is living in a socially, financially and academically devastated condition. His real name is Gopalan. After passing an exam in traditional wisdom, he began visiting Paraya settlements with action plans to uplift his community. He advises them. He makes them understand the need to organize themselves. Shastrikal is saddened by the fact that the community is split into Hindus and Christians. They have to be united ... raise the awareness of their unity ... this is his goal.

He makes ceaseless efforts to eradicate the divisions, street-fights, conflicts and quarrels among the Parayas. To unify their different groups ... to make them conscious of their unity ... to act towards that.

That is his mode of operation.

The Parayas are divided into different groups.

Ariparayas.

Podiparayas.

Vemparayas.

Kolamparayas, or puzhuparayas.

They can't marry among each other. They don't interdine. They don't cooperate with each other.

'Disintegration is the negation of strength.'

They must organize and become powerful.

That is what the All Travancore Hindu-Christian Paraya Upliftment Association is trying to achieve.

In Ilavattam Shastrikal's opinion, the Parayas are the owners of a high cultural legacy. They were born in the Brahmin clan. Because of a minor impurity, they lost caste and became Parayas!

That is a story.

That story, obtained through old tongues, is now brimming within them.

Long, long ago ...

There was a renowned Brahmin family. They were divided into two branches, the Southern Illam and the Northern Illam. In those days, there were no cows on this earth. People polished their floors with dogshit.

Those days, there were cows only in heaven.

They threaded a string that had come from above and fashioned a chariot, climbed on it and went to the upper world and proclaimed the sorrow of not having cows. The cows were not prepared to go down to the earth that lay between the higher world and the lower world. Saying that the men of the earth would harm them in various ways, the bovine community ran away.

Finally, an aged cow with sores all over agreed to come down to earth. That cow reached the earth with the Brahmins.

There was a lot of grass on earth. The cow grazed around on a hill with light grass. That aged cow regained the youth of a newborn. A virile bull from heaven came roaring, and mated with her. She gave birth to a cocky young one with a beauty mark on his forehead and spots on his legs. If you milked the cow, she gave two and a half measures in the morning and one and a half measures in the evening. The morning's milk went to the elder sister and her children at the Southern Illam and the evening's milk went to the younger sister and her children at the Northern Illam. That's how it was when the inmates of the two Illams quarrelled over the quantity of milk.

With festering horns and hooves, the cow died. The inmates of both Illams jointly cremated her corpse. The cow's flesh from the burning pyre spattered onto the bodies of the children of the Southern and Northern Illams. The Brahmins of the Southern Illam wiped it away with their spit. The Northern Illam inmates plucked leaves to wipe it off. Those who had wiped the flesh with their spit were called 'cow-eating Parayas' by the others and were made outcasts. Drawing boundaries on land and water, they placed them beyond that.

There's another legend doing the rounds. The inmates of both Illams joined to cremate the cow's corpse. The smell of the rotting cow corpse spread from the burning pyre ....

One of the inmates of the Southern Illam was seven months pregnant. When the smell of burning beef spread, the Brahmin woman's mouth began to water. She craved to eat beef.

The craving became unbearable.

That Brahmin woman crept outside and stole the meat. She hid it and ate until her craving subsided ....

The Northern Illam people discovered her secret.
They howled in derision ....
'Shame, shame! Beef-eating Parayas!'
So the Brahmin woman who ate beef and her descendants became low-caste, they became Parayas ....
When Ilavattam came to a Paraya settlement, he will visit each Paraya home. And at night, he will request all the Parayas to assemble in one house. Everyone who is a Paraya, and irrespective of the gender, would assemble there. Shastrikal would make a public address about unity, the awareness to organize, the ways to reform society.

'Beloved brethren, we are the owners of a noble culture. What is the meaning of the word Paraya? Those who can speak (parayanka) was parayar. The famous poetess Avvayyar, the famous scholar Tiruvalluvar and others were Parayas. Who was the renowned Pakkanar—also a Paraya.'

He would go on to recite a poem ...

Born in the Paraya clan, we humble folk—
Few understand the truth we speak
Paraya-born Pakkanar of great renown—
Distinguished Paraya, now so widely known.

Thus he described the greatness of the Parayas.

Following which, Shastrikal would elaborate on his action plan to uplift the Parayas ...

'In a settlement of thirty families, one family buys ten eggs and hatches them. In 30 families, we will hatch 300 eggs. Let's say, fifty eggs are rotten. The remaining will hatch and there'll be two hundred and fifty chicks! These two hundred and fifty chicks will grow and lay eggs. At ten eggs each from the two hundred and fifty hens, two thousand five hundred eggs will be hatched. If five hundred among them are rotten, what's the remainder ... two thousand. Those two thousand chicks grow. They lay ten eggs each. How many then?' Shastrikal's question.

Twenty thousand eggs.

Shastrikal continues.

'Including the initial hundred and fifty mother hens, there are totally two thousand two hundred and fifty hens. Along with that, twenty thousand eggs are hatched. A thousand are rotten. Nineteen thousand hens remaining, so totally how many hens?' Shastrikal's question.

Some of them would calculate and reply. Two thousand two hundred and fifty. Plus nineteen thousand. In total, twenty-one thousand two hundred and fifty hens. These hens again lay eggs. So, how many?

Similarly, lakhs of chickens! Crores of eggs! If these crores of eggs are sold, lakhs of rupees come into our hands. Then, homes for the homeless, factories, schools, colleges, educational fund ... with money, various programmes for the upliftment of Parayas ....

Shastrikal would elaborate excitedly on the hen-raising project.

Shastrikal would continue ...

'Lakhs of hens will still continue to lay eggs. Crores of eggs will be sold every week. Money would pile up. With that money we can build big institutions.'

When Shastrikal's speech gets intensified, a small doubt from a youngster. His mischievous question—

'Shastrikal Sir, it will become impossible to walk on the paths because of the droppings of lakhs of chickens.'

Everyone burst into laughter.

Shastrikal becomes angry.

'This is the curse of our community. A lot that obeys no one. A brainless community. A lot that listens to the words and advice of no one.'

Shastrikal would begin to curse.

It was to establish a branch of the All Travancore Hindu-Christian Paraya Upliftment Association that Ilavattam Shastrikal had come to Mayiladi. That's when he came to know that Chennan was lying there unconscious. Shastrikal went straightaway to Mathias's house.

Even from a distance, Shastrikal heard the sound of the percussion and the songs and the Hallelujah cries. Counsellor Caleb and his wife and the faithful were standing in a circle and singing, praying and talking in tongues. When they saw Shastrikal, they temporarily stopped their prayer.

Shastrikal has learned attack, defence, the craft and also medicinal system of Marmam. He tested the pulse of the motionless, corpse-like Chennan. He gently touched a sensitive marmam (vital nervespot). All at once, Chennan opened his eyes. He looked at the people crowded around him.

'Water,' he whispered.

Mathias's wife immediately brought him hot coffee. In a cupped jackfruit leaf, Chennan was given coffee, a little at a time. After drinking the coffee, Chennan looked at the people surrounding him.

Chennan had regained his life.

* * *

The Rat Snake Concoction

Counsellor Caleb's and his friends' song and prayer had not worked. Understanding that there was absolutely no use in song and prayer, and going around Paraya settlements with his social work, Ilavattam Shastrikal now took over the medical treatment of Chennan.

Years ago,

When Ilavattam was a young student, his father Pirungan was a 'Siddan'. With some special medicinal herbs he used to cure incurable diseases. Pirungan's Mulleli thailam concoction was famous for treating sicknesses like rheumatism, jaundice, phlegm, piles, and infant diseases like polio. Two drops, and the illness was sure to be suppressed. Pirungan was also a renowned 'Marma' practitioner.

Once, a Paraya lad's thumb was crushed. He came to Pirungan. Pirungan went to the back of his hut, plucked out a herb of amazing strength, crushed it in his palm and applied it on the crushed thumb. What a miracle! Within a few hours, the crushed finger became whole again. The pain vanished. Complete relief. Pirungan knew herbs of such magical strength.

Before Pirungan died, he had taught Gopalan about various herbs with medicinal virility and amazing strength. Gopalan had learnt from his father the art of making special varieties of concoctions, syrups and oils. He was equipped to make Siddha medicines for certain terminal diseases. If he treated and cured a patient, his father had warned him not to accept any remuneration for it. He had advised him not to consider healing as a means of livelihood.

Ilavattam had some special line of treatment for those who suffered bodily harm from being beaten, fisted, kicked, clobbered, etc. Porcupine balm, fox soup, rat snake concoction, tortoise essence, crab syrup were among the things that Ilavattam knew how to prepare.

Ilavattam got ready to begin his treatment to heal Chennan's bodily injuries and make him healthy again. An important youngster of the community becoming tubercular and, inch by inch, coughing his way to his death after being beaten and fisted? That shouldn't be. That youngster should be treated and made to recover. He should be cared for. He should be brought back to his former condition. He should be transformed into a pillar of society!

In order to do this, he began a special line of treatment.

Various medicinal herbs, roots of plants, leaves, flowers, raw fruit and skins were all beaten and mixed with milk and given to Chennan on an empty stomach. Fit medicine for bodily injuries, wounds and physical torture.

Following which, under Ilavattam's leadership, a group of youngsters went out in search of a rat snake. At the edge of ditches, in outer yards, in coconut groves, in areca groves, in gardens, they wandered in search of a rat snake. A yellow rat snake was what they wanted. Looking in the bunds of paddy fields, in plots, in buildings, even after searching exhaustively for the oft-seen rat snake for two days without rest, they couldn't find one. That's how it is with anything. Search for something in an emergency and you may not find it.

Two whole days they sieved that locality. They couldn't find a single rat snake. Disappointed, they were going to wind up the day's mission when their eyes fell upon a yellow rat snake crawling on the edge of a ditch.

They were happy.

Wielding stick, club and other weapons, with the enthusiasm of attacking a formidable enemy, they surrounded and captured the rat snake. They snipped off a piece from near the head. P.G. rolled up the remaining part. Removing its fangs with an extra-sharp knife used for cutting bamboo, he washed and cleaned it. Cutting out a leaf, he finely shredded the yellow snake and placed the pieces on it. P.G. had collected herbal medicine consisting of a hundred and one herbs with vital healing properties. The rule is that you are not supposed to speak when you are plucking the herbs. The mind should remain focused.

The herbal medicines that P.G. had brought were crushed and rolled into a mixture like butter and placed in a special container. The sliced rat snake was placed in another container. Afterwards, the crushed and rolled herbal medicine and rat snake were put into a jar. Twenty-five pots of water were added and the mouth of the jar closed with dried banana leaf tied to it. With the protective covering of the banana-plant fibre tied around it, the jar was made even more secure.

In the courtyard, a stove was made with three stones. The stove was filled with firewood. P.G. lit a twig. Turning to the east, he stood meditatively for some minutes, moving his lips in a chant. Kneeling, facing eastward, with great reverence, he lit the stove. The fire should burn in the same way for two nights and two days, that is the rule.

After two nights and two days, the fire is to be removed. The heated concoction is sieved through a coconut frond. The sediments are kept secure in a special container. The essence is shut up in a jar.

Chennan consumed the rat snake concoction. Morning and night and evening. Kept smearing the sediments of the rat snake concoction all over his body. And massaged.

A month passed.

Miraculous transformation.

Chennan's figure was completely transformed. His exhaustion fell away. Flesh swelled on his body. His hands thickened like clubs. His chest expanded and became vast. It seemed that the touch of a finger would make the blood spurt.

Chennan regained his old vigour and health.

He grew huge and smart.

—*Translated by Shreekumar Varma*

The Pulaya Ghetto

Paul Chirakkarode

The anniversary of the congregation on the hill dawned. It was a grand affair. Pallithara Pathrose and wife Maria, Paulose and Outha, and other new Christians also arrived. As always, they arranged themselves in front on the woven-leaf mat. The benches at the back lay vacant, and would be filled by the elite, who would arrive only when the meeting was about to start, wearing wrist watches.

It was a Monday. Even so, there was a good gathering. A feast that included everyone present was being prepared in the mission bungalow.

Custodian Thomas went around supervising it all. He had no time to sit down. He would run to the mission house; dash back to the church, then you would see him taking four rounds in the yard thickly laid with sand. He ran about like a caged civet cat. Yet he never reached anywhere in time. He pulled off his fine shoulder cloth and wiped his streaming forehead. He appeared at the church door, his mouth smeared with betel froth.

'It is our anniversary today, is it not? I have called one or two people to speak. They'll arrive quite late ... Womenfolk ... go in and start singing.'

The women entered, shook the dust off the mat and spread it again, sat down, tugged at their fine upper cloth to cover their heads, and thick hair that tumbled down, like a black poem to beauty. It was the rule. A saintly disciple who wrote epistles in the Gospel had said: a woman must cover her head with a cloth and sit silently in the congregation. Though these were all rules that could not be broken, they could sing. Their melodious voices could be used to praise God, was that not so?

The women began to sing.

Paulose stood in the corner of the yard, restless. There were many things he wanted to say. There were many things against which he wanted to object. But he had not yet acquired a clear language. That would take time. Perhaps he might die and dissolve in the mud without saying anything. Pallithara Pathrose and the old Outha Pulayan would not believe him. They were all just slaves. They would all isolate him; that's what would happen. Should he clear the path for that?

Behold! Through the open windows of the church the combined sweetness from the women's throats flowed, breaking barriers. Paulose listened to the song. He thought: like granite lying submerged in the pond; when you break it open, there will be no wetness at all inside.

The song continued to rise. It rose and rose, vibrating with energy; it took on life; a wonderful world of God unfurled its petals through its lines. The musical streams reached their crescendo. Were their waves spreading in the atmosphere? It seemed as though they were flowing towards the limits of the horizon.

Outha Pulayan came towards him. The expectation of a good lunch filled the old man. On every anniversary of the congregation, Outha Pulayan would fill himself with a good lunch. That day had arrived this year too. Outha Pulayan asked, 'Eda, Paulothe, is the lunch ready? Everyone has to eat, *alle*?'

Paulose looked at the greedy man with contempt mixed with sympathy. Displeased, he asked 'Achaan*, do you think only of lunch and eating?'

Outha Pulayan did not understand what was wrong in thinking of food. He was old. He could no longer make bunds in the paddy fields or ply or ride the wheel. Thus he no longer got the breakfast he used to get from the landlord's house. The stomach of the old man's wizened body churned. If he went to the landlord's house he might get a meal. But now youngsters were the ones who had able hands and the will to work. New slaves had been appointed. Those men bent double, toiling,

---

* Achaan: Uneducated way of saying Achayan a term of respect used to address an older man.

would gobble their breakfast and leave. Outha Pulayan struggled with insatiable hunger and a wrinkled body. The old man asked, 'What is this, Paulothe, you after all have a bit of sense! What's wrong in eating the church's lunch? I too give the monthly subscription and fistful of rice, okay!'

The old man was clearly provoked. His smothered, crushed pride awoke. He had many things to say. It was the congregation's lunch that he ate every anniversary. No one need to curl the lip to give him that. Not only that, he gave the fistful of rice, and the monthly subscription and other earnings as well.

Paulose was at a loss. The old man had totally misunderstood him. He said, 'Achaan, you flare up even before I finish talking! This is what I said. Listen carefully, Achaan.'

In the voice of one delivering expert interpretation of a grave and complex problem, Paulose said, 'Achaan, you, myself, and Pallithara Pathrochan are all committee members, aren't we?'

The old man nodded in agreement. 'True, true. All of us are in the committee, after all.'

Paulose spoke more sharply, 'Why were we elected to the committee?'

Outha Pulayan did not know much about the responsibilities of a committee member. Paulose's question struck somewhere in his heart. But he did not understand it entirely. Outha Pulayan said casually, 'Why we became committee people—because we wanted to be committee people.'

Paulose corrected him. Not just that. In truth, it was a matter that needed a lot of speaking and explaining, was it not? Paulose began to speak, his enthusiasm rising as he spoke, 'You know, I'm asking because I don't know. If it is wrong, forgive me. We are said to be committee people. Do we get to know anything? No. They, the Father and the Custodian decide. And it happens.'

There was the Father, the Custodian, and certain other committee members .What they think, takes place. There were any number of examples and past experiences. Paulose asked excitedly, 'If that is not true, Achaan, just think. This anniversary celebration which is being held, did we committee members know anything about it?'

That was not it. No decision about celebrating the anniversary was taken in the committee meeting. Then how did this decision happen? How was this meeting organized? All these things should be done with their knowledge, was it not so? Today some stranger is coming here to speak about the Gospel to God's true lambs. It was because that gentleman was late that the meeting was being delayed. Who was coming? They should find out.

A light flashed in Outha Pulayan's mind. For this long, he had been proud to be a committee member. He used to mention it to several people. For the first time that consciousness lost its firmness. It wavered. He thought for a while, then said, 'Then I'll go into the church and ask Father. Ho! We have to know this k'datha!

The old man became excited. Paulose understood this. Concealing his satisfaction he said, 'Achaan, don't go there now. That's not how it should be asked.'

The priest was extremely cunning. Paulose knew that very well. A white smile would blossom on that flushed tomato-like face; with gentle soothing words that fell from his clever tongue, Father would easily tame Outha Pulayan. Even a tempest would be suppressed. The situation should not be one that rose like the mountain, only to vanish like mist. Paulose said, 'The time for that is yet to come. Then we will ask.'

Songs resonated within the church as their dark-skinned womenfolk sat in a row and sang. Melodious music poured into the air with rhythm and cadence. A song that could submerge all the sorrows of the material world in the intoxication of the soul seemed to gain life as it flowed. Paulose listened intently. So did Outha Pulayan. Were they taking in the message of the song that said that this world and everything in it were illusory. What lasted was only up there, in the world above. There the Saviour, with His pious brides would live for thousands of years. Everlasting life and everlasting happiness. No trials and tribulations nor afflictions.

Were those women not aware of these troubles? The church that was blessed by their vital music was full of caste-based jealousies; did they not know it? Here there was no light. No spirituality. A place wholly darkened by superstitions and caste sovereignties. O people who come here hoping for light! Go back! This was an organization built by rich men who had made God a witness for the prosecution. In this religion which had turned into an organization, there was no purity, no spirituality. It was now place gone dark where good people could not see their way at all.

A car drew up on the main road below and a thick-set man emerged from it. Custodian Thomas ran to greet him. He said joyfully, 'Come, come. Saar, it is because you were late, that the meeting did not start. I was a little anxious.'

That fat man smiled sympathetically. Before the smile faded he said, 'Oh, if *I* say that I'll come to a function or place, I *will* come. I'm very particular about these things'.

'Yes, yes. I know that', replied Thomas, quickly.

With the conscientious care of a guide, Custodian Thomas walked ahead, the speaker behind him. The church on top of the hill could be seen above, facing the open sky and the expanse of paddy fields. The rays of the sun fell on its whitewashed surface and cross, making them glow. They climbed the hill. On both sides of the path stood boundaries of mud. Tapioca branches, bent and tied together formed a fence above it. The speaker glanced at both sides along the path as they climbed up. Tiny, tiny yards all filled with tapioca, banana trees, pumpkin creepers, and ladies finger. As he looked into the whirlpool of that greenery, he saw small huts—the thatched homes of the new Christian members of the Church on the hill congregation, believers of the true faith.

The esteemed person who had come to speak had a question to ask, 'All these huts are occupied by new Christians, is it not so?'

'Yes,' Custodian Thomas continued with enthusiasm. 'Our sympathy for them, led to their being allowed to dwell here, during various times. But they all seem to be rascals.'

'Why? Why is it so?' asked the speaker gravely.

'Oh, is there a reason for all that? Rabid communists, all of them!'

That was a hint that said that the speaker should respond to it. But the man did not say anything. He just grunted. Custodian Thomas looked at him sharply. The fat man's face had begun to look glum. A shadow had fallen over it. Just that. Custodian Thomas felt tired. He wondered what the man's speech would be like.

People filled the yard and the church. Now the meeting had to start, that was all. Pallithara Pathrose and Outha Pulayan entered the church. There were other new Christians too. Anna kidaathi sat among the women on the southern side. Her husband had not come. Thoma had gone to the hill slope on the other side that day, to clear land to plant tapioca. He had tied the minnu around his woman's neck; made her his own. He was determined that she should not go hungry. He did not need rest.

Anna kidaathi's eyes swept the inside of the Church four sides. Many of her friends had come and their husbands too. Even if one had to forgo work for a day, even if it meant forgoing a meal, one had to take part in the congregation's anniversary and should partake of that day's festive lunch. Such a meal could be had only next year. Her husband alone had not come. 'It's the anniversary and you are alone, Anna kidaathi? Where's the man who tied the minnu?' asked a friend.

'Didn't come. Went for work.' The bride's voice cracked. The corners of her eyes grew moist. Her lower cloth was new. She wore it neatly pleated. Her fine gold bordered upper cloth had not lost its sheen. If her husband too had come it would have been so complete. Now a sense of dissatisfaction flitted in her heart.

She no longer looked about. She bowed her head, pulled the shining gold bordered edge of her upper cloth over her head and sat still on the mat. All around her, her happy friends were singing. The song seemed to rise and fall like waves in the sea. She listened to it. Her lips did not part. She could not join in that joy around her.

One who sat beside Pallithara Pathrose asked, 'Achaya, who is coming to speak today?'

Pathrose did not know and gestured to express this. 'How do I know, k'datha'?

The young man who had asked the question, was angry. He asked, 'If you do not know that, why do you continue as a committee man, Achaya?'

Pallithara Pathrose bowed his head. What an insult! Pathrose wanted to make some reply. He felt stifled, but he could not think up a quick repartee. Yes, this irresponsible stance was wrong. It must not be repeated.

Father entered the church, the speaker behind him. Custodian Thomas appeared at the door on the northern side, a hitherto unseen gravity on his face.

'Let us pray. Let us remember the blessings of the congregation and the astonishing manner in which God led us this year,' said Father.

Everyone knelt and bent over. An unworldly peace descended on the house of prayer. Three or four seconds went by, in this manner. Again Father said, 'Now Pallithara Pathrose will pray for the growth of our congregation and for the increase of God's might.'

Pallithara Pathrose's prayer was well known among the congregation. No one else could pray that loud or long. Many times youngsters had become enthused by the prayer. This time too Pathrose's voice rose, and gathered volume.

The prayer was over. The next was a 'welcome' speech. The priest called Custodian Thoma. He went towards the table cleared his throat and began, 'My greetings to God's holy servant, reverend Father, and the congregation ....'

Paulose murmured something in Pallithara Pathrose's ear and then turned towards Outha Pulayan who shook and tidied the second cloth draped around his thin shoulders when he tried to rise, Paulose stopped him.

Custodian Thomas continued, 'I do not have the task of introducing today's honourable speaker, because he is that famous and loved by all.'

Outha Pulayan stood up suddenly. A forceful question shot out from the old tongue, 'Who invited this man?'

The assembly was shocked into immobility. Insult! A grievous insult! Father rose and spoke in the unique voice of priestly gravity, 'Outha Pulayan, be seated.'

But Outha Pulayan did not sit down. He somehow grew brave and it showed. With the seriousness of his newly awakened courage, he repeated, 'None of us committee members knew about this. Father and Custodian Thomas together brought him here. Let him speak. We will listen to it. But you must at least ask us before you do this.'

The visitor broke into a sweat. He looked at Father. It was a pitiable sight.

Father gave a casual excuse. 'The decision was taken in a hurry. That was why we could not think as we should. I am sorry about that.'

In such situations Father expressed regret. If necessary he would even beg pardon. The Pulayan could never focus or think of anything consistently. He would soften quickly. Father knew this very well. He began to speak conciliatory words. Paulose's question rose from a back row.

'What about last year?'

That was indeed a question! It had strength. Father was truly shocked. What was the nature of last year's function? It was the same as this year. Someone was brought to speak, without the knowledge of the dark-skinned committee members, without their consent. Accounts of income and expenditures were presented and passed. Till now it had always happened that way. For the first time dissent arose. Where had it come from?

Father looked at Pallithara Pathrose. A glance loaded with meaning. A look seeking help. Pathrose leaned forward. Stretching his arm he caught hold of Outha Pulayan's left arm. 'Achaya, what craziness is this? Sit Achaya.'

Fury made Outha Pulayan sightless. The old man's body trembled. He swept his hand energetically and roared, 'Let go, young Pulayane, I have to know this. They should not cheat without the knowledge of the committee members. This is a sin against God.'

Words that blossomed from the fury of the lowly ones, swirled like a cyclone within the stone walls of the church on the hill. Were the walls shaking?

Outha Pulayan said, 'You carry on with your anniversary. Our group is leaving.'

The old man led the way out. Paulose and some other low-caste Christians followed. Some women also stepped out. Anna kidaathi watched. Her father Pallithara Pathrose sat motionless. She was in a dilemma. Finally she too went out.

In that manner the first cyclone hit the congregation hard. It was very strong. A great trembling. What were the things it would dash and scatter?

* * *

Pallithara Pathrose was troubled. On one side, there was Father and the Custodian. On the other side were his people. Whom should he join? There was substance in what Paulose and Outha Pulayan said. The present situation should not be allowed to continue. The domination of the elite held sway in the congregation on the hill. For a very long time they had been ruling it. Only what Custodian Thomas desired happened there. Why? What was the reason?

The wife saw Pathrose's distress and understood it. Maria's tongue moved. 'Adi, what is it that you are thinking, all the time?'

Pathrose became even more upset. Maria did not stop. She asked, 'If that Custodian and Father get angry, let them. This is foolish! Is it greater than our own people?'

A pale smile spread over Pathrose's rough face. That new Christian who was a true believer, shook his head and said, 'Sshe! Edi, that's not it. What our people say is also true. But what will Father think?'

Maria understood the essence of that sentence. Father liked Pathrose very much. Whatever meeting was held, it was to Pathrose, that Father turned asking him to pray. Father had said several times that there was no one else in the congregation who could pray with as much spiritual intensity as Pathrose. All that was true. Pathrose was satisfied by an intense, inspiring prayer. Till today that man had had no complaints. Today, for the first time, he had grievance. Did that not mean that he was gaining awareness? Pathrose was proud to be just a member of the congregation on the hill. The tinge of egoism mixed into his pride had been shattered. Father, Custodian Thomas, and *their* people were dominating them in the congregation. His own Pulaya people were mere slaves. There, the songs that he and his people sang within the thickly white-washed walls of the church on the hill, were all denials of truth. Those songs had no vitality. It was just a feeling. Could the manifestation of slavery have vitality?

Pathrose felt irritable. Was there anything to be proud of in his, a true Christian's, life? Nothing. He silently obeyed what Father, the Custodian and those who had been Christians from very early times, said.

As he understood that shameful truth a change came over Pathrose. His enthusiasm withered. He could no longer sing loudly, or call out 'Praise the Lord.' That old Pulayan told himself, 'Pelayan will remain Pelayan, always. Joining the church was useless, completely useless.'

That was a terrible revelation. Pathrose thought about it continuously, like one who is sick of drinking sour medicine. His heart felt heavy. He could not bear it. Worry throbbed in his heart. Unable to bear it, afflicted by the burden that made his heart grow heavy, Pallithara Pathrose called out, 'Oh my God ...'

Outha Pulayan and Paulose came to see him. When he saw them Pathrose felt a flash of fear within him. That old fashioned man wished he could disappear. All the Harijans who joined the church should unite. In some unknown manner the idea had sprung up. The elite Christians controlled the wealth of the Christian congregation and they enjoyed it. The poor Parayan and Pulayan had no right to it. Where did the huge income from all that wealth go?

As soon as he came Outha Pulayan said, 'Eda, Pathrothe, I know that Father has frightened you with his words. Even so, you'll have to come.'

Paulose supported him. Not just that, the young man had something more to explain.

'Pathrochaayan, you are the big man among us. That being so, it's not right for you to distance yourself.'

Pathrose did desire to acknowledge that leadership. For this long he had acted as though he had it. He had never compromised it. For the first time he began to feel that the leadership was a myth. But there was one consolation. Parayan and Pulayan had joined the church. By having the baptismal water sprinkled on their forehead, they had taken on the names of the wealthy Christians and lived with those names. The new

Christians still wanted his acknowledgement. It had not become totally meaningless. He could feel relief now.

Pathrose asked, 'What should I do?'

Paulose was the one who replied. 'If you ask what you should do ... Achayan, did you not know anything, till now?'

Pathrose replied like one, held guilty, 'No, I did not know anything.' He scratched his head, and as though asking forgiveness for the lapse, continued, 'What is it? What is it?'

This time too Paulose explained, while Outha Pulayan nodded in agreement. 'Achaan, did you not hear? Then it is very sad. We have decided to have a meeting.'

'Going to have a meeting!' The true believer Pathrose, recalled meetings which echoed 'Halleluiah!' and 'Praise the Lord,' and asked, 'Who is speaking?'

Infuriated, Outha Pulayan spat out, 'Ha, Ho!' The old man continued energetically, 'Eda Pathrose, listen. The thing is, our people have been cheated by Father and Custodian Thomas. Their songs and prayers are meaningless, utterly meaningless; our people are their slaves.'

Pallithara Pathrose stared, amazed. He was reminded of a story Father had said, when he was reading and studying the Bible. Apparently a donkey had begun to speak! It was at a time when God's prophet stood like a dull-witted man, that the donkey opened its mouth and began to speak. Amazing! Even old Outha Pulayan has started to explain things!'

Paulose continued the explanation. 'Why did they included our people in the church? For what? They profit from it; that was why they included us.'

Paulose could not clarify what that profit was. There *was* something. His instinct nudged him to recognize it. Did Custodian Thoma, Father and their folk need the help of simple people like Pallithara Pathrose and Outha Pulayan? A doubt rose in Pallithara Pathrose's mind and broke out from his tongue, in the form of a question, 'What do they gain from our people joining the church?'

That was indeed a question! Was it not right? They who depended on the upper castes, who lived somehow on their kindness, what gain were they for the upper castes? Nothing. Pathrose laughed when he thought of the illogicality of the statement. Paulose saw it.

'Why are you laughing, Achaan?'

'What do they gain?' Pathrose repeated his question.

Paulose was in a quandary. That was obvious. Paulose who bore the responsibility of explaining everything was at a loss. So too was Outha Pulayan. He had not expected such a question from Pathrose. Somehow, a quickly conceived reply appeared on Paulose's tongue.

'If you ask what that is, I do not know the whole of it. But there are those who know. They are the ones who will come and speak at the meeting.'

Outha Pulayan let out a deep sigh. Paulose had brains which woke up at the right time and acted. When they included Harijans in the church, they saw some obvious advantages. That advantage did not end with the expansion of Christ the King's kingdom. But neither Paulose nor Outha Pulayan were capable of explaining why. They did not know enough to provide an explanation. But because of that, could the great secret remain unknown? No, that too was not possible. It was said that somewhere, there were Harijans who could explain these things. They did not know the place or address. But even the knowledge that there were such people amongst them was such a relief!

Pathrose asked, 'Will Father and the Custodian allow this?'

It was not just Pathrose, but Outha Pulayan too had the same fear. The meeting had to be held in the mission-owned property. Such a convenient place was not available anywhere in that land. The vast sand covered yard in front of the church, on the hill. Any number of people could sit there.

Outha Pulayan said, 'I too have the same thought. What will we do if Father does not agree?'

Paulose was not bothered. He was filled with enthusiasm. The passion to resist anything and anybody. The feeling that he could sweep aside whatever resistance sprouted before him. The enthusiasm awakened within him when he realized for the first time, that he was marginalized. Would it die out?

Paulose said, 'Father, need not agree. We will hold our meeting despite that. Or else, watch out!'

When he spoke it was in a firm voice, determination mixed into it. Let Father, the Custodian and the dominant upper castes, jointly resist. Parayan and Pulayan who had joined the church would hold the meeting. The new generation would resist. This was the first enactment of that great resistance. Paulose once again said, with verve, 'Or else you watch what happens!'

* * *

An obvious split appeared in the congregation on the hill. The elite Christians continued to assume their earlier dominance. No one resisted openly. Yet a change appeared in the behaviour of the new Christians. That change spread like a film of oil floating on water. Anyone could see it. A single look was enough.

Even today a great many people arrive to worship on Sundays. As usual the upper-caste Syrian Christians sprawl against the back-rests of the benches at the back of the church. A large mat was spread in front. There were two big mats. The new Christians sat on them like a flock of tamed sheep.

The old songs continue to be sung even today. But they had lost their vitality. The curiosity in the hearts of the Pulaya women which gave the songs rhythmic vitality and melodious sweetness, died. They understood. The Kingdom of God would not arrive all that soon!

The worship and the song dragged on, somehow. But everyone seemed to notice the dullness. Nobody did anything about it. Somehow an issue had churned up. It would settle down, clear up; that was all.

But Parayan and Pulayan awoke. Everyone's goal was that meeting. On that day people from their lowly community, who had gained education and risen, who could speak at a meeting, would come to address them! They would enumerate and catalogue one by one, all the injustices that the upper-caste Christians had been routinely inflicting on them for over a hundred years. They wanted to hear it. Wanted to see them. Old Outha Pulayan was amazed, 'In spite of everything, people who could speak a few words had come up in our community too!'

When he thought about it his greying eyelashes grew moist. The old man rejoiced to see his people progress. Did he not have the right to it? In his youth none of them had held meetings. No one made speeches. In those days as he ploughed the fields that yielded a thousand paras of rice, sowed seeds and drew water to irrigate them, he had seen the landlords hold meetings. So many such festivals had taken place in Kuttanad. People came in big snake boats, sitting in rows, enthusiastically singing songs. They held meetings; there would also be fireworks on a large scale. The vast fields lay in darkness at that time. Parayan and Pulayan who had become part of that darkness often stood in the muddy paddy fields and watched the far away lights. The sights he had seen! Many years had gone by. Today Outha Pulayan too could sit in the front row of such a meeting. That change was progress, was it not?

Tears filled the old man's eyes and dripped on to his bony chest. The tears were an offering to an exhilarating experience. He wept with joy.

One Sunday, adoration over, people got moved into the yard. Some went and sat down in the shade of the mazhavadi tree. That was quite common. They would sit there and tell many stories.

Paulose came forward. He seemed to be in a hurry. 'Look, we should all get together. We need to discuss something.'

Some who did not quite understand its seriousness, asked, 'What is it? What is it?'

'*You ask what!*' Paulose was cross and infuriated. 'This is why it is said, our people will never prosper. We forget so quickly!'

When his anger dimmed, he explained, 'Have you forgotten that we are holding a meeting?'

A man asked jokingly, 'Why, is the meeting today?'

'Not today, but don't we have to think?'

The new Christians gathered in a circle. One of them asked, 'Should we not call the women?'

'Of course. What did you think?'

The women stood in a group towards the south, talking idly. Anna kidaathi and her mother were talking. Paulose went towards them. Maria asked him, chattily, 'What's the news Paulocha?'

Paulose smiled. 'Does Maria sister not know? We are going to hold a meeting.'

Pride throbbed in those words. Other women listened. Maria said, 'I know. When is the meeting?'

Another asked, 'Who is speaking?'

A beautiful sari-clad young woman with a thick layer of powder on her face simpered, 'You should include my song.'

She was one bold woman!

As though she had just remembered it, a woman said, 'My younger daughter dances well. You must include her dance.'

Paulose gave a general reply to all the suggestions. 'We'll do all that. We are holding this meeting to decide what all should be included. Come, we'll go over there.'

They gathered. In the shade of the mazhavadi tree, men and women folk, the new Christian members of the congregation on the hill gathered. It was indeed a sight. They would think and decide.

As an introduction, Paulose said, 'We have assembled here for a purpose. As to explain what it is, though our people joined the church, our people still experience exclusion. The upper-caste Christians and we are two groups.'

A Pulayan who stood far behind, away from the group, asked, 'So what should we do? Can our people and the upper castes become one?'

Some of the old fashioned ones were of the same opinion. They had not voiced it, that was all. They all nodded in agreement. The old became more enthusiastic. Another question arose from that old tongue. 'Eda k'datha, let me ask you something. So are we holding this meeting to turn our people into upper castes?'

A contemptuous laugh rose from the crowd. Paulose was in a fix. He had not expected that sort of a question. If there was to be resistance, it would be from the upper castes, he had thought. Here, his own people were laughing and howling at him! They were ridiculing him.

Paulose woke up. He zestfully asked a counter-question. 'We joined the church to be Christians, right?'

A man said, 'Yes. So what happened?'

Paulose did not know how to explain. If he were to begin to narrate the many intolerable experiences, there were so many to be said. Had they all forgotten those experiences? Will they ever learn anything! The bondage could well continue tomorrow and the day after!

Again the question arose, 'So what happened?'

'What happened! What more can happen? Our people joined the church not to continue as landlord and slave, it was to worship God.'

That struck home. People lowered their voices and listened. The silence was noticeable, meaningful. Paulose's words dug into their hearts like a chisel. It pierced hard. Each one had memories to recall. Experiences in one's own life. The Syrian Christians in the church on the hill were always the Thampurans. Though the Parayan and Pulayan were baptized, they were still excluded, and that continued even today.

'Friends, should we not seek a way out?' Paulose asked.

'We should,' they replied in one voice. 'There should be a way.'

That was a momentous occasion. Paulose had won. He looked around in the exhilaration of victory. No one was resisting. Everyone had fallen into that stream of thought. That was a relief. Now he could talk. He could go forward.

Paulose continued, 'Therefore we have this meeting, to think of that way.' His glance swept four sides once, and said, 'Now have you understood?'

'Oh,' everyone nodded their heads, as a proof of agreement.

Someone was coming along the long lane that led from the church to the common road below. Outha Pulayan said, 'Someone is coming. Who is it?'

Another said, 'That's Thoma, isn't it? Pallithara Pathrose's son-in-law?'

Thoma drew near. He had changed, looked a different person. He was no longer the handsome young man he used to be. The time—when he had thick curly hair and an ink-black body, when he wore a waist cloth that was not smeared with mud—was gone. He looked wild. His hair would no longer lie neatly, even if patted down. He had become thin; bones protruded in places. Life had appeared before him in its true colour.

Thoma sat among the crowd. He showed no enthusiasm.

Outha Pulayan looked him over, then said, 'Look, shouldn't you youngsters show some fervor and enthusiasm? Look, I'm asking because I don't know. Shouldn't the youngsters be doing all this?'

Paulose continued, 'There are expenses to hold a meeting. And we should conduct it well.'

Yes, that should be so. The meeting should be conducted well. There should be songs, speeches, a lot of people should assemble. The crowd should be as thick as the flowering blue valley. No one had anything against that. But a young man with an inclination to resist, asked, 'What about expenses?'

Paulose said, 'Yes, there are expenses.' He explained that too. Some good speakers have come up among the Harijans, in recent times. Some of them are writers as well. They must be brought to speak at the meeting. A meeting was held in far away Mavelikkara. Paulose had gone for that meeting as a visitor. That time a young man who wrote stories in magazines spoke. That was some speech. Words flowed endlessly like a stream.

Recalling the occasion, Paulose said, 'If you want to hear a speech that is the one you should hear. But that is not what I'm thinking—that young man's father was a preacher.'

A man asked, 'Isn't that a problem?'

'Aa, perhaps there might not be. That young man is a smart one. People were clapping throughout his speech.'

Outha Pulayan grunted in agreement. 'That's true. I too heard it.'

Immediately, a man in the crowd asked, 'What is his name?'

That Paulose did not know. However, there is a way, he said. Someone should go to Mavelikkara. They could send some young man who rode a bicycle, that was enough. He would bring all the information about that speaker. There should be others too.

'Who else will we call?' Outha Pulayan asked energetically.

'We should bring that achen*.'

'Should we?'

'We should. Now our people should make our separate congregation. That achen will be the bishop.'

Someone in the crowd began to laugh loudly. A Pulayan could at the most, become a priest. Could he come a Bishop? Of course not. Even God in the heavens above would not allow it. If God's anger flared up would not the whole world be consumed by that fire?

Thoma alone did not say anything. He could not speak. Why did he go and become a Christian? He saw a girl, fell in love with her; destroyed everything he had to make her his own. Today what did he have that was his own? Nothing. He had even his name lost. He yearned to hear the call 'Kandan Kora'. There was sweetness in it. It was a relief to hear that name. No; no; he would never again have the comfort of hearing someone call him that name affectionately. Why did this name 'Thoma Pulayan', happen?

A man sitting beside him asked, 'Don't you have anything to say, friend?'

He grunted to say no, then shook his head. He was a lowly Christian— was it not better to be dead?

Those who could not make them human, were they the ones who would take them to the heavenly kingdom? Thoma felt doubtful. Would there be lords and slaves in the heavenly kingdom too? Would God Jehova allow the lordly Christians and the slave Christians to sit together? In that heaven .... For the first time in his life, Thoma thought: Lies! ... all this is a big lie ... it was all lies.'

Detailed programmes of the meeting were discussed and decided. They should ask for contributions. There should be lights, a mike and other things. A member of that group worked in the electricity department. He would do the wiring for free. There should be a bright tube light where the women were seated. The decision was thus completed.

---

* Achen: Priest.

Now they had to elect a committee. They should get the contributions in two weeks. A notice should be printed a week before the meeting. Notice should be sent to the chief guest, speaker and some others.

'In which press are we printing it?' asked someone.

'It can be any press.'

Someone suggested Thoma's name for the committee. Another seconded it. Thoma said, 'No, I don't want to. I can't.'

Outha Pulayan was not pleased. 'Why not? That's impossible. It's not right for young men to stay away.'

Thoma said, 'It's not that. I can't leave the hut and go anywhere after dusk. It is at night that we go for subscriptions, isn't it?'

Everyone understood his difficulty. Thoma's wife Anna kidaathi was pregnant. If he went out at night she would be alone. She was scared.

Paulose said, 'Then we can exclude Thoma.'

It was a relief. But he should not keep away for that reason. He should take part in the day time activities. If he too did not join the venture, it would not be a success. Was he not clever!'

Outha Pulayan said, 'But listen, k'datha, you must contribute.'

'I will,' Thoma got up and began to walk. That he was troubled, was obvious.

When he reached the hut he saw Anna kidaathi lying on a woven mat. She was not asleep, just lethargic. He went and sat near her, pressing his body against hers. Her body was slightly warm. It slowly spread to him. She opened her eyes and looked at him. The gaze was not sensual, there was affection in it. Like a mother petting her son, she ran her fingers through his curly hair. She asked kindly, 'Is the meeting over?'

'No. They are still talking. I came away.'

'Why?'

He did not reply. He let out a sigh. It mingled with the air around. He stared at her belly. It was growing by the minute.

—*Translated by Catherine Thankamma*

The Death Wail*

P.A. Uthaman

The lore of my forefathers that was passed down to me,
That which I felt in the blood and in my being,
That which I heard and all that I tasted.
That which I grasped and much that I imbibed,
I have tried to put in words.
To those who have died and become one with the land,
To the many whom time passed by,
Where, how, nobody knows.
To them who know and the many more who don't,
Who have chronicled their wisdom or lack of it,
To them who taught me to speak,
Who committed me to write,
To all of them, these lines are dedicated.

* * *

The astrologer sat cross-legged.
He scattered the shells and spread them out.
He smeared sacred ash on his forehead, rubbing it backwards.
Shells that echoed the sea.
He arranged the seeds.
Seeds which held the secrets of life.
He prayed, 'All you thousand gods, lords, and protectors; you witches and demons, you who hover over us, who inform our vision and speech, I beseech you to make crystal clear, the right and the wrong. Reveal to this poor soul the sins of his body and soul. So you want me to tell you who has possessed this young girl named Velutha, taking her to be alone and unprotected. If I reveal it what will you give me? You must keep your promise understood.'

The shaman danced till dawn. He threw the shells and the dice and all was revealed. He asked for offerings of plantains, rice flakes and jaggery; for betel leaves, toddy, the blood of a black fowl, for red silk. He danced in the light of the flaming torches.

---

* Original title *Chavoli*.

When he had danced to a frenzy, when his trance faded and his dance slowed and ended, when the rooster blood had all been drunk and droplets had been sprinkled on Kochembi, the shaman called out in a voice loud enough for all to hear, 'Your daughter is a virgin. I will prove it. But you mustn't forget me. The gods are my witness, your offerings have been accepted. I will perform all the necessary ceremonies. Happy? The shaman leapt away, his forehead and crown covered with sacred ash. Another beseecher moved forward and bowed.

* * *

Nilembi came from Aruvikkara. In fact, he was sent for. Three bushels of paddy were measured out and placed before him. Kunjankaran, the elder thampuran ordered, 'This is Kochembi, my labourer. He has a daughter. You there, does she have a name?'

'Yes my lord.'

'Oh so she has a name. Well, you accept this gift, Nilembi, and marry her. I will gift her some land. You look after the land and the girl.'

With hands hardened from working on his own land, Nilembi accepted the gift. Velutha carried it in a basket.

At night, the lamps were lit and betel leaves and toddy were arranged.

Kochembi called, 'All you elders and ancestors, you who have passed away yet listen and reply, you who protect us, and stand guard over the four directions, who make firm our footfalls, listen and bless us. Put your hands on our heads and grant consent. The elders and guests had gathered. 'When is the wedding?' they asked.

'No need to delay it,' Kochembi told his brother-in-law.

'The time is auspicious. And the toddy has been drunk.'

'Then call Nilembi, send for him.'

Nilembi said, 'When the thampuran's men summoned me, I thought it was only about work. I was tilling when these people told me to drop everything and come immediately. They wouldn't even let me put down the raised spade. There would be many days work they said. I was very busy with plenty of my own work and no time to spare but when they said it was the thampuran who called, I was scared. So I just put my spade down and rushed down here. As for the wedding, I have folks, elders and friends. They must be told.'

'So what, that's all right. You are go and tell them whenever you want. We will come along to inform your father and mother. But right now you give the pudava to the girl.'

* * *

'I agree. But I don't have a puduva to give her.'
'That's not a problem ...'
Velutha's maternal uncle removed the towel wound round his head. 'Here's the bride cloth.'
'Very good,' the seniors approved.
'Does anyone object to the marriage of Nilembi, son of Keyavan and Paru of Aruvikkara and Velutha, daughter of Kochappi and Chakki. This I repeat thrice.'

The dowry and the brother-in-law's fee was paid with borrowed money. With the towel of double weave, Nilembi wed Velutha.

Having accepted the bride cloth, as she was about to step on to the veranda, Velutha felt a flash of pain in her belly. Giving the wedding cloth to her father, she fled.

Not wanting to have Nilembi face the guests alone, Kochembi took him to the inner room and seated him on the bamboo cot. Leaving the bridegroom in the room.

Kochembi sat near the platter of betel leaves and started crying. His brother-in-law saw him weeping and said, 'Isin't it better to rejoice?' and he started laughing.

* * *

In the room which women used on the days of their periods and during birthing, Velutha stood confused, not knowing whether to laugh or cry.

The women started preparing the tubers and vegetables for the feast. When it got dark, pots of toddy were brought in by the elders. They also pulled out some cannabis which they smoked and passed round. Everyone was very happy and sang happily.

Kochembi brought his son-in-law before the gathering. He introduced him. He said, 'Son-in-law, these are my friends. If I fall, they will hold me. And they will support you also. Now take this.' And he gave him a coconut shell full of toddy. He was also given cannabis to smoke.

* * *

After her periods, followed by the ceremonial bath, Velutha left the confinement hut, looking as radiant as a lighted lamp.

In the bedroom, Nilembi was lying on the bamboo cot. When she lifted the mat curtain, he saw her. A little light filtered into the room. Nilembi swallowed hard in the face of her beauty. Spirited as a calf, she came lovingly and nestled next to him. Nilembi was embarrassed; he sprang up.

'What is it?' she asked.
'Nothing,' he answered.
'Then why did you jump up?'
'You mustn't misunderstand me.'
'Ask me anything.'
'Is your period over.' Velutha laughed. Nilembi was embarrassed.
'Don't laugh so loudly. Your father and uncle will hear you.'
'Look at me. I am burning like a baked tile.'
Nilembi fell on the cot as if he was on fire.

* * *

As they were tilling the soil, the young thampuran hurried up to them, very angry. Kochembi stopped ploughing. The thampuran Velaynaru roared, loud enough to upturn the field. 'Come here, you.'

Not knowing who was being called, they all put down their spades.

'You rascal, I am calling you.'

'Kochembi, he means you.'

Kochembi came out of the slushy field, careful not to splash even a drop of mud on the thampuran. He stood humbly some distance away, scratching his head.

'What did you tell your senior thampuran about Velutha, what did you tell my father?'

'I never said anything my lord.' Kochembi stood obsequiously with his hand on his mouth.

'If you didn't tell him then how did he come to know. Is he a god or what?'

'Not you, not even your lord can stop me marrying Velutha if I set my mind to it.'

'My lord, leave us alone ...,' Kochembi bowed down in the slush.

'Where is she?'

'She is married. It was the senior thampuran who chose the bridegroom.'

'Do I know him?'

'I don't know.'

'Where is he from?'

'Aruvikkara.'

Only after Velaynaru left the place and could be seen no more, did Kochembi go back to his work in the slushy field. Only then did he take up his spade. By that time the others who had been working with him had gone halfway across the field. Kochembi went after them. No one said a word.

* * *

Nilembi prepared the field for planting. He burnt the weeds. He sowed the field. He set the poles and planted the black pepper. He also planted different types of vegetables and tubers. He put in betel and spinach.

The land became fruitful. Nilembi was busy. So was Velutha. Very busy.

At dawn, Nilembi would leave with his spade on his shoulder. His presence was needed everywhere. The land called to him. Velutha took the goats to graze on Lionhill. Returning, she fried the grain, pounded it and got enough rice to make gruel. She strained it, plucked some chillies and then went in search of Nilembi. He could be anywhere in the field.

When Velutha reached the place, he was murmuring endearments to the paddy.

'Oh my, whom are you talking to?'

'To these stalks.'

'Why, do they have ears to hear and a tongue to speak with.'

'The grass has its own grievances and so do the plants. Even the birds and the worms air their sorrows. Only we must have a ear to hear and a feeling heart.'

'Then tell me, what did the rice stalks say?'

Nilembi laughed happily, stroking the rice stalks that reached the level of his chest. 'It's pregnant.'

'Only the stalks.'

'This and this and these.'

The stalks laughed, as if they couldn't help themselves.

Velutha left, carrying the gruel bowl.

She had to go to Lionhill. She had to round up the goats and come home before sundown. She had to collect the green feed, otherwise the goats would give her no peace. Rubbing against her, shaking their heads, they would cry, 'Ma, give us something to eat.'

Harvest time was fast approaching.

The vegetables were plump and ready.

The plantains were loaded.

The pepper vines had sprouted.

The birds had arrived; the pigeons and the swallows were hungry.

In the plantain groves, the squirrel, the bat, and the hedgehog waited.

Right on time the fox too had come.

It was feasting time for land and sky.

'Mustn't we go and see the thampuran before the harvest?'

'Of course we must.'

When Nilembi returned from ploughing, Velutha said, 'Come and help. To make some riceflakes.'

Velutha took out the seasoned rice that she had kept safely in a box.

She dampened and roasted it. Nilembi pounded it and made the rice flakes. By the time they had cleaned it, removed the husk and tied it securely in a bark, it was dawn.

'You'll go ploughing only after seeing the thampurane.' Nilembi agreed.

They went into the thampuran's courtyard and stood in a corner.

Koyinaru the overseer, pretended not to have seen them.

The thampuran, Kunchakaranaru, made his appearance.

'So Nilembi?'

'Your servant.'

'What did you do about the land and the woman.'

'Your servant is taking care of them.'

'Anything special?'

'Nothing.'

'We have brought an offering,' Velutha added.

She put the bundle in front of the senior landlord.

'What have you brought. Open it.'

'Just some rice flakes.'

The scent of seasoned rice-flakes reached them.

'All right, go to the backyard.'

As they were leaving, after having eaten their fill of leftover gruel, Velutha asked, 'Why didn't you say anything about the harvest.'

'The thampurane didn't ask,' said Nilembi, savouring the aroma of the tobacco the landlord had given him as they were leaving.

'You really are a simpleton.'

If he opened his mouth it was full of betel juice, if she leaned into him she got the full fragrance of tobacco. She liked that aroma. Breathing in all the fragrances, Velutha leaned on Nilembi.

After his marriage, Nilembi had not gone to his village. Nor had anyone come asking about him. Nilembi would explain that people would say, 'Why bother about anyone who has been sent for by the thampuran.'

When they lay together, as fertile as the land, Nilembi would say to Velutha, 'You must plant coconuts on the hilltop. As the lowland is covered by vegetables, the hilltop will surely be turned into a coconut grove. Then whom should we fear. Let them reap, cut the fruit. Take the grains, then ...'

'Then ... what will you do?'

When she asked that, Nilembi would close his eyes.

'Mustn't we give *them*?'

'Whom?'

'The birds, the squirrels, the hedgehogs, the thieving owls ... let them eat. What is left over is enough.'

'It is they who really own the land.'

'So true.'

Nilembi left to till the land. Velutha went to the hill that was called Lionhill to graze the goats. While the goats fed, she sat in the shade, lulled by the breeze, half asleep.

* * *

The rock platform. Velutha remembered. Could she ever forget. For aminute there was a lull in the wind. The frantic waving of grass ceased. There The same odour. Beneath the Jambu tree. Now here

Velutha looked down. Her breast. Her belly. A hand slid down her belly. She felt the rocks moving apart .She fell flat on the grass. Her head hit the rock. Assault. When she opened her eyes, blocking the noonday sun, looking like a giant black rock himself, stood Velaynaru.

He snatched her garment away. She sprang away. She was pressed down. She felt as if a dark stump was pumping into her. He got up panting. It was as if everything was being burnt away: the jambu tree, the rocks, the shade, her dreams. Lying where she was, she said, 'Young Thampurane, you need not have attacked me. Don't you know I am beholden to you. I would have taken off my robe myself. Don't touch me ever. I never want to see you again.'

After Theyi was born, Nilembi never told Velutha what the gossiping cowherds said ...

Once, just once, Nilembi pointed out to Theyi, her father.

That was just before leaving Koshavarakodu.

* * *

The senior thampuran, Kunchankaranaru, stood a distance away from the hut. Outside the hut, Theyi was playing with coconut leaf sticks, hiding them. Nilembi came panting and stood with head bowed.

'Coconuts can be grown on the hilltops, is it?'

'The trees are loaded.'

'Bring two tender coconuts.'

Nilembi climbed the hill and brought them down. He cut two plantain leaves. The bailiff snarled, 'Why did you cut the leaves.' Nilembi cut the tops of the tender coconuts. He placed it on the leaves and presented it to the thampuran.

'You have one.'

'I don't want to, thampurane.'

'What! You won't obey me?'

'Please forgive my foolishness.'

'Do you know where Koshavarakodu is?'

'I have only heard of it, thampurane.'

'All right, you come and see me. Now drink up and give the kernel to your child.'

After the thampuran and the overseer had left, Velutha came out.

'What did the thampurane say?'

'To go and see him.'

'Why?'

'I don't know.' Nilembi returned after seeing the thampuran

He returned with two pieces of tobacco and a pot of toddy

Velutha saw the rare sight of Nilembi drinking. She didn't stop him. His happiness. Wasn't it given by the thampuran! Wasn't it the thampuran's gift? It must have been the liquor, but all night, till dawn, Nilembi roamed about in the fields, crying and wailing. It was always so, after sowing he never could sleep well.

At dawn, he called Velutha and Theyi out. He asked Theyi to call her grandfather.

'Get the luggage packed.' He was speaking very loudly.

'Whatever happened to you.' When they took away the harvest, you said, 'Aren't the seeds, the thampuran's? His own.' When they pulled out all the vegetables, you said, 'The soil is the lord's. The arecanut and the tender betel leaves have sprung up in the thampuran's soil.' You only said that. But we will get a bit of arecanut and a small betel leaf. You said this so happily. 'And now what happened.'

'It is the thampuran's soil. And so is the produce.'

* * *

He took the dry coconut bark and two pebbles and rubbed it together. It caught fire. He set fire to the heap of dry leaves. He lit a beedi and puffed. He put it out after a few puffs and tucked it behind his ear.

He said softly, 'So many came. Tell that man we will teach him a lesson. I gave him everything. Even myself. And they made the profit. With my single eye, I went and danced in Delhi. I took their breath away with my art. So many people came and gave me money. They touched my head. But I did not get even stale gruel out of it. Now no one remains, neither the people who took me nor those who made money out of me. But all that my masters taught me, that's kept safely in my heart. No one can take that away. No machine can take it. Of course, some are playing with the bits and scraps they have got out of me. Well, let them.

I never expected it to turn out this way. There I was without eyes and ears when a woman kept me company, I had two children by her. A boy and a girl. But then she was trapped. Someone in the locality couldn't keep his eyes off her. I had the use of only one eye and didn't know what was going on. My children used to go to his uncle's house, where he gave them leftover gruel. My children did not like the way that upper-caste dog looked at them I think they complained about him to the uncle.

That day was just like any other. I went out to look for work but didn't get any. At lunch I saw people come running. I threw my spade and ran, seeing only half the way, only half the soil.

I saw everything blurred. Half images. My children, their pet dogs, the old man who gave them gruel, the children's mother, realizing what she had done, hanging from the roof of the hut.

The children, the dogs, the mother, I buried them all in the hut.

The lust of that high-caste rogue.

His eyes filled and overflowed.

—Translated by Sushila Thomas

Legacy of Blood*

Raghavan Atholi

The religious organizations and political parties of Chandravalli always isolated the Pulayas. A government official from the southern region came to live in Chandravalli. He came in search of Thevan. Thevan and Matha received him. The children gathered round him. Without anyone having informed them, Mayyan and Mathu reached the colony. The newcomer introduced himself. He had come to Kozhikode from Pathanamthitta as the sales tax commissioner. Everyone made much of the man who had arrived wearing a suit and in his own car.

'I have heard a lot about Thevan. That's why I came to see you,' the official said. 'We are the ones who are ignorant of history. Who have been ignored by history. So we have become history. Yet we have a saga of our own. Let me tell the details of a search I undertook, mainly for our children to benefit from after our time.

Many Pulayas reached Thevan's hut, having heard of the official who had all these modern views. They sat in the veranda and in the courtyard. The official continued his story.

'Long long ago, we were a divine race who were the masters of the land. A people noted for their honesty, mutual trust, love, and virtue. At that time, as mentioned in the Puranas, there occurred a great flood.'

'We have studied about it in the Bible, Sir. It was the time when Noah made the ark.'

Madhavan commented, deeply interested.

'Yes. The Great Flood of 5000 BC. All the territory between the southern tip of India and Australia was submerged. During that time, the ascetic Shukra along with Dasaratha and his followers came to India via Baluchistan and Burma. Probably they brought cattle too. When they came, the chief of our tribe, Shiva, met them in a battle that lasted for centuries.

Arrogant demons destroyed our places of worship. They killed our kings. There was a furious battle between the illustrious gods and the demons. It was when the battle was at its fiercest that Brahaspathi and his followers reached India. They camped in the Ghandava forest.

---

* Original title *Choraparisham*.

The Aryans who came later did not directly attack the gods. They had mastered several magical practices. They combined the souls of their ancesters with other awful elements and created horrible creatures. These terrible powers when infused into the gods, strengthened them. The Aryans, though, remained spectators. The story I want to tell you is how, in the ensuing battle, the gods won and the Aryans tried to gain ascendancy in our land. The demons stole our sacred texts and hid it in the palace that lay submerged in the sea.'

'All these facts are being discovered by the archaeologists. The Lemuriya land mass. The palaces in it.' Dasan commented, deeply fascinated.

The official continued, 'It was around that time that the first incarnation of the chief deity of the gods—Paraasakthi—came into being. Paraasakthi took the shape of a tortoise and retrieved the sacred book and gave it to the gods. At that time it was our practice to make offerings at shrines and temples to the souls of our ancestors. In those days our gods would appear immediately when called upon. But we lost our strength and fervour when the Aryans, demons, Muslims, and Christians started performing their religious rites. Now we must regain our original power. Only then can we recover our lost land and honour.'

'But our book mentions that the incarnations were of Vishnu,' Neeli wanted to know.

'That is just a myth that has been circulated. Vishnu, Brahma, all of them are the symbols of the dictatorial tendencies of the Aryans. All of them are in chains now, they are imprisoned in the equatorial oceans.'

'What about Shiva?' Matha asked.

'Shiva was a powerful tribal lord. He married Sati, the daughter of Daksha. Daksha did not like Shiva. He made arrangements for an elaborate sacrifice. But he invited neither Shiva nor Sati. When she came to know about the sacrifice, Sati stubbornly insisted on attending it. So Shiva permitted her to go. But at the site of the sacrifice, she was insulted by her father. Unable to bear the humiliation, Sati committed suicide in the sacrificial fire. His inner vision enabled Shiva to see how the sacrificial fire had become a funeral pyre. Shiva started his dance of destruction .As the dance increased in frenzy, Shiva threw a spear. From the place where it landed the incarnation of Virabhadran sprang up. Shiva prostrated himself before the evil annihilating deity.'

'Then what does Shivashakti mean?'

Kanchiram said, 'It was much later that Shiva married Parvathy. Or rather Parvathy married Shiva. At that time the Arabs and other foreigners who had settled in India, made plans with the Aryans and the Asuras to destroy Shiva's power. They cut off Shiva's penis which was endowed with Shakti's power.'

'Isn't that the reason why Dravidians worship the sivalinga?' Leela asked.

'Is that the reason why Shiva and Parvathy are constantly having lovers' tiffs?' Neeli added. Kanchiram continued his story of Shiva.

'Once Shiva and several gods were conducting the worship of Shakti. It was the time of the Great Flood which happened in 5000 BC. This was also the period of the Buddha. The Emperor Asoka, a Buddhist, sent his disciples under the monk, Rajasekharan to Sri Lanka and Kerala. They fell out with Udayavarman who ruled Madurai and because Udayavarman's wife failed to have children, they had invited Hindu priests and converted to Hinduism. They conducted the puthrakameshti yaaga to ensure the birth of children. The sacrifice was conducted under the guidance of the chief priest of Adi Sankara's Kanchikamakodi monastery.

Following the dictates of the high priest, thousands of Buddhist monks were killed. This massacre took place at a place called Sharamkolli, which still exists, many miles from Madurai. At that time there was a Buddhist nun called Sabari. Rajasekharan and his followers made the Adivasi nun's convent their headquarters. The king of Pandalam invited martial experts trained in the northern and southern traditions for the protection of the Buddhist missionaries. At that time, Trivandrum, Cochin, and Malabar were part of Tamilnadu. Trivandrum was ruled by local chieftains. This was the time of the Pandya kings. They gave special honours and titles to the experts trained in warfare. Some of these titles are Pandya Regiment, Tiger Regiment, Parambaanda Regiment and Meenaparaya Regiment.

The chief commander of the Tiger Regiment was Karuppan. He was the nephew of Udayavarman. According to the prevailing matriarchal system he was the heir. As Udayavarman had become a Hindu, he ordered Karuppuswamy to capture Rajasekharan and to kill the Buddhists. In order to assess the skills of the maestros of the martial arts (kalari), he organized a demonstration at the Sabari hermitage, where all the kalari arts experts gathered. The young and handsome expert from Ambalapuzha martial arts academy, Ayyappan, excelled all the others and earned everyones respect. Another maestro, Valiyakadutha, his wife Mohini and his younger brother, Kochukadutha, acknowledged him as their guru. Mohini was drawn to the maestro. Mohini was very fair, had a supple body and remarkable prowess in the martial arts. She used all her charms to conquer the expert. But Ayyappan's Buddhist austerities helped him to resist her. It is a fact that a beautiful girl is attracted to martial experts. The maestro would give a pudava* to the girl and make her his wife. As Mohini was completely infatuated with Ayyappan, she had no time for Kadutha who was so filled with despair that he made mistakes in his martial exercises. He was aware that his wife was beautiful. He was also aware of the fact that she was now obsessed with another man. He made so many mistakes that he was killed in an encounter. His brother Kochukadutha spread the word that his brother had died of a heart attack. Kochukadutha made Mohini his wife. It was when he was the head of the kalari that the group of Mappila kalaris reached Pandalam from Musiris. There was an encounter between the experts of the two different traditions. In a tournament, Vavar the guru of the Mappila kalari lost to Ayyappan and surrendered to him.

Vavar, the head of a Mappila academy, was also young like Ayyappan. Kochukadutha's wife Mohini was attracted to Vavaru. Once Kochukadutha saw Vavar coming out of Mohini's bedchamber. Crazed with anger, he sent for all the martial arts experts. There was a fearful combat. In the encounter, all the warriors from the Ambalapuzha, Travancore, and the northern academies were killed. On hearing of Kochukadutha's death, Mohini jumped into the fire and committed suicide. All those who escaped death, fled the place. When Vavaru was not among the dead, Ayyappan sent his disciples in all directions and finally Ayyappan himself found Vavar in Erumeli, on the shores of the river Pampa. Vavar entreated Ayyappan to accept him as his disciple but Ayyappan said that as his life was nearing its end he planned to go to Sabari Ashram to attain nirvana. Vavar followed him.

'But sir, isn't the one called Ayyappan, a Pulaya of our tribe?' Matha expressed a doubt.

'You might be right. But if my guess is correct, Ayyappan was a Buddhist monk.' Kanchiram's lips quivered, his body shivered, he prayed for strength. It was not just a mere story as far as he was concerned.

'That's what I said, Sir,' Matha stated firmly. 'As you said, in those days, there were neither Ezhavas or Thiya castes. We were the original inhabitants. And Ayyappan was the son of some Pulaya woman. Ayyappan was a Buddhist. In those days of Brahmin supremacy, many Buddhist monasteries including Kodungalloor had been seized by the

---

* Pudava: A gift of clothes signifying a bond of marriage.

Brahmins. They captured the ashram, gave it the name of Sabari and made Ayyappan their god. The Aryans killed the low caste Ayyappan when he was meditating. Or probably he attained nirvana.'

'Whatever. Let us go on with the story,' said Kanchiram. There was a vision of divinity in which our ancesters believed. The disciples who had gone in search of Vavar found him. Seeing him alone and unarmed, the soldiers ambushed him from behind and stabbed him to death. They tied his hands and feet to a branch and carried him from Erumeli to Sabarimala. Elated at having killed a brave warrior, they were dancing with joy when they were suddenly intercepted by Ayyappan. He ordered them to carry the body back to Erumeli and to erect a tomb over it. To commemorate this journey, the pilgrims to Sabarimala participate in the ceremonial dance, the *petta thullal*, even today.

When Ayyappan reached Sabarimala he saw Sabari lying dead. He had her buried according to the rites. Ayyappan sat in meditation. Having heard of the death of the kalari practitioners, all the relatives and family members flocked to Pandalam, Erumeli, and Sabarimala. They prepared a repast in honour of the departed heroes. As forty-one days had elapsed, they paid homage to the souls of their ancestors. Then it became the practice to visit every year during the Makara Sankranti or the vernal eclipse to participate in the anniversary funeral repast. As there were no roads or vehicles at that time, people used donkeys to reach the place. The king and the local chieftains used palanquins. Seeing Ayyappan on the back of a buffalo, his soldiers called out *eruma, eruma*, buffalo, buffalo, which gave the town its name, Erumeli. Ayyappan once wrestled with a tiger and that gave rise to the legend of Ayyappan riding a tiger. It was to commemorate the tiger regiment that the Sri Lankan Tamil soldiers called themselves the Tamil Tigers.

The soldiers of those times, the kalari gurukkal, were of the Ezhava community. That is why, till the formation of the State of Kerala and also of the Temple Boards, it was the Ezhavas and the low castes who used to carry the provisions required for the commemoration feast. As I told you, the first contingent of relatives reached Sabari hill on the forty-first day after the mass deaths in the kalari, the gymnasium. When they reached Sabarimala, Ayyappan had already attained nirvana. The relatives saw a large eagle overhead circling the corpse.

Sabari hill is the only pilgrim centre where people come fasting and dressed in black. The reason why the Ezhava community is prosperous, and why Sri Narayana was born amongst them is because they faithfully performed funeral rites to honour their ancestors. You must have heard of this. From ancient times we also had the custom of honouring our heroes and ancestors, and perhaps that was why we too had an Ayyankali amidst us! But when we gave up these rites of ancestor-worship after the 1930s our disintegration began. If we want to come up again, we must revive our age-old practices.

Forty-one days had elapsed since the death of the soothsayer Rayan. Thevan and Matha with their children reached Rayan's house. Chirutheyi the unmarried younger sister of Chiruthakutty received them. Chiruthakutty, Chirutheyi, and Maya had come when Rayan died and had not returned home. Earlier, Chirutheyi had been fully involved in caring for Rayan Soothsayer.

Chirutheyi and Matha exchanged greetings. Matha and Thevan made all the preparations for the rites. The children ran about playing.

By evening all the relatives had arrived. But Mayyan and Mathu were yet to reach. In the light of flaming torches, everyone gathered round the tomb of Rayan. Matha poured oil over the torches. She performed the purification ceremony, sprinkling from a platter, water mixed with rice flour, basil leaves and turmeric powder. They made a totem of rice powder, turmeric powder, and charcoal-ash and placed it on the grave. Rice and rice flakes were placed on banana leaves and distributed by Thevan. Columns were drawn on the ground and rice was thrown into the certain spots to the accompaniment of chanting. The gathering repeated the chants.

Carrying all the articles needed for the rites they moved towards the sacrificial Gulikan* platform. A torch was lighted for the spirits and a palm leaf placed on the ground. Everything was ready and Dasan, Mayyan's son and Madhavan, Thevan's son picked up small drums.

Thevan asked them, 'Do you know how to play the funeral beat?'

'We will try.'

Dasan and Madhavan had not learnt to play but they drummed liked experts and sang:

Oh my Ganapathy, my lord ... Muthappa
My Ganapathy, muthappa
Oh! Aaratiyaan Kuruvamme
May we merge with that family
Oh Aayiravalli Komaram†!

---

* Gulikan: A temperamental low-caste shaivite diety.
† Komaram: A human medium that receives divine commands in a trance.

I vow on the komaram, Muthappa!
Oh my lord.

Mayyan and Mathu arrived during the chanting. Thuluvandi placed an upturned ural in the shrine and Dasan and Madhavan sang the funeral songs with abandon.

Thevan rubbed rice flour paste on Mayyan's face. He drew lines on it with turmeric. On his back, Thevan drew certain patterns. He made a paste of lime and turmeric powders and drew lines on his chest and on his back. He marked his eyebrows with charcoal powder and his face with red and yellow lines. His head was covered with a piece of red silk and it floated down his back. A piece of bark was shaped like a wreath and placed round his head and covered with black cloth. He was given a sickle and a broom to hold in each hand. The tempo of the chanting rose and Thevan trembled where he sat. Two persons stood with lighted torches on each side of Mayyan. The chanting continued. A shower of incantations was frenziedly sent up to their ancestors, to their earliest ancestors, praising them and entreating them to receive the new soul. With great agility Mayyan danced round the tomb and the shrine, occasionally making prophecies. When the night had far advanced, Mayyan said:

I ... AM ... VERY ... HAPPY. I WANT SOME ... BLOOD ...
I ... WANT ... ROOSTER ... BLOOD.

One of the elders, Kariathan, gave him a rooster. Mayyan put down the sickle and broom on the ground. He held the rooster firmly and bit into it, tearing it apart. Biting its neck, and severing it, he threw it to the ground to the beat of the music. The head scattered. The rooster shuddered and was still.

Paraayi went into the kitchen with the rooster. Mayyan took up the torch and sickle. In a frenzy he ran ten yards forward. Without turning round he ran six yards backwards. Ten yards forward, six yards back again. Everyone moved towards the bank of the canal with lighted torches. Mayyan cut a palm leaf. Thevan took the palm leaf from Mayyan. Mayyan went up to the shrine and stood by it. The chanting continued. Late into the night, Mayyan climbed on to the rafters with the broom and sickle. On the rafters Mayyan stood on one leg in the pose of Shiva's dance and again on both feet in the stance of Kali the goddess of destruction. Dawn was approaching when Mayyan slowly came down the rafters beating the air with the broom and making chopping gestures with the sickle. The incantations continued. Mayyan sat on the upturned ural. Thevan removed Mayyan's ceremonial garments one by one. He wiped his face and body clean. Mayyan washed his face and hands. There was still time for the break of dawn. Paarayi called Matha. Chirutheyi served the offering on leaves. Taking the offering, Thevan went towards the shrine. Everybody gathered round. Dasan and Madhavan untied the drums and hung them up in the sit-out. When Thevan reached the shrine, and the torches that had burnt down suddenly burst into flames, and filled everyone with fear.

'Don't frighten us,' Thevan entreated.

Suddenly he heard a sound. Had the others heard it? Thevan turned in the direction of the voice. 'I am here. I haven't gone anywhere. Even if I wished to I wouldn't be able to. I will always remain with you all.'

It was the voice of Rayan the soothsayer.

Palms pressed together reverentially, Thevan stood still.

Suddenly they were bathed in the light of the dawn.

* * *

A scene flashed in Thevan's memory. Kandan and Rayan. They were meeting after a long time. Kandan said, 'I have come to tell you something.'

'What is it?'

'We must make an offering to Muthappan, the family deity.'

'Now who is there to go about it?'

'As for Devan, he has to go to meetings every day.'

'Where is the time after the meetings?'

'Let me see. I will tell my brother-in-law Theyyon.'

'That won't work. He hates it.'

'His wife is a party worker isn't she. Party workers do not like making offerings.'

'But then who is going to make offerings to our ancestors, now?'

'They are great lords aren't they? They say we are being ruined because of our useless beliefs.'

'We are backward because they don't give us work, isn't it? They say they are unable to.'

'What do they mean by 'unable to'. Do you know how costly grass is?'

'All that is true. But what do they say now?'

'That everything has been done by the party workers.'

'But what about them?'

'No brother-in-law. They mean why we are without work.'

'Have *they* provided all the work?'

'If not them, then has the Congress provided work?'

'It's not that the Congress has not done anything. It's because of them that at least two or three from our Panchayat have got government jobs.'

'That's true. But will the Congress members come to our houses. Aren't they upper class.'

'Nowadays it is the comrades who consider themselves upper class.'

'You know Thevan's son Madhavan who gave him a job in the Panchayat?'

'What good is that to us?'

'Brother-in-law, why do you speak like this?'

'I had gone to see him.'

'And what happened?'

'He acted as if he had never seen me before.'

'That's just *your* way of seeing things. Madhavan is doing a lot of good for our people.'

'What he says is correct. What's your problem.'

'I was thinking of Madhavan's father.'

'Yes?'

'Our Thevan. Isn't he a communist?'

'Yes, yes, yes.'

'And Madhavan?'

'Congress.'

'And what good is Congress for us.'

'Who will fight for us?'

'You needn't say that. Even without the comrades, we would have somehow ...'

'We would. Have you heard what Muriyalan and Thevan say?'

'What?'

'That Ayyankali who held demonstrations for the freedom and education of our people was a Pulaya.'

'That's true. Chanthuparayan too.'

'Raman, the landlord also said the same thing.'

'And now do you know what the communists are saying?'

'What?'

'That they provided everything for our people.'

'The comrades are lying.'

'If you come to that, who *are* these comrades?'

'The Brahmins, the Thiyas, the Muslims, and the Christians, who else?'
'Let me ask you something.'
'What?'
'Weren't the Thiyas, the Namboodiris, and the Muslims originally with the Congress?'
'Yes, they were.'
'Who made them comrades all of a sudden. Did anybody consult us? What good did it do us?'
'Nobody asked *us* about *our* needs.'
'Our lands and fields are now in others' hands.'
'We don't want others to hear us.'
'What do you mean?'
'This is a toddy shop.'
'So what?'
'It belongs to the Thiyas. They are comrades too.'
'So true. They will tell us not to drink. And what are they going to do with the toddy.'
'That's not what upsets me. Do they mean to stop us from offering a little liquor, a little light to our gods.'

Rayan soothsayer had no further vision. Kandan also got stone drunk. Each leaned on the other as they left the toddy shop. They were chewing betel and singing. Kandan sang loud and clear:

It is for my gods I plead,
I want tender toddy for my gods,
It is not for me but for my gods,
Why do you want to break my heart?

Give me tender toddy for my gods,
It is two pots of tender juice that I crave,
It is not for me but for my gods,
My heart yearns, and that is true,
And that is true, is true, is true.

Both of them walked along the fields singing and dancing. Far away in the darkness, they saw a torch flash. It was Kumaran, Mayyan's son. Kumaran saw them. 'Achacha' he called aloud.

'What is it? Where is your father?'

'Father is waiting. He asked me to tell both of you that he wants to see you.'

'Mayyan wants to see *me*? Why?'
'I know nothing about that.'
Rayan turned to him. 'Which class are you in?'
'I am in the ninth.'
'Sing a nice song, do.'
Kumaran couldn't refuse. He sang. Kandan and Rayan sang the refrain:

Oh my gods, oh ye gods,
Why oh why did you give us life?
Oh ye gods, oh my gods,
Why oh why did you create us?
The gods are good that's why,
The gods are good that's why,
And that is why they created us.

* * *

The modified land rights movement was carried out with great fanfare. No one bothered about the outcome. The new land reform bill only served to take away the farmlands from the rightful owners and distribute it to the landlords and the plantation owners. By the time they realized they had been deceived, it was too late. Thevan remembered how his parents had owned vast areas of land and how he had taken them to the register office and made them sign various papers just to get it back. Kunjananthan Nair, the Ezhava Kanaran, and the other landlords must have signed papers in the same way. But with a great difference. They were cheating the government and the Pulayas to become owners of vast tracts of land. Even in Chandiravalli, there were many who besides owning land which could legally be held by one family, managed to grab vast lands in the names of any odd claimant. They even managed to acquire land under the category of plantations. Thevan remembered what Ramdas and Mukundan had said about the speech made by EMS in the meeting of the Yogakshema before the land bill was passed where he tried to protect his community's land in a similar way by listing it under different names. The indigenous tribes, the Parayas, the Pulayas, the Paanars and the Vettuvars were left with no land. Who will write the history of the cruelty of looting the farmlands from the Pulayas who were once the kings of the land? Which book has recorded the treachery perpetrated on the Pulayas by the Asura Dravidians, the deceitful Aryans, Muslims, and Christians. Thevan could not but think about the helplessness of his people who were unable to protect even the minimum that they had gained after repeated strikes, demonstrations, incarcerations and police atrocities. Moreover the organizations and leaders had never consulted the really deserving or their leaders before planning the demonstrations or formulating the land acts. Every law benefited mainly the upper class. The supporters of the lawmakers knew all the tricks to bypass the law and to make it invalid.

So the law was of no use to the poor.

The Thiyas for whom tapping and selling toddy was the main occupation, soon became prosperous. Moreover, since Malabar was part of the Madras province even those thiyas with minimum education got jobs during the British rule. But as South Kerala was under the king, the Pulayas got none of these benefits. The Nair community depended on the king's favour had to be satisfied with the concessions they received from the ruler. The great leader Ayyankali and other leaders of his Sadhujana Paripalana Sangham (Organization for the Welfare of Backward People), intervened from time to time in the assembly and got waste lands allotted for the Pulayas and Parayas of Travancore. The Pulayas of Malabar could not become landowners as they lacked farsighted, energetic, and commanding leaders. It was K. Kelappan, a leader who was not from their community who managed to get some land here and there for a few of them. And EMS and other leaders helped them when even the occupancy rights were hanging in the balance.

The highhanded behavior of the Nairs who were the king's dependants, drove many Ezhavars, Pulayas, and Parayas to Christianity and Islam. Kumaran Asan tried to put a stop to the large scale conversion. In Chandiravalli of North Malabar there was not even a single Pulaya convert. Whenever Mayyan and Thevan met, they would indulge in reminiscences. They feared that theirs would be a community, cut off from their own land and eventually ruined. They thought that when the highway passed by Chandiravally, there would be development. But after the highway and the bus came, there sprang up new claimants for their lands. Those who had gone abroad, both in the past and recently, appropriated the waste land. They levelled the paddy fields and constructed huge mansions. They started cutting down huge trees for construction. For these purposes, mills sprang up. Mills were set up for grinding grain. Rice fields gave way to beautiful houses. People who were rolling in money paid bribes to get government jobs. Trade and commerce flourished. The newly rich procured every luxury for themselves. The Pulayas who did not have the finances to seek work in the gulf, could not get work in the fields either. Some of the young men turned to the construction field. At least they would get daily wages. Those who had their houses near the fields were moved far far away to the hills. Where Thevan's house had once stood, there now flourished a film theatre. With the money received, he had bought an acre of land in the hilly region in Chengore. He cultivated tapioca, cashew and pepper.

When Mayyan saw Thevan's land, his craving grew. Many times he laboured on Thevan's land. And his thoughts were all of working on his own. Even now Mayyan's thoughts were all about the different land and fields and their varied odours. The scent of Punja rice. The scent of the full grown tapioca plant. The scent of mature bitter gourd. The scent of ploughed land. He would forget everything in these scents. For him the scent of the rice splitting from the husk was like that of mother's milk of which he had got but little. He remembered what his mother had said of making a hole on the bank of the paddy field and placing him there when he was a baby and herself going to work in the field and how a black scorpion had entered the hole and bitten his little finger. To this day like a curse, he bore the mark. On the days when there was no work to be done, Mayyan would lose himself in the sound of crickets on the banks of the fields. Or he would listen to the sound of hoof falls in the virgin fields. Covered in perspiration he would lie on the floor in the veranda paved with dung. Even at night he would stand on the edge of the field communing with crickets. One day, with great longing, he said in a voice loud enough to be heard, 'Even if we cry aloud, the authorities will not listen to us. We will not get our land.'

Mayyan used to think that the crickets were the souls of those dead and gone. He felt they were crying heart broken because their descendants would not inherit their land. The Ezhava, Kanaran of Olangot, kept his fields for cultivation alone Mayyan became a regular worker of Olangot. Even when his work was over he would sit for for hours on the newly turned soil. He would sit their till the mud and sweat on his body caked and fell off. Mayyan would sit there for that special feeling when it fell. He felt that as he scraped it off each flake felt similar to that of a decade of time. He felt a special pleasure as he peeled off the flakes. And also, when it grew dark, the bath in the stream. The special fragrance of the koova leaves as he rubbed his body with it. After his bath he would stand among the cactus plants. On moonlit nights, he had frightened passer-by standing utterly still. Those who saw him like that circulated stories about him. Some said it was impossible for anyone to walk safely through the cactus grove. Some said that it was the god of death that they saw. The older people said that was a sure sign that disaster would visit the land. When he heard the stories, Mayyan laughed. Someone said the god of death had no feet we could see Dasan was sure that it was just a myth. Because of these stories, people stopped walking on the bank of the stream at night. Some of those who got frightened said that on moonlit nights, the spectre's feet would not touch the ground and that it was so tall that it would touch the sky. Instead of the five cents he owned at Thevambalam, Mayyan would stand on the banks of the stream dreaming of vast fields. Thinking of how to give money for his son Dasan's education. Seeing Dasan walking to town, as he did not have the money for bus-fare, Mayyan said, 'Our problem is that we don't have ten coconuts. Only those who have land and wealth can study and get ahead.'

Mayyan had planted coconut trees, areca nut palms, and vegetables around his house on the five cents of land he had been given as occupancy. As a boundary for his plot he had grown hibiscus plants and shrubs. Leela and Karthiyayani helped their mother. On holidays Leela would go to Chandu's house to help in chores outside the house. Karthyayani would always be in deep thought. Sometimes Mathu would scold her, 'What's the use of your studying ... to become a collector ...'

'Let her study ... Mayyan says. Even if she does not become a Collector .... What's the harm if she studies?

'My! I didn't say anything. Look at father and a daughter!'

'Let her study. It's when she gets a job that we must buy some land. That man gave two hundred rupees for land .We might get it for less. A little land of our own. When we buy it we must build a good house. They are going to fill up this canal and make a road aren't they? If we buy land somewhere close by we will get a good price for it. Then we can go somewhere far away and buy a lot of land. And then to lie down and enjoy the smell of new earth ...'

'What dreams! It would be enough if we had food and drink every day!'

'That's not it. What is Chandu's son studying for?'

'I don't know. Its three years since he passed the tenth standard, isn't it. He took him to Ernakulam.'

'Not to a kulam (pond), Amma,' Devi teased her.

'And from where will he get the money for all that. You need to pay high fees to study. Then you need more money for living expenses. How much will all this be?'

'Don't they get about four to five thousand coconuts? Moreover they have paddy, pepper, cassava, and other produce,' Matha said.

'That's what I said. If we had some land we too would have been able to educate our children.'

'Kumaran stopped his studies, didn't he? I told them to let him study. He would have been a comfort for us too. But they didn't listen.'

'It's not that I didn't listen. When he reached the tenth, there was a change in him. And he went to Kozhikode saying he wanted to study something. And how expensive that was. And what did he learn? Don't make me say anything.'

'What use is it to say anything now? Didn't he leave this very place? When he found a girl, didn't he just disappear? Didn't he decide he needed only her and no one else? Didn't he forget us all?'

'When they are children they are like that. The times are different now. It all started when Kelan Parayan came here …'

'What's the use of blaming Kelan Parayan? We couldn't control our son.'

'What all will we have to hear when we have boys. After all he is your son.'

'And what is wrong with me?'

'Nothing. Only in those days you wouldn't leave me alone. How many days you starved just to get me to marry you.'

'That's true. But is this case similar? She has used potions and magic …' Thevan said.

'My father was like this. But in those days customs like Pulaya-fear, Mannan-fear and Paraya-fear made people wary and controlled them.'

'That was then. Now all that has changed. What happened to your brother Thuluvandy? Who gave him potions? The landlords. As soon as he passed the tenth standard he got a job. Somewhere in Kollam. He married a Namboodiri girl working in his office. A rich girl .

'Not bad! What hopes!'

* * *

Kumaran was lying with his head in Anima's lap. Running her fingers through his curly hair she said.

'I have to go home.'

'Why?' Kumaran was angry.

'I want to see my mother.'

'Your mother can come here.'

'You said you loved me very much.'

'Any doubts?'

'Then let's go.'

'Why? You want to start a fight between the two families.'
'No. Let's go to your house. When my mother hears about it she is sure to come.'
'These are people who conducted your funeral rites aren't they? They expelled you from the clan, didn't they?'
'What I did was wrong, wasn't it?'
'What wrong? Then go right now. And don't come back for my sake.'
'I don't want to make you angry.'
'Don't you have to go to the company?'
'I can take leave.'
'Aren't you pregnant?'
'I am into the fourth month. That's why I said I want to see mother.'
'I don't have any leave this month. We will go next month.'
'That's enough. Now, even if we don't go, it's all right. At least you have agreed to go.'
'Yes, I agreed. Now just for that, do sing a song.'

—Translated by Sushila Thomas

DRAMA

There are elements of theatre in almost all the Dalit ritual performances of Kerala like Theyyam, Thira, Chimmanakkali, Thalika Kali, and Kakkarassi Natakam. They mark Dalit community life, reflecting their protest, resistance, and life-consciousness.

Unlike mainstream theatre, which is the product of a leisurely life in folk performances there is no rigid separation between performer and spectator.

A cursory look at Kerala socio-cultural history will reveal that it was drama that provided a common platform for people to assemble and experience a work of art irrespective of their caste and religious differences. In other words, drama played a vital role in secularization and integration. This democratization of art owes more to Dalit folk tradition than to the theatrical tradition of the hegemonic. Whereas most of the classical arts were performed within temple walls or stately houses and reserved for upper class, high-caste persons, folk performances were staged in available open spaces where no one was denied entry.

The written tradition of Malayalam drama began with the translations of Sanskrit plays. In the latter half of 19th century the translation of *Abijnana Shakunthalam* by Kerala Varma Valiya Koyi Thampuran gave a fillip to Malayalam drama. It soon achieved a didactic and propagandistic form. V.T. Bhattathirippad's *Adukkalayilninnu Arangathekku* (1929) and K. Damodaran's *Paattabakki* (1937) problematizing many social evils that the writers found detrimental to society. In Pandit K.P. Karuppan's *Balakalesm*, written in 1913, one could see the traces of a written dramatic tradition where caste and Dalit life predominates. This is the first drama in which a Pulaya character, Kochalu, makes his appearance.

In the Left-wing socio-realistic plays, the strategy is, as usual, the same: in the garb of speaking for the other, one speaks for oneself. But with the entry of K.J. Baby and his *Naadugaddika* (1982), with its simultaneous critiquing of the internal Emergency proclaimed in India (1975–7) and projection of tribal rights, the socio-realistic tradition was under immense attack. Although the play was written by a non-tribal writer, who lives among the tribal people of Wayanad, the play could overcome many of the conventional assumptions and dramatic strategies of the 'speaking-for-other' plays of the socio-realistic paradigm. A significant feature of non-Dalit playwright K.J. Baby's *Naadugaddika*, which was staged in more than 200 venues during the Emergency is that the actors were tribals and not professionals. Unlike the realist theatre, which reduced every experience into the life-world of the urban middle-class family, this drama demanded a different sensibility and the awareness of a different time-space.

Sam Kutty Pattankari has also done some experiments in rewriting and creating visual texts exposing the caste prejudices in the epics and mainstream plays. Many professional and amateur playwrights have produced plays with subaltern themes. They include Dalit theatre practitioners like Pappan Pantheerankavu, Purushan Kadalundi, and non-Dalit writer-activist like Ramachandran Mokeri and well-known literary figure and academic like N. Prabhakaran. Yet another name to be reckoned here is that of Manoj Kaana. His play in 2005, *Uratti* (a tribal) ritual is one in which tribals themselves were engaged as actors to talk about their own issues.

The theatrical activities of the late 1970s and early 1980s were primarily led by small amateur groups belonging to the Left and extreme Left camps. They staged/performed many fringe theatre and impromptu street plays dealing with contemporary socio-political issues. Among them Vijayan Venattusseri's experimental plays are significant. He was instrumental in forming a theatre group called Flaming Arrows in the 1980s which staged a number of plays. His *Krishikkaran* (Farmer) was a Dalit rewriting of Thakazhi Sivasankara Pillai's short story of the same title. In order to bring out the Dalit perspective on feudal landlordism and Dalits' right to land he created an additional Dalit character in his play. His *Marakuthira* (Wooden Horse) is a satire of the left politics and class analysis. His *Kroosithante Mozhikal* (Words of the Crucified) is a leap in the experimental theatre tradition where the experiences of the characters who played the role of Yesu (Jesus Christ), Judas, and Mariyam were enacted.

Other Dailt theatre practitioners from south Kerala include Jayachandran Thakazhi, Santhosh Thakazhi, Dr Baburaj, Kochin Babu, Unni Thrippunithura, and others and one of the distinguishing features of these amateur theatre groups is the focus they gave to children's theatre. *Kannadiyum Komalikalum* (Mirrors and Baffoons),

Omankkuttan (Beloved Son/Boy) are examples. Yet another significant theatre activity by South Kerala Dalit collectives was the itinerant troup which toured around a vast area comprising Alappuzha, Ernakulam, and Thrissur for six months staging the play *Arangilninnu Adukkalayilekku* (2005*)* a satirical subversion of V.T. Bhattathirippad's *Adukalayilninnu Arangathekku*. Santhosh and Jayachandram were significant figures behind this unique attempt. Jayachandran who has been actively engaged in this field for more than a decade has also made his presence felt in solo performances like *Josephinte Radio* (Joseph's Radio, 2010) which is a good example of how powerfully Dalit politics could be conveyed through theatre. He also led the Deepthi Nataka Sangam during the 1990s under which banner they performed skits and one-act plays dealing with themes related to Dalit life and experiences.The introduction of television was a major distracting influence and when Dalit communities assembled around a single TV at dusk the troupe took the opportunity to perform to those same groups, reminding them of the real issues in their lives, and silently warning them against collaborating with fantasy.

This collective was also active in children's theatre and performed plays like *Njangalkku Chilathu Parayanundu* (We Have Something to Say). They are now in the process of forming a theatre group consisting of Dalit theatre practitioners (actors, writers, directors, and so on), which could perform at least one play in every three months.

In North Kerala much of the theatrical activity was under the patronage of the Left parties and their plays dealt with issues related to poor peasants, unemployment, feudal exploitation, land rights, and so on. These socio-realistic plays looked at social issues from the point of view of Marxist theories. During the late 1970s there emerged small groups within the Left who wrote and staged amateur performances on Dalit themes—their lives and experiences and aspects of their specific culture and spirituality. The extreme Left groups (Naxalites as they were called) also used theatre, especially street theatre as a major tool for propagating their ideology and challenging the dominant discourse. Many non-Dalit theatre practitioners dealt with themes related to Dalits and tribals.

Among the theatre practitioners of North Malabar, Dalit actors, writers and directors like Pappan Pantheerankavu, Purushan Kadalundi, and Santhakumar are the significant names who brought Dalit themes and sensibility onto the amateur stage.

Pappan Pantheerankavu's *Thudippattu* later staged as *Vanchippattu* brought to the stage for the first time Dalit rituals and showed caste hierarchy and power embedded in the ritual traditions. These amateur Dalit theatrical tradition—especially its bold experiments—were ignored by mainstream literary and critical discourse.

Among contemporary Dalit theatre practitioners, the writer-actor-director Santhakumar's plays like *Daaham* (Thirst), *Karutha Vidhava* (Black Widow), *Sukhanidrayilekku* (Sound Sleep), and *Swapnavetta* (Dreamhunt) are instances that bring Dalit life and experiences to public performances. Though they do not reflect the kind of militancy and ideological significance as done in Tamil by Dalit playwright Gunasekharan (*Baliaadukal*) they are initial attempts to foreground life and experiences from a Dalit perspective. *Swapnavetta* projects the conflicts within the (Dalit) Theyyam performer between his dream world and reality. Santhakumar is the recipient of the Kerala Sahitya Academy Award for the best script and many other awards as well.

Notes

Theyyam: Popular Hindu folk ritual form of worship of north Malabar—the performers belong to indigenous Dalit/tribal Communities.

Thira: A sub-division of Theyyam. A ritual dance drama performed in Kaavu. The performer of Thira, through appropriate costumes assumes the roles of divinities they hold in veneration. The dance, to the accompaniment of indigenous instruments takes place mostly at night.

Kakkarissi Natakam: A folk theatre form of Kerala with the distinct feature of social satire. Dance and songs are integral part, with instrumental accompaniments. Originated in later half of 18th century. Performed by Kurava/Malaveda communities in the early stages, but now other communities also partake in it.

Chimmanakkali: A folk art from Palakkad district, Chimmana means fun–full of humour. Current and day-to-day affairs come to centre stage-inequalities and antisocial elements come under harsh criticism. Pulaya community usually renders it.

Thalikakali: Performance carrying plates in both hands. Mostly performed by Thiyyas during marriage ceremonies.

Dreamhunt*

A. Santhakumar

This is Kannan Theyyam's home; the one-room shanty is both a sleeping and cooking area. Theyyam ornamentations and paraphernalia can be seen hanging from the clothes line and wrapped in bundles. A single-plank cot. In a corner of the shanty, daughter Parvati's sewing machine and a wooden chair. Every article in the room lies scattered, like parts of a dream that cannot be read as a whole.

Night time. Smoky light from the kerosene lamp that Parvati forgot to extinguish. Kannan Theyyam lies curled up on the cot, asleep. Daughter Parvati sleeps, head resting on the machine's table top, having fallen asleep as she sat stitching, because a half-done garment hangs from the machine. Parvati's thick hair lies loose.

Soft dreamy music, Light as air, soft dreamy music is heard in the background. A brightness falls on Parvati. She appears to be in some deep magical sleep. Yes, we too are entering her dream, softly.

A young man in white enters her dream, accompanied by flowers and butterflies. He gathers a bunch of her curly locks and takes in its fragrance. He talks, like one intoxicated.

BRIDEGROOM: This is Parvati. Kannan Theyyam's daughter. Tailor Parvati. I ... I'm her invisible bridegroom. We are lovers who meet only in dreams. . . .

Romantic music. Parvati wakes up in her sleep. She moves towards him, leans against his chest.

PARVATI: I don't know where you are from, what your name is .... When I wake up I do not recall your face. Why do you come into my dreams and awaken desire in me?

BRIDEGROOM: Reality is so terrible, that I am incapable of offering you a life in the real world.

* Original title *Swapnavetta*.

PARVATI: Waiting endlessly for the bridegroom who will never come, hearing father's endless curses every day ... I'm fed up; look (*pointing to the sewing machine*), this is my only relief. I want to live as long as the wheel of this machine turns. Till then I'll stitch dreams ..., waiting for my invisible bridegroom.

BRIDEGROOM (*Smiles adoringly*): My dear tailor girl, stitching garments during the day and dreaming at night, when the world becomes beautiful—like a dream, like music, I'll come climbing the steps of your home, and take you away as my partner for life.

PARVATI: Impossible (*weeps*). Don't speak about the impossible and fill me with desire.

BRIDEGROOM: Don't cry. Don't let tears fall on dreams. Look Parvati, dreams—is it not dreams that keep us alive? (*He comforts her, running his fingers through her hair. He lifts her hair and takes in its fragrance.*)

BLACKOUT

It is dawn. Parvati's head rests on the machine. She dozes in after-dream lethargy.
A rooster crows.

KANNAN THEYYAM (*Sits up suddenly, cursing the sleepless night and spitting in the face of the new day*): Ho! Inauspicious night; couldn't sleep a wink (*looks at Parvati*). Oh, you are dreaming! Hasn't realized it is dawn. Parvati, ediye Parvati!

PARVATI (*Jerks awake. Stares at him sleepily*).

KANNAN: You needn't stare at me. I'm your father, Kannan Theyyam.

PARVATI (*Lazily, still dreamy, sleepy*): Oh! Is it dawn?

KANNAN: The day's dawned, bright. I'm shivering. I didn't sleep at all last night (*yells*). Get me a glass of hot black tea.

PARVATI (*Angrily*): Oh, have Kannan Theyyam's curses begun? I'll give you black tea immediately. (*She busies herself in a corner, preparing tea. Kannan Theyyam turns the theyyam decorations this way and that, reliving some glorious event. Parvati takes a cracked mirror from near the stove and looks at herself, happily expectant. Kannan Theyyam happens to see her doing this.*)

KANNAN THEYYAM: Rotten eyes and saliva smeared face .... Why do you look at that cracked mirror, the moment you wake up? (*Continues to look at his theyyam decorations.*)

PARVATI: Why do you, with your heaving chest and weakened limbs, finger those theyyam decorations you can no longer wear?

KANNAN THEYYAM: It's a pleasure, remembering the good times. It's like having a good dream.

PARVATI: Yes. I was searching whether the dream I had yesterday, was here somewhere in the mirror.

KANNAN: The tattered theyyam decorations please and comfort me. When I look at the dusty theyyam crown the happy past trickles into my memory. (*Rhythmic beats on the chenda and sounds of bygone festivals enter his memory.*)

KANNAN (*Sadly*): All the Bhagavathi groves have been turned into temples ... it's Ramayana reading and Bhagavata reading ... theyyam and theyyam performers are ousted. How can this Kannan Theyyam live, without Bhagavathi groves to perform in?

PARVATI (*Running an unfinished garment on the machine*): Achcha, it's festival at the Palliupuram grove today. There's mimicry and music at night. May I go, with Suluchechi from the southward house?

KANNAN THEYYAM (*Bewildered*): What! Today?

PARVATI: Aa ... yes. Today is the first day of Vrischikam, isn't it?

KANNAN THEYYAM (*Appears troubled and sad*): I forgot. In Vrischikam when the mist on Kooman Hill descends, it's festival time in Pallipuram grove.

(*He begins to arrange the theyyam decorations with the bewilderment and anxiety of having forgotten something important.*)

PARVATI: Achcha, you have forgotten everything (*laughs mockingly*), that theyyam performances in Pallipuram grove were stopped, long ago and mimicry and music are held instead; why do you unnecessarily get the theyyam decorations ready?

KANNAN THEYYAM (*Throws the decorations angrily*): Stop your mockery. (*He moves towards her, crazed with anger; at the same time he reminisces with nostalgia.*) Do you know ....

When the month of Vrischikam arrives, when the mist on Kooman Hill descends, the festival flag goes up in Pallipattu grove.... It was the day this Kannan Theyyam became king. He would roar and dance as

Gulikan Theyyam, through the glowing embers in the grove (*kavu*), not feeling the cold of Vrischikam. In harmony with the chenda's chembada rhythm Gulikan would move to the front of the ritual space and suck the warm blood of the live rooster ... people would watch this Kannan Theyyam with awe.

Then, waist pouch full of coins; rice, and coconut, the chicken offered to Gulikan, I would tie everything into a bundle, and reach home by dawn ... you and your dead brother would be waiting for me. (*He is exhausted.*) Why did you remind me of it all? That Vrischika month has dawned, that mist has descended from Kooman Hill, ... let it all lie in some corner of my heart as some old memory. Do not touch and awaken them. (*He shivers in the Vrischika cold.*) I'm shivering with cold, edi ... get me some black tea.

Parvati pours hot tea for him. He drinks it greedily.

PARVATI (*As though describing a pleasant dream*): Mist and chill and the clear sky of Vrischika month. The month when dreams flower in the hearts of girls who have reached the marriageable age. The month when girls perform rites to get a manly husband, who will give them a life, who will climb the steps of their homes and take them away. From the dawn of Vrischika month to mid Idavam, it's dream time for us girls. Once it is mid Idavam, panting like the Idavam wind, ruing the extinguished dreams, weeping like the Idavam rain.

KANNAM THEYYAM (*Throws the empty glass into her hands*): You are crazy. Crazy because you're unmarried.

PARVATI (*Shaken by his words, she stands immobile for a moment, then walks towards her father angrily*): I had an elder brother who went crazy and died, hanged himself from the ceiling! Me, I too will go mad. But let me ask you something, achcha. How did ettan go mad? Why did ettan hang himself?

The daughter's question falls on him like lightning. Kannan Theyyam cups his hands over his ears and roars; then moves toward Parvati like a mad man.

KANNAN THEYYAM: I do not know why your ettan committed suicide. His dreams reached the sky. I did not know any of his dreams (*remembers*). Maybe I disgusted him, I Kannan Theyyam, who enacted Gulikan theyyam in Bhagavathy's grove, who climbed the steps at dawn, reeking of rooster blood and arrack. But I nurtured him, watching every limb grow. (*He sits down exhausted. Parvati goes to him, tries to comfort him.*)

PARVATI: Achcha, This is how we talk, isn't it, rambling aimlessly. Finally we hurl stinging words at each other and curse. I reminded you of what you wanted to forget. You must forgive me achcha.

KANNAN THEYYAM: Cannot forget anything. The sight of your elder brother hanging, his eyes staring, upward, towards the sky. This Kannan Theyyam has not slept since then.

PARVATI: I too remember. The rope hanging from the ceiling, twisted around ettan's throat like a dream creeper climbing towards heaven.

KANNAN THEYYAM (*Cannot bear it*): Stop. All you can talk of is dreams ... life is not like that. Life is frightening, like the rope from which your elder brother hanged himself.

PARVATI (*Hands over her ears, upset*): I do not want to hear anything that frightens me.

They stare at each other.

BLACKOUT

The scene is depicted in a manner that makes it difficult to distinguish whether it is real or a dream. A rope hangs from above. Kannan Theyyam and Parvati stare at it aghast, as it swings frighteningly.

KANNAN THEYYAM (*As though asking his dead son*): Didn't you hear what your sister asked?

PARVATI (*Speaks, looking at the rope as though at her brother*): How did you go mad, etta? Why did you hang yourself?

KANNAN THEYYAM: Son, Prabhakara, you suppressed everything, told no one anything ... why did you leave us?

PARVATI: You were our support and our shelter. Why did you end everything on this rope, Prabhakaretta?

KANNAN THEYYAM: You must not question him like that. Everything ... Achan's fault.

PARVATI: At least now you realize you made a mistake ...

(*They quarrel again.*)

KANNAN THEYYAM: Yes, edi, in those prosperous times, ... when without sleep, when I danced like one in a trance, in Bhagavathy's groves ... I forgot my children, ... I forgot life.

PARVATI: Your dance over, when you climbed down the steps of the grove, could you not have turned back once, and prayed to Bhagavathy, ... for us ....

KANNAN THEYYAM: This Achan ... forgot everything, edi.

PARVATI: How could you not forget? Once you descended the steps of the grove, all you could think of was arrack and loose women ....

KANNAN THEYYAM (*Upset*): Edi, what is this that you are saying? Don't bring up things that I'm trying to forget ... (*Looks at the rope sadly*). Did you hear Prabhakara, ... what your sister said? Did you commit this horrible act because you hated me that much?

(*He is exhausted; holds the rope to prevent himself from falling; bows his head and weeps.*)

PARVATI (*Looking at the rope*): Like a dream creeper spreading out to heaven ... ettan had many dreams, isn't that so? Big ... big dreams.

Prabhakaran appears in their memory.

PRABHAKARAN (*Breathing heavily, tired*): This Prabhakaran had some tiny dreams—a secure job, a small house, Parvati's wedding; then a life with the girl to whom I had given my heart. But who was it who hunted down even these insignificant dreams of mine? Yes, I remember. The night I thrashed about on the rope, from the ceiling. The night I entered death in search of my lost dreams .... Achan was asleep, exhausted, dreaming of Gulikan Theyyam and chicken blood. As for Parvati, she was flirting with her yet-to-come bridegroom in her dream.

The light goes out, then slowly comes on again. Prabhakaran is raising and lowering the wick of the lantern. Parvati is asleep, her head resting on her sewing machine's table. Kannan Theyyam lies curled up among the theyyam adornments.

(*A man comes, holding a carefully wrapped sketch. He calls softly.*) Prabhakara.

Prabhakaran looks at the visitor who has entered at an unearthly hour.

PRABHAKARAN: Oh! It's Sivadasan. I was expecting you, though it is very late.

SIVADASAN: Your Achan and sister?

PRABHAKARAN: They are asleep.

SIVADASAN: Then do not wake them.

PRABHAKARAN: No, I won't. Let them sleep.

SIVADASAN. Look, I drew the picture you wanted. I spent the whole day, drawing this picture for you. Your Sreedevi's picture.

PRABHAKARAN (*Takes the picture eagerly; he looks at it, smiling sadly*): The gift my artist friend gives me, for the first and last time, a sketch of my Sreedevi, the girl I loved (*starts laughing, hysterically*).

SIVADASAN: Why were you so adamant that you wanted it this very night?

PRABHAKARAN (*Looking at the picture*): Sreedevi, you forgot me, forgot my love, you are getting married tomorrow. You leave me to become the wife of some bank officer.

SIVADASAN: She'll have a secure life, like gold ornaments secure in a bank's locker. Could you give her that?

PRABHAKARA (*Addressing the picture*): This night when you became a stranger to me, I want to sleep, kissing your picture.

SIVADASAN (*Contemptuously*): Oh! Was it for this, that you wanted the picture? You and your pulp dreams.

PRABHAKARAN: Stop. Everyone has their pulp dreams. What about the dreams we shared as we roamed the roads, in sunshine and rain, in search of work? A secure job, life with the girl we loved. (*Sivadasan looks irritated, tries to leave. Prabhakaran stops him. Desperately.*) Those hopeless evenings when we lay on our backs staring at the sky, what all dreams we saw! (*Sivadasan looks away. Prabhakan turns it forcibly towards him.*) Did we not sit in bus shelters, late at night, weeping silently over our dwindling youth?

SIVADASAN: Yes. It is all true.

PRABHAKARAN: Then why do you blame me?

SIVADASAN (*Angrily*): I am disgusted—with myself and with you. We are good-for-nothing chunks of flesh.

(*He thrusts aside Prabhakaran's hand and leaves.*)

PRABHAKARAN (*To himself*): What Sivadasan said is so true! Without a job, without income, just a good-for-nothing bit of flesh. (*Looks at his body with disgust, then at Sreedevi's picture. With self-loathing.*)

Sreedevi, and yet ... why did I desire you? Why did my veins throb for you? A useless life is as heavy as the mountain, its death is as soft as a bird's feather. Why should this good for nothing bit of flesh thrash about on earth? (*Despair and sorrow mingle in his smile. The rope swings before him. His trembling hands move towards the rope. Kannan Theyyam is asleep, exhausted, the theyyam adornments lie around him. Parvati is flirting with her dream bridegroom. In her dream she is seated at a machine sewing a garment.*)

BRIDEGROOM: Can't you stop this stitching, at least in your dreams?

PARVATI: What else can single girls do? Stitching a beautiful garment is as pleasurable as dreaming.

BRIDEGROOM: My darling tailor-girl, with the scent of new clothes ... (*he kisses her thick curly hair passionately*).

PARVATI: When will you stop this dream love-making and take me into life? When will you give up your supernatural form and come to me as a human being?

BRIDEGROOM: Real life is not possible for me. Isn't that why I come to you only in dreams? ... To love you without taint, to kiss without the taste of sourness; that is possible only in dreams.

(*He presses his face into her thick hair and kisses it. Meanwhile, Prabhakaran can be seen staring at the deadly noose he has prepared for himself. He looks at his lover's picture and speaks his last words.*)

PRABHAKARAN: Sreedevi, these sunken eyes of mine, hollow cheeks, lean body, eternally empty shirt pocket, I do not blame you for hating these and seeking a secure refuge. You are smart and fortunate. But before I die, I must tell you at least, what I wanted to tell the world. This society which is out to grab everything—if I had emerged first in its race, if my pockets were full, I would not have lost you tonight (*with self contempt*). Hmm. This wasted youth of mine, discarded by society, why should you want it? But these dull eyes have seen many dreams.

He sobs, kisses Sreedevi's picture. He lies down beneath the rope, embraces the picture madly; finally exhausted, panting, he tears it into bits and scatters the pieces. As he slips his head through the noose, Parvati and her dream bridegroom are locked in a passionate embrace.

The light dims then brightens again. Kannan Theyyam and Parvati look worn out, scorched by memories of Prabhakaran.

KANNAN THEYYAM (*Sadly*): Many more scorching things remain to be seen and heard. Then why did we remember this? (*Parvati remains silent, impassive*). You're still lost in dreams.

PARVATI: Yes, I'm dreaming. Isn't it because his dreams burnt out, that ettan died, thrashing about from that rope? Why did you give us life at all, Acha? To thrash about?

KANNAN THEYYAM (*Trembles as he hears her words*): What did you say?

PARVATI (*Loudly*): Why did you bring two worthless bits of flesh into the world?

KANNAN THEYYAM: You daughter of a dog! (*Slaps her hard.*) How could you ask that? (*Weeps, penitent, Parvati tries to console him.*)

PARVATI. Acha ... it is a question that all children whose youth is over, ask; only theirs are silent questions. I said the words out loud. Forgive me ... let me live in my dreams.

She walks towards her machine, head bowed. Begins to stitch the rest of the clothes. The grating sound of the sewing machine. Kannan Theyyam moves towards her.

KANNAN THEYYAM: This old man does not have a single dream to live for. (*She hears it, but continues to stitch without responding. He moves about like a caged civet cat, muttering.*) No sleep even, to dream.

(*Parvati continues to stitch.*) Stop it. Your blasted stitching! You said this and that to tear my heart. I too have something to say. (*He prevents her from stitching and pulls her up, querulously.*) What can this father dream about you, a daughter past the marriageable age, who fills the house. What dream can I have, of a son who hanged himself?

PARVATI: Acha, stop it. Let's not quarrel and hurt each other with scorching words.

KANNAN THEYYAM: No. We will. You will again say things that break my heart.

PARVATI: When the heart sinks, I somehow say those things ....

KANNAN THEYYAM: If you say them again, I'll kill you.

They stare at each other.

BLACKOUT

It is night.

Parvati is fast asleep, waiting for her dream bridegroom to appear. The rhythmic pounding of the chenda from Pallipattu grove. This is followed by the thottam song to rouse the theyyam. Kannan Theyyam turns this way and that, unable to sleep. Finally he sits up, cursing.

KANNAN THEYYAM (*To himself*): It's festival time at Pallipattu grove. Mist, chill, Gulikan theyyam. Rooster's blood. Ho! If I could forget myself and perform just once, my heart would cool a bit. (*He takes up the theyyam adornments.*) Nobody wants Kannan Theyyam. But I want this GulikanTheyyam's dress and crown. I'll dress up and perform in my own courtyard.

In the background, the theyyam song reaches a crescendo.

KANNAN THEYYAM (*Dons the theyyam costume in a mad frenzy and looks at himself in the cracked mirror*): Magnificent. Let me dance my fill this Vrischika night without chenda, chenda artist or audience. (*Ponders over something then with the same mad frenzy.*) This Gulikan does not need rooster blood to drink. (*Looks at Parvati with bestial glee.*) There is this good-for-nothing being that I gave life to. (*Moves towards her in fury, and tells the sleeping Parvati.*) Never again must scorching questions come from this throat. No unfulfilled dreams should appear before your eyes again. And that is this father's last dream. To become Gulikan Theyyam and perform in my courtyard. Let it happen by drinking blood from your throat. The rooster offered to Gulikan, its life is not in vain. That's all you need to think about. At least in that way let your life be sanctified. (*He bends towards her neck, his lips, teeth, and face furious. The rhythm of the Thottam song becomes faster; Parvati cries out, her body thrashes about. Kannan Theyyam's roar. Sound of things falling.*)

At dawn when the light brightens ...

The bloody unconscious form of Parvati. Kannan Theyyam scatters rooster feathers in the air, then bows his head into his theyyam adornments and weeps. The unseen bridegroom enters Parvati's dead dream with love-filled eyes .... He looks at her unconscious form, then kisses her curly tresses. He looks at her half-closed eyes.

BRIDEGROOM: Even in death, you dream with your half closed eyes. Your tresses still have the scent of dreams. Words of love still tremble on your lips. As you lie underground, with dreams that death cannot end, you must call out, call from your grave, ask who hunted down my dreams, why did boiling youth wither and die ... ask, aloud! Ask!

He kisses her passionately, pressing his face against her hair.

CURTAIN

—Translated by Catherine Thankamma

LIFE WRITINGS: Autobiography and Biography

Mainstream historiography has never perceived Dalit as subjects worthy of attention. Dalit lives were a presence marked by their absence. Their struggles, their resistances, their emotional and social agonies were less important than plant life. They were not even seen as a people with a history. They were outside history. If this is the status in the historiography of the collective, it should be easy to understand their status in the historiography of the individual: autobiographies and biographies. There, too, the Dalit is defined by his or her non-presence.

History writing of this sort was made possible by two strategies of erasure: (1) an erasure from history and therefore memory; and (2) an erasure from the lived context when the former strategy of erasure did not work. In this context it is appropriate to recollect two subaltern experiences. The tribal hero, Ekalavya* who became a formidable archer by training before a statue of his chosen guru (a guru who never knew of his existence and who would never have accepted him as a student) and Sambooka the Sudra who tried to acquire knowledge. Their caste status places them outside the scope of history, but their valorous actions place them in the heart of historiography. However distorted the Brahminical representations of these individuals, an outstanding fact remains: they *had* to be included in History. In other words, these rebellious

---

* The puranic story has Ekalavyan hidden and watching archery classes because his caste would not permit him to join master-archer Drona's group of students. Drona recognizes the threat to Arjuna's pre-eminence posed by Ekalavyan, and when it is time for Ekalavyan to make an offering to Drona, the guru demands his low-caste student's thumb thus destroying Ekalavyan's true destiny. This story is traditionally retold as an example of devotion to the guru but it has darker caste implications.

heroes gate-crashed into history and paid a terrible price for it: one was incapacitated and the other was beheaded.

If one looks closely at the contemporary practices of historiography, one is surprised to find that the same strategy of containment and erasure from memory is at work. E.M.S. Namboodiripad did not think it fit to mention the contributions of Ayyankali in his work on Kerala history. The first volume of subaltern historiography, when it arrives at a contextualization of the subaltern, fails to mention 'Dalit' as a category worth including.

Despite E.M.S. Namboodiripad's amnesia, Ayyankali was eminently qualified to be included as a hero in mainstream historiography. Other lower-caste lives that deserve equal treatment are: Sree Narayana Guru, Poikayil Appachan (later Yohannan), Pambadi John Joseph, and Pandit Karuppan. In short, they are excellent subjects for biography-writers. In the modern context, one could mention Kallara Sukumaran.

The collections in this section point out that there is another form of memory, another form of narrating life. It may be biographical or autobiographical. What is recalled in this section are not heroic deeds but quotidian life in all its diversity and specificity. It is seen that these life writings depict a struggle for education, equality and democratic rights. They are not celebratory of individual lives, but pleas for tolerance towards the differences of other lives and for safeguarding human dignity.

Dalit autobiographies referred to as narratives of pain do not harp on victimhood, but use writing as a tool against the inhuman social order. A noteworthy feature in Dalit autobiography and biography is the powerful narrative agenda which contests both the basis of caste discrimination and the claim that caste no longer functions as a social force in modern India. There is explicit reference to caste in Dalit autobiographies and biographies, in which most often the paramount concern is caste-oriented discrimination. On the contrary it is interesting to note that there is almost no reference to caste in mainstream life writings, evidently because savarnatha is already encoded in all its linguistic and cultural constructs. Thus Dalit life writing serves as a space for dissident within the literary public and within the public sphere. They depict a struggle for education, equality and democratic right. They exhibit great control over questions they want to address and invest a lot of energy and commitment into an empowering construction of Dalit selfhood. They are pleas for tolerance towards lives of every sort and for safeguarding human dignity.

Kallara Sukumaran's struggles become significant from a historical point in the context of Dalit entry into politics in the post-Independent period. Kallara's lifelong struggles stretch across a long political period from the formation of Kerala Harijan Federation to the formation of Indian Dalit Federation. He joined the Bahujan Samaj Party and contested in the Parliamentary election. The significant aspect of Kallara's poltical intervention is that unlike other Dalit politicians who entered the corridors of power through political parties, Kallara entered the political platform by asserting his Dalit identity.

Kandal Pokkudan's autobiography is an unusual Dalit experience in Kerala. This dictated writing posited somewhere between biography and autobiography has become noteworthy in Kerala's narratives of the self.* His life is fashioned by a consciousness rooted in community and nature and an alienation from political parties and mainstream society. Pokkudan's most noted political gesture has its roots in an alternative Dalit ecological understanding: despite ridicule and ill-treatment he planted mangroves on the river banks, which earned him the name Kandal Pokkudan. The specific inbuilt knowledge of taxonomy and aquatic lives inherited from ancestors, helped Pokkudan to construct his life in a unique and significant manner.

Adiyar teacher offers yet another slice of life from the perspective of the lived experiences of an educated Dalit woman. This portrayal of life, so far absent in dominant histories, does not conform to the established pattern of life writings. It deviates sharply in spirit and form from mainstream writings and interrogates the latter creating an uproar against it.

If history cannot capture life, it means the course of history has to change, not life. That is precisely what the quotidian lives of Pokkudan and Adiyar teacher teach us. These sketches of different lives reconstruct history and document the socio-cultural specifications of the Malayali Dalit's world.

---

* First person narratives not scripted by the self, but written by another person to whom the life story is narrated. The autobiographies of C.K. Janu, the Adivasi leader and Nalini Jameela, the sex worker belong to this category. Pokkudan's autobiography was dictated to his son.

AUTOBIOGRAPHY

My Life* (Excerpts)

Kallen Pokkudan

Untouchability

I am a man who has long borne the humiliation and misery of untouchability, particularly that associated with caste, money power, and slavery. It was the priest (*Adi*) from the Ezhothu Cheermakkavu who reminded me that according to the caste system I could not approach Brahmins, Nairs/Nambiars, and Thiyyars. I am not very clear about this, but I do remember vaguely. Thus did I slowly form an idea about pollution and untouchability. Those days I used to visit the house of Advocate Sreedharan, a local Congress leader. The house was named 'Padikkal'. By the side of the wetland near our compound, they had some coconut trees. When my father felled the coconuts, I went to deliver them at Padikkal. This was the routine. Once when I made the delivery, they gave me two *annas* for a cup of tea. Since it was evening time, they did not offer me *kanji*. The tea shop-cum-residence of Koran Vaidyar, who was also a member of the Harijan Welfare Committee, was near the Anjeengal Temple. A single tea and a snack cost two *annas*. I decided to have tea. I sat on the ground outside the shop and sipped it (as done to maintain the caste). When I tried to give him the money, Koran Vaidyar brought water in a tin vessel and poured it into my glass. I dropped the coins in the glass and sprinted away, without a backward glance. Thus, I learnt something new. Koran Vaidyar who was a member of the Harijan Welfare Committee, wanted me to wash the glass in which I had tea. This was the new understanding.

* Original title *Ende Jeevitham*.

Later too, I was placed in a similar situation. Kathiri, who owned a small-time shop near Edakkeel House, asked his maid Janaki, whom she could take along with her when she went to Aniyikkarakkavu to sell dried prawns. She chose me. We took a sack of dried prawns and started selling them in the neighbouring village of Aniyikkara. A young man came to us at noon, someone with the same looks, height, and complexion as me. My father and Kathiri were friends. Kathiri had asked this person, his son, to get us lunch.

'Your lunch is ready. Women can have it here,' he said and took me home. Near the gate of the house stood a pot of buttermilk. He poured me a glassful and drank from the same glass himself. Later, while having food from banana leaves spread outside the *padinjatta* (west-side hall) of the house, his mother asked me.

'You belong to which house?' There was no way to wriggle out of this question unlike in the earlier incident. I thought hard and replied, 'I am the nephew of Krishnan Nambiar of Chemmancheri House.' Suddenly, the mother started picking up the banana leaf and the food.

'Krishnan Nambiar belongs to our ancestral house. So, it is improper to seat and serve you here. You better have it indoors,' she insisted.

'Don't bother. I will have it here. It is better to finish where one began eating. I am not going to report this to anyone.'

After lunch, I returned with the packet for Janaki Edathi. Sometime later, the Nambiar met Kathiri.

'What's wrong with you? Why didn't you tell me that he is Krishnan Nambiar's nephew?'

'Who? He is only a Pulaya boy!'

Kathiri came to me when Nambiar left.

'Better run! Or, they will beat you to a pulp.' Since I knew the consequences, I handed over the prawns to Janaki Edathi and escaped to Cheruthazham.

Those days, the workers used to get small loans from the businessmen (*muthalali*) before they went to work in the hills during the harsh rainy month of Karkatakam. They repaid the money on their return. A man used to carry a load of rice and a long spade on the trip. They carried the load to the mountains, walking an entire day to Koyippra and another one and a half days to Edakkuva. We went as the labourers of Hazinar *Muthalali* to Koyippra. Every morning, we would go from Koyippra to Panapuzha to work and return in the evening. Edacheriyan Kannan, Kottan Kunhiraman, and others were part of my group and the three led while the women and children followed us. That day, we reached the workplace early. A Maniyani Nair was managing the tea shop in Muthalali's land. The people with me knew that untouchability was practised there. I suggested that we have some tea. We sat on a bench and ordered tea for three. 'What's for snacks', asked one of us. We got a *kadalakka* stew and three leaf-spoons to scoop it up. When it was finished, I asked them to walk ahead. I had four *annas* with me. When I asked him how much it cost, the shop owner said 'four *annas*'. When I was counting the coins, he asked me to wash the glasses.

'You set up shop to get money so you wash the glasses. I will not pay if I have to wash my glass.' He was not pleased with what I said.

'Are you trying to teach me what is right?' he asked. I threw the question back at him. I had to address him disrespectfully as '*Nee*'. Then, he abused my mother. In return, I abused *his* mother. It became a scuffle. Mammu, who was the supervisor, intervened. 'You abused Pokkudan's mother, that's why he abused your mother. Anyway, they are each one's mothers.' He pacified both of us and sent us off. After a while, I saw the Nair's daughter falling into the slush in the canal when coming from home. People gathered together and made me pull her out. I carried the girl to the Nair's house and laid her on the veranda. The Nair was dumbstruck.

'I don't practise untouchability. The Thiyya community people come to the Cheermakkavu nearby and they will not come here again if the place is polluted by a Pulaya or if I don't make a Pulaya wash his own glass. I'll have to close shop. That's why I behaved the way I did. Please forgive me,' he pleaded.

We returned home after our work.

After the landlords had divested me of ownership of the farmlands, I went once to Appukutti Eledath's house (*illam*) to pay the rentals. Since I could not find anyone outside, I had to call out many times. When I got fed up, I picked up the *Mathrubhumi* newspaper lying on the veranda to read. Immediately, Appukutti Eledath called out from inside asking who the visitor was. His crippled second son came out to see me.

'You can't do this here. Do it on the road below. Stay away, now, get off.'

I made no reply. I came back without paying the rent. The next day, Krishnan Namboodiri's manager (*karyasthan*) came and collected the payment. After many years, Appukutti Eledath died. The *illam* was partitioned. The second son met me once outside the Ezhom Panchayat Office. He grabbed my hand and told me he had something to discuss.

'There are five granaries for sale. You should have a look and find someone to buy them.' He took me to the *illam* and showed me the granaries. I did not react. Just came home.

Party meetings used to be organized in the houses of all castes. I have not seen any discrimination in the houses of Tayalapiri Kannan or Chemancheri Krishnan Nambiar. There was no serving of tea since they were secret meetings.

I had another experience at the hands of political party people. I can't mention any name. When I finished the *kanji* they poured water in my plate and asked me to wash it. I threw that plate with the *kanji* and water into the bushes by the courtyard and came away.

Mangroves and Environment

In 1989, I was supervising the building of a bund on the wetland by the riverbank for Ibrahimkutti of Pazhayangadi. It was then that the idea first came to me for that one should plant mangroves to control and break the force of the waves as they surged. I collected around two hundred seeds from various places and planted them. But, none of them sprouted. The seeds were wasted by the heat from a kind of wild grass in the slushy soil. Next year I thought of planting mangroves alongside the road as it could be protection against the storms and the force of the water as it beat against the banks. I had seen many children losing their umbrellas in the lashing rain storms. The girls suffered most. I remembered that some children had died in storms slipping and falling into the river while crossing the narrow plank on the makeshift wooden bridge in Neriyachira. I thought such mishaps could be averted.

I planted three hundred seeds alongside the road near the bund. Within two years the plants grew and looked healthy. This attracted the attention of Lakshmanan Master teaching at the Talipparambu Sir Sayyed College who was invited for the anniversary of the Club at Muttukandi. While inaugurating the function, he shared his happiness with the audience and appreciated me for what I had done. The people belonging to my community did not like this at all. Someone threw the mangrove seeds I had collected and stored near the bund in the river. And, someone started damaging the plants every day. Some people who witnessed this told me that the workers fixing the net on the prawn bund were doing this. The plants were on a stretch of about a kilometre. 'Damaging the plants' activity continued every day. The same year, on Onam eve, about twenty-five plants were damaged at a stretch. I met C.V. Kunhiraman, the Ezhoth Local Committee Secretary of the Communist Party of India (Marxist).

'Twenty-five mangrove plants have been damaged. The Panchayat should take action. It will happen only if you speak to the concerned.' Kunhiraman tried to play down the issue.

'What do we gain from taking action? What good does it do to the Party? What's the use of the plants being there? Can we pluck the fruits and eat them?' Kunhiraman asked me.

'You can address this question to Lakshmanan Master of Sir Sayyed College. You've often heard him speak about this. I don't know much.' I said and returned. Kunhiraman filed a complaint at the Pazhayangadi police station.

'It is true that Pokkudan planted mangrove trees for about a kilometre. Because the land belongs to the Panchayat, it is the duty of the Panchayat to look after them. Therefore, the police should find the people who damaged the plants and arrest them.' This was the complaint. The police sent for me.

'I haven't actually seen anyone or anything. I can't make assumptions. Because it was the day before Onam, many people were near the Club. This can't happen without their knowledge.' I told them. They made enquiries at the Club.

'If even one more mangrove plant is found damaged, you will be held responsible.' The police warned them and left. A week later, when I was planting a mangrove seed, the sister of a lackey of the leader and her husband saw me on their way to Pazhayangadi.

'Pokkuda! Are you mad? I will smash your spectacles. People can't walk this way if these plants grow thickly,' she accosted me. Her husband quickly led her away. I did not respond.

Though I had left active Party work, I had still not forsaken politics altogether. One day, the classmates of my second son Ananthan who were also workers of the Sastra Sahitya Parishad, came and met me and joyfully invited me for a meeting to felicitate me as stated in the pamphlet they brought with them.

'I did not plant all these trees with this aim. Earlier, there were mangrove trees beyond the prawn-bund. I planted them here so that they will block the severe winds. So, I can't come for the meeting.' I turned them away. They were greatly disappointed. They called Ananthan at Alappuzha and informed him. Ananthan came home and explained.

'You should attend it, Achan. Those teachers were my classmates. That's why they printed the pamphlets without asking you. You should not object,' Ananthan said. Meenakshi reminded me of something else. 'You should attend. Or, they will hate him. You should not make anyone hate him,' Ananthan said.

I attended the function. So did many people including teachers and students. The programme was organized in Neruvambram UP School. The next day, it hogged space in the all Kerala editions of newspapers. Thus, environmental activists began to trickle in to meet me. Also, journalists. *Deshabhimani* did carry it, but stopped reporting after that. Except *Janmabhumi*, all newspapers and television channels approached me. Nandu, a lecturer at the University College, Thiruvanthapuram, began to visit me every second month with SEEK (Society for Environmental Education of Kerala) activists. They always returned after promising me all kinds of help.

In the meantime, I was invited to a meeting organized by the 'Sanskriti' Nattarivu Gaveshana Kendram at Pariyaram which was operating under the leadership of Rev. Fr J.J. Pallath. Later, I participated in the meetings organized by them at Kozhikode and Thiruvananthapuram. Wherever I go, I carry mangrove seeds. In a week-long workshop organized by them at Kannur, I distributed the seeds to everyone. Pallath snapped a photo of me with the bundle of seeds and sent it for publication. Once, Nandu and his SEEK activists came to meet me. He had offered me financial help many times. 'I don't have children. So, why can't you take money from me?' he would ask.

'This won't do. We should do research on this. I came here to tell you that. For doing research, you will have to travel a lot. Are you ready for that? If money is the problem, you can ask SEEK's Pappan Master,' he said.

'I'll do as you say,' I saw them off. He shared all the information he had with researchers and ecologists and also informed the newspapers. Ecologists and environmental activists applied their minds to it. They did research on an all Kerala level. They inquired whether anyone else was planting mangroves. They could not find any. They came back to me. I was not well informed about this. But, I shared my limited knowledge with them. Nandu was very happy.

'Pokkudettan was the first one to plant mangroves. Now, let ecologists observe their uses,' Nandu said. In the meantime, I had to chop off the branches of some mangroves I had planted because of a larvae attack that was damaging the leaves.

As the mangroves grew, so did the number of my enemies who were mostly my own community people at Muttukandi.

But, the intervention by environmental activists and researchers against destroying mangrove trees had been growing. The High Court delivered a judgment that slapped six months imprisonment and two thousand rupees fine for damaging mangrove trees. This made a great legal impact in Kerala. The Coastal Protection Act came into being. Out of the Central funds sanctioned for planting mangroves, the Kerala Government allocated fifteen lakh rupees to the district of Kannur. The Taliparamba Forest Officer Uthaman and the Kannur DFO Chandran came to Ezhom Panchayat and informed everyone about the fund allocated and enquired whether there was any governmental land to plant mangroves within the area of the panchayat. The panchayat said, 'No.' Then, they came and asked me. I tried to turn them away saying, 'It is not correct on my part to say there is such land when the panchayat has said no.'

'We are leaving. But, we want you tell us certain things. Where can we get mangrove seeds? In what seasons will the seeds be available?' When they asked me to collect seeds for them, I agreed. In June, along with my children, I collected seeds for them. The Forest Department started the activities for planting mangroves in Thalasseri. I planted them near the Komath bund. In Thalasseri they planted the mangroves block-wise. They also started a mangrove nursery near the river. By 1994, the Fisheries Department decided to convert the Komath Bund, which was eight metres wide from Pazhayangadi to the Mosque in Ezhom Moola, into a road. Narikkote Pappan got the contract for thousand three hundred metres. From Pazhayangadi to the Muttukandi national club, a contractor from Kasargode got the contract. Then, the mangroves I had planted near the bund posed a problem. O.V. Narayanan, District Panchayat President, formally inaugurated the road work. 'Land cannot be used from inside the bund, but only from outside. Only then can the mangroves can be uprooted,' the Club members spread this message. They were angry because of the earlier incident. I met the SEEK workers many times to do something to stop the road work. I thought something could be done through the Fisheries Department. I shared this with T.P. Padmanabhan Master, but he ignored me. One day, when I was about to go and meet him in Payyanur, I found the Club members in towels wrapped around their waists and on their heads preparing to start work. Before I reached Pazhayangadi, with 'Govinda' chants, under the leadership of a young Dalit local Congress leader, they started slashing down, one by one, the mangrove trees that had been growing for the last four years, tall as men, blocking the surges of wind and wave.

Thirteen people from my community participated in slashing down the mangroves. A Thiyya from Chengal supplied them with drinking water. Around noon I came back from Payyannur. I heard about the slashing of the plants while sipping tea from the tea shop of my friend Pappan in Pazhayangadi. I saw the destruction on the way back home. I did not say anything to anyone. I called the *Mathrubhumi* photographer Madhuraj and he reached the spot immediately in a jeep. The people who had cut down the plants tried to block him from photographing it.

'You should not go there or photograph it. This issue is related to building a road. You should not report it,' saying which they tried to stop him.

'Whether it is the issue of a road, or canal, or even an airport, I *will* photograph it. No one can prevent me,' Madhuraj retorted. He told me this when he came home after snapping the photos. Though he compelled me to pose near the cut-down mangroves, I declined. He snapped some photos at home and left. The next day, this news flashed on all the Kerala editions of the newspapers. The next morning, when I went to buy the newspaper at Pazhayangadi, I saw Pappan Master of SEEK and Babu Kambrath near the Muttukandi Club talking to the people who had cut down the mangroves. I exchanged pleasantries with them and walked home. After some time, I heard them speaking to each other in raised voices. Meenakshi, Raghumon, and Rekhamol came out on to the road thinking I was involved in the scuffle. When I walked back with my wife and children, ignoring them all, one of them physically attacked us claiming Raghumon had stared back at them. 'There is nobody on your side in this area,' Meenakshi's brother-in-law warned us. Babu Kambrath picked up my fallen spectacles and walked home with us. This attack also made news. I did not file a complaint. Political workers and environmental activists from all over asked me to file a case against those who slashed down the mangroves.

'They are now cut down. Nothing could be done to prevent it. I pleaded with you many times to do something. I am not starting a revolution by filing a case.' I stated my position. Krishnan Master, who was earlier the Ezhom Panchayat President, and Balan Master, Vice-President, met me after a few days. We started conversing in the office room.

'We were not aware that the mangroves were destroyed. We came to ask you to file a case against those who did it. We knew about it when the Road Development Committee member Hamid called and informed us,' they said.

'I know who cut them down and who made them do it. Though I am not well-read about Communism or anything, I have enough knowledge from experience. So, I don't intend to start a revolution by filing a case. For now, you can drink the water Meenakshi gave you and leave. I already knew it was happening.'

I did not speak after that. They left. It was the Party and the Panchayat that filed a complaint when twenty-five plants were damaged. The very fact that neither the Party nor *Deshabhimani* reacted when more than ten thousand plants stretching over one-and-half kilometres were slashed down was indicative of their silent approval and role in it. Later, when environmental activists and the people began to force the issue, the same Dalit Congress leader managed to insert a report in the *Malayala Manorama* that said, 'savarnas are creating caste conflicts in Muttukandi'. 'Whatever they may say, we need Pokkudan', is how *savarnas* who met me reacted. Meanwhile, the party people and the Panchayat decided that 'whatever has happened in the past, Pokkudan should be given fifteen thousand rupees to plant mangroves.' I did not respond immediately.

'I will not plant mangrove trees anymore in Ezhom Panchayat,' I declared to the press. Research and observation of the mangroves at the initiative of Nandu and other SEEK activists meanwhile, continued. One day, we visited the snake shrine and the woods around it in an islet at the river mouth at Madakkarara Mattool. There are eighteen acres of mangroves on this island. The shrine was in a small hut in the middle of where there was also a well with fresh sweet water. We went around and videographed everything and walked untill the sandy, shifting wasteland left over from tidal waves near the marsh at Madakkara. Fifteen acres of a vast expanse of sand without any mangroves. The Hindus around claim that the snake shrine was a place where women divinities used to meditate. The belief is that the well water is sweet because of this. But, what we inferred was that the mangroves spreading around it for acres were the real cause.

I came back home. After the mangrove destruction events and after this first visit, I went back there, this time alone. I had a good look at the wasteland lay quite close to the river mouth, and came back and returned home. It was difficult to carry the seeds that far on my own. Even if it was done with great an effort, if someone threw them away, the seeds would go waste. I met the forest officer Uthaman and told him the facts. Together we met the Kannur tahsildar.

'If you plant mangroves there, we will not be able to do any developmental work,' he reacted. Uthaman was disillusioned.

'That is unclaimed land. No need for any permission. They cannot bring up any legal obstacles if we plant the seeds. Let's not waste time,' I told Uthaman on our way back. I collected seeds. A road was cut through the area where fisherfolk from Kochi and Dalits were living to reach that unclaimed land. It coincided with the time when the people there were clamouring for a road. So they helped us. They called a meeting; organized awareness classes. A local man Sudhakaran was entrusted with the job of supervision on a temporary basis. The Left Front was in power at that time. One day, the Payyannur Municipality Chairman Jyothi drove up to my home in a jeep. She shared her happiness in meeting and talking to us.

'We have to learn certain things from you. We will organize a seminar, awareness should be built and we must plant mangrove trees,' she said before leaving. SEEK's President, T.P. Padmanabhan Master, asked a man in Mattool to supply one thousand seeds. A thousand mangrove plant seeds were planted at Kotti under the Payyannur Municipality in which I also participated. They did not inform me about how they got the seeds. None of them came out well. The Municipality had decided to plant mangroves for the next five years along with organizing seminars and other programmes and videotape them to show the then Chief Minister E.K. Nayanar. Madhava Panikkar, a teacher at the Kasargode Government College, sent the college peon Rashid to my home, after reading about it and realizing that I was not being given any sort of recognition by the Municipality. On 5 June (World Environment Day), at Madhava Panikkar's initiative, I was felicitated by the college and after that, including the Kerala Government's Vanamitra Award in 2006, my work received around twenty-five felicitations. Left Front workers from Karivalloor, Thrissur, and Pappinisseri, and more than sixty organizations felicitated me. The writer G. Madhsoodanan, IAS, at a simple function attended by Perumbadavam Sreedharan and P. Surendran, presented me with the award amount of ten thousand rupees he got as an award from the Kerala Sahitya Akademi for his book, *Kathayum Paristhithiyum*.

Above all, the greatest pleasure and recognition I got was from the opportunity to share with students from more than a thousand schools and colleges, from the north to south of Kerala, the knowledge gathered by an unmistakable man named Kandal Pokkudan' about the mangrove forests and nature and laws of nature. I have preserved the names and addresses of those schools and colleges and their certificates as valuable records. The concern that the next generation has for the environment is very crucial. I have gained in knowledge from interacting with Lower Primary school students to research scholars. I have no faith in human gods. My gods are Nature, People, Truth, and Justice. I have not so far faced any grave consequence because of this faith. My family joins me in all these efforts to the extent possible to them.

—Translated by Ravi Shanker

BIOGRAPHY

Excerpts from Ayyankali

Velayudhan Panikkasseri

Hundreds of thousands of the poor had been living a life of forcible suppression, carrying the yoke of slavery like animals in the dark depths of ignorance. It was the social reformer, Ayyankali, who shook them awake and brought them back into the mainstream of society. He is the warrior who, without faltering till the end of his life, fought for the multidimensional enhancement of the toiling, depressed section of society. He mobilized this community and gave them the awareness with which to recover their human rights which they had been denied all along. He is also the leader who led the first strike of agricultural labour in Kerala to victory.

Ayyankali was born in August 1863 in Venganur near Thiruvananthapuram. Mala and Ayyan were his parents. Kali was the first child of Mala and Ayyan. Kali was a common name in the Pulaya community in those days. In order to distinguish this Kali from others of the same name his father's name was added to his and he came to be known as Ayyankali. After him came his brothers Chathan, Gopalan, Velayudhan, Velukutty, and the sisters Kanna, Chinna, and Kunji.

Dalits were not admitted into schools those days. Neither did they have any other means of receiving education. As a result the able-bodied Ayyankali did not learn the alphabet and became an agricultural worker at an early age. Kali's father was different from the other members of his community in that he owned five acres of agricultural land. This was given to him by a local landlord for whom he cleared many acres of forest land and made it suitable for farming.

It was the practice of the landlords to inhumanly treat these sons of the soil who laboured from dawn to dusk. Refusal to pay fair wages commensurate with the labour involved, unjustified reprimands, use of abusive language, physical violence were all common occurrences. The workers had to accept whatever the landowners said and there could be no dissent. They did not have the right to use the roads which they had built through hard work or bathe in the ponds which they had dug. They could not enter public places. In case of sickness they had to wait in hospitals at a prescribed distance from the others. (Pulayas, Parayas and other low castes had to keep a 64-foot distance between themselves and the Brahmins.) They would be attended to after all the other patients had left. The doctors would not physically examine them but would only listen to the symptoms shouted out. Medicines such as tablets would be wrapped in paper and thrown to them. Liquid medicine would be poured into containers brought by the patients who would withdraw after lining them up.

They could not enter tea shops but regardless of the weather had to sit outside at a distance on the ground. While everybody else was given tea in glasses these low-caste people were served tea in coconut shells.

When they returned tired after a day of hard labour for their masters they were served rice gruel not in any container but in leaves placed in shallow depressions dug into the ground. No worker, man or woman, was allowed to wear any clothes above the waist or below the knee. Women were not permitted to cover their breasts, but could only wear necklaces made of shells and stones. Wearing of white clothes was banned and new clothes had to be covered in dust or dirt before use. Umbrellas were not allowed, rain or shine. Wages could not be demanded or asked for. They had to accept the wages without demur as and when the landlord paid. These landlords had to be obeyed unconditionally. Overseers had the power to punish physically or even kill without a valid reason. In either case no question would be asked. The workers lived in small hovels. At the height of farming activity they would spend the nights in the fields in guard huts. Sun, rain, mist, or wind would be of no consequence. These bipeds did not even receive the consideration given to the quadrupeds. This pathetic treatment of his brothers caused proud Ayyankali much anxiety. All these unwritten laws built Ayyankali's arrogance. Who had made these laws? He decided to defy all the restrictions. When work in the fields was done Kali, his brothers, and friends of the same age used to meet on the maidan. The topic of their discussion was how to break the shackles of slavery. After long days of contemplation a way emerged. 'If we are to free ourselves from our pitiable state we ourselves have to wake up and act. We have to devise a plan to achieve freedom and implement it. If we wait for others to come and rescue us it will only lead to disappointment.'

Physical strength was the workers' asset. Hard work on the farms and in the fields had made their muscles firm and strong. This strength had to be used to win back their rights. A group of strong young men was mobilized. An expert in martial arts was summoned from outside, various exercises were learnt and training was taken in self-defence and handling situations wherein they were outnumbered.

Fight for Right of Free Movement

Their first effort was to establish their right to use the roads built by the sons of the soil and which were freely used even by lowly animals. That was the first sign of social change. Most people travelled on foot in those days. Long distance travel was in bullock-carts and the well-to-do had carts that were mounted on springs. Ayyankali acquired a well-sprung cart and two healthy, beautiful white bullocks. These animals had bells that jingled tied to their horns and round their necks. Ayyankali travelled along the road in this beautiful, well-sprung cart drawn by white bullocks. He himself wore the famous and most expensive '703' mark mulmul dhoti, a white singlet and a fancy turban. Endowed with an impressive physique and bearing Ayyankali moved along the road in regal style. A Dalit wearing white clothes and travelling in a spring-mounted bullock-cart! What a spectacle! Those who witnessed this sight just stared in disbelief. The caste fanatics were enraged. A defiant Dalit? Entering the road was itself an offence—and that too in a fancy bullock-cart wearing a turban and white mulmul mundu, not tied above the knee but let down to his ankles! This was something which could not even be imagined and it shook everyone. Those who knew of Ayyankali's martial skills were reluctant to approach him. But then this could not be permitted. They first tried to obstruct him by pelting stones but he, agile and brave, skilfully evaded the stones. Finally, they threw caution to the winds and stood on the road. One of them shouted 'Remove your turban, get down from the cart!' Ayyankali slowed the cart and took out a big knife tucked into his waistband and swirled it around. 'Come close if you dare,' he roared. 'I shall then show you who Kali is.' Seeing Kali's fearless stance and the glitter of the knife no one had the courage to close in. They could neither move forward nor go back. 'So you have got so far, have you? Then we shall teach you a lesson' was their response packed with rage. Kali's anger 'matched theirs. 'Yes, Kali is learning and he will teach you a lesson too.'

Ayyankali completed his journey and returned successfully ignoring the opposition. This incident needs to be inscribed in letters of gold in the history of the Dalit struggle for the right of free mobility. This historic journey marked the beginning of a series of struggles that lasted many years. This was the first time that the upper caste dominance had to bow before lower caste resolve. News of this spread instantaneously with added frills not only in Venganur but all over Travancore. All Dalits accepted Ayyankali unanimously as their leader. Ayyankali knew that the consequences of his journey would be terrible and that the casteists would not lie low for too long. A virtual army of young men was readied who were willing to make any sacrifice for the right of unrestricted travel. He travelled not only in Venganur but in neighbouring areas creating awareness in young people and setting up volunteer groups. Many folk arts popular among Dalits were used to spread the ideology of the movement.

In Ayyankali the untouchable community saw their saviour. If the first phase of the struggle for the right to unfettered travel was undertaken alone by Ayyankali, he was not alone in the next phase. He was accompanied by groups of his followers. Fully prepared, they started from Venganur and walked along the public road to Balaramapuram, Aaralummoodu Puthenkada market. This was in 1898. All along the route there was stiff opposition but it reached its crescendo in Balaramapuram Chaliyatheruvu. Those of the intolerant upper caste had congregated there but the Ayyankali volunteers moved ahead determined to face the opposition at any cost. Ayyankali's instruction to his followers was that they should not hurt anybody but that if they were attacked they should return two blows for every one received. The attackers fell on the Ayyankali group from all sides. What followed was a true armed conflict. It was literally a bloodbath. The blood of the upper and lower castes flowed in a single stream. Despite indescribable physical violence and wounds Ayyankali's men stood their ground.

The news of the Chaliyatheruvu conflict spread with lightning speed all over the region. The suppressed classes who had been put through hell began to stir. The entire region shivered at the loud cry for rights that rose from them. They came forward to answer Ayyankali's call and were ready to face any situation. The reaction to the struggle for rights began to manifest itself in different places in different forms. The Dalits dared to defy unwritten laws that had existed through generations.

The uncompromising privileged communities tried to nip the Dalit movement in the bud. However, just as cutting off one shoot produces two new ones, the Dalit fight for rights gathered strength and spread all over Travancore. Unconditional obedience to any demand of the landlord and submitting to physical abuse became old memories. The workers began to question unreasonable instructions and countered any attempt at physical violence. The landowners could not bear this uncontrollable stir among the workers.

Ayyankali travelled all over the area addressing his people in an effort to create awareness of their rights. His words, coming as they did from the depths of his heart, carried a special and unique persuasive power. Volunteer groups of young people started sprouting in the villages and working for the cause. They came to know immediately if and when Dalits were attacked anywhere. They would mobilize and promptly arrive at the trouble spot. Those in power could not control this. Abuses from the upper castes were met with worse abuses. Violence was met with violence. When hovels were set on fire, mansions began to burn. In the face of the organized strength of the Dalits the false notions of the upper castes and their various restrictions began to wither one by one. While the tolerant section of the privileged community welcomed the change the majority was unable to accept it.

The freedom to travel as they liked was not enough. The Dalits had to have the opportunity for total education. They should have free access to schools, both government and government-aided. Education was essential to enable them to live as others did and to have awareness of their human rights. At least the next generation should cease to be the proverbial frogs in the well. Ayyankali became totally immersed in the mission of achieving complete freedom for his people.

Sadhujana Paripalana Sangham (Society for the Protection of the Poor and Downtrodden)

Ayyankali was convinced of the need for an organization to channel the new-found Dalit power through the right courses, to spread awareness regarding their rights and to acquire those rights through mobilized strength. He was encouraged into this line of thinking by the advice of Sri Narayana Guru and the renowned poet Mahakavi Kumaran Asan and the growth of SNDP organization set up in 1903. In 1907, he formed Sadhujana Paripalana Sangham to emphasize the importance of their aims of winning the right to unrestricted travel and access to schools, reforms of traditions and practices, cleanliness, awareness of good ways of life, mutual love and respect, and of protecting the rights of all Dalit sections.

'Strength through organization' was the message that Ayyankali and his followers propagated as they travelled through the length and breadth of Travancore. This effort was not in vain as branches formed all over the State, capable workers and all sections of the Dalit community rallied under the flag of the new organization. Those who rose through their work for the organization and became Ayyankali's trusted aides are Gopaladasan, Kurumban Devathan, Vellikkara Chothi, Vishakhan Thevan, and Thiruvarpu Kuttan among others.

Freedom of Education

As a result of their joint representations the government issued an order in June 1907 giving Dalit sections access to schools. The diwan of the time took special interest in issuing this order. However, fearing opposition from certain sections or communal jealousy, senior officials showed no inclination to implement this order. The leaders of the Dalit organization who knew about the order approached the school authorities with the children to seek access to schools. Not a single school responded positively. The Dalits intensified their struggle and sent several representations to government. They called on the Director of Education, a European by name Mr Michael, and the new diwan, P. Rajagopalachari, and conveyed their grievances. Both of them were interested in enhancing the status of the depressed communities. They issued a fresh order allowing children from these communities to have access to schools. There were many who disapproved of the Diwan's sympathetic attitude to the requests of the Dalits. It is suspected that this was the reason for some so-called reformers criticizing not only the order but also the diwan's personal life.

Swadeshabhimani Ramakrishna Pillai was one of them. On the other hand, Changanassery Parameshwaran Pillai, C. Raman Thampi, Ramavarma Tampan, and Mannath Padmanabhan held the view that the demands of the Dalits should be conceded. Ramakrishna Pillai wrote three editorials in *Swadeshabhimani* criticizing the 1910 order granting school access to Dalits. On 2 March 1910, he wrote, 'I see no merit in supporting the view that all children without exception should be allowed to sit together in schools in total disregard of their caste status just because some are demanding equality in the matter of traditions and practices. Putting those who have been cultivating their intelligence for generations together with those who have been cultivating the field for even more generations is like putting a horse and a buffalo together under the same yoke.' Apart from this, Pillai lined up many ideas and examples in his three lengthy editorials. All these led to his conclusion that students from the Dalit communities should not be allowed to sit with upper-caste students in government-aided schools.

On the strength of the government order Ayyankali arrived in Ooroottambalam school with a girl student, Panchami. With prior information that Ayyankali would be on his way to Ooroottambalam to enrol Panchami, a Pulaya girl, in the local school against past practice members of the privileged community had gathered in the school premises. Anticipating this Ayyankali was also fully prepared for any eventuality. He was escorted by his 'army'. No sooner had Ayyankali and his followers entered the school area than the members of the upper caste pounced on them. It was a clash between hands calloused by the use of the hoe and hands which had only rolled balls of rice. Weapons came out into the open and were used freely. Supporters on both sides who got the news of the clash rushed to the scene. The fight continued until dusk when the venue changed. Dalit homes were destroyed and some were burnt down. The Dalits retaliated more strongly.

The owner of the school was a landlord called Kochappi Pillai. He decided that the school building polluted by the presence of Panchami had no right to exist. He burnt down the building the same night and derived a perverse satisfaction.

Following the Ooroottambalam incident Dalit students approached schools elsewhere and they all led to more Ooroottambalams in effect. Thanks to the combined opposition from the communally jealous the government order of 1910 also did not benefit the Dalits. It became clear that without a change in the attitude of the upper castes a government order by itself would not succeed in resolving this issue.

Ayyankali in the Legislature

It was the practice to nominate members to the legislature only from the tax-paying section of the public. However, tax-paying Dalits were not entitled to nomination for the reason that they were from low castes. All other castes and landlords had their representatives in the legislature to plead their cause and for the resolution of their problems. The year 1911 saw the introduction of a new provision by which the issues concerning Dalits would be presented in the legislature by members of the upper caste nominated by government for this specific purpose. The person nominated to represent Pulayas and other Dalits at that time was the editor of *Subhashini*, P.K. Govinda Pillai. Speaking in the seventh assembly of the legislature he narrated in detail the travails of the depressed classes. He concluded his speech with this request, 'If the people have no objection and the government is kindly disposed towards this request, it is my appeal that at the next assembly (in 1912), one of them (the depressed classes) should be allowed to represent them and directly present their case.' This appeal had its effect. It was supported by many backward communities and Ayyankali's Sadhujana Paripalana Sangham launched a strong movement in its favour. As a result, on 15 December 1911, Ayyankali was nominated to the legislature.

In the eighth assembly in 1912 Ayyankali who never had the opportunity to even learn the alphabet made his maiden speech in a House filled with landlords and the elite. Without blaming anybody he presented the needs and problems of his people in his characteristic style that touched one's heart. While a section of the assembly found Ayyankali's presence and speech disagreeable it evoked pleasure and respect in the vast majority, particularly Diwan Rajagopalachari, who had taken the lead in nominating Ayyankali. While Ayyankali's speech covered the right to travel freely and receive education he brought up a new issue for the consideration of government. This was the fact that agricultural workers had no land of their own and, therefore, it was necessary to transfer some government land to their ownership.

Mannath Padmanabhan, in his 'Memories from the Past', has recorded his impression of Ayyankali in the legislature: 'Seeing Ayyankali enter the legislature wearing a turban, a kumkum *pottu* on his forehead, a coat and a *veshti* draped around his shoulders, several visitors present wondered whether this was the diwan.'

Rights Must be Conceded

Despite many public demonstrations and agitations, although Ayyankali presented his grievances in the legislature and government issued many favourable orders the attitude of the upper castes and the like underwent little change. They viewed the Dalit struggle for rights as defiance and rebellion. Ayyankali and his followers soon realized that their aims could not be achieved through a favourable change in the attitude of the privileged community. Their subsequent activity was marked by their strident demand that their rights be conceded. He made his followers promise that what they were not given would be wrested by force. He gave a call to his followers to start a life-and-death struggle for their rights and not to wait for anybody's charity. All of Travancore felt the tremors of this call and some saw this struggle as the 'Pulaya rebellion'.

When Ayyankali went to Venganur school to enrol his children there, an attempt was made to prevent them from even stepping into the veranda. When this did not succeed hooligans waiting outside were brought in and violence erupted. There were casualties on both sides. The headmaster locked up the school and went home. So did the students. This conflict could not be contained and it spread in even more serious form to Nedumangad, Balaramapuram, Kovalam, Kazhakoottam, Pullad, Perinad, and Chennithala. When the situation reached a stage in which school authorities deliberately flouted government orders and even forcibly drove away parents and children seeking admission Ayyankali appealed to the diwan for direct government intervention to ensure admission of Dalit children. The seriousness of the situation soon stirred the government machinery into action. The Director of Education, Mr Michael, himself participated in the admission process but in the meantime, hooligans removed his vehicle and set it on fire.

Establishing his Own School

When Ayyankali discovered that Dalit children were not being admitted into the existing schools he put together another plan—set up his own school. The school shed came up without delay and the furniture also arrived. But where were the teachers? The Dalits had no literate persons. There were no volunteers from the upper castes. He approached Mahakavi Kumaran Asan and through his effort got a *pundit*, Parameshwaran Pillai by name. The teacher and students had assembled in the shed, but by the time the first lessons ('Hari Sri Chant') started the rowdies engaged by the upper castes attacked the school. Ayyankali's followers were standing by and they pitched in. They evacuated the teacher and the students to a secure place and then faced and drove the rowdies away. These battered rowdies set the school on the fire at night. By dawn another shed had arisen. Groups of volunteers were mobilized, one to escort the teacher to and from the school, one to guard the school and so on. There were fights and arson from time to time.

The First Strike

No amount of effort showed much progress on the education front and Ayyankali thought of another form of agitation—a strategy untried before. What provoked Ayyankali to use a new strategy—pressure tactics—was the realization that those who obstructed the education of the children were the landlords themselves; it was the granaries of these very landlords that the Dalits had toiled to fill for generations. Ayyankali took a solemn oath that if the landlords opposed the education of the Dalit children he would see that the paddy fields would be overrun by weeds. He briefed his followers first on the new strategy. Then he formed groups that were sent around the State to publicize this programme and the benefits that would accrue from its success. Committees were formed in the regions to oversee the programme. Ayyankali's oath caused waves that spread across the State. Dalits all over Kerala began to organize themselves to enable Ayyankali, their God on earth, to realize what he had set out to do. They declared repeatedly that even if they had to starve to death they would not take a step back.

The workers set out their demands. Right to free travel and to education continued to be their main planks. Other demands included regular hours of work, commensurate wages and a humane approach towards them. They had realized they were human beings and as such were entitled to human rights. They also knew that their future generations would live as human beings only if sacrifices were made at this stage.

The fields went dry, there were grave threats, but not a single worker went to work. There was an attempt to import mercenary labour but this failed in the face of determined opposition. A few landlords entered the field themselves. However, they were more used to enjoying the fruits of other people's labours and not to doing the work themselves. This failed.

The workers faced starvation and then came disease. Starvation was not a new part of their life but then how long for this time? Ayyankali resolved this by liaising with the fishing community nearby who were their kindred souls. The workers were invited to join them in their fishing operations. This improved the situation from total starvation to half that. Despite all these hardships that confronted the workers their spirit did not flag.

Granaries lay empty, avenues of income closed, and the landlords began to panic. One more attempt was made to bring in local goondas to work but they faced strong reaction and failure. Months went by and this strike turned out to be the first long-term strike in the country. The government had been intently watching the developments following the strike. The diwan was of the view that the crises were necessary to clear the churned up, muddied state of the society. The landlords tried to get the police to intervene but the diwan refused.

The government also could not be silent spectators for long in such a grave situation. Both sides were weary. The diwan decided to initiate mediation to resolve the issue and appointed the First Class Magistrate, Kandala Nagan Pillai, as the mediator. Pillai summoned both sides for detailed talks. He then ruled that the demands of the workers were justified and should be accepted. The landlords were in a dilemma as the ruling was too bitter to swallow, yet too sweet to spit out. However reluctantly, in the absence of an alternative, the landlords decided to yield.

Hours of work and wages were settled. Freedom to travel, right to education were conceded and the strike that started in June 1913 was successfully terminated by Kandala Nagan Pillai in May 1914. This strike, the first of its kind not only in Travancore but in all of India, for human rights demonstrated the power of the dark skin. With this Ayyankali's organizing skill and his fame crossed the borders of Kerala. One has to remember that something as daring as this strike happened nearly a hundred years ago. The worth of this struggle can be truly assessed when we recognize that it happened a few years ahead of the Russian Revolution, it lasted nearly a year and the workers who took part and won were those who eked out a living from day to day.

One cannot assume that this strike solved all the problems of the dark skinned community. All it means is that the venomous serpent of communalism had lowered its hood temporarily. From time to time it continued to spit its venom. It is not easy to cleanse minds of pollutants which had occupied them for centuries. Whenever the Dalit students entered the classes the upper-caste students began to hold their noses and walk out complaining of stink. This was a new form of their protest. School authorities were tormented by the refusal of the upper-caste parents to let their children sit with the Dalits. It came to a stage when many schools would have had to close down. Ayyankali apprised the diwan of this ruse to defeat the purpose of the government orders. This crisis was resolved at government level.

Reforms to Traditions and Practices

When problems relating to unrestricted movement, access to schools and agricultural labour had mostly been resolved, Ayyankali and his organization concentrated their attention on reforms in their traditions and practices. Ayyankali advised his people to give up their orthodox practices, superstitions, and unrefined dress habits. Following this their women in many places gave up their shell and bone necklaces which were the symbol of their lowly status. Those who were half-naked and covered in dirt bathed, wore clean clothes with blouses and more modern ornaments. This did not please the privileged classes and many clashes resulted on this account. Ayyankali and his co-workers called meetings in various places and spread awareness among members of his community Dalit women participated in these meetings with great fervour. They were not allowed access to public venues and their meetings were held on unused or government land. Although the subject of discussion at these meetings was reform of their own practices they faced opposition from the casteists. On these occasions it was the women who, armed with the tools of their trade—the sickles—stood in front to face the attackers. The most serious of these attacks was on the Dalit conference in Perinad. The women turned into goddesses of destruction and turned on the attackers cutting them up with sickles. It was a bloodbath and the attackers fled. However, the vanquished returned under cover of night and set fire to the Dalit homes. The Dalits, not to be outdone, lighted torches from their burning homes and retaliated by burning down the homes of the attackers. The damage they caused was many times what they had suffered. Both sides indulged in mindless violence. The flames that rose in Perinad spread to other places and there was no peace anywhere. Nobody could step out of his or her home. Ayyankali rushed there to restore peace. The progressive elements among the upper class and social workers also arrived. The government also went into action, recognizing these conflicts as inevitable in the Dalit effort to get into the mainstream of society and the need to restore peace. In all these clashes in the name of human rights there was never a single instance of the Dalits hitting first. They were only defending or retaliating, but the retaliation was always very strong and bloody.

No More Shell and Stone Necklaces

Violence is never a permanent solution for any problem. Without peace no country can progress. It was not possible to suppress Dalit demands for their rights. The government desired to find a peaceful solution to this problem. Social activists were encouraged to intervene and Changanassery Parameshwaran Pillai and C. Raman Thampi came forward to help. They had talks with Ayyankali and on the basis of these a formula emerged. It was decided that a conference should be called involving all communities and to resolve with unanimous concurrence problems relating to traditions and practices, thereby restoring peace. This had government support. The conference was held on the Big Maidan in Kollam under the chairmanship of Parameshwaran Pillai. Over 4000 Dalit women participated. Other communities also were well represented. The chairman spoke at length on the need for communal amity, the dignity of labour and the invaluable contribution of the Dalit brothers and sisters to the economy through their work. He then reminded them that all communities had to progress for the country to progress and that none should obstruct this process. C. Raman Thampi in his speech declared that no community was against Dalit women wearing clean clothes and blouses and the opposition came from misunderstanding in the minds of a few traditionalists. His statement that there would be no opposition in future was received with loud applause. The next speaker was Ayyankali and when he rose there was great excitement among the crowd. He spoke calmly and said, 'As a result of the work of my organization in South Travancore my Dalit sisters have begun to abandon their shell and stone necklaces and wear clean clothes and blouses. The members of the upper castes have stated here that this is what they also wish. Therefore, I call upon my sisters present here to discard their shell and stone necklaces.' The entire assembly supported this call. Ayyankali invited two Dalit women to the dais and suggested to them that they publicly cut their shell and stone necklaces which they promptly did with their sickles. Following this all the Dalit women including many grandmothers present there mounted the dais and discarded their necklaces which then lay in a huge heap. This was an inspiring moment in the history of social reforms and the reconciliation ended successfully.

Although this blunted the edge of organized opposition the sporadic incidents continued here and there but were not serious. There was no open opposition but many minds continued to nurse their dissent.

Sadhujana Paripalana Sangham intensified its effort to nurture the new vigour and confidence of the lower castes and to channel them through useful courses. In 1916, they launched their monthly magazine, *Sadhujana Paripalini*. Each office and educational unit of the organization functioned as centres for reforming traditions and practices. Ayyankali's main slogan was 'Development through Education'. He emphasized the importance of women's education and enhancing their social status. It must be recalled that Panchami was the first Dalit girl whom Ayyankali escorted for enrolment in a school.

Community courts were functioning under the auspices of Sadhujana Paripalana Sangham to settle disputes amicably. Only disputes that could not be resolved by these courts went to Ayyankali. His decision was final and accepted as such by all. This avoided animosity and wasteful expenditure.

Running up the Steps of Progress

The annual assemblies of Sadhujana Paripalana Sangham were held in VJT Hall in Thiruvananthapuram and representatives of thousands of their branches participated. The diwans of the time presided as the Maharaja's representative. All senior government officials including the Chief Secretary would be present. Ayyankali would make the welcome speech in the course of which he would list out the disabilities, cases of neglect of his community and its needs. The relevant official would respond then and there to issues in his domain. Where immediate action was possible the diwan would direct that it be taken. Other matters would be listed and sent for the Maharaja's approval. Each of these assemblies helped the community run up the steps of progress.

As a result of Ayyankali's effort more members of the depressed castes were nominated to the legislature enabling more attention towards the Dalit needs. For twenty-eight years from 1912 Ayyankali served as a member of the legislature and worked for the multidimensional development of his community. Apart from the freedom to travel without restriction and to receive education, he tried his hardest to get farmland and homes for his constituents.

Mahatmaji and Ayyankali

Thanks to Ayyankali's efforts many hostels were set up in different parts of Travancore where Dalit students could live while studying.

When one of them who resided in one such hostel while studying, K.R. Narayanan, became the president of India, Ayyankali's soul must have found fulfilment. When Mahatmaji visited Venganur he asked Ayyankali, 'What is your next desire?' Pat came the reply, 'To see at least ten BA graduates from my community.'

When Mahatmaji visited Venganur in 1937 to felicitate Ayyankali he was given a rousing reception. He described Ayyankali as the Pulaya King. Mahatmaji then addressed the tens of thousands of Dalits and said, 'You have got in Ayyankali, your uncrowned king, a tireless worker and I understand that under his leadership you are making steady progress.' With this visit the renown of Ayyankali's unique work spread all over India.

Ayyankali was an active participant in the temple entry struggle of the harijans, arguing that everyone was equal in the eyes of God and the right of worship was not a monopoly of some. Until the temple entry proclamation was made in 1936 by Chithra Thirunal Balaramavarma Maharaja, Ayyankali continued to raise this issue. He also encouraged mixed marriages.

All of Ayyankali's activities had the blessings of Sri Narayana Guru. In overcoming any crisis he had the unlimited support of social reformers such as Mahakavi Kumaran Asan, Changanassery Parameshwaran Pillai, Mannath Padmanabhan, C. Raman Thampi, Dr Palpu, T.K. Madhavan, Sahodaran Ayyappan, Mulur, and others.

Ayyankali was married in March 1888 to Chellamma of Manjankuzhi tharawad. Ponnu, Chellappan, Kochukunju, Shivathanu, Thankamma are his children.

Unending struggles and ceaseless work took a toll of Ayyankali's health but he worked hard till his last breath. By 1941 he was considerably weakened and on 18 June that year the sun set on that dark-skinned hero.

We have always been showing criminal neglect in the matter of honouring the architects of modern Kerala. Have we adequately honoured this great man who played an important role in the resurgence of modern Kerala? What exist today as standing memorials to this towering personality are the commemorative structure near the Venganur school that he set up and his full-scale statue which was unveiled in 1980 in Vellayambalam Square.

Ayyankali was honoured at the national level on 12 September 2002 when the Postal Department released a memorial stamp which contained a representation of his services to the backward classes and his picture. A pamphlet released with the stamp said, 'Ayyankali was a great man who worked untiringly to bring his community into the mainstream of society.'

—*Translated by T.C. Narayan*

Poikayil Sreekumara Guru— A Historical Record (Excerpts)*

K.T. Rejikumar

From Lineage Rituals into the Churchyard

He started working on the farm and in the fields from about the age of twelve. He cleared mud to make ridges, dug canals, sowed, worked the waterwheel, and helped those who guarded the fields prepare for harvest. Those days he used to attend the Mar Thoma assemblies with his family. As the Sankaramangalam family was a prominent member of the Mar Thoma sect their retainers were also admitted into the sect. Although they were members of the Christian community these retainers were not admitted into the church. Those in the Iraviperoor and Vellikkara areas were admitted into the Kumbanad assembly. The upper castes in the region did not wish to see these Christians as anything but their retainers. These retainer communities continued to follow their old rituals and practices.

One day there happened to be a death in Iraviperoor Vellikkara. A man aged nearly fifty, Kuthoran, was found dead under a tree by some persons returning home after work. This information was conveyed to the Sankaramangalam landlords the same night and the instruction was 'Bury him in the morning'. It was generally believed that the dead man was killed by an evil spirit and in the morning he was buried near his hovel. On the sixteenth day, the body was taken to a hilltop and buried under a paala tree, where all the dead folks were interred. There on Onam day or Changranthi day at the beginning of specified months toddy and coconuts were left as offerings to the dead. Whenever the landlord reprimanded them or there was no food or they felt the pain of

---

* Original title *Poikayil Sreekumara Guru—Charittrarekhayil.*

grief, the local folks used to gather at that spot and cry to their hearts' content. After he became a Christian and joined the Mar Thoma sect, Kumaran began to read the Bible and seek to understand its inner meaning. This knowledge of the Bible helped him to receive recognition as a keen student of the Bible and move into the role of an adviser. Kumaran was seventeen when he was initiated into the Mar Thoma sect. The bishop of Ayiloor inducted him. After entry into the assembly one had to have a Christian name. The father asked Kumaran what name he wished to have. 'Lohannan' was the reply. They knew what he meant was 'Yohannan' which meant 'cleansed of sin by Jehovah'. Kumar became an active member of the assembly towards the close of 1897.

Yohannan began to address the assembly. He was very impressive with his clear voice and his speech blended with songs. He became an itinerant speaker and preacher. He travelled around to various places and spoke at street corners, cattle markets, and wherever people gathered. Those who heard him speak wished to hear him again. That was a time when twelve powerful speakers were in the arena. Eminent among them were Punjamannil Mammen Upadeshi, Kozhencheri Kurunthottathil Daniel Munshi, Itayaranmula Muthon Paakkal Kochukunjupadeshi, Sadhu Kochukunjupadeshi, K.V. Simon, and others, and they rose because they conducted 'awakening' assemblies. Poikayil Yohannan was prominent among them.

At the age of twenty-two, Yohannan married Maria in 1901 at the Mar Thoma Church. She was from the Pulaya community and was the daughter of Poovathur Melathethil Kuthadi of Vellangur. Over the next few years they had four children.

Around this time, at the Maramon Convention held on the sandy banks of Pamba river in Kozhencheri, it was Yohannan who spoke. The theme was 'God's children and the devil's children'. Who are God's children? He quoted from the Bible the comparison of the rich man entering Heaven like a camel squeezing through the eye of a needle. Is it a matter of credit that members of God's assembly should refer to a large section of the community as the untouchables, the lowly, and the unworthy? He sang:

In a home fashioned by your hands
The saviour will not seek abode
Heaven is His throne
And the earth His footstool.
Think all of you now

The Day of Judgement is nigh
All of you begin to pray.

If God is to reside in one's heart that heart has to be free of sin. When, on the Day of Judgement, He comes galloping through the skies on his white steed is there anybody who is sure he or she will rise to the drumbeat? They realized that these questions were really intended to question the baseless beliefs and practices of Syrian Christians.

There are many right here
Who squander the light
No home, no country, nothing do they have
Not many to keep them company
They hide beliefs within
Uttering empty boasts they live
Let us see Him as our Guide
Let us follow our Saviour.

Using the content of the Bible as the basis his speech and song he questioned the discrimination that existed within the Mar Thoma Church against those from the lower caste.

Church after church appears in line
But no difference do I see
A church for the father, a church for the son
Yet another church for the family
A church for the lord, a church for the slave
A separate church here and another one there
A church to the south, another to the north
A church to the east, another to the west
A church for the Pulaya, another for the Pariah
A separate church for the fisher folk
Those who declare to the beat of the drums
Those who seek ways to make life safe
And despite all that they try to do
Safety's something that's not so sure.
Complaint boxes are ever so full
Complainants are now driven to drink
Drinking seems to be the only way
And the time for this has come, I say.
My mother fed me milk, this I didn't know
Smeared oil on me that I didn't know
My mother wept at the working place
She wept at the gate where the wages were paid

I've bathed in Christ's blood
I am no longer defiled
If a Pulaya I am now called
No more will I attend that church
If a Pariah I am now called
No more will I attend that church
Road after road in front of us we see
The wearers of silk just have to join us here
Our witnesses have taken leave of us
Having received their wages of slaps and blows
Speakers of truth were cut and sliced
Their cries are heard around this land
It's imperative that those tears are wiped
The time for this too has come, I say.
Church after church ....

Yohannan openly questioned the truth of the beliefs that the low-caste members would enjoy comforts when they reached Heaven while others enjoyed comforts on earth as well and that charity and faith in the Bible would help gain entry into Heaven. He said this was propagated by Satan. Since the Apostolic Society ceased to exist the Bible seemed to be the only route to salvation. But then did the Bible route guarantee salvation?

Those trapped by the written word
Should let go of it
For the written word is not for the likes of us.

The Bible laid down the new code through four Gospels and twenty-seven Epistles. The Epistles addressed to twenty-seven sections of the community. The question is 'Have you received any epistle?' Yohannan led the low-caste members out of the Maramon Convention and to Iraviperoor in a procession. Later those who boycotted the Maramon Convention met in Kunnanthanam to debate the subject 'Who set up the Assembly on Earth?' Human history begins with Adam. Speeches based on the Bible caused a stir among the believers. They sang at this meeting:

Stricken with grief we are
Stricken with grief we are
Regret we have to speak out
In the Old Book God created Adam
And placed him in the Garden of Eden
All day and night happily did he live

When evil entered through Eve
Then Adam sinned
Expelled he was by God
Sins spread the world over
And Noah was summoned by Him
And to this tenth patriarch
God revealed his plan
Eight souls chosen by God
Saved themselves in the Ark
The sinners left behind
Drowned in the great deluge
God's call and His voices
Like God's will from time to time
Summoned patriarchs one by one.
He called Abraham
Who heard His voices till they died.
Then Jesus appeared
Jesus walked this earth
Jesus chose twelve men
Like His father
He gave them assurance
Then He died on the cross
He rose again and reappeared
Gave orders and went to Heaven.
For the promised Holy Spirit
The Apostles did wait
No sooner did the Holy Spirit descend
Than three thousand lives were saved Thessaloni, Colossi,Philibin
Other assemblies appeared
Became the Christian foundation
An assembly appears now
But God's voice is not heard.

The assembly that the apostles established on Earth ceased to exist. Thereafter, God's presence was not felt on Earth. It has been a period of darkness from then till now. Today's assemblies are not extensions of those set up by the apostles. This is to say that there is none who secured safety as a result of apostolic activities. The one who offered safety to His followers was Jesus. Poikayil Yohannan's Redemption Conference became a matter of debate in Mar Thoma circles. The Mar Thoma bishop instituted an enquiry to go into the view that Yohannan's teachings were unacceptable to the Mar Thoma Church; that they were against the principles of the Church and his boycott of the Maramon

Convention. The enquiry commission was chaired by one of the most eminent priests, Father Thengumannil Kochuvarkey.

Father Kochuvarkey and his four co-members arrived in Kunnanthanam, the venue of Yohannan's meeting that was in progress. A long discussion followed at the end of which the committee came out unable to accept Yohannan's firm stance. Father Kochuvarkey said to the others on their way back, 'This is not possible. He seems to say he is greater than Jesus Christ. Jesus Christ is the lord of the Jews, my God on earth. He cannot be a member of our church or be allowed to speak at our gatherings.' Therafter, Yohannan was not permitted to speak at Mar Thoma events.

Following the death of a low-caste member of the Pullarikkat Mar Thoma Church the priest permitted the family to inter the body in the local cemetery. By that evening the upper-caste members made an issue of this and threatened the members of the dead man's family. They dug up the body and threw it outside the cemetery. Yohannan arrived on the scene and consoled the family. The body was buried again near his hut.

Later there was a conference in Katapra where the theme was the construction of a 'convention city'. Syrian Christians took part in this meeting in which Yohannan sang this song pregnant with meaning:

The fathers of Israel Abraham, Isaac, and Jacob
Gave their parents space to rest
Father Abraham and mother Sarah rest there.
There also lie safe, untouched
The bones of Joseph, son of Jacob.
And the fathers of Israel rest there
Secured by walls and forts
Called the city of their fathers' tombs
Where do our fathers and their fathers lie?
In jungles, mountain canals, rivers,
On hilltops, beaten and thrown,
Torn apart by wild animals,
Skulls and bones scattered around the land,
Many dumped in wells and covered with mud,
Thrown alive in canals,
They rise everywhere
To the cries in those dying days.
Corpses saved somehow must keep safe,
Must have resting places known,
The resting places of some children
Are already decided

And are known to the All Powerful One.
God has already decided on the meeting place and town for the believers.

Those who listened to Poikayil Yohannan's speeches were moved to tears and to deep thought.

—*Translated by T.C. Narayan*

Pampadi John Joseph (Excerpts)

T.H.P. Chentharasseri

Armed with the information that his community was essentially that of Adi Cheramar who were later downgraded as Pulayar, John Joseph proceeded to Kottayam. He held discussions with the elders who led his community and who loved it. They reached certain conclusions based on these discussions. They, who were called Pulayar, were originally Adi Cheramar. Therefore, they should henceforth be known only by their original name. The caste name Pulayan should be discarded. On the basis of this decision, in 1921, an organization by the name the Travancore Cheramar Maha Jana Sabha was formed. Both Hindus and Christians became members of this organization. There was an air of excitement all around. Many of the young men and women working for the Sadhu Jana Paripalana Sangham were drawn to the new organization. M.I. Kunjappi, Sethu, M.T. Ashirwadam Asan (Thiruvalla), P.J. Joseph, P.O. Mathu (Kurichi), T.C. Kuttan (Tiruvarppu), Joshua Mistri (Alappuzha), and others were elected to the Executive Committee and John Joseph was elected as the General Secretary.

The first General Body meeting of the Sabha was held on 14 Jan 1921 at Podippara near Thiruvalla. Even Sadhu Jana Paripalana Sangham leaders like Vellikkara Chothi participated in the meeting. John presented his new concept before the meeting eloquently and skilfully. Following that, he presented his case at many other places. People who heard him were enthralled. The notions that they maintained till then had bitten the dust. The speaker's elegant way of dressing, powerful demeanour and oratory skills caught the attention of everyone present. There was no need to distrust an educated man. More than that, he was presenting his case with facts and figures, logically and quoting from documents. By the time he finished, he had followers without any great effort. Yet, he had to face a certain amount of opposition unsubstantiated by ideas or historical facts.

Some opposed the idea of starting a new organization under the name of a community. In the premises of the Prakthyaksha Raksha Daiva Sabha (PRDS) headquarters at Iraviperoor, a meeting of the supporters of Cheramar was convened. Poikayil Yohannan, the founder of PRDS, was also present. In his speech, he condemned the idea of creating an organization segregating the Cheramar. He opposed the idea of differentiation. He made it a point to sing a melodious song in every meeting of the PRDS depicting this opposition:

If the Pulayar all become Cheramar
will pollution vanish for the Pulayar?
Will any change occur ever?
If the Parayar all become Sambavar
Will pollution vanish for the Parayar?
Will things end well ever?

The Riddle of the Aikkara Landlord

John Joseph carried on with his work confronting all opposition. He came to know that a family belonging to the lineage of the last feudal landlord of the Chera dynasty was living in Aikkara in Kunnathunadu and that the last Aikkara landlord had exchanged much correspondence with the Travancore kings. Enquiries in Kodungalloor revealed that Aikkara Kurup was a follower of Christianity and that his new name was John (Yohannan).

John Joseph decided to organize a big meeting with the participation of the Aikkara landlord, who was the last link to the prosperous days of the Cheramar. It was thus that on 9 March 1923, presided over by the great poet Ulloor S. Parameswara Iyer, a mega conference of the Cheramar was organized in Thiruvananthapuram. People flocked to get a glimpse of the last Chera King of Cheranadu. Aikkara landlord was seated on a podium in the middle of a sea of people. John Joseph delivered a speech delineating the history of the Cheramar. And, declared Aikkara landlord as their King.

News spread that the Maharajah Sree Moolam Thirunal was enraged by the mega conference of the Cheramar and the speech by John Joseph. He summoned John Joseph and questioned him. John Joseph elucidated the facts available to him, but did not reveal the sources. He merely explained that this was knowledge handed down traditionally.

'Whatever Mr Joseph said is right. But, it is not yet time for the Cheramar to inherit the kingdom. They will get it when the time is ripe.' Saying this, the Maharajah confabulated with the Chief Secretary. Later events made it clear that they were discussing how to put Joseph down. What John Joseph was theorizing was overtly harmless but covertly disastrous. There was no offence he could be charged with. He was just laying historical facts on the table. It was decided 'not to kill the snake, but to crush its hood.'

John Joseph was dismissed with a small pouch of cash prize money for the speech and simply could not comprehend what it meant. The pouch had the stamp of the kingdom. Since there was no permission to walk along the main roads, he took the side streets. When he reached Vellayambalam, two horsemen confronted him and snatched the pouch. They punched him up brutally and warned him, 'You expect cash for talking nonsense? Don't utter a word to anyone about this.' He realized then that this was the real reward he got for uttering the truth! No wonder, the slogan of the upper castes was, 'Truth Prevails!'

There was an eyewitness to this. A young man named Panthukalam Karutha Yakoob, who was cutting firewood from a tree nearby who later became a follower of the PRDS. Those days, whichever was the organization, all Dalits respected the leaders. I learnt of this incident later from that very same eyewitness who was an old man by then. I met him while searching for the house that John Joseph built near the premises of the Kowdiar Palace.

Organizational Work

A meeting was organized at Nemom for publicizing the Cheramar Maha Sabha. In those days, such meetings were presided over by those who had some influence. Thus, M. Govindan, a judge, presided over the Nemom meeting. John Joseph eloquently described the history of the Cheramar with supporting records. But, in his concluding speech, the Presiding Judge thought it fit to run down his arguments. He began thus. 'If the uncle rode an elephant, will the nephew develop calluses on his bottom?' John Joseph did not like this even though it came from the Judge. He replied with a double entendre.

'Govindan said this because he is a Judge.'

The concluding speech was concluded then and there as if the Judge had swallowed his own words.

After John Joseph became a member of the Sree Moolam Praja

Samiti (Member of the Legislative Council), he was given a reception at Thiruvalla which is one of the rare places where the notion that Cheramar/Pulayar all belong to the same fraternity still exists. Kottayam and Changanassery also follow that tradition.

Welcoming the first MLC of the Cheramar community in a befitting manner is respect paid to that community itself. Holding the leader in high esteem means upholding that community itself.

The followers of John Joseph gave him a royal welcome at Thiruvalla on 5 January 1932. Thousands of people joined them at Vennikulam with decorations, flags, and festoons. The reception lasted four days. It was towards the end that his second book titled *The Tale of a Cheramar Child* was released.

The Memorandum Submitted to the British Parliament

Disgusted with the non-cooperative attitude of the upper-caste Christians, John Joseph prepared a Memorandum against it to be submitted to the British Parliament. It was pointed out therein that the upper-caste Christians were maintaining double standards towards the newly converted Christians and that they still followed caste differences and practised a discrimination policy towards the newly converted in weddings and religious ceremonies.

He had also argued that there were 1.2 million Cheramar in Kerala out of which 0.8 million were Hindus and 0.4 million Christians, and that for the Christians a separate parish might be assigned under him.

In 1935, this Memorandum was submitted to the Maharajah of Travancore to be forwarded to the British Parliament. Maharajah Bala Rama Varma was a minor then. His mother Setu Parvati Bai was the Regent. The dewan was Mr Austin. The Memorandum submitted to the Parliament needed the approval of the Maharajah. Before, countersigning it, the young Maharajah raised some questions.

To his query whether the Hindu Cheramar will not object if they learnt of the Memorandum, John Joseph replied thus: 'I believe that my people will not object.'

Thus, this Memorandum was presented to the British Parliament on 4 April 1935.

—*Translated by Ravi Shanker*

Kallara Sukumaran

Elikulam Jayakumar

The Commander of the Slaves

The Dalits are on the path of a great struggle even sixty-three years after independence—a struggle to restore the rights that are still denied. There are a few people who have passed on after playing the central role of a commander in this battlefield. Kallara Sukumaran can be counted as one of the foremost of such great persons who sacrificed their lives for the Dalit liberation struggle.

The Dalits are now shielded by many kinds of protective measures. Some of them have also been able to reach the top echelons. They also continue to be involved in the struggle for better opportunities. But, forgetfulness memory, the sorrowful yesteryears, and to imbibe the message that they hold will act as a hurdle to the total liberation of society. (*Underground Memories*—Kallara Sukumaran)

These observations of Sukumaran relate to the activities of some Dalit bureaucrats. It should not be forgotten that some have been able to reach higher levels due to the tireless efforts of Dalit leaders who came before them. The 'Aryan thought process' that encroaches on the mind when they reach positions of power alienate them from the common wage labourer. This creates a block in the smooth interactions between different Dalit masses. Social unity is the foundation of the total progress of the society. The so-called 'self-sufficient' bureaucratic class should also work for the progress of their community. With this in view, with great introspection and far-sightedness, Sukumaran had appealed to the bureaucratic and legislative sections of the community for their unequivocal support.

The sorrowful memories of the past were what prompted Sukumaran to become a revolutionary. He knew from his childhood how horrifying the cruelty and mental torment were that the prevailing caste feeling generated. He had learned from his mother how even a six-foot grave was denied to his dead grandmother and how she had to be sunk in the backwaters tied to a boulder. The seeds of hatred were planted in his infant mind. This was one of the reasons that prompted him to fight till his death the rotten system and assume the role of the commander in the Dalit liberation struggle.

Bearing Ammumma's body
Appuppan laid her on the boat gently.
The ones around burst into tears;
She, to whom, no one was 'the other'.

These lines are taken from Sukumaran's poem 'Soil'. The situation that his grandparents had to face was like a stab in the heart of any Dalit. There must have been many such incidents that they had to face. Sukumaran believed that knowing such stories of Dalit repression and drawing valuable lessons from them was essential for forging Dalit unity. The present Dalits who take upon themselves the sufferings of their forefathers would be the messengers of that unity. They would also be spokespersons for Dalit liberation. Unfortunately, it is difficult to meet likeminded people now. Sukumaran's style of functioning was an exception to this.

There should a strong base for the growth and personality development of a Dalit. It should be a strong social system that takes pride in one's indigenous culture and identity. Sukumaran was one of those great men who tried to rebuild that social structure that was destroyed by someone. One tends to accept his view that only those Dalits who imbibe the sufferings of their ancestors, who sacrificed their lives as slaves to their landlords, can think of social progress and that they should be firmly rooted in historical truths while their activities are oriented towards social transformation in the contemporary world.

Sukumaran had subjected the current events and their aftermaths to scrutiny from a Dalit perspective. Comprehensive studies and objective analyses had helped him to delineate the entry of the monstrous caste system. He was a true humanist over and above being a courageous activist who took upon himself the sorrows and sufferings of his community and struggled relentlessly for their liberation. He never misused the matchless status that he had acquired through self-developed personality traits or leadership qualities for himself or the members of his family. This is another feather in his cap. Sukumaran who desired only the well-being of his people and who became a guardian angel for the subaltern classes who lived an insecure life for centuries well deserves the title 'Commander of the Slaves'.

In the history of Kerala, there is no other leader after Ayyankali who loved the Dalits so much. He became a unique leader because of his approach to them, fluid articulation of new thoughts and ideas, and his responses to the unscientific nature of caste. The methodology of studying the problems of the people by living as one among them can be seen in all his organizational activities. His efforts are commendable in uniting the different castes or sub-castes among the Dalits after the formation of the Kerala State. Beginning with a small outfit like Peerumedu Harijan Federation and progressing further with the Indian Dalit Federation, Indian Labour Party and the Bahujan Samaj Party, Sukumaran, who was the central pillar of the liberation movement of the subaltern classes, was an excellent organizer, orator, and writer.

Sukumaran, who had discarded sentiments for reason and had approached issues with a critical eye, always questioned irrational faith. Basing himself on a free and practical approach and following his conscience, he forged ahead subjecting to scrutiny the traditional forms of worship that went unquestioned and the various attributes of castes and sub-castes formed allegedly for maintaining its sacred nature.

Sukumaran, who was essentially an atheist, always believed that the caste and untouchability feelings that the Hindu faith generated were an obstacle to the growth of the liberation of the subaltern classes and desired that there should come about the development of a casteless society along with intellectual renaissance among the Dalits and other communities.

How meaningless
and laughable
is the worship that men do
to a dumb god
who has his abode
in a palatial house!
(From 'The Fuel Shed')

Sukumaran had declared unequivocally that idol worship was meaningless and that God was Brahma and one could do worship only if one had the Brahma inside oneself. He said that the rest were all external manifestations and proclamations and that such an approach to God could never help the cause of the liberation of the subaltern classes.

There are two kinds of people in world history—the ruling classes and the slaves. In this divide, we observe the classification of the haves and have-nots. But, the case of the suppressed classes of India is different. Here, with the existence of castes, sub-castes, and religion, human beings have been divided into several tiers or ranks. The upper castes have been able to turn into a riddle the issue of the liberation of the oppressed people who have been rendered subservient to religious sentiments and rituals and denied the possibility of a brotherhood. Here, new equations for the liberation of the Dalits are a must. Sukumaran's effort was a harbinger of that.

The Dalits, who converted to Christianity in the hope of receiving consideration love and interaction, have also recognized the fact that they have not been able to achieve the social progress that they hoped for. The Dalit Christian struggle that Sukumaran led helped in making this a social issue and to attract public attention to it. It was a crucial moment in his endeavour to unite the Dalits beyond the confines of religious beliefs. What acts as a hurdle to the Dalits finding their path of liberation is the fact that they do not realize that it was because of the unholy influence wielded by the upper-caste society that they were alienated from priesthood or from the practice and interpretation of the holy books created for dominance and reign of their favourite religions and movements. But, Sukumaran entered the scene as the saviour of the Dalits by questioning the very authenticity of the holy books.

Sukumaran, who studied the Hindu puranas in a critical manner and subjected them to reinterpretation as a Dalit, was a critic with a touch of genius. He was not the one to surrender his rights and sense of revolution to God's grace and to repose under the shade of fear in the fortresses of blind religious faith.

He always tried to transform the Dalits into a people with proper organizational awareness, political approach, and modern outlook though they were now acting as the vassals of different political parties and as believers and spokespersons for sub-castes with no sense of unity or ability to contribute anything to the cultural development of their own. It was a great struggle for him to even get the basic truth recognized that equal participation and consideration is the fundamental right generated from one's civic sense and not dependent on any movement. Even now, it has not reached the level of actual practice.

It will not be erroneous to say that Sukumaran was an epic figure who showed the way for the cause of the liberation of the Dalits armed with a ray of light from the lamp lit by social reformers like Ayyankali, Ambedkar, or Mahatma Phule. The conservative classes, who are wary of changes, will always act as poison weeds blocking the total progress of the oppressed classes, however much the latter grow or transform themselves. The 'Commander of the Slaves', who questioned their authority, will always stand tall with his head held high for many epochs to come.

Kerala Harijan Federation

Empathy for his community was evident in Kallara Sukumaran from his childhood. When he realized that the mental anguish and pain of slavery because of caste and religious beliefs he began to research the Hindu religious books. He tried to question any faith that was irrational and to criticize it in a manner common people could understand by going deep into its varied levels of meaning. He realized that 'It needs explosives to shatter the stone portals to deaf ears in a momentous time as this when the arguments of the oppressors grow in relevance and prominence and the outpourings of the oppressed end up as cries in the wild', and was himself turning into shattering force on the social firmament.

Sukumaran struggled day and night to restore human rights to Dalits who toiled silently like animals without any consideration in the fields of their owners and lived at the pleasure, and condescension of landlords. He transformed them into a force to reckon with. He was inspired by the courageous Ayyankali who scored a historical victory leading the struggle of the agricultural labourers. He was influenced by the deep knowledge and tireless efforts of Dr Ambedkar who sculpted the Indian Constitution. Pampadi John Joseph, who worked among the Dalit Christians, Poikayil Yohannan, and Kandan Kumaran were his leading lights.

Sukumaran himself experienced oppression in the name of caste. Even in school he viewed with concern the practice of abusing someone by calling him by his caste name. The teachers would order the 'pulaya students' and the 'paraya students' to stand up. Or, abuse them by calling them 'freemeal students' or 'subsidized students', hurting Sukumaran's sentiments. From his perspective, the starving skeletal figures of the Dalit children and the prosperous children of the conservatives who ate and slept well were poles that never could meet. The duty of a real social activist was to reduce that gap. Hence, he had to act as an organizing force among the Dalits.

It was in this situation that Sukumaran thought of an organization for the Dalits that did not recognize any differences in terms of caste, sub-caste, creed, or class in which everyone toiled and no one exploited anyone. He carried on hoping for a cultural revolution and social transformation.

Thirteen people, including Sukumaran, assembled in the house of M.C. Gopalan Mullankuzhi in Glenmary Estate of Elappara village in the taluk of Peerumedu on 20 September 1957. After protracted discussions it was decided that an organization for the Dalits that stood beyond the pale of caste, religion, or political thought should be formed. Everyone agreed to Sukumaran's suggestion that the name of the organization should be 'Peerumedu Taluk Harijan Federation'. M.C. Gopalan (President), V.C. Viswanathan (Vice-President), P.C. Pappi (General Secretary), G. Jnanayya Vadhyar (Jt. Secretary), P.K. Kutti Vadhyar (Treasurer), Kallara Sukumaran (Office Secretary), and Job Kangani became the office bearers to start the organizational work. Sukumaran was just seventeen years old then.

In December 1957, they rented a room as their office, but had to vacate it within four months because they ran out of money to pay the rent. It took another after two years for work to start again. Sukumaran became the Organizing Secretary. But, during this period through the efforts of the organization the Rani Koil Harijan Colony and Peerumedu Welfare Hostel had become realities.

In those days, Sukumaran and his colleagues used to go from house to house for the organizational work. To attract listeners they used to organize shows of *Katha Prasangam* (a narrative performance with stories, songs, and music) before Sukumaran started speaking about the organization. He became the General Secretary in the third organizational election of the Federation. Many prominent persons welcomed this movement. In this meeting, it was decided to change the name to High Range Harijan Federation to encompass the entire district of Idukki.

It was in 1964 that Kallara Sukumaran organized a bitter struggle for Dalit rights. A hunger strike under his leadership was declared against the ABT lockout on 15 August. He continued to be the General Secretary from the age of twenty-two.

In 1969, it was decided to form a Coordination Committee bringing together seven small Dalit organizations and make Sukumaran its convener. A huge rally and a strike was organized by the Committee in April 1970 in front of the Peerumedu Taluk Office giving a memorandum signed by ten thousand people to the government to assert the legitimate rights of the Dalits.

In 1972, the Harijan and backward Christians Federation joined Sukumaran's organization. A two-day workshop was organized for the workers of the organization. Sukumaran had always tried to bring up good volunteers for the organization from the very beginning. In the annual December 1972 meeting, he became the Chairman and the name of the organization was changed to All Kerala Harijan Federation.

From 1973, the Federation's work began to spread to other parts of Kerala. In August, the Federation became a member of the Kerala

Harijan United Committee. Sukumaran became a member of the State Secretariat. A peaceful agitation was conducted by this Committee in front of the Secretariat in Thiruvananthapuram in January 1974. In the same year, the Idukki District Convention of the organization was held but even before that date its name had been changed to Kerala Harijan Federation (KHF).

Kerala Harijan Federation was a movement of the scheduled castes and tribes and backward class Christians without the limitations of party politics or sub-castes. Its policy statement is quite different from that of the other scheduled-caste organizations. Kerala Harijan Federation grew opposing both party politicians and the sub-caste organizations among Dalits.

KHF had very clear objectives to end:

- Suppression on the basis of castes.
- Economic dependence.
- Educational backwardness.
- Lack of political and organizational persuasive power.
- Social and cultural retardation.

The aim of KHF was to study and analyse these objectives comprehensively and work accordingly. The organization was meant to be a working medium to achieve these objectives. The title Federation was meant to signify a coming together. Sukumaran said that there was no harm if the Dalits found a spiritual guru from amongst themselves and worshipped him.

After it grew in strength and confidence the KHF tried to put its stamp on the election politics of Kerala in accordance with the ideas of Dr Ambedkar. In 1977, Sukumaran fought the elections to the Kerala Legislative Assembly as an Independent candidate and lost. He, who began as a Communist, had then joined the Congress party and it was after working in the party organizations that he realized that the liberation of Dalits was not possible through such movements. This eventually resulted in the formation of an independent political movement.

Kerala Harijan Federation had many mass organizations under it like the Harijan Youth Federation, Harijan Mahila Federation, and Bala Jana Sakhyam Voluntary Corps. Sukumaran knew that the organization would endure only if empathy towards one's own community was inculcated in children, youth, and women. He had also picked up some experience in the formation of trade unions.

Kerala Harijan Federation organized a big rally in front of the Secretariat in November 1977. The main demands were: 'Make suppression of the hairijans an act against the State; implement the Tribal Land Protection Act; establish free examination centres in every district; organize noon meals in every school.' A Rights Manifesto listing twenty-five demands was handed over to the Chief Minister of Kerala in the same month.

With this, Kallara Sukumaran's movement became the main organization fighting for the harijans of Kerala. Marches were continuously organized to district headquarters and the Secretariat. In 1979, bringing together the activities of different Dalit organizations in different states, the Confederation of the Depressed Classes Organization of India (CDO) was formed. Kallara Sukumaran became the General Secretary of the Confederation. Kallara Sukumaran was not someone to compromise with anyone and would go to any extent to accomplish what he set out to do.

Kerala Harijan Federation organized a mass hunger strike in July 1980 in front of the Kerala Secretariat demanding that special courts be set up to hear cases of atrocities against the harijans and that special police squads should be set up to look into such cases.

Till 1986, when KHF was renamed the Indian Dalit Federation, Sukumaran and his colleagues had to surmount many difficulties in the growth of the organization. They will always be remembered in history as those who created organizational awareness among a people who had no proper direction. The movement had gone ahead with the objective of liberating those who were disintegrating into many small and different organizations serving different political masters.

In the Malabar Region

Six northern districts of Kerala from Palakkad to Kasargode form the Malabar region. This was a part of the Madras Presidency before the formation of Kerala State. It was in 1974 that Kallara Sukumaran and his colleagues reached Kozhikode to explore the possibility expanding of the Federation's activities to the Malabar region. He met the Dalit workers there. The Malabar Regional Harijana Samajam was a big organization doing cultural work among the scheduled castes/tribes of Malabar.

The Harijana Samajam that functioned beyond party politics had organized several struggles to assert fundamental rights to temple entry, for using the public roads, to have tea in the tea shops along with the others and get a haircut in barber shops.

After discussions with Dalit intellectuals at various levels and also with

Sukumaran about the formation of a single fighting organization for the Dalits, the General Council of the Harijana Samajam assembled at the end of 1974 and decided to merge with the KHF. Thus, Sukumaran's selfless work resulted in making the scheduled castes and scheduled tribes a crucial organized force in the Malabar region.

The Indian Dalit Federation (IDF) is the only movement that is growing strong in the Malabar region for the protection of the rights of Dalits and tribals. The Federation runs numerous discussion forums and study centres. It was Sukumaran's powerful leadership that helped them achieve all this. Sukumaran, who joined in the joys and sorrows of his fellow Dalits in their little hutments and shanties, was an inspiration to the Dalit at large. There is a portrait of Sukumaran in every Dalit household in Malabar.

Many struggles that Sukumaran led began originated in the Malabar region. The Tribal March, the Anti-Caste Rally, the Protection of Rights Rally, etc. are some of the examples. It is known from many of the prominent activists in the region that they all had the opportunity of working with Sukumaran. It has been opined that the study classes that helped the Dalit youth in learning the meaning and essence of the word 'Dalit' had a great influence on the new generation. A committee has been formed in Kozhikode to publish Sukumaran's collected works and to discuss the various viewpoints posed in them. In short, Sukumaran has earned a permanent place in the minds of the Dalits of Malabar.

—*Translated by Ravi Shanker*

Adiyar Teacher

Taha Madayi

The children used to make fun of me calling me 'Adiyar teacher, Adiyar teacher' (low-caste teacher, low-caste teacher). Their guardians merely stood watching from a distance. I used to wonder why God gave me eyes and ears. I could not even go out to answer the call of nature. People used to pelt stones and make fun of me. Then there were the drunks. But there was one boy who was very fond of me. He was Balan and he used to sit beside me always.

What was the experience historical of being a pulaya? Did the dispensations of the leftist parties which grew parallel to the reawakening reform the worlds of the isolated people? Through the experience of

Sulochana, who was forced to resign her teaching job, sixty years ago unable to bear calls of 'Adiyar teacher, Adiyar teacher' the manner in which a suppressed community saw the modernity of Kerala is being subjected to a study.

March is generally known as the month of farewells. It is widely known that those who are retiring from government after 'laudable service' are accorded appropriate farewells by their colleagues and, in the case of teachers, joined by the PTA. In most of these programmes in which leaders of organizations, leading citizens, and others take part. A community feast, release of a souvenir, fine arts performance, gifts, and donations to the retiring person—but none of these happened in the case of Dakshayani, also called Sulochana teacher. Her life is a textbook which was shut before it could be opened and read. It would be true to say, 'There is blood around the edges.' However much she searched in her mind she could not find any memory of a pleasant conversation. Nobody ever addressed her as 'teacher'. The new generations around her did not even know the historic paths that this seventy-eight-year-old had traversed. She had never expected that she would at some stage share her memories with someone. For that reason alone a lot lay buried in the depths of her lapsed memory.

Sulochana teacher's replies carry two other voices. One of them, heard to more frequently, is Stephettan's. He is the person Sulochana would traditionally have married. Stephettan and Sulochana used to go to school together but later went their separate ways. Stephettan was good at history and was in Coorg for a long time. The other person was Gopalan, also known as George, Sulochana's husband, generally a quiet person. He had memories, was witness to Sulochana's path through life and her companion. They had no children.

SULOCHANA VALLYAMA*: Has anyone ever called you teacher?

SULOCHANA: Nobody knows now that I was a teacher. Wasn't all that long ago?

True that it was all long ago but father, mother ....

SULOCHANA: Father was Itacheri Vatyan. Mother was Thekkathi Prikkathi.

Do you remember joinng school?

SULOCHANA: I studied here in Basel Mission School.

* Vallyamma: elder aunt, a respectful form of address.

Auntie, do you remember the old teachers?

SULOCHANA: I remember only Daniel master.

STEPHEN: I'll tell you the names of the teachers. The first was Robert from Thalassery. In the second class it was Samuel who had a limp. The third was the headmaster, Devadas.

What subjects did you study in school?

STEPHEN: Modern Malayalam Lessons.

SULOCHANA: We learnt to write in the sand.

STEPHEN: Because the slate and pencil were not in use at that time.

Vallyamme, do you remember songs from those days?

SULOCHANA: I have not bothered to remember anything? What good does it do anyway?

STEPHEN: Not songs but verse. Songs mean sowing songs, country songs, and so on. It was verse that they taught in school. There was one about Naranath Bhranthan. I remember it, don't I, Sulochana?

SULOCHANA: I have forgotten all that. I don't recollect anything.

STEPHEN: I haven't forgotten even Sri Krishna Charitham Manipravalam. I like Poonthanam's verses. I can recite the verse on Naranath Bhranthan.

He is blessed
Who with his learning
Who with his courage
Establishes himself
He who like a dog
Depends on others
Is a mere ... (*Stops here and then ... I shall tell you something about living beings*)
Talk not of beauty
In a lifetime
It fades like a dream
Like a corpse that lost its soul
It is not what it seems
How real is life however pure
In life is this not a burial ground'

This is a song about death, about living beings.

Up to what class did you study in Basel Mission School?

SULOCHANA: Up to fourth standard.

Then?

SULOCHANA: I went to Kozhikode and joined a Harijan hostel—Puthiyara Harijan Hostel.

Kozhikode was far away those days, wasn't it? Who escorted you there?

SULOCHANA: Chatayan MLA. He was then our leader.

Where did you study in Kozhikode?

SULOCHANA: In Chalappuram High School.

How was life in the hostel?

SULOCHANA: There were many of us. They were all poor, and destitute. Everybody was fed. There was cholera then (*pointing towards Stephettan*). Ask him about cholera.

STEPHEN: I shall tell you.

SULOCHANA: Not the first cholera but the last one.

STEPHEN: The first cholera was when we were young.

GEORGE: Before that was the bad eye infection (conjunctivitis)

STEPHEN: Eye infection everywhere, oh my!

GEORGE: Water has to be boiled and one has to stand and look into it. There was no medicine. It was so painful. The eye was full of smoke. Couldn't see a thing.

SULOCHANA: After that came cholera. Many died—night and day, no caste, no community. People just died.

STEPHEN: What caste, what community for diseases? The people died and the corpses piled up on the mud banks of our canal—corpses with none to care for them.

Was there anyone to offer medical treatment?

SULOCHANA: There is no cure. There are bad infections and runny stomachs three times a day. One lived for three or four days and then died—cannot even cry.

STEPHEN: While cholera was raging there were good sardines available on the beach but there was no one to buy them.

How long did you stay in the Harijan Hostel?

SULOCHANA: I studied up to ninth class in Palappuram High School. Then I came home and did different kinds of work. While doing this, Reggie master sent an application for me to Beypore. 'You must study and get a job' he said. In those days there was a training school in Beypore that taught many handicrafts. My application was accepted. Reggie master himself took me there to get me admitted. He was a good man. I joined a coir training course. There were people who twisted coir fibre to make rope. It was expected that learning this scientifically would provide a good future.

How long did you train there?

SULOCHANA: For two years and then I got a Coir Teacher's certificate. I returned home. For a while I did nothing. Then I had some people I knew in Payyanur Block with whom I got in touch. They brought me some yarn and a charka. Those days in Madayi Moola the caste system was very strong. Harijans could not go anywhere near the station. We live and move in fear. I was good at the charka. I was the first girl in these parts to scientifically learn weaving. I have seen pictures of Gandhiji using the charka. I could not make a living out of the charka. Nobody would buy the yarn touched by a harijan. My training on the charka was futile.

STEPHEN: I also did weaving for a year. I had to make light yarn out of heavy yarn and the finished yarn would be given to the khadi store. Sulochana did the same thing. When Sulochana worked on the charka she came to know many persons in the Block. Let her tell us the rest.

SULOCHANA: There were some good nurses in the Block. They registered a coir company in Mattool and appointed me as a teacher. The company then moved to Payyanur and I went there as teacher. There was a major problem as I was from the Pulaya community. At that time I was appointed Coir Teacher in Karadukka School in Kasargode district. I considered it a great boon but all my training was a waste.

What happened?

SULOCHANA: It was all about caste—something which I cannot even imagine today. I go to sign my attendance the headmaster would open the register and move far away. When I had signed, the register would be wiped with paper or a cloth before the headmaster touched it. It hurt so much. I would weep out of everybody's sight. Not that it mattered if anybody did see me cry for pulaya tears did not have any value. One had to just suffer.

Were there not other Pulayas in the school?

SULOCHANA: No, only nairs. Children were not allowed to do handicrafts. The headmaster had ordered that students were not to be touched or to be seated beside me. I taught the children Malayalam. The masters were nairs. There was a teacher from Thalassery who was thiyya. She liked me very much. She was not trained like I was.

So the masters were the problem, were they?

SULOCHANA: Nairs, Brahmins and nambiars were the masters. So were the students. The children used to make fun of me calling me 'Adiyar teacher, Adiyar teacher'. Their guardians merely stood watching from a distance. I used to wonder why God gave me eyes and ears. I could not even go out to answer the call of nature. People used to pelt stones and make fun of me. Then there were the drunks. But there was one boy who was very fond of me. He was Balan and he always sat by my side.

Did you not complain to anyone about the children calling you 'Adiyar teacher'?

SULOCHANA: That would have been of no use. When this contempt got worse I wrote to the DO that I did not wish to work in the school. When I was transferred elsewhere I did not go. I asked the DO, 'If I cannot even sit outside what use is a school? What use is education?' There was no reply.

STEPHEN: Adiyar, pulayas—in those days they had no status, no honour. Saying you were educated meant nothing. Isn't this a play scripted by Sankaracharya earlier? But who defeated Sankaracharya? An accursed low caste. A low-caste fool! He blocked Sankaracharya's path and declared, 'Your blood and mine are the same.' Everything went topsy-turvy when the Aryans reigned. I have studied history. History is not what the masters teach. You want to know about Sulochana and I don't wish to divert your attention.

SULOCHANA: When I was teaching in Karadukka real Adiyars used to visit me. They never washed or bathed. I used to give them soap and ask them to come back bathed and with clothes washed. They would laugh. Will a bath change caste? Why does everybody call a teacher 'Adiyar?' How did I manage those six months?

Then you switched to Christianity?

SULOCHANA: It was Father Francis who admitted us into Basel Mission—many years ago.

Did you join Christianity to escape from this caste problem and the contempt?

SULOCHANA: When the Basel Mission came, Pulayas converted to Christianty in large numbers. We hung on to the pulaya community but gradually we got isolated. Then we also converted. Now this area is full of Christians and Muslims. There are few Pulayas.

Did you get any benefit by becoming Christians?

SULOCHANA: We received none. It was the Roman Catholics who got them. We joined Basel Mission because of caste problems.

How did you feel when you switched to Christian faith?

GEORGE: We felt nothing. All humans are the same.

Now that you have changed your faith are you looking down on your old caste?

SULOCHANA: No. As Pulayas we were not liked by many people. After we changed our faith there has been some change in this. People began to come to our homes. The isolation ended.

STEPHEN: I converted in my younger years. Do you know there are sub-castes amongst Pulayas also?

SULOCHANA: Not castes but kinship.

STEPHEN: Family problems but really not serious. Long ago there were high-class families and low-class ones among Pulayas. Those days if you went to a wedding the first question you would be asked would be the family you were from. Thaliyil folks, Cheran folks, kozhi folks—these would all be mentioned and laughed at by the high class families. This used to be a big headache among pulayas in Kannur district. The change happened when there was a marriage in Vilakriyan family in Mattul desham. All pulaya families were invited to the ceremony. Times have changed. It was a person by name Pallan Choyi who did away with this division in the community.

What was the menu for wedding feasts in those days?

STEPHEN: Mainly rice. There would be ray, shark and other fish. Cucumber curry too but ray and shark were the main items. Ray was the equivalent of today's chicken.

SULOCHANA: Weddings were at night in petromax light.

After giving up the Karadukka teacher's job what did you do?

SULOCHANA: I did sundry jobs. Carrying stones, moving sand. As a teacher my salary was forty five rupees. When I worked part-time in Payyanur I got thirty rupees. It was adequate those days but the harassment was terrible.

STEPHEN: In the schools the masters taught that all humans are the same but what we saw was the opposite. Let me narrate an experience. In 1949, I was working in Pazhayangadi with Abdul Rahman Sait. He was also known as Babu Sait. He was a congressman, a freedom fighter, a humanist, Even the Brahmins rose when they saw him. In summer his well dried up. My job was to carry water in vessels from the Matayappalli well to his house. After finishing my work I was planting a banana tree within a fence near the tombs of the senior Muslim religious leader. At that time a lady, a fat lady, went that way to the shop to buy rice. She was a pulaya and the shop-owner was a thiyya. She had a fish-basket which only pulayas carried. The thiyya pulled off the mundu she was wearing. She was not wearing much else and she stood there naked not knowing whether to stay or run. I witnessed this through the fence. I ran up, gave her my mundu to hide her shame. People used to pull off the pulaya women's mundus whenever they could, that was how things were in those days.

SULOCHANA: Pulayas were not allowed to wear white clothes. They did not wear blouses but a short, thin, loosely woven towel was tied round the shoulders. Even that was not spared.

Was it after you joined Basel Mission that things changed?

SULOCHANA: By changing our faith we had peace of mind. We did not desire any monetary benefits. As I had resigned my teacher's job I got nothing from that either.

STEPHEN: When I had finished my yearly work near home I would go to Coorg. That was how poor we were. When I was once returning from Coorg what I saw was the trained teacher, Sulochana, doing menial work. She said she had enough of being called 'Adiyar teacher' and did not want a teacher's job any more. I know history but I have a disappointment.

What is that?

STEPHEN: I did not study English. There was no English teacher in my school.

SULOCHANA: My disappointment is that I have no children.

Have you faith in politics?

SULOCHANA: When I was studying in Kozhikode Balika Sadan Kelappaji and Kuttimalu Amma would come there. I have received many prizes from Kelappaji.

Have you spoken with Kelappaji?

SULOCHANA: Umm. He was a great man, a loving man. Kuttimalu Amma was the same. All human beings were the same to Kelappaji. When I was in the hostel I did not feel I was a harijan.

What are your politics?

I grew up hearing about Congress. I had not even heard of Communist party. Congressmen used to visit us in the hostel. So I used to have faith in Congress. Now I have no faith in any party. I am old now and I know that I can only live if I work.

You said that after you left your teaching job you took up menial jobs. What was the job market like?

SULOCHANA: For some time I worked in the China Clay Factory in Matayippara. We were the only two Christians employed there—myself and Leelamma. Sandy Aaron was the Manager. Sunny Mooppar was the supervisor. There was once a huge landslide. I was stuck neck-deep in mud, barely escaped death, barely stayed alive. Two persons died. I was sent to hospital. Thereafter I did not go back to quarrying china clay.

Do your old acquaintances visit you?

Reggie Master still lives in Pilathara. He is ninety years old and visited me recently. He is weak. There are others who worked with me and who are still alive. Many are dead. We are old and are forgetful. We have forgotten the pain inflicted on us by people. However, we are unable to forget Kelappaji's laughter.

This conversation should have been complete with its transfer from microtape to print. The avenues that words open up are many. Even with extreme modernization, increased pay scales, revised employment, and compensation systems, caste and community seek entry into the Kerala psyche lurking behind the dark mask of discrimination. In the midst of the contradictions like apolitical Dalit chauvinism, politicized savarnatha, equidistant communal interests, the problems of a marginalized people continue unresolved. Sixty years ago a Pulaya lady resigned her job unable to bear the pain of humiliation at being called 'Adiyar teacher' and of harassment by the general society. Later struggles gave Kerala a new face. But will this new face of political renewal be like a cosmetic make-up which washes away in the slightest wetness? Is the red of Kerala turning into another apolitical compromise?

History: Dakshayani. Born in 1928, was driven by communal harassment to join Basel Mission and take on the name 'Sulochana'. A teacher discarded forever the blanket of her caste and religion became her support.

The present: On the night of 31 December 2005 some antisocial elements set on fire the autorickshaw driven by the Dalit woman 'Chitralekha' who lived on Edat island in Payyannur. Chitralekha is a communist and the complaint is that these elements called her 'Pulachi'.

Conclusion: In the cycle of history black humour repeats itself. Instead of caste some seek refuge under the cover of religion and others in Communism. Where will the Malayalis with their half-burnt bodies flee when these refuges also catch fire?

—*Translated by T.C. Narayan*

CRITICAL INTERVENTIONS

The mainstream tradition of literary criticism in India was primarily text-centred hermeneutics, paying close attention to the infinite potential and possibilities of words, expressions, and their meanings to the exclusion of other ways of making sense of the text. The quality of a work of art was adjudged by inflexible aesthetic standards, based on concepts like *rasa*, *dhwani*, and *alankara*, a system which was constructed on the triad of *kavi* (poet), *kavyam* (poem), and *sahrudaya* (sensibility achieved through learning in poetics). The approach is idealistic because it consists of the idea of an archetypal good and that everything that follows is merely a copy. The hermeneutics thus acquired the function of judging the good from the bad, depending on the degree of correspondence between the copy and the archetype.

In contrast to this idealistic approach, the charvaka[*] philosophy projects a materialistic approach, which contested the *varna*/spiritualistic discourse, and thereby projects an alternate aesthetics. This aesthetics relates enjoyment to the tensions of worldly existence. The following quote bears testimony to it:

Fire is hot, water cold,
Refreshingly cool is the breeze of morning;
By whom came this variety?
They were born of their own nature.[†]

There were many other thought systems that contested the Brahminical one, including Buddhism and Jainism. But, as later history shows, these other traditions were brutally silenced.

---

[*] A rationalist philosophy of ancient India, around 600 BC. Named after Charvaka, the author of the Brahaspathy sutras. Classified along with Buddhism and Jainism as 'faithless system'. Also known as Lokayatha, it does not recognize any knowledge which is not based on sensory perceptions and physical verification. Considered as atheistic, materialistic, and hedonistic thought it defends every citizen's right to equality, justice, and liberty.

[†] From Madhava Acharya's *Sarva Darshana Samagraha* (Trans. E.B. Pavell and A.K. Gough, Kegan Paul, Trench and Turbner, London, 1914).

One way of looking at Dalit critical writing is to see it as a continuation of a silenced tradition's resistance. It draws its energy and sustenance not from the scriptural elite/*savarna* aesthetics but unconsciously from other traditions. This critical paradigm evolved through the speeches and conversations of Narayana Guru, Ayyankali, Poikayil Appachan, Pandit K.P. Karuppan, and others.

A significant feature of the Dalit discourse of Kerala is that due to the nature of the public sphere and the publishing industry of the State, its critical writing quantitatively surpasses its creative expressions. For a very long time, prior to the proliferation of electronic media, Kerala's public sphere was governed by issues generated by its newspapers and periodicals, which outstrip other Indian languages in sheer volume and which privilege critical writing over literary works. But this does not mean that the journey of caste-based issues to the mainstream periodicals was smooth. On the contrary, these issues had been sidelined and silenced in the mainstream press before they started appearing in Dalit-run periodicals like *Pithrubhumi, Soochakam,* and *Saindavamozhi*. In short, the entry of Dalit issues into the periodicals was ultimately necessitated by Dalit self-assertion that could no longer be overlooked.

Many easily discernable trends are available in Dalit critical writing: pro-Ambedkarite, pro-Buddhist, pro- and anti-Marxist neo-Marxist, pro-feminist, pro-liberal, etc. At times, the writers even adopt an eclectic stance, drawing from different, and often conflicting, sources. But all share, under the veneer of heterogeneity and plurality, a tendency toward unearthing the politics of caste in its manifold manifestations in history, society, literature, and cultural practices. The styles of presentation are as diverse as the ways the writers encounter and negotiate their world and its issues.

The selections in this section represent an interconnectedness between the past and the present, a bridge across the years from Kaviyoor Murali to Pradeepan Pampirikunnu and his contemporaries. They reflect a period of tumult, which changed the direction of critical writings in Kerala, by opening wide the door to so far undiscussed topics. Each one of these essays, in their own ways are fraught with political ramifications and they employ varied and individual strategies of negotiations. These strong voices of dissent are attempts in the direction of the making of a counter culture which has been either weak or simply inconsistent. These writings, by developing an alternative Dalit epistemology also mark a break from brahminical representations in the critical interventions of Kerala.

The Uncompromising Dalit Language*

Kaviyoor Murali

There were three kinds of dialects in the category of the native (desi): (1) the tribal dialects made use of in the settlements; (2) a common dialect of Trāviḍam developed from the blending with the tribal dialects (or the refined Prakrit); and (3) Thravidam that was polished to a fine degree or Tamil, the language of literature, in the same period.

It is said that there are 700 languages in India. Another view pegs this number at 1652. All these belong to six linguistic families, namely, the Negroid, Austro-Asiatic, Sino-Tibetan, Dravidian, Indo-Aryan, and others. Of these the only language that has no relation to any other language outside India is the Dravidian. And, of the linguistic families, Dravidian is placed second in the extent of its spread. Malayalam is the youngest language born into this family. The considered view is that modern Malayalam is not more than a thousand years old.

Before Malayalam changed into this state, Tamil and Trāviḍam were the spoken languages here. Tamil was subdivided into Pandi-Tamil and Malanattu-Tamil. Linguists have analysed why two kinds of Tamil were in existence and found that it was caused by permeation from outside. This is true only to a certain point. The fact is that there were internal reasons for this apart from permeation which was not limited to Cheranadu alone. So, the main causes must come from within. Let us examine them. Tamil was born from Thuravida language. Thuravidam is an open space. It means a space where anyone can move about freely. The visitors came mainly from the west. And, it was in the west-open Thuravidams that pepper, that rare commodity unavailable elsewere, was available. Therefore, in order to be of more convenient use to majority of the people to the west of the Western Ghats, a kind of liberalization has occurred in the language. The Namboodiris laid their hands on the language as a sequel to this. To the east of the Western Ghats, no such liberalization was necessary.

---

* Original title *Sandhi Cheyyatha Dalit Bhasha*.

The Tamil that the ancient Dalit people (they were not 'Dalits' then) of the Cheramandalam region developed was beautiful in all respects. It was this Tamil that the Vaishnavites mutilated. They made Tamils pick on Sanskrit words. They were having fun like children forcing dragonflies to clutch small pebbles. There are numerous instances of this great deception in Ceeramakavi's *Ramacaritam*. The following words will suffice to prove this point:

1. *Sanskrit words*
   Niśicarāthipati
   Pavanasambhavan
   Dadhimukhan
   Dasāmukhan
   Dāśarathi
   Gandhamādanan
   Bhayam
   Śatakoṭi
   Daāarathan

2. *Their Tamil form*
   Nicicarātipati
   Pavanatampavan
   Tetimukan
   Tecamukan
   Tācarati
   Kentamātanan
   Payam
   Catakoḍi
   Teyaratan

Kerala Panini views *Ramacaritam* as belonging to the Karimthamizh (unrefined Tamil) period. The period of *Ramacaritam* could be the 12th or 13th century CE as per Attoor, Ulloor, Ilamkulam, K.M. George, et al. We have seen the linguistic style of *Ramacaritam*. We have also considered that changes are occurring in language almost on a daily basis. A doubt could occur here—why is it that in the writings of Tolan alone (one or two centuries earlier) we find a somewhat purer version of Malayalam. Professor P.V. Krishnan Nair had actually raised this question in response to poet Ulloor's opinion. Quite a relevant point. But, neither the poet nor the professor paid attention to a very crucial factual truth. In Krishnan Nair's opinion the period of a text cannot be determined based on its language. His argument is that a poet in the 20th century can write a poem in the language of the 15th century. But, it is also true that a poet of the 20th century will not write in a language that could belong to the 22nd century. This means that the writer's eye tends to look to the past. If this be so, how could the language of *Attaprakaram*, belonging to 1000 CE or before, become synonymous with the language of the 13th century CE and after? Only Dalit linguistic researchers can answer this question. Dalit language has remained unchanged and will remain so in any era. No one has done any acrobatics with it. Dalit language is the language that has not compromised with any other language.

Ilamkulam points out numerous words that are found in *Attaprakaram* (believed to be authored by Tolan), and *Bhasha Kautileeyam* (believed to be of the 4th century CE). Ilamkulam is not aware that most of these words are currently in use among Dalits or that Dalits are quite familiar with them. It will be useful here to make a comparison of some similar Dalit words alongside the words from *Attaprakaram* and *Bhasha Kautileeyam*. Non-Dalits may be astonished to know that many of these words do not differ much in meaning even now.

Words from *Attaprakaram* and Similar Dalit Words

1. Words from *Attaprakaram*	2. Meaning	3. Dalit words	4. Meaning or usage
Akkaram	Syllable	Accaram	Syllable
Ayyam	Alms	Ayyam	(Inferior)
Āti	Beginning	Āti	Beginning
Iḷa	Give up	Iḷa	Give up
Kuṭi	Ancestral house	Kuṭi	Homestead
Teyam	Homeland	Teyam	Homeland
Naṭa	Gate	Naṭa	Gate
Niravu	Fullness	Neravu	Fullness
Nuruññu	Bit	Nuruññu	Bit
Pāññu	Wealth	Pāññu	Wealth
Paḻi	Discredit	Paḻi	Discredit
Poli	Gift	Poli	Gift
Poṭṭa	Hillock in a scab	Poṭṭa	Protuberance
Śanam	People	Cenam	People

Words from *Bhasha Kautiliyam* and Similar Dalit Words

1. *Bhāṣā Kauṭilīyam*	2. Meaning	3. Dalit words	4. Meaning or usage
Aḻivu	Expense Deterioration	Aḻivu	Weakness Deterioration
Aruti	Destruction	Aruti	End
Āṭṭuka	Abuse	Āṭṭuka	Abuse
Irikka	Seat	Irikka	Seat
Illam	House	Illam	House
Iraku	Wing	Irakalu	Wing

Uvar	Sea	Oru	Salty
Kakkam	Armpit	Kaccam	Armpit
Kaṇṭu	Carefully	Kaṇṭu	Carefully
Canaccu	Pregnant	Cana	Pregnancy
Cā	Death	Cā	Death
Karuvi	Tool	Karuvi	Tool
Kūra	Cloth	Kūra	Cloth
Cūlu	Pregnancy	Cūlu	Pregnancy
ñerippu	Fire	ñerippu	Fire
Tamappan	Father	Tamappan	Father
Tānam	Spot	Tānam	Spot
Tīma	Evil	Tīma	Bad

Among the words that find a place in this 1000-year-old text, non-Dalits are using only words like 'poli', 'potta', and 'illam' but *all* the words in this text are used with the same meaning by the Dalits. Our investigation as to why these words were abandoned by others while Dalits did not do so will lead us to another truth. The Paanans and Parayans who were managing language and literature were uprooted from society a very long time ago. The ones who were on the margins moved to the centre. They became the elite and the Dalits became the outcasts and made untouchables—reviled, abhorrent scum!

To those who were eliminated from society, proximity to the other languages was something they could not even dream about. On the other hand, the elite had the back-up of languages like Sanskrit and Konkani. It goes without saying that the elite tried to develop the language here under the shadow of Sanskrit. Since they were denied the opportunity of mingling with other languages, the people of the southern regions—specifically the people of Keralam—had to depend completely on the same language that they had long been practising. The pressure from this social situation was what prompted them not to discard Dalit language or Tramidapazha. Since the others had no such necessity, they pushed Tramidapazha to the rear.

Even though it was relegated to the background, Tramidapazha was not totally forgotten. The authors of that time were forced to use many Dalit words in their texts. In the 'aadal' done by '*kūttaccakkaiyans*' the jesters used only Dalit language. But, it was not possible for them to handle Tramidapazha in its original form. When they adopted the words of that language and used them, they came mixed with Sanskrit diction or the syllables themselves. As time passed, this amalgamation grew stronger. It is seen that out of the 173 words that Ilamkulam retrieved from *Āṭṭaprakāram*, 24 end in half-syllables. In three words, the syllable 'sa' has found its way in. It could be an error in copying the text. But, if the words are pronounced the way they are written, it will not go with the Dalit manner of speech. Dalits never pronounce the half-syllables clearly. Even now they speak like that, not to speak of that time! They manage correct pronunciation only when half-syllables are added to other words. They do not deliberately do it, but it just so happens somehow. They prefer to add the *anusuāram* to the end of the word. Given below are some examples of how Dalit words with half-syllables are pronounced.

1. kāl   kaalu
   kaal rūpa   kārūpa
2. mīn   mīnu
3. ter   teru
4. teḷ   teḷu
5. caṇ   caṇu

It is without knowledge of such intricacies that many write Dalit words with half-syllables and publish them.

What we see in *Āṭṭaprakāram* and *Bhāṣā Kauṭilīyam* are merely Sanskrit terms. In *Ramācaritam*, Sanskrit words take their form as they are. This indicates the development of Sanskrit as a textual language. The usage of the terms and words mentioned above help us in determining which text came first and which last in the case of *Āṭṭaprakāram, Bhāṣā Kautileeyam* and *Ramacaritam*. On this basis, we can conclude without any doubt that *Attaprakaram* came first. *Bhasha Kautileeyam* was written next and then *Ramacaritam*. *Āṭṭaprakāram* is the text closest to Tramidapazha and *Ramacaritam* is the text farthest from it. Whoever be the author of *Āṭṭaprakāram, Ramacaritam's* author is without doubt a Brahmin. In determining its period, as far as *Ramacaritam* is concerned, we can completely agree with the view of Hermann Gundert that 'it was written before the entry of the Sanskrit alphabetical system'. The views of K.M. George, Attoor, Ulloor, Ilamkulam, et al. that it was written in the 12th or 13th century CE may also be correct.

In all this, there is something that the Dalit linguistic researchers should comprehend. The Vedic religion with the Sanskrit language became a tool of social transformation and for 800–900 years has been butchering the Dalit language.

Dalit language has not disintegrated totally though it has been rendered lifeless. Many words in *Attaprakaram* (kuṭi, teyam, neravu, paṅṅi, pāṅṅu, poli, potta, pokku, muruka, cenam, etc.) and in *Kauṭilīyam* (irikka, iraku (irakalu), orutili, cutuvattam, kida, ila, kūra, cūluka, ñerippu, tangu, teema, teke, tembadijnaru, etc.) are still in vogue with the same meaning among the older Dalit's. The educated Dalits know the words, but do not comprehend their meaning. Many young people have demanded that I write* down the meanings of the words given at the end of this book. Not only the usage of the Dalit words but also the Dalit diction and the Dalit language are discernible even now in its entirety. This way of speech may become extinct after a generation.

—*Translated by Ravi Shanker*

Language and People†

K.K. Kochu

Language binds together social groups, otherwise divided on the basis of ethnicity and *varna*, to form a uniform mindset. Such social groups will be able to resist various discriminations and oppressions as a people. This particular aspect of language makes it into a discourse of sociopolitical transformation.

Language played a significant role in constructing a national community during the 17th and 18th centuries. Even in the face of economic inequality, social groups with shared customs and rituals, thoughts and feelings, and cultural traditions became united as a people through language. These peoples became a national community when they took a stand on the rights for their habitat. In Europe, those who spoke French became the people of France and those who spoke English became the people of England on the basis of acquiring a uniform mindset through language and establishing political sovereignty. Language, hence, becomes the foundation of the nation-state.

As far as Malayalam is concerned, it could neither become the basis of a nation-state, nor even unify diverse social groups into a people. An evaluation and assessment of the reasons for this may enable us to study contemporary issues concerning language development.

* Reference to his *Dalit Bhasha Dictionary* published much later.
† Original title *Bhashayum Janathayum*.

Professor C.L. Antony, who examined the developmental history of Malayalam language, identifies the political reasons behind language formation.* According to him, when Chentamizhu (classical Tamil), which had existed as *varamozhi*—written language—under Chera–Chola–Pandya, became the language of the rulers; *vamozhi*—oral language—which embodied native-regional discourses, through persistent transformations displaced Chentamizhu and established itself. Hence, Malayalam language, as the language historian Chelanatt Achutha Menon notes, owes more to tribal languages than to Tamil.† From such observations it can be gathered that it was the unified struggles against political domination by people who were divided, both in terms of tribe and community, that consolidated the Malayalam language.

But the later stages in the development of the Malayalam language was to a large extent influenced by values that came into vogue in about the 4th century AD, being collected from the Vedas, Upanishads, and Epic-chronicles, and became institutionalized through Sankaracharya during the 8th century. Soon enough, strict casteist ritualism and ideological construction stilted the growth of the Malayalam language. As a result, it was Brahminical values, rather than the values associated with native-regional resistances against Tamil domination that the language thereafter percolated into peoples' lives. Such dissemination through language paved the way not only for the reinforcement of casteism, but also the emergence of various caste groups that lay claim to distinctiveness akin to the Brahmins. The course of language evolution thereafter took a different turn as the *savarna* sections in such caste groups attempted to internalize Brahminical values.

Texts from *Vaishika Thanthram*, written in the 13th century, to the later *Chandrolsavam* reveal that the socio-political domination of Brahmins had begun to decline in those respective periods. As a result, wealth and knowledge that these traditionalists had reserved for themselves began to spread to other social groups as well. Thereafter, it was the cultural identity acquired by non-Brahmin communities, especially the Shudras, which facilitated the development of language. Even as these groups submitted to the values of the Vedas, Upanishads, and Epic-chronicles, in material life they existed as 'lower' castes. Hence, their cultural expressions were predetermined by Hindu-Brahminical ethos.

---

* 'Bhaasha Gadhyam' in *Sahitya Charithram Prasthananagalilude*, ed. K.C. George (Sahitya Pravarthaka Sahakarana Sangham, Kottayam, 1958).
† C. Achuta Menon, *Pradakshinam* (Current Books, 1968).

Niranamkrithikal is a product of such a conflation. Though Niranam poets' *Ramakatha*, a collection of native-regional oral languages, set the stage for the dawn of a new language, it could not repudiate Brahminical values. That is to say that though *Ramakatha* incorporated all necessary elements, for the growth of a language identified by C.L. Antony, it was the exclusion of tribal languages that disabled it from becoming a common language. In the middle of the 16th century, with Thunchath Ramanujan Ezhuthachan, language became delimited as the sole 'upper' caste mode of communication and cultural interaction. Ezhuthachan's language, which was different from that of the Niranam poets, knitted various 'upper' communities together through religion, incorporating various streams of the *Bhakthi* movement. About the cultural vocation of Ezhuthachan, P.K. Gopalakrishnan, remarked: 'The Bhakti movement, though it could not destroy the feudal structure, reorganized it on a broader basis. As far as Kerala was concerned, Brahmin authority was replaced by "upper" caste domination.'* Not only did this change negate the distinctive cultural attributes of 'non-upper' castes, it also wiped out their native language resources. More than unifying society, language became a means of social domination.

Language evolution, as described above, had the following repercussions: (1) lack of development among the majority of the population due to the unequal distribution of wealth, authority, and status within the caste structure; (2) absence of a social unification whereby differences could be overcome. Consequently, social philosophies and literature that emerged through language failed to create a common Kerala mindset. Language devolved into a *varna* language. Such a *varna* language, suitable for caste-ownership of property, Brahminical values and menial jobs, could not integrate diverse caste-communities as a people through cultural assimilation. The subordinate and 'lower' caste status of non-Brahmin communities sustained the *varna* language. They were forced to accept all kinds of physical labour as a means of livelihood. Depth of the poverty, dependency and degradation of such 'lower *savarna*' communities is evident in the tragic biographies of numerous poets and artists, including those of Ezhuthachan and Kunchan Nambiar. The draconian embrace of Brahminical values constrained these poor and oppressed writers and caused the content of the Vedas, Upanishads, and Epic-chronicles, hitherto limited to a small minority among the

---

* K. Gopalakrishnan, *Keralathinde Saamskarika Charithram* (Kerala Bhasha Institute, Trivandrum, 1991).

'upper' class communities, to permeate *avarna* communities, through literature, visual spectacles and ritualistic performances. The best example of such a phenomenon is Kunchan Nambiar's *Ottam Thullal*, which blended the rituals and oral knowledges of tribal people with the Epic-chronicle-narratives. Not just the visual arts, but the literary works which followed them, one and all, were also written as a medium for propagating Brahminical values. Even *Unnineelisandesham*, attributed to the 5th century AD, which embodied a different social milieu, is not an exception. As Brahminical values pervaded folk literature, folk songs and rural art forms, even those in the lowest strata began to give expression through *vamozhi* and *varamozhi*, the lives of mythological characters and not to the real life.

The transformation of Malayalam language reinforced *varna*-caste contradictions. C.L. Antony writes: 'As a result of the fourfold *varna* system and the associated social regulations, new forms became prevalent in place of pronouns like "me", "you", and "he". According to the dictates of caste-hierarchy, words like *nam, nom, adiyan, raan, pallikuruppu*, and *neerattu* infiltrated the language.* The plight of those in the 'lower' social strata who had internalized this language is illustrated by Elamkulam Kunhan Pillai[†]: 'The price of male slaves with *vayapirapithi* and *theerani* for work was 250 *panam*; the price of females was up to 300 *panam*, and those with children aged 12–18 were sold with mother for 25–75 *panam*.' Such people comprised the majority of the population, notes C. Kesavan.[‡] In Malabar alone, as per the 1835 census report, there were 144,000 slaves, which increased to 159,000 by 1842. In the beginning of the 19th century, when the total population of Thiruvithamkur (Travancore) was 906,357, 48,974 people were agricultural slaves. As far as Kochi (Cochin) is concerned, 32,668 of the total population were agricultural slaves. Malayalam was unable to take cognizance of the miseries and discriminations suffered by these half-humans to whom the letters of the alphabet were a taboo. Artistes and littérateurs, who were generally poor, also did not bother about them. EMS proclaims: 'There is every reason for a Malayali to be proud of Kerala's early culture. We can boast of Malayalis who were renowned,

---

* C.L. Antony, *Bhaasha Padanangal* (Kerala Sahitya Akademi, Trichur, 1989).

† Elamkulam Kunhan Pillai, *Kerala Bhashayude Vikasaparinamangal* (Sahitya Pravarthaka Sahakarana Sangham, Kottayam, 1967).

‡ C. Kesavan, *Jeevithasamaram*, vol. 1 (Kaumudi Publications, Trivandrum, 1953).

even outside Kerala, in sciences like Ayurveda and Astrology as well as in art and philosophical traditions like Vedanta. Their individual greatness and their contribution to Kerala's as well as world culture cannot be denied by anybody.* The realization that the cultural tradition which gave EMS goose pimples, the consecrated offering of caste system, prohibited to the majority, enabled socio-political reform movements of the 19th century to modernize language so as to facilitate a cultural renaissance.

* * *

British rule resulted in manifold miseries, but it also led to the downfall of many a Jack-of-Spades' rajah, without popular representation, political will or expertise in governance. It also revived protests against the values embodied in the Vedas, Upanishads, and Epic-chronicles that had for centuries constricted the life of the people. But the developments in language that ensued were not conducive to reflecting new realities, because art, literary and cultural fields continued to be under the purview of rajahs and Koyithamburans. These petty kings and the feudal aristocrats who lost crown and sepulchre to the British had already, by and large, abandoned socio-political initiatives as they conveniently focused on cultural enterprises. The abodes of those without any contact with peoples' lives and without any notion of social transformation were soon to become the scene of play for art and literary ventures. Publication and reinterpretation of Sanskrit texts, hence, dominated the cultural field. Alongside, classical music and *Kathakali*, which tickled the sensibility of a minority even as it was rejected by the vast majority, were also revived. The proclivities of the palace-approved artistes and littérateurs further reinstated Brahminical values. To name a few of the personages who reigned over Malayalam literature: Kodungallur Kunhikuttan Thampuran, Keralavarma Valiyakoyi Thampuran, Kadathunattu Udayavarma Thampuran, Venmanimahan, Oduvil Kunhikrishna Menon, Sheevoli Narayanan Namboodiri, Pandalam Keralavarma Thampuran.

Not one of these works by any of the above-mentioned littérateurs, who were *savarna*s and *thampuran*s, was able to create a uniform mindset among the general population. But their dependency and servility to the British rule ensured that their works were accepted and acclaimed

---

* E.M. Sankaran Namboodirippadu, *Vedangalude Naadu* (Shastra Sahitya Parishath, Trichur).

as well as officially prescribed as school textbooks. (Keralavarma Valiyakoyi Thampuran, for instance, was the chairperson of the first Language Reformation Committee.) The conflation of religiosity, as constructed by such cultural reformers, and the official patronage helped in establishing the cultural representative rights of the *savarna* communities. The nationalist movement facilitated this process further. In general, it was *savarna* communities who were initially attracted by the nationalist movement. For example, it was the Kozhikode Zamorin and the Nilambur Ilayaraja, having lost their authority as well as army, and their dependent landlords, like Kodungallur Kunhikuttan Thampuran and Rarichan Moopan, who first hoisted the Indian National Congress flag over Kerala. (Moreover, the second Indian National Congress meeting, on 23–24 April 1917 at Kozhikode, was chaired by C.P. Ramaswamy Iyer.) The Indian National Congress flag was to slip from palace-personages to other *savarna* communities. This metamorphosis of the Indian National Congress was reflected in its policy decisions as well. The Indian National Congress meeting held in Vadakara on 5–6 May 1917 declared its allegiance to the British government. During the following years, the meeting held at Palakkad passed a resolution thanking the British for the creation of a special military regiment of Nairs, while the meeting at Kozhikode resolved to thank the British for recruiting Indian volunteers into the Defence Force as well as to request the British to provide necessary facilities for pilgrims to Rameshwaram. Hence, the entry of the Nair community into the nationalist movement predicated it, not as the *Shudra*s of the fourfold *varna* system, but as the nascent Kerala community. In accordance, a politico-communitarian claim was also raised. Institutionalizing such a claim, the historian K.M. Pannikar noted: 'In social standing, Nairs were just below the Namboodiris. They were not a caste. They were a class. Amongst them, there are several castes with varying social privileges. The highest among them were the *Saamanthars*, who were the ruling class in Kerala. All the great *Maadambi*s in Kerala from Western Karnataka to Kanyakumari were Nairs.'* The coming-to-community of the Nair as Kerala's representative community, being involved in nationalist movements and opposed to the fourfold *varna* system, bolstered visual art forms, like Koothu, Koodiyattam, and Mohiniyattam, as well as fostered Ezhuthachan as the precursor of Kerala's cultural renaissance.

---

* K.K. Kochu, *Kalaapavum Samskaaravum* (November Books, Kottayam, 1998).

Simultaneously, Kunchan Nambiar's texts, *Unnineelisandesham, Unniyachi Charitham*, etc. were reinterpreted. The wide communitarian base, amply supported by the nationalist movement, enabled this cultural stream to ever-so-easily merge with earlier initiatives, like that of Keralavarma Valiyakoyi Thampuran.

Reform initiatives within the Nair community were thereafter shaped by its disassociation with the fourfold *varna* system and its self-determination as the socio-political community of Kerala. Consequently, C.V. Raman Pillai and O. Chandu Menon refashioned the future of literary work. C.V. Raman Pillai's narratives that argued for the right of the Nair community in Thiruvithamkur for a share in governance did not attempt to link with Epic-chronicles. Rather, the endeavour was to connect with the political history of Thiruvithamkur. Similarly, O. Chandu Menon's writings which were not inimical to Brahminical domination bore the torch for communitarian reformations. Works, such as mentioned above, which exhorted the Nair community to merge with the general populace without breaking away from caste and communitarian structures seemed to have used oratory logic to modernize language.

The break of *savarna* communities from the fourfold *varna* system, their internal social reforms and their switch to the patrilineal scheme created deep cultural resonances. Consequently, through poets like Vallathol Narayan Menon, Kuttamath, and other cultural activists, a distinctive Kerala consciousness was also fashioned alongside the national one. As a result, *savarna* social groups' participation in the independence struggle widened and paved the way for a linguistically unified Kerala. The extent of *savarna* representation in the overall social transformation also resulted in the reformation and resurrection of Christian and Muslim communities. In short, language was capable of incorporating the socio-political pressures faced by *savarna* Hindus, Christians, and Muslims and the transformation in the family structure by acquiring rural diction, common speech patterns and a Kerala atmosphere. But the fact of the matter is that, as this language continued to exclude the thoughts, feelings and the cultural signs of people of the 'lower' strata, it did not become a common language. Rather, it was to some extent the missionaries of the time who managed to evolve a language capable of addressing the people belonging to the 'lower' strata. Though language was simplified as it absorbed *vamozhi* and rural diction, it was a dead language as it failed to integrate the essence of a whole people's insurgency.

* * *

Though the socialization of Malayalam was a progressive move, it could not create a common mindset because it failed to incorporate the lived reality of the caste groups belonging to the 'lower' strata. (Works which represented the real-life conditions of caste groups 'lower' than the Ezhavas, like Changampuzha's *Vazhakula* [1937], Thakazhi's *Randidangazhi* [1948], P. Valsala's *Nellu* [1972], Malayattoor Ramakrishnan's *Ponni* [1967], and K.J. Baby's *Maveli Mantram* [1991], ignored the conceptual realm as well as the tangible realities of the caste system.) In brief, all art and literary activity with a social commitment was secular and anti-religious, but not anti-caste. In a society where division of labour was based on caste, and not religion, anti-casteism is more important than secularism. When this fact slipped through art and literature, communitarianism that predetermined the progressive individualism that displaced the democratic and came to dominate art and literary productions. The resolve of such a progress was to shape society in accordance with the mindset of the educated among the *savarna* communities. As cinema and other media became useful in this endeavour, artistic productions lost touch with life in the 'lower' strata and were no longer representative of the whole of society. As a result, artistes and littérateurs did not emerge from Dalit and other social groups and language degenerated into a means of *savarna* communication.

It was in 1920, when Congress raised a demand for the reorganization of the country on the basis of language that the idea of linguistic States became prevalent. The demand for linguistic States, which stood for a decentralization of State power, was soon to create conflicts between Brahminical and other regional *savarna* communities. It was in such an atmosphere that the Kerala State was formed on the basis of language. Though it was able to become secular through struggles against *varna* language, the absence of an anti-casteist perspective led it to favour *savarna* communities, thereby becoming unacceptable to *avarna* people. Exposing the vested community interests underlying the linguistic state argument, in 1936 Dr B.R. Ambedkar noted: 'In a linguistic State, what opportunities can there be for very small communities? Can they hope to be elected to the legislatures? Can they aspire to jobs in government service? Can they believe that their economic development will be a consideration? In such circumstances, linguistic state formation means the handing over of one's land to a majority community. What an end to Gandhiji's *swarajya*! Those who still cannot understand this aspect of the problem, will be able to grasp it when, instead of linguistic provinces, one were to say Reddy State or a Maratha State.'* In Kerala, the linguistic State argument was raised in the interests of the Nair community. They were a minority among the Hindu society. The reformations of the Nair community were not aimed at uniting, integrating with other communities to form a people, but to attain a unique communitarian identity of their own. It was more a cultural, than an economic, agenda. Dr Ambedkar points out: 'The prerequisite for linguistic State formation should be that States are capable of survival. Only States that can survive can become independent states.' Since Kerala did not have such a capability and was, moreover, dominated by community-based interests, it could not augment the Malayalam language.

The intellectuals of Kerala today are anxious about the future of Malayalam. Economic backwardness coupled with social insecurity had alienated the Kerala people from their own land, forcing them to migrate to other States and nations. As a result, Malayalam is being surmounted by other languages (mainly, English) and values. In such a situation, when Malayalam is just a mother tongue for the 'upper' classes and castes, the economic, socio-political, and cultural development of the people belonging to the 'lower' strata is essential for the invigoration of Malayalam.

—*Translated by M.T. Ansari and P. Shyma*

The Return of the *Thampurans*[†]

A. Soman

The Malayalam cinema today has been emptied entirely of the renaissance spirit it possessed. Our cinema has lost forever—not one stone left upon another—the democratic, humanistic values, and the multicultural nature of the Kerala society that were foregrounded by films like *Olavum Theeravum*. Their place is now wielded by images and diction of the dominant religion. *Thampurans* and *Thampuratties*[‡] impose upon the living discourses of other communities their

---

[*] B.R. Ambedkar, *Complete Works*, vol. 1, *Malayalam* (Kerala Bhasha Institute, Trivandrum, 1996).
[†] Original title *Thampurakanmar Thirichuvannappol*.
[‡] Terms used in the past to address feudal/upper-caste masters and mistresses.

kalabhakkuri, kathakali head, and *sandhyaseeveli** as signs of hegemony, whereas these other communities are the ones that preserve Malayali life as it is. In this worship of the past, however, cultural images and signs that rupture historical stages are abundantly mixed. By strategically evading temporal and spatial references, our film world has turned out to be a food for fantasy.

It must be noted that a social atmosphere is already formed in Kerala— an atmosphere conducive to the smooth circulation of the images and diction of the dominant religion. Recently, as the Indian national consciousness grew busy with a rethinking of nationalism, it has become imperative for our middle and upper classes and castes to define their position within such a problematic paradigm. Consequently, in the last two decades that resounded the slogans of saffronization, these classes found a way out to their predicament in conceptualizing nationalism based on religion. When anxieties about nationalism grew on account of various social and political factors, it became necessary for the upper classes of the dominant religion to reinforce the framework of their religion more close-knit. One of the easiest means to achieve it was to construct an Other, an identity with hostile and inimical characteristics. Contemporary Malayalam cinema has now faithfully taken up, almost as an obedient servant, the production of subjectivities that are capable of reproducing this process of Othering.

There was an almost perfect correspondence between the signifiers of the renaissance cinema and the real-life signifieds. On the other hand, recent films keep a safe distance from temporal and spatial relations; their signifiers float in cinematic discourse without even touching the signifieds. It is this futile play of signifiers that build a supernatural world for commercial films in Malayalam. For instance, since they do not provide any reference to time and space films like *Maanatthe Vellittheru* and *Chandralekha*,† can happen anywhere at any time. It may even be possible to take their thematic environment and replace one with the other.

Until recently, it was common for the ordinary viewer to wonder about the shooting location of the movie while watching it. He was then in need of certain signs of time and place. On the other hand, the

---

* The reference is to various practices, rituals, and arts that were typical of upper-caste/feudal traditions. Their abundant reappearance in contemporary movies is indicated here.

† Both films deal with supernatural experiences and characters.

false universality and a fake sense of vastness created by the metaphysical or supernatural world of the contemporary cinema cleverly distances the viewer from such thoughts. It is thus by overlooking and distorting materiality that the ideology and capital of the cinema formulates subjectivities required for it.

Aaraam Thampuran (Thampuran, the Sixth) is the latest instance of how cinema replaces reality with a constructed fantasy world. Moreover, it sneaks in a certain hidden agenda pertaining to the construction of subjectivity. In this film where the family feud between two *kovilakams** is delineated on a wide canvas, except the lives of those nobles and their bootlickers, no other section of the society finds a mention. All signs and symbols of village life have been kept aside. Further, it is not accidental that graffities or bills and flags that are integral to social life have been strategically removed from the eyes of the camera, when the hero and the villain fight in the marketplace.

The film, *Aaram Thampuran*, seems to be duty-bound to protect the hegemony of the dominant religion. The only non-Hindu character in the movie is 'Thangalangadi Bappu'. As for the treatment of this character, he is presented as a loyal servant of the hero who in turn is an embodiment of modern sensibility (evidenced by his craze for archaeology, familiarity with JNU, handling of art magazines, stay at Gwalior Gharana, and so on). In short, the film warns Bappu that he has no other alternative but to remain subservient to the hero's monopoly of modern values and the consequent possession of power and knowledge. This film unilaterally determines that the subject position of other communities is at the point where the dominant religion completes the process of subjugation.

The renaissance Malayalam cinema had possessed, as its salient features, certain democratic assumptions about social life. It was never intolerant of multicultural and multireligious social situations. Instead, it provided within cinematic discourses space for subaltern lives as well as for communities outside the dominant religion. It will be interesting to think of how films like *Neelakkuyil* or *Asuravithu*, if made today, would be accepted. Today, names like 'Chathan', 'Koran', and 'Mammad'† are mere butts of ridicule within cinematic discourses. Even a movie

---

* Term for upper-caste feudal households. These were also centres of knowledge and art as they were patrons of art and artists.

† Localized names. The first two are typical lower-caste names whereas the third one is a typical local version of Muhammad.

like *Kaliyattam*, which attempts to delineate subaltern life-situations, has been created within the psychological framework of Shakespearian characters who exemplify elite, academic, and classical aesthetics.

In Malayalam cinema, Muslim life was once shown undisparagingly; but the ideological reasons for the same to have become unthinkable today requires to be examined. Further, we must also enquire about why even the Muslim film-makers in Kerala do not attempt to break the Hindu paradigm. In our society where cast-mindedness remains despite the disappearance of caste system, it is really regrettable that even the avant-garde film-makers with an aura of radicalism do not share any anxiety about the invasion of violent Hindutva ideology into various social discourses and aesthetics.

Apart from a few films like *Agraharathile Kazhutha* and *Harijan* which apparently problematize Brahmanism and upper-caste Hindutva (even in other Indian languages), our avant-garde film practices have only rarely dared to confront the challenges of religion-centred ideologies.

—*Translated by Saji Mathew*

The Dalit Presence in Malayalam Literature*

Sunny M. Kapikkad

An equiry into the Dalit presence in Malayalam literature becomes meaningful only when it opens up new vistas of aesthetics. Dalit literary studies which includes anything that is written about Dalits in the purview of Dalit literature parades 'Duravastha', 'Vazhakkula', and 'Kurathi' as Dalit literature. It is as ridiculous as categorizing Thakazhi's *Chemneen* as literature of the community of fisherfolk. A healthy debate on Dalit literature and aesthetics would be possible only if we reject such basically untenable categorizations. To the aforementioned theoreticians and also to those who in opposition to the former, who blindly deny Dalit literature its due, Dalit is only a common term for designating the untocouchable. But the word has a history that they refuse to acknowledge. It became part of the socio-political discourse of the

* Original title *Malayala Sahityathile Dalit Saanidhyam*.

turbulent 1960s, as an epitome of India's dreams of liberation. It carries the weight not only of strife but also of centuries-long philosophical enquiry.

'How do those who have buried their heads in clouds realize the problems and setbacks that we face?' When Mahatma Jyothi Phule posed this question a century and a half ago, did he visualize an irrevocable dissociation of sensibility that might take place in aesthetic experience and appreciation? And who doesn't realize this day that this observation which he made apropos the Indian psyche which tends to turn a blind eye to hard facts took root and spread all over India through E.V.R.'s Dravida concept, Ambedkar's social democracy, the *avarna*s empowerment through appropriation by Sreenarayana, Sahodaran Ayyappan's liberal thought, and Ayyankali's concept of social justice! This incursion into all realms of human existence created a new understanding of the rebuilding of the Indian psyche. These bold and unending efforts to refashion man opened up new vistas of human liberty. Dalit literature burgeoned in the creative engagement that the Indian psyche had with this peculiar formation of history.

Human freedom is realized in man's possibilities to rebuild and metamorphose himself. In India, where one is born into a particular caste and destined to die in it, the possibility of rebuilding and changing himself is connected to the possibilities that his caste offers. It is only when one understands the full implications of these sanctions put on human freedom that we realize the organic nature of the relationship that anti-caste traditions have with human freedom. It is when we miss this source that we fall into the error of categorizing as Dalit literature everything scribbled by people sympathetic to the Dalit cause. It was with India's aesthetic heritage that Dalit literary discourse had to contest. In India, values have always been ascribed and interpreted in relation to one's caste: good/evil, ability/inadequacy, beauty/ugliness, humility/impertinence, and so on. The Malayalam proverb according to which 'there are no fools among Brahmins' is the result of this value system. When one says that 'though she is dark she is beautiful', it implies that a dark-skinned person being beautiful is somehow against the laws of nature. It was only by contesting this wild and warped sense that Dalit aesthetics could develop. Dalit literature has been misunderstood as anti-*savarna* propaganda precisely because of the failure to understand this different aesthetic sensibility.

Dalit literature is a mode of self-expression that history has invented against class and caste values and their aesthetics that bind us in a vice like grip. As in the case of any other literature, the life breath of Dalit literature is also its anxieties about human liberty. It advances by making intrepid incursions into language and the value system toward its realization. This is an attempt at subjecting certain texts in Malayalam that have substantially influenced the aesthetic sensibility of the Keralite, to a rereading.

The theme of *Nalukettu* by M.T. Vasudevan Nair, the famous Malayalam littérateur is the break-up of the *tharavadu* system of the Nairs. What is the world that unfurls itself before us through Appunni's thoughts and anxieties? It is regret at his inability to be a part of the tharavadu aristrocracy that haunts him and shapes his personality. This takes root in him not as a rejection of the status quo but as a cheap grudge against being denied a share in the bounty. Amminiyedathi is the personification of a felicity that evades him because he is an exile from the tharavadu aristocracy. Fair and slender like the inner pith of the plantain, with beautiful eyes half veiled by their lids, wearing a velvet blouse and glass bangles, Amminiyedathi smelt alluringly of bath soap and at first sight strikes Appunni as the personification of lust. And he is unable to reciprocate the love of Malu, who is dark and thin and is always shabbily dressed and unstinting with her love. At a close analysis one is sure to arrive at ample reasons for this particular instance of acceptance and rejection, which appears to be random. It is only when we relate the Amminiyedathi/Malu binary to the fair/dark binary that the aesthetics that this text subscribes to, shocks us. It is the collective mindset that has been trained to view female beauty in relation to a fair skin, that works in Appunni.

Beyond experiencing a gross physical pleasure engendered by the memories of his affair with Amminiyedathi, Appunni is incapable of even a trace of human feeling. Bearing a grudge against the whole world in general, Appunni leaves home to amass wealth and comes back to buy the tharavadu only to revel in the thrill of a cheap revenge. We are taken aback by Appunni's sudden realization that he was never an outsider in his world. That would naturally make us wonder what exactly Appunni's problem had been to begin with. The only thing that bothered him was the loss of power. Appunni who buys the tharavadu, dismantles it to build a new house (one which would let in air and light), is slowly growing into a new figure wielding of power, the custodian of wealth, and tharavadu aristocracy. It is the riddle of the continuation of communal power that unravels itself here. Why did Appunni's unreasonable craze for power and suppressed sexual drives become acceptable to the Left leaning Kerala? Does Appunni's endless craving for power and lust lurk behind Malayali pretence of progressiveness? Indeed the times cry out to us that it does, and to a very great extent.

It does not require much linguistic knowledge to realize that the language that has been celebrated as purely rustic was actually that of the Nair and Ambalavasi communities of Kerala. It is only when the language which bears the imprints of Namboodiri *sambandham* and tharavadu aristocracy became the powerful medium of Hindu revivalism, that we realize that the aesthetics of Nalukettu has become a liability.

The central concern of Thoppil Bhasi's play *Ningalenné Cammunistakki* which created quite a stir in Kerala is the conflict between a crumbling Nair aristrocracy and the Communist Party. Chathan and Mala become characters in the play as a means to elucidate this central theme. Why does Mala's love for Gopalan become futile and unrequited? Why does the relationship between Sumam and Gopalan appear most natural and acceptable to Thomas who admonishes Mala for crying over lost love when she has to lead the class struggle? Here behind the apparent irrational acceptance and rejection is an aesthetic bias which in a Communist shocks us. This is not to imply that Gopalan should have loved Mala. But we have to concede that it is caste consciousness that fills the deep recesses of our collective consciousness. Paramu Pillai who consents to join the Karshaka Sangham, condescendingly invites Chathan who is waiting outside, to enter. There is also an absurd scene in which Chathan the untouchable touches Paramu Pillai and joyfully jumps up and down. Mala enters the scene with a red flag held aloft and Paramu Pillai who has had his eyes opened, accepts it. Here, Chathan and Mala are inertia personified to whom nothing will or can happen. It is not difficult see that an aesthetics tinged with caste consciousness is behind the spectacle of Chathan and Mala becoming such entities.

There is a frightening parallelism between Paramu Pillai who welcomes communism into his debt-ridden tharavadu, and Appunni who dismantles his old and decaying tharavadu to build a house that will let in light and air. But this is not coincidental. There is the presence in them of an ancient aesthetic sense that had always been acceptable to the Indian casteist mind. The Malu–Amminiyedathi and Mala-Sumam duo are the inevitable tragic results of this.

When we praised these works as being revolutionary and offering vignettes of Malayali experience we were being forced to relinquish a whole lot of other things. At the utmost we refused to acknowledge the caste elements at work in experience and appreciation. We had been a progressive people, hadn't we? The Malayali, who mistook these collectives of caste experience for national consciousness was lulled into a bogus sense of self. It was the inevitable tragedy of the Malayali's refusal to accept the role of caste and class as social institutions in shaping our emotional and intellectual worlds.

The conflict of identity faced by the Malayali who carried a baggage of socialism in his public and unbridled casteism in his private lives was something terrible. The 1960s witnessed the publication of texts which bore the stamp of angst and identity crisis of a middle class which had strayed into an urban scenario. Ayyappa Paniker's *Kurukshetram* inaugurated the trend. The poem incorporates the problem of Dhritharashtra as its central imagery; the blind Dhritharashtra who seeks to find out the fate of the Kauravas and the Pandavas in Kurukshetra. Could it be an accident that this myth permeates modern man's search for identity and sensibility? Again we come across the same myth in K. G. Sankara Pillai's *Bengal* which is said to have changed Malayali poetic sensibility during the onslaught of extreme Leftism. Why does an Aryan heroic tale alone fill the consciousness of these so-called middle-class people? The reason is that their aesthetic sense has been shaped by the social consciousness of belonging to a middle order caste. Was the Malayali who sought to establish a new identity for himself eating *kaalan* and *olan* (purportedly the quintessential Malayali food) and enjoying the beauty of a woman, newly bathed and wearing a sandal-paste mark (the typical dress of the Malayali woman is still *settu-mundu*!) declaring once again that Kerala belongs to Appunni? Oh Lord, do Appunni and Paramu Pillai come creeping out of the deep recess of the postmodern minds which, working or asleep, pretend to be controlled by Foucault and Lacan?

Khasakkinte Itihasam is another text that appeared around the same time. What was the universe that Ravi approached in the novel that has been described as magical in its use of words? Distant memories of his mother and guilty ones of the clandestine affair that he had had with his stepmother and uncertainties of events yet to come, lead Ravi to aimless and meaningless drifting. Ravi was the unclaimed body floating around in the sea of existentialism discovered by Malayalis. As an alternative to pseudo-spirituality the disinterestedness of self-destruction is strong in him. Drowning in liquor and sex, there was nothing for Ravi to do in Khasak, a continent of nightmarish ignorance. What accompanies this descent into disinterestedness is his anxiety about the lives yet to come.

It is not quite accidental that Ravi's mind wanders through astrology and Upanishads.

It was the threshold to India's eternal tragedy. In the Indian context the agnostic in Ravi can attain only the knowledge of Brahma. If the mask of unrefined basic instincts were to be shed, what is left in him is the passive social mind that keeps its face turned toward Parabrahman (Great Reality, Truth). The growth of this Indian mindset is always toward fascism and the aesthetics tinged with communalism that we encountered earlier. In Vijayan this assumes the shape of pure Hindutva of philosophic dimensions. The pitfalls contained in this are deep indeed. The langage of Khazak was for the Malayali a new experience. Shedding the marks of caste it showed signs of developing into a level at which it would interact with middle-class sensibility. But since a middle order class consciousness predominates in the Malayali middle class the language of Khasak nosedives into pure Hindutva.

Anand and Basheer were those who engaged themselves in a kind of writing different from this. The narrative style of Basheer is a legend in its own right in Malayalam. The Kerala that unfurls itself in his writings is very different from the one that reveals itself in the texts mentioned earlier. The liveliness of his characters is something which only the unfettered vision of a Sufi can create. The Malayalis will have to go a long way before they can understand Basheer, who unveiled the world of Suhra and Majeed and Pathumma before them and went laughing out of the world. We can observe the fearlessness of a philosophical stand in Anand's writing. Anand who refuses to view Hindutva as a prop makes fearless incursions into the dilemmas of human freedom. Here history is not mere fable. It is an active presence experienced by the characters. Anand who approaches the conflict faced by Ekalavya in *Nishadapurana* with philosophical angst strikes a hard blow at the narrow aesthetic sense of the Malayali. Anand is the only modern writer to have overcome the casteist inertia of language with philosophical rigour. The Malayali can approach him only when he breaks open the narrow confines of his small world. Or the writings of Anand become significant only when they are read that way.

Dalit literature came into existence in Malayalam as the self-expression of those Dalits who had access to higher education. They approached their experiences with a new sensibility or insight and sought the possibilities of their expression. In their writings the Dalit achieved a dynamic existence with an emotional and intellectual universe and revealed their hopes for freedom. Foremost among them was T.K.C.

Vaduthala. His story 'Achante Ventinja Inna' ('Here's Your Scapular, Father') depicts with unusual felicity the existential angst of Pulaya who embraced Christianity. This opened a door into a world hitherto unexplored in Malayalam literature. But the Malayali who was browsing in the dark recesses of caste consciousness could not take in the story. And he also did not possess the wherewithal to assess the writings of Paul Chirakkarode who entered the scene in his wake. In the place of either accepting or rejecting it, it was the Chanakya strategy of ignoring it that was staged here.

Another collection of short fiction that Malayalis refused to acknowledge was C. Ayyappan's 'Uchayurakkathile Swapnangal' ('Dreams in a Siesta'). The pieces are blessed with lively and rare observation and a dreamlike quality in narration. The fundamental fact about these characters is that they confront us as Nairs or Namboodiris or barbers or Chrstians or Pulayas. The Pulaya woman in 'Pretabhashanam' ('Ghost Talk') asks God a question: 'How can a Pulaya woman be sister to a Christian, old man?' At this question, it was as though someone had stuffed a plantain in God's mouth. The Pulaya woman who stuffed a plantain into God's mouth is a powerful symbol that haunts the Malayali's pretensions of progressiveness and values. It is only with a shudder that we realize that the question would render the average Malayali also speechless.

The father who comes to realize that his son has an affair with the maid tries to dissuade him. The son in question is Syrian Christian and the maid is Pulaya. The son's response is that he is not going to marry her anyway. The response makes the father feel that someone has stuffed a plantain into his mouth. The father lapses into silence before the commonly held impression that it is perfectly permissible for a Christian (generally a *savarna*) to have an affair with a Pulaya (a Dalit) woman so long as he does not propose to marry her. It is this wild assault on the sham morality of the Malayali which turns Ayyappan's stories into a new aesthetic experience. It is this strange process in which each character matures through their social identity and confronts one another that makes Ayyappan's stories Dalit stories.

'Aanabhranthu' is the story of impoverished Unni Namboodiri who becomes mad in the craze to buy an elephant. Unni's mother asks a young man, their neighbour and an *avarna*, to help cure her son's craze. And the young man promises to buy her an elephant. Unni Namboodiri's mother is an *antharjanam* who is secretly happy at the thought that if he brings her a *Kuzhiaana* (a bug) she will be able to curse him to her heart's content. Since *illams* and antharjanams constitute the quintessential personifications of good in the Malayali mind, this depiction has a sort of violent beauty. This is the negation of the tradition that values are caste-specific. The aesthetic sense of the Malayali which he has internalized by rote is not strong enough to bear this antharjanam. This style which is at once revolutionary and dismissive of dominant values makes Ayyappan's stories Dalit narratives.

It is in poetry that the maximum Dalit interventions have taken place. Though there are not many that stand out due to their aesthetic sense and the felicity of expression, it is noteworthy that Dalits have started expressing themselves through poetry. K.K.S. Das is a name to be reckoned with among Dalit poets. His poems are the aesthetic expressions of angst, tribal memory, and the negation of upper-caste values. The poet who strives to regain the ritual grounds of knowledge by tilling the land carries the richness of a truly ancient tribal memory in him. He exhorts the Dalit to look the tiger in the eye. There is an ocean of self-knowledge beneath his querulous questionings. The poet, who is in constant strife with Aryan bestiality, is conscious of the quantum leap that Dalits should perform in the interests of self-expression. The poet, who sang of growing by chewing thorn upon thorn, by taming the viper and partaking of gun powder from the skulls of men, may perhaps have been turning into the custodian of the most resplendent dream about Dalits. 'I will be born again in history in the ritual grounds of knowledge. Dressed in the clothes of the dawn and bearing the lion's teeth you wait for me. We must share the spring of the earth.' How can one justify turning a blind eye to the music and hope in these lines? Yet some of his poems tend to loose their impact due to the ideological baggage they carry.

Kerala's most creative Dalit poet is probably G. Sasi Maduraveli. The poet who opens up new worlds of experience with every word he writes is a wonder. In his poem 'Shambukam' appears a certain image: Shambuka, what were you in that impure social state? An intelligent horse both driven by the whip and restrained by reins.' How can we explain the strength and depth of that world hidden in these words? 'When his expectations were unfulfilled Valmiki reverts to his true self—wild and uncivilzed.'

Sasi who sang these words deals Indian cultural consciousness a huge blow. Sasi, whose definition of culture is the distance between the forester and Valmiki, stubbornly turns back towards the forester— another blow to mainstream aesthetics. 'When my mother is called a suckling mammal ....When my father is called a creeping reptile...' the utter lack of feeling the words convey makes us collapse. Grown insensitive to repetitive cycles of misfortune and humiliation, poetry goes beyond mere lament.

'Mother Kali, whose severed heads form the garland around your neck? Whose chest do you mount to cool your rage?' It is these questions that concern the poet. In such poems, identity becomes something deeply perplexing. Poetry grows madly from the realization that these gods kill to eat. The emotional and intellectual world of Dalits and their perplexity is developing into a new experiential world. 'Saumini, didn't you say that Black is beautiful? And haven't the poets sung so too?' is the poet's gentle question. Before that searing question, the Keralite simply shrivels in shame. It is when the beautiful symbols of aesthetics that we have raised begin to crumble, that we are reminded that the poet stops us from saying 'You had better not merely sing or say that Black is beautiful.' When you understand 'That black is the colour of love' the *kaapiri* in your soul will sow the seeds of your own revolt.

—*Translated by Ravi Shanker*

Caste and Accumulation of Capital[*]

Sanal Mohan

The accumulation and circulation of capital has an important place in understanding the social, economic and political problems of Dalits. Historically, Dalits were part of the agrarian social classes even as they were prevented from owning land or any other form of property.[†] As a result they could not evolve as a class engaged in accumulating capital. In the first part of this study I intend to analyse the relation between Dalits and agricultural land. The growth and development of various trends in political economy provides the template for the ensuing analysis. One may refer to colonial agrarian transformations that led to the development of capitalist agriculture as a decisive point in this discussion.

---

[*] Original title *Jaatiyum Mooladhana Roopeekaranavum*.
[†] This had been the case in most parts of India. For the South Indian case, see Dharma Kumar, *Land and Caste in South India: Agricultural Labour in the Madras Presidency During the Nineteenth Century* (New Delhi, Manohar, 1992).

An enquiry into the specific stage in the agricultural development in which land began to be perceived, as intrinsically valuable property as we understand it now, assumes a larger import in our study. Such a shift in perception also resulted in a consequent transformation of the structure of land control and the hierarchical rights to land and our notions regarding them. The nature of such a transformation as well as the resultant economic relations form significant issues in my enquiry. The transformation of land in the political economy can also be studied in the context of India's overall historical experience. The fundamental changes in the social structure and the relative position of the agrarian social classes who had toiled on land or who had established various kinds of control over the resources of land are to be closely observed. Such a perspective will give a clearer picture of the agrarian relations that change over a period of time. This will enable insights into the processes by which groups of primary producers belonging to the subjugated castes come under the hegemony of dominating castes.

Under British colonialism, the general expectations about land or about the value attributed to land in India underwent a transformation. Land came to be perceived as something to be developed for increasing market-oriented agricultural production. One could also observe similar trends in Kerala following British colonization. The economic value that had been ascribed to land before colonization has already been widely theorized. These debates focused mainly on whether private ownership in land had existed or not. At the same time, scholars have argued that various social groups had different hierarchical rights over the resources produced. Economic historians are however divided over this. Authority and rights over land continue to be an important issue for both economists and economic historians.

But, with colonization, one can see a precise definition evolving about authority and right over land. From 1793, after the introduction of the Permanent Settlement agrarian social classes and their rights to land were redefined and it became the fundamental law that determined authority and control over land.* The main principle behind this policy was to identify a specific social class, the Zamindars who would improve the land according to the demands of the market. In other words the new land settlement was aimed at identifying a social group that would be held responsible for the improvement of land. This evidently led to the

---

* For introductory observations on the Permanent Settlement in the context of agricultural production, see B.R. Tomlinson, *The Economy of Modern India 1860–1970* (Foundation Books, New Delhi, 1998, pp. 42–5).

creation of a class of Zamindars whose juridical position was redefined as landlords to suit the requirements of colonialism.

In the course of the Permanent Settlement, it was the peasants who lost out. However, human labour in the agrarian sector continued to be provided by the untouchable lower castes in most parts of India. In the colonial agricultural production they were gradually transformed into agricultural labourers.* What is more striking, however, is the peculiar persistence of caste-based division of labour. This aspect is often overlooked by social scientists even as they talk about agrarian class differentiation. It was the newly obtained land relations that determined various aspects of colonial mode of production in agriculture. This change in the mode of production in agriculture and the structural conflicts that were endemic to them were not adequately analysed. One may bring in here various forms of extra economic coercion under which agricultural labourers worked in different parts of India. The situation becomes complex if one brings in conditions of slavery as well as other forms of bondedness that had been observed as persisting from the 19th to the 20th century in various parts of India. The situation becomes even more complex when the question of caste is also brought to bear on the problem. For example, the implications of the changes in the structural position of agricultural labourers before and after the transformation to colonial capitalism have not been studied. There seems to be a reorganization of caste according to new demands. Put another way, even as colonial capitalist mode reinterpreted the value of land, reinventing it, the social relations of the previous mode of production, including caste structure, seems to be retained in the new mode of production. They, thereafter, continued as part of the agrarian social structure. Though the discussions in the 1970s had precipitated detailed research on the mode of production in Indian agriculture and even on agrarian populations, it cannot be said that the influence of caste structure in the relations of production within the colonial mode of production was ever seriously studied. This is true for the studies of postcolonial agrarian class formation. Consequently, a situation has risen wherein we aver that such discussions were futile.

This study intends to analyse the transformation of land into an object of value that could be bought and sold, and the subsequent changes in the agrarian social structure. This process had solidified dominance in

* Utsa Patnaik, 'On the Evolution of the Class of Agricultural Labourers in India' in *The Long Transition: Essays on Political Economy* (Tulika, Delhi, 1999, pp.181–207). Also see Dharma Kumar, *Land and Caste in South India.*

the agricultural sector and reinforced caste structure in various regions of India. The agricultural labourers who performed the actual labour in most cases belonged to the 'lower' castes. The relation between caste hierarchy, ownership, and control of land is evident everywhere in India. For example, 'middle' castes anywhere in India can be seen to have more control over land. Similarly, if one looks at the agricultural labour community, the majority may be seen to belong to the 'lower' castes. The modern agricultural labourers in Kerala emerged from those castes that were traditionally agrestic slaves. Their slavery cut across pre-colonial and colonial periods, contrary to the opinion of many a social scientist. It may be argued that their transition to modern agricultural labourers might have been a slow process. Historians in Kerala have argued that slavery was abolished to make way for the planters to resolve the scarcity of labourers in the plantations and thereby develop capitalist agriculture. However, there is not enough evidence to assert that the labour force required for plantations in the eastern highland of Kerala emerged out from freed slaves. Spatial mobility of the freed labourers was very much limited if we go by the available source materials. Likewise, it cannot be said with any certainty that slaves of the old system became labourers in the capitalist agriculture without much structural constraints. There was no such sudden transformation, which is supported by the fact that even half a century after the abolition of slavery, and through the middle of the 20th century, the spatial mobility of former slave castes was limited.

Though the agricultural sector has changed into the capitalist mode, old social relations continued to hold sway in the relations of production. Even as land became property, a significant section of the society has not been able to assert any authority over land because of the peculiar relations between their position in the caste hierarchy and their economic condition. The form of landownership in the colonial period may be seen to be continuing in the post-independent period as well. In the newly evolving political economy of land control, it would have been difficult for the class of agricultural labourers drawn from Dalit communities to become landowners unless they accumulated some capital to invest in buying land. After land became property, Dalit communities have not been able to establish control over it. In regions where Dalits could own land it happened through migration and similar contingent factors. At the same time, it can be seen that they possessed immense practical knowledge of agriculture. However, the possession of agricultural knowledge never enabled them to stake a claim on the wealth that they produced. Such a situation continued in the post-

Independence programme of the Green Revolution that never took into consideration the knowledge of these social groups in agriculture. Soon new agricultural norms and newer technological innovations changed the face of cultivation. In the emerging scenario, the age-old skills of these social groups no longer had any currency. In places like Kuttanad in Kerala, the introduction of new agricultural technology completely devalued older forms of knowledge.

A good instance of the efforts made by Dalit communities to acquire land is the internal migrations of the 1950s.[*] These internal migrations from the southern Travancore region of Kerala to various parts of Malabar and the highlands of Travancore have not yet been carefully examined. The stories of internal migration by Syrian Christians, however, have obliterated the narratives of other social groups.[†] The internal migrations of the 1950s can be seen as a movement for control over land, though other socio-economic factors continued to delimit this process. The land reforms of the 1970s was the most important factor in determining landownership as it conferred ownership of a minimum of ten cents of land to the agricultural labourers. After all, agricultural land to the farmer was the rallying cry of land reform. But the question as to who was the farmer, despite being central to the initiative, was not quite clearly defined. As a result, Dalits, who actually tilled the land, were not recognized as farmers in the new system and thus did not become landowners. At the same time, those who did not directly work on the land were categorized as farmers. In actual terms, the pro-tenant land reform initiative limited the right of landownership of Dalit agricultural workers to a mere ten cents (4360 square feet). Thereafter, Dalits, who

---

[*] There are quite a few settlements of migrant Dalit Christians from the Travancore region in the Calicut Wayanad, and Kannur districts of Kerala. The villages of Kottukappara and Parakappara in the Kannur districts are very important in the history of Dalit Christians in the postcolonial period as it led to the establishment of exclusive Dalit Christian Catholic parishes after the Dalits moved out of Syrian Christian dominated St Thomas Church at Karikkottakkari due to caste oppression during 1957–9.

[†] V.J. Varghese, 'Migrant Narratives: Reading Literary Representations of Christian Migration in Kerala, 1920–70', in *Indian Economic and Social History Review*, June 2006, vol. 43, no. 2, pp. 227–55. For a different perspective, see Michael Tharakan, 'Migration of Farmers from Travancore to Malabar, 1930 to 1960: An Analysis of Its Economic Causes', M.Phil Dissertation in Applied Economics, Centre for Development Studies, Thiruvananthapuram; Jawaharlal Nehru University, Delhi, 1977. In addition to the academic studies, there is a huge literature in Malayalam narrating various aspects of Syrian Christian migration to Malabar.

from time immemorial had worked the land and produced surplus became agricultural labourers.

Some people believe that agriculture does not have much importance in a period of modern technological development. It is also reported that technical expertise will soon provide food for every table without large-scale cultivation. Hence, one might argue that there is no basis for any anxiety over agricultural land. But such an argument was not prevalent during the land reform initiative. Considering the technological advancements and the resultant increase in agricultural production the struggles over ownership of agricultural land may become inconsequential. Perhaps newer technology will completely displace traditional mode of farming and make the agricultural labourer defunct. In such a context, the concept of rights over land may become paradoxical. But this study assumes that older forms of agriculture, and knowledge will persist for many more years. Moreover, caste determined hierarchies in landownership may even be carried over, as in the past, to emerging contexts sans critical reflection as everyone talks about the magic wand of technology in resolving the issues of agricultural production that would make any argument for redistribution of land to Dalits insignificant. Since recent reports indicate that concerns over food and agricultural/farm products may become even more complex in future, this study would like to further underline certain facts and facets related to agrarian questions in Kerala.

In connection with land reforms and Dalit groups, a few more things have to be indicated. The basic issue is regarding the question 'Who is a peasant?' Many prominent economic historians have already discussed this issue. The general consensus seems to be that though agricultural labourers are not peasants, they are an integral part of the agrarian social structure. Hence, they deserve a special place in the agricultural sector. When it was pointed out to E.M.S. Namboodiripad that there is a viewpoint that Dalits have not got any agricultural land though the slogan of agricultural 'land to the tillers' helped to establish the Party which implemented the policy, his reply was that people belonging to the Dalit sections were able to develop 'a sense of self-confidence in getting organized in the struggles against injustices'.* Self-confidence for Dalits, and assets for the others!

---

* P.K. Michael Tharakan, 'Social Change in Kerala: E.M.S. Namboodiripad Talks to P.K. Michael Tharakan', in *India International Centre Quarterly*, Special Issue on Kerala: Progress and Paradox, vol. 22, no. 2–3, Summer-Monsoon, 1995, p. 221.

Clearly, it becomes imperative that the Left should seriously engage with the contradictions within the agrarian society. That these contradictions were a serious concern for the Communist Party is evident in the party documents. But, when land reform became a governmental initiative, such contradictions were not seriously addressed. Maybe, this omission points to the necessity of a different social order. The central issue is that the situation demands a restructuring of the notions of rights in relation to the history of landownership.

The main debate in the agricultural sector today seems to be about commercial crops. But the commercialization of Kerala's agricultural sector had begun in the first half of the 19th century itself, with the selection of crops being determined by the anticipation of a large market. Even the production of essential food items like rice, was commercialized. Agricultural production, therefore, has been market-oriented.

In the 1980s, agricultural labourers had 175 working days per annum. By the 1990s, the working days were reduced to almost a half; implying that job opportunities were severely reduced. Hence, not surprisingly, there is a widespread discussion about innovative crops. Floriculture, with plans of catering to an international market, is an example. Meanwhile, newspapers like *Malayala Manorama* opine that backwaters where paddy was cultivated can be more profitably used for tourism, the argument being that the loss incurred in the agricultural sector can be compensated by tourism, which will also generate more job opportunities. Such endeavours, if embarked upon, will definitely change our agricultural profile. But, what also happens simultaneously is that discussions about issues related to the ownership of land get postponed, if not terminated.

A salient part of the problem is that it is the developmental model that continues to dominate discussions. The 'Kerala Model' of development has had its supporters and detractors. But the issue of agricultural land for Dalits was not on the agenda of any of these discussions. The rights over land and its resources for people belonging to the lower strata do not seem to be important for the Kerala model of development. But in a larger Indian context, the alienation of Dalits from agricultural land seems to be a very serious concern. It is because the radical groups, in Andhra Pradesh and Bihar, were able to raise the issue of land that they continue to receive support from rural Dalit groups. In other words, the control over land and survival on it becomes a crucial political issue. But the Kerala scenario is different. Since there is a prevalent belief that the land issue has been resolved once and for all, political movements that demand a re-examination of land relations have not been able to gain momentum.*

It is in connection with the Adivasis that the question of land has been recently raised in Kerala. Even then it is being discussed as a question limited to one or two regions. In reality the conflict is centered on the perspectives of two social groups regarding the productivity of land and the transformation of land into property.

If Kerala is generally considered to be developed, it is because discussions about the Kerala model have never examined caste issues. In connection with ownership and rights over land, it would be pertinent to ask whether such a rosy picture conceals the problems faced by Dalit groups. It would not be wrong to consider that right over land would remain a pertinent problem, given the fact that India is not likely to quickly switch over to technology-based agriculture. Another facet that can be considered in connection with control over available resources would be the peculiarities of accumulation of capital. Accumulation of industrial capital also happened on the basis of caste-based social networks; an aspect that has never been analysed in depth.† Generally, economic history never indicates the caste background of Indian bourgeoisie. In order to study the accumulation of capital in India, caste background also has to be taken into account. However, Marxist historians like Bipan Chandra have always adopted a methodology that negated any influence of caste structure in the accumulation of capital in India. Though one may find occasional references to other factors, most discussions are based on the notion of a national bourgeoisie.‡ But old social relations based on caste have played a significant role in the growth of Indian capitalism. The history of capital accumulation among the Marwadis of North India makes this more than evident. Caste-based social relations may disappear in a capitalist mode of production. But

---

* There was a huge debate on this issue in the last few years and the traditional Left in Kerala fights shy of another phase of land reforms fearing the cost of losing the support of the propertied classes. Hindu Right outfits of late have openly demanded a second land reform, in order to woo Dalits to their sectarian politics.

† For a recent argument on the imbrications of caste and capital, see Barbara Harris-White, *India: Working Essays on Society and Economy*, chapter 7, Caste and Corporatist Capitalism, pp. 176–99.

‡ See for example Bipan Chandra, Mridula Mukherjee, Aditya Mukherjee, K.N. Panikkar, and Sucheta Mahajan, *India's Struggle for Independence* (Penguin Books, New Delhi, 1989, pp. 375–85).

instead, what we find are diverse social relations that evolved out of the caste system and caste practices that underwent modifications in order to help the accumulation and reproduction of capital. Later, the accumulation and the reproduction of capital became, particularly during the post-Independence period, a governmental policy. This discussion leads us to a fundamental question regarding the very nature of the Indian state itself. Even a traditional approach to this question would have to take the class aspect of the nation into consideration. Such an investigation is also relevant to the study of the redistribution of resources.

What is the nature of capital accumulation that is happening in the reorganization of the present economic structure of India? There seems to be an influx of foreign capital as well as accumulation of national capital at the same time. Economic powers are also able to accumulate capital here itself. In such a context, where economic activities such as capital accumulation and distribution have more or less been based on caste, contemporary changes gain significance in the discussion of resources.

Another important problem related to resources is the growth of modern workers and the rise of the working class. We ought to examine the kind of working class that has emerged from Dalit communities. Modern workers should have naturally emerged from the social groups that were involved in manual labour. But it cannot be said that the available studies on the rise of the modern working class have taken this problem seriously into account.

For a working class to emerge, certain cultural contexts are required. In the absence of such cultural specificities, it is impossible for communities without resources to develop into a working class. We have already referred to certain instances from the case of agricultural labourers in Kerala to show the imbrications of cultural factors in the formation of the working class. Certain examples of Dalits in the larger Indian context will further illustrate this. Modern industrial workers in Bombay were once organized on the basis of caste. Even when working class organizations came into existence, caste-based gatherings and events were quite prevalent. Initially, these appeared as 'upper'-caste collectivities. Without the structure of an organization, these sprang up from their everyday relations and interactions. People belonging to the untouchable castes were kept away from these relations. That is why Ambedkar had to organize only those belonging to the Dalit community.

Today we find that the economic sector is greatly influenced by caste and the social relations that emerged from it. Likewise, the history of the working class in India will give us an indication of people, if not of Dalits, who lost out because they belonged to particular classes and castes. As mentioned before, the Dalits in India have not been able to become a modern working class. If we take the example of Kerala, the Dalits' share in the job market is predominantly in the agricultural sector.

Let us take a contemporary example. As mining started in the tribal region of Jharkhand, all the Adivasis were evicted. Later, when a town came up, the Adivasi share of jobs was low and limited to unskilled manual work in the unorganized sector which did not require any technical knowledge. A situation prevailed whereby Adivasi women were subjected to extreme exploitation and forced into sex work.*

The Adivasis of Jharkand found themselves in a context which could have enabled them to grow in accordance to modern industrial demands. But certain social limitations thwarted their growth. And they ended up as the downtrodden and oppressed community in the industrial cities. They cannot become a working class, a fact attested to by many Indian cities. Dalit and Adivasi communities are yet to reach a situation whereby they can acquire cultural capital to even *become* a working class.

Most studies usually address the withdrawal of the labour force from the agricultural sector. Such being the case, a couple of observations can be made regarding the withdrawal of the Dalit labour force from the agricultural sector. Primarily, in the prevalent atmosphere, being an agricultural labourer is seen as an impediment to social acceptance. Secondly, by withdrawing from the agricultural sector they lose even their traditional skills nor at the same time, they can acquire new technical knowledge. The contemporary phase of technological developments demands technological advances to achieve social mobility.

—*Translated by M.T. Ansari and P. Shyma*

---

* Susan Devalle, *Discourses of Ethnicity: Culture and Protest in Jharkhand* (Sage Publications, New Delhi, 1992).

Identity, Alienation, Expression: Dalit Writing in Kerala

K.K. Baburaj

Those who upheld the hegemonic discourse of ancient rituals and manuscripts were keen on attributing a Brahminic ancestry to Ezhuthachan and to celebrating him as a bard of *Harinamakeerthanam*, whereas, those who expressed themselves through the medium of print, ruled out Ezhuthachan's Brahminic parentage and established him as the author of *Adhyatma Ramayana*. It is the very same people, belonging to the latter group, who through the production of books on history, philology, translation, novels, children's literature, and other such texts, translated into the written word, the ambivalence of the social milieu and that of a particular historical juncture. These writings and readings made anachronistic the historical consciousness of 'Keralolpathi' and the reign of Perumals, thereby making the public sphere of 'Draveedam' acceptable. They contested the premise that Malayalam originated from 'Prakrith' the early form of Sanskrit and established that it was part of the language family, which included sister languages like Tamil. Also there were arguments that the world views reflected through these texts and their readings were mimetic in nature and had a slant towards western nationality and Victorian morality. Anyway, without further ado on those debates, what is suggested here is the fact that Kerala's epistemological sphere is more or less influenced and controlled by a cultural capital reinforced by various elements of upper-caste identity formations.

Dalit Identity and Alienation

During the Kerala 'renaissance', the salient feature of which was the widespread belief that people's collective movements would integrate social revolutionary ideologies, Nair–Ezhava communities entered the historical–linguistic domain, though in unequal proportions. Agitations for equal opportunity and participation in colonial administrative reforms helped these communities to forge ahead in the larger movement. Moreover, they were able to overcome sub-caste division through the process of community formation.

This background enabled these communities to ensure political power through radical interventions and to produce competent and dynamic bodies which were pluralistic. As against these identity constructions, organized movements became weak and transformed themselves into mere agencies that protected community interest. The religious framework of Muslim and Christian sects helped various other sects to consolidate exclusive interest of their respective communities. In the same context, Dalits who did not have either a strong written tradition or an intellectual representation, or an offshoot of inter-textuality, were excluded from the historical–linguistic consciousness.

But it was impossible to construct a cultural geography of Kerala excluding Dalits altogether, since the notion of unity in diversity was still prevalent as a part of the national movement. The fact that during the renaissance Dalits were confined to agricultural and manual labour sectors, also influenced the constructed cartography of Kerala. Here, the mainstream revised the Dalit representation based on certain mechanical constructions. Their official propaganda is reductive in portraying ritual art and lifestyles based on customs and traditions as Dalit representation. Along with such constructed stereotypes, mainstream social and cultural representations claim that such portrayals are true reflections of Dalit life. Thus the genuine Dalits were excluded from the mainstream mapping. This amnesia is genocidal. Many tribal societies of the world have faced genocide either through the violence of such representations, or through the erasure of self and identity by way of hegemonic cultural maps. Marginalized communities which are denied entry into the organic cultural expressive paradigm of texts, reading and dialogue would mould their survival strategies through constructing their own paralleled micro worlds, which hegemonic symbolic systems could not account for or even comprehend. This is made possible through a process that transformed memory into history, personal into political. The subalterns still retain their rituals, traditions, collectivity, spirituality and festivals as cultural capital. Some of these are subversive and have immense potential for resistance. *Bharanippattu* and *poorappattu* are two instances of such cultural capital. Community construction is carried out not just through the oral elements, but also by making linear texts of collective memory from personal anecdotes and experiences. Most significant among such memories include conflicts and personal sacrifices that Dalits confronted during the renaissance period. Thus Dalit identity survives outside the periphery of language consciousness and official historiography through the recreations of such memories across generations.

Dalit Identity and Expressions

Though the historic sense that evolves from memory is subversive and reactionary, it need not be humanistic at all times. Many elements of outdated lifestyle and conventions could accumulate on it. Therefore, Dalit identity has to be reconstructed giving primacy to Dalit discourse and struggle for existence. It is against this possibility that traditional icons are being propagated through a deliberate erasure of Dalit discourses, their primary objective being attempts to prevent the dialogic subjectivity of Dalits.

As far as Kerala is concerned, no attempts have been made to deconstruct these official discourses that present Dalit in a non-dialogic subject position. All signifiers of Dalit community formations were selectively avoided from the written history of Kerala 'renaissance'. In the post-renaissance period when socialist consciousness became prevalent, the fear of the mainstream towards the dialogic subjecthood of Dalits was again not discussed. Moreover, in the high noon of modernism these communities were subjected to the most dreadful notion of the constructed 'Other'. They were strictly categorized as agricultural labourers and poor landless peasants. The reason behind such categorization was the same old hegemonic mainstream world view, by which Dalits were seen as 'sons of soil' and adivasis 'sons of forests'. What was rendered invisible in the formation of Kerala history is the subaltern space created by the marginalized through their struggles for equal opportunity. Dalit movements of the 1980s have to be examined in the light of this forced invisibility. The Dalit movements that emerged in this period, gave priority to and projected mass movements, unlike the obstinate caste and community leaders of the earlier phase. A significant aspect to be emphasized here is the fact that these movements tried to bring in Dalit perspective to writings and readings. It is the selfsame movements and the writers who debunked and deconstructed the traditionalist–modernist historiography.

What is noteworthy of this Dalit movement is their reinterpretation of Sree Narayana Guru's thoughts. The Dalit writers of the 1980s fragmented the Hindu homogenous and hegemonic discourse by producing subaltern hermeneutics to Sree Narayana Guru's thoughts, which have been linked to idealist, mechanical and materialistic vantage points. When the socialists and new democratic movements of the time thrived in textualizing the *savarna* cultural capitals, these Dalit writings transformed the real experiences of the periphery in Indian contexts into historical facts. Consequently in Kerala, these interventions have given rise to a public space for 'the coexistence of diversity' and also a new dialogic space where all kinds of marginalized identities could receive social justice and equal treatment.

Notes

1. A medieval Vaishnavite poem in Malayalam in praise of Hari/Vishnu/Rama, popularly believed to be written by Ezhuthachan, again traditionally/pedagogically held as the father of Malayalam and its poetry.
2. An early/pre-medieval Brahminical treaty, imagining and legitimizing Brahmin-centredness and subjecthood in the creation and sustenance of the geographical and cultural territory of Kerala, through the legend of Parasurama, the Brahmin wielding an axe.

—*Translated by Ajay Sekher*

What did Literary Histories Say to You?*

Pradeepan Pampirikunnu

History writing is not merely an innocent desire to document the past. It is related not only to justice, but also to power. The consideration of power always depends on the Law's focus on laws. Social powers also predicate, and perpetuate, unwritten and written aesthetic rules, very much in their own interests. By the same process, social powers also degrade and debase aesthetic-knowledge productions outside their own interests. Hence, descriptions such as Sanskrit/Prakrit, literate/illiterate, classic/folk, are also signs of marginalization. After categorizing people into *varnas*/castes, looking at those who were outside the system the '*varnadarmas*' wondered as to who these beings were! After all, power is hardly reflexive about its own knowledge-aesthetic self-constructions. Given that a natural order of power does not exist, the notion of a human hierarchy is merely an interpretation of power. It is through such interpretations that man synonymous with Brahmin, colonized the earth. Such exercises also alienated the knowledge of the first indigenous peoples. According to Foucault, the urge to construct history through

* Original title *Sahitya Charithrangal Ningalodu Samsarichathenthu.*

interpretations is the disguised desire for power/knowledge itself. It is power that hegemonizes a particular form of the aesthetic, which in turn determines interpretation and appreciation. Such predeterminations became the yardstick to measure literary merit and were canonized as literary history. Thus, literary history is, simultaneously, a justification as well as an institutionalization of a particular form of the aesthetic. Its judgements are hardly impartial or in the interests of the general populace.

Any literary work is a sign structure and can only be interpreted, not immortalized. A text survives through history and time because of its various interpretations. But established literary histories tend to trivialize such interpretational possibilities by institutionalization and imputation of immortality to the texts. By enshrining a text in a particular period of time by virtue of its supposed singularity of signification, such literary histories preclude the potential for other readings. Thus, literary histories limit these texts within the hegemonic structures of interpretation and appreciation. Even the most radical of texts is often mummified by literary history. Revolution, thus, becomes a museum artefact.

By subscribing to a linear and continuous concept of time, literary history has forsaken intertextuality, which makes possible heterogeneous times. The meaning of a text produced in the 16th or 18th century is not exhausted by available interpretations of that period. Likewise, a particular interpretation by the literary history of a period of any text does not delimit the inherent potential of that text for multiple or plural significations. Obviously, it is such a potential of a text that enables a person to quote *Bhagavadgita* even today. It is even possible for someone to redeploy a text in a period outside that of the determinations of a literary historian, because literary history takes the author and not the text as the standard measure of time. Just as the time in which a text is produced could differ from the time represented in that text, a text's time is also not just the time of its creation. Thus, literary history's period-wise classification of texts, even as it accorded priority to the author, becomes insignificant. In fact, Formalists had already maintained that the period in which the author lived and wrote cannot be considered a criterion for studies on literature.

It is quite possible that a text's potential for other, dialogic readings will only be realized centuries later. Omar Khayyam's *Rubaiyyat* and Potheri Kunhambu's *Saraswathivijayam* in Malayalam are familiar instances of such possibilities. Time in literary history is not a sacred entity. Setting apart the idealizations of the text, Benedetto Croce's opinion may be relevant here: 'That each text is indefinite cannot be contained in classifications or generalizations. But classifications and generalizations are required for literary history, which are formulated because of practical considerations and are often informed by personal interests.'*

It is not time alone that works against marginalized peoples and texts, but (literary) history's classifications as well. A text cannot be a history. Its narrative may identify an idea or value system as the dominant feature of a period. Such standardizations naturalize fields of perception and appreciation, thereby producing a normative literary history. In Malayalam, it was *savarna* aesthetic that became lauded as the literary mainstream. *Paanan pattu, Parayan pattu, Pulayan pattu, Mappila pattu* and *Vedan pattu* are, for instance, marked by extra-literary concerns, or by their caste names. Such a classificatory method adopted by literary history precluded the possibility of later social movements from accepting a wide range of cultural forms as common capital. While Malayalam literary history classified 'lower'-caste art and literature under caste names, the 'upper'-caste practices were determined as mainstream. Can a history which denigrated some arts as caste arts while celebrating others as mainstream be considered democratic? Especially when all the 'native' art-forms of Kerala have caste associations! The fact that all the so-called mainstream arts are associated, even dominated, by 'upper' castes but not referred to by their caste names questions the innocence of such nomenclatures. How many are the 'lower' castes in Kathakali or Koodiyattam? How much of 'lower'-caste lives find representation in their historical and aesthetic elements? The Kerala identity is indeed informed by an othering of 'lower'-caste life. Hence, everything and anything that did not belong to the 'lower' castes became the mainstream. Is *Keraliyata* the tradition of an 'upper'-caste aesthetic and history, especially since they form only eight per cent of Kerala's total population? How is mainstream culture and art then defined? Ulloor's literary history underscores the point: the eligibility criteria of the literary history of the 17th, 18th, and 19th centuries found only one *Dheevaran* and two *Kanniyans* as worthy of mention.† If so, who ripped off the socio-cultural assets of the Dalits, who form the majority of the

---

* David Perkins, *Is Literary History Possible?* (Johns Hopkins University Press, Baltimore & London, 1998).

† N.V.P. Unithiri, 'Keraliya Sahitya Mathanirapekshathayum' in *Ramanayana Padanavum Mattum* (Chintha Publishers, Trivandrum, 1998).

population? Therefore, any attempt to include the contribution of the occluded Dalit community has to be welcomed as the essential process of democracy. On the other hand, those who continue to see such attempts as communal/sectarian take a twisted view of literary history.

Let us also examine the caste questions raised by literary histories. Ulloor's exemplary Malayalam literary history is well-trained in the art of detecting the caste of most writers. Such an approach, generally adopted by other literary histories also, describes caste as a Keralite's history and inscribes it as a sign of poetry as well. But how can caste be an important criterion in textual analyses by literary histories which simultaneously claim to espouse secularism and place themselves as being above caste, creed, and religious considerations? While writing about Ezhuthachan, why does it bother the historian whether he is a son of a Namboodiri or not? In short, apart from unearthing the caste, religion, region, father, political party, god, etc. of the author, our literary histories have not made any significant leap. Moreover, when it is a 'lower'-caste author, literary histories become contradictory, often discourteous, if not offensive.

About Pandit K.P. Karuppan, Ulloor observes: 'Overall his style is brilliant. Very rare are verses without merit. A highly talented poet is evident in each of his works.'* On the other hand, Leelavathy judges Karuppan in a very negative manner. Not only does Leelavathy who usually uses emotionally charged comparisons become toneless in her description of Karuppan, she also belittles him 'as a poet who cannot lay claim to any greatness though he has more than 10–20 works to his credit'.† It should be remembered that Leelavathy, in the same text, advocates: 'Literary history is not a catalogue of books. It should be able to examine the real blood connection between social life and the literary work, describe its stylistic features, offer a critical appreciation based on an in-depth analysis' (1996, p. 8). Observe how the claims of such aesthetic–historical projects become hollow before Karuppan, whose poetry was a social weapon, to the extent that Swadeshabhimani Raamakrishna Pillai made fun of Karuppan's poetry saying it smelt of fish! The face of literary history becomes even more sullied when we understand how these same literary histories eulogized Manipravala poetry, which basically extolled the mental decadence and historical

---

* Ulloor, *Kerala Literary History* (Publications Department, University of Kerala, 1990).
† *Malayala Kavitha Sahithya Charithram* (1996, p. 162).

discontents of the brahminical caste. Moreover, a commonsensical notion of beauty and merit as a simple and self-evident attribute, outside of history, is unashamedly latent in all such writings.

History writing is also marketing. It was the 'upper'-caste market of Indian literature which determined the acceptability of a Dalit. The blueprint of 'upper'-caste markets are the literary histories. Kerala's literature and its history are also the constructs of the 'upper'-caste market, where the tragic beauty of social survival, in all its squalor and splendour, is considered counterfeit. Literary history reveals, not facts, but attitudes. The democratization of literary history occurs not when the sincerity of the writer is unquestionable but when the writer is able to accept the possibility of literary histories from diverse perspectives. It is not a question of the sincerity of Govinda Pillai or Ulloor. The problem before literary history writing is the social right of every community and even every individual for self-determination. Hence, the Dalit perspective on literary history is also a decolonization of *savarna* sensibilities.

Let me conclude with Ellis Cashmore's idea in *The Black Culture Industry*: 'That for the white, the only difference between a black Olympic champion and a black cobbler is that while the cobbler is just a clown, the Olympic champion is a 'fast' clown.' Those who are not in history, hence, have to interpret it anew.

—*Translated by M.T. Ansari and P. Shyma*

The Issue of Self-liberation*

Lovely Stephen

The status of an individual in Kerala society is based on two factors: caste and gender. Access to knowledge, wealth, and power depend on these factors. Reactions on issues and their analysis are also based on the same two factors.

Fifteen years ago in our Kurichi village, a Dalit student by name Amminikutty was raped and murdered. She had gone at dusk to buy mango and dried fish and the next morning her body was found hanging from a young coconut tree. The children from the neighbouring school

---

* Original title *Swayam Vimochanithande Prashnam*.

protested by staying away from classes and blocking roads. They demanded that those guilty should be punished. However, the students of the Girls' School at the nearby Mandiram Junction itself did not participate in the protest. The truth of the matter was that the teachers did not allow them to. The reaction of a lady from the area was: 'The cat goes around and creates all kinds of trouble. What can the citizens do?' Within a few days a former non-Dalit student of the same Girls' School, Jolly Mathew, then a college student, was killed in the same manner. On this occasion the teachers of the Girls' School took the initiative and called a huge protest meeting at Mandiram Junction. The people from around the area spoke at length on the girl's many fine qualities. Such differences in the reaction are seen all the time in our rural areas. We do not pay attention to these or do not take the trouble to analyse them—or the truth is, we take our time over it.

Let me narrate another incident which happened in our village in 1995. Kurichi is a village where communal strife is common. Conflicts among anti-social elements ending in communal violence were a regular occurrence. Towards the end of 1994 some of these conflicts reached a stage when every dark-skinned man was beaten up on the roads. Dalit men stopped work and stayed at home. Dalit women who took up this issue formed the Dalit Action Council and on 3 January 1995, under its auspices, organized a peace rally and held a public meeting. Hundreds of Dalit women took part in this rally and meeting. The women raised slogans like 'One caste, one religion, one nation for human beings'. It was the women who were in charge of the meeting and the rally. Only then was it possible for the Dalit men to even step out again after a week. Following this, discussions and peace efforts at the government level took place and peace returned. Unfortunately, those in political parties and communal organizations did not take too kindly to this intervention by women. A communist leader, a Dalit, came home and said: 'This was not necessary. There are communal organizations and political parties here. Is it not adequate if they do what is necessary?' When asked whether the women had to act as the others did not, he disagreed saying the women did not have to intervene. I was reminded of Lenin's statement: 'If you scratch a communist, you will find a philistine. But the scratching has to be in a safe place as the reaction is psychological in nature.'

Like any other man a communist also has difficulty in acknowledging a woman's ability and right to deal with matters to do with society and take decisions. They think that her place is within the confines of the family. They advise us that we should vote only for those whom they suggest. They need women comrades only to take part in protest rallies and to cook rice and curry for their conferences. As if women do not have the ability or the right to acquire and practise intellectual skills. The fact is that progress does not apply in the case of women. The men cannot find the time to arm their women's intellect with ideology.

The State planning programme is the latest example. Our panchayats have for many years been run by communists. When a seminar was held in connection with this planning there were only 17 women including ward members among the 300 participants. Nobody saw this as a shortcoming. I find it difficult to imagine that all these comrades had no mothers, sisters, or wives.

A situation exists now in which there is no recognition of the Dalit woman's right to think for herself, organize herself, and liberate herself. Dalit women have always been in the forefront of struggles for their own and public causes but there is no mention of them in the history of any social or women's movement. The Dalit woman does not even seem to have the status of a *woman*. She is for ever dominated by others. In short, in all areas Dalit women appear to have been kept far away from any position of power.

It is in these circumstances that Dalit women are compelled to seek and take the path of liberating themselves and enhancing their knowledge. As far as they are concerned their problems are inextricably and only related to the larger problems of their community.

A survey of 100 Dalit families conducted in 1992 by the Dalit Women's Society pointed clearly towards today's situation. Out of 100 families, 16 have no land of their own. Of those who owned land 24 families have less than five cents. The rest had a maximum of ten cents.

Of the 345 adults 115 in 100 families were without employment, of which 70 are women, 214 are casual labourers, and 11 work in private companies (Travancore Electro Chemicals). Only five are in government service and one of them is a woman. Women make up 82.4 per cent of agricultural labour. They have 60–90 working days. Six are illiterate, 165 have studied up to or below sixth class, 127 have a maximum education of tenth class, and 43 have failed in their pre-degree examinations. Four have gone as far as the degree level, 68 families have no toilet or bath facilities. Not a single house has drainage facilities, 57 families have no drinking water sources of their own, 78 families have no electricity, 95 families do not get newspapers. Only 30 families have radios and two have television sets. Studies conducted in other areas in 1996 only served to strengthen the Kurichi findings. A survey conducted by K. C. Aniyan in 1996 in Karinkal Mata in Perumbayikkat village in Kumaranallur Panchayat covered ten women engaged in menial work and came to the following conclusions:

Three out of ten are illiterate; two have studied up to fourth class and one up to tenth; three have no homes of their own and two have single-room homes; four have two rooms each and one has three rooms; only two families have bath and toilet facilities; none of them has a television or gets newspapers but one has a radio. The men in these families are engaged in the same work and the hardship involved in this work has driven them to smoking, drinking, and gambling. This has cast the domestic responsibilities on the women.

In 1996, K. Appukuttan did a study of ten agricultural workers, all women, in Manjoor village in Kottayam district. The findings of this study showed a remarkable similarity to the findings of earlier surveys. Out of ten families two have no land of their own; nobody among them has over ten cents; only eight have their own homes; three women out of ten are illiterate; two have studied up to second class and two up to fourth. The highest level of education was sixth class. The academic record of their children is no better. There are no graduates or those studying for a degree. Out of 12 who sat for pre-degree exams one had passed. Of the 17 who completed school education, seven passed SSLC.

This is part of a serial story—part of a story beginning with slavery. This is the story of 67-year-old Kunjamma, daughter of Vezhapra Poliyathara Yohannan of Alappuzha and Kathri, who at the age of 17 married Ennaikachira Etayatiparambil Kunjerukkan. This forms part of the serial. Kunjamma's parents had no land of their own. They lived the life of tillers. 'My parents left for work at dawn. All the work in the fields was done by Pulayas but work is supervised by Ezhavas. Our people made two stupid mistakes. They taught these Ezharas how to work in the fields. They received instructions from us and learnt our work.' An aspect of the caste system can be seen in the fact that there was no job security for those Dalit families who had, for centuries, been field hands. Prohibition which affected the livelihood of those who produced arrack, was offset by government promises of alternative work. Even this would not have been forthcoming had the producers of arrack been Dalits.

Kunjamma entered work in the fields at the age of 13. Three measures of rice were the wages and this was barely enough for two meals. Food was provided in many places and this was given in earthenware pots out in the open. Though there have been changes in this situation there are upper caste people who even today refuse to see Dalits as human beings. The fact that Dalits see themselves as human beings and respond unlike they used to in former times has influenced the intensity of offensive behaviour against them.

Very recently, a Dalit woman, Eliyamma, shared her experience. She accompanied some men to an upper caste home to help with some urgent work. The lady of the house gave Eliyamma coffee in a cup unwashed after the master of the house was served coffee in the same cup. Eliyamma openly discarded that cup and poured out her coffee in another cup which she herself washed.

Kunjamma had six pregnancies. The first ended in the pre-natal death of the baby. The second child died at the age of two of a skin disease. The fourth child died of the same problem when three years old. This shows the pitiable state of the health of the Dalit women and children and the usually indifferent attitude towards them within the families. Childbirth and skin disorders are generally not fatal but they turned out to be so in many Dalit families.

Kunjamma has been staying at home for years, unable to go to work due to ill-health. The family barely survives on the wages which the husband and children earn from menial labour. She applied for the agricultural worker's pension but it was rejected on the grounds that her known income exceeded the prescribed limit. A question which has not been answered is why there should be a prescribed income limit only for the agricultural worker's pension which is intended to offer some support during sickness or age in the lives of these Dalits who sacrificed their years and health working in the fields. It is also not understood why this amount itself is so low. It is not unlikely that in the coming years in changing circumstances there could be fewer Dalit workers available as a result of which there could be a higher pension and no prescribed income limit. Getting the benefits of any Dalit welfare programme is as difficult as winning an obstacle race—there are too many hurdles. When students from upper-caste landowning families are able to get income certificates tailored to suit their needs most of our village officers scrutinize from all angles the yield of a couple of sick coconut trees owned by a Dalit and after complicated mathematical calculations issue certificates which show a decent but non-existent income. The only remedy is to cultivate the awareness of rights and the power to react.

Kunjamma is a Marxist sympathizer and has taken part in many processions. It was mostly Pulaya and Paraya women who participated in these processions. The number of women from other castes like

Ezhavas could be counted on one's fingers. Kunjamma's view is that if all the hardships faced so far were to be taken into account, the benefits have not been commensurate.

As in the case of any individual in society her history plays a large part in determining the social status of the Dalit woman also. What is the history of the Dalit woman? What is her heritage? Her heritage is her slavery. Her ancestors have been through a period in which they could be bought or sold at will. She has been denied the right to live with her family. She had no power or right over anything and is therefore invisible in history. The reason is that written history begins and continues on the basis of stories sourced from those who wield power. This is why a Dalit woman has never been projected as an image of the Kerala woman. Even progressive historians begin their history of women's movements with references to the problems of Namboodiri women. That is why the low caste women who fought for their right to wear a top cloth and the Dalit women who discarded their kallumala do not find places in history. That is why the Dalit woman who paid the toll by cutting and offering her own breast does not appear in history. That is also why the two-piece set *mundu* (dhoti and top cloth) which have recently become the dress of the upper-caste woman has been depicted as the traditional dress of all Kerala woman.

Slavery is the heritage of the Dalit woman and hers alone. Caste-related harassment is her experience and hers alone. The consequences of these two realities are also her experience and hers alone. All historical compositions and agitations for women's rights which hide and ignore the above are biased and incomplete.

As mentioned earlier the factors that play a decisive role in understanding and dealing with women's problems are caste, wealth, power, knowledge, and gender status. The interplay of these factors obstructs the growth of a women's movement. When faced with women's problems the questions raised are: 'What caste is she?' and 'What are her financial circumstances?'

The only women's movement which can find an answer to all these problems is the one that presents a united front pledged to the cause of the tormented and those subjected to communal harassment. The Dalit women have a decisive role in putting together such a movement. The first condition for this is that Dalit women should begin to acknowledge and respect each other. They have to exit the world of self-justification and create a heaven for themselves. They have to discard the upper-caste attitude of 'I do everything, I am the only one who can do it, everything is possible only under my auspices'. The roots of the slave mentality have to be severed. Disrespect towards one's own caste has to end. We have to firmly believe and loudly declare that we are also human beings, that we also deserve equality and religious equity, that this world belongs to us also and that we have the right to make it better.

We have to investigate whether it is an awareness helpful to the cause of liberation that drives the Dalit woman. We must also participate in a move to ascertain if, in political programmes, we are being given the status and rights that help our liberation. We must also have programmes that enhance our awareness and intellect.

Dalit women must establish their own organizations in all parts of the State. They have to study and face their own problems. We have to accept our historical responsibility by engaging in healthy debates on our liberation and joining the mainstream of society. In establishing our rights we would be motivated by the memory of thousands of our mothers and sisters who lost their self-respect.

—*Translated by T.C. Narayan*

Dalit Women and Political Empowerment*

Rekha Raj

During this election, development and participation in political power are as relevant as the discussions on coalition politics and policies. The introductory phase of reservation for women in local self-government institutions is over. Our discussions move beyond the romantic idealization of serving the people to the concepts of power and representation. Dr Ambedkar envisaged political power as an important goal. He recognized it as community power. It was when he demanded political power that Ambedkar faced criticism and challenges from the leadership of the national movement. Rejecting his vision and praxis for total political representation, the national leadership relegated Dalits to the beggars' alms known as reservation. Dalit movements demand that their representation and participation in the micro and macro spheres of power need to be ensured. What determines power is the ability to control and manage resources. This ability is determined by caste and

---

* Original title *Dalit Sthreekalum Rashtriya Adhikaravum*.

gender status. As long as gender and caste fail to remain homogeneous, the relationships produced by it will act differently in different contexts. The power dynamics existing between gender and caste is molecular, complex, and diverse and as a result it is extremely aggressive. Within the caste hierarchy, gender relations vary among various castes. That is, power dynamics work differently in the male–female relationship in different castes. Also, caste relations and their religious and ritualistic moorings make the above scenario more complex. That this complexity will influence political power is inevitable.

The main force of our coalition politics and political parties is the nexus of the middle and upper castes, who dominate resources. They are able to determine their interests and define them as public interests. It is these very interests that decide who rules which part of India, not withstanding the recent differing trends. In other words, what determines political power is their power over discursive systems that are inextricably linked to positions in gender and caste hierarchies. Dalits remain outside the above-mentioned processes. They are not yet become capable of achieving their community requirements.

In the first decades of the 20th century, upper-caste women pointed out that in a patriarchal society, every space sanctioned to men is linked to power, and woman's life is confined within the realm of domesticity. Even as they were subject to gendered oppressions, because of their high caste status, they could exercise limited rights. This is what made the upper caste women more powerful than Dalit men.

While the early women's movements demanded education, freedom of mobility, the women's movements that followed focused on inheritance rights and equality in family. In fact, these demands must be read as demands for an equal share in the resources that had been available to the community as a whole. Only a community that has resources and control over it can claim equal rights when it comes to sharing resources. The issues generated in this manner become universal, and 'the woman' becomes the upper-caste woman, and the 'woman's issues' become the issues faced by the upper-caste women in their families and communities. The representations of this sort marginalize Dalit, adivasi women's identities. The simplification of the term 'woman' results in the suppression of the identities of different groups of women. This suppression is reinforced by communal power dynamics.

These things must be considered while the notion of women's reservation that extends from local self-government institutions to parliament is to be judged. It should not be seen as unnatural that most of those who were elected as women representatives into the local self-government institutions belonged to either upper-caste communities or family members of the male political leaders. Excepting a few women who came to the forefront through political movements, the eligibility of the rest is often decided by communal preferences. Not a single political party is an exception to this. One does not hide the fact that there are many efficient social workers emerging from them. But the approach which considers merit as a community product will in no way be beneficial to women.

Some other women also entered the corridors of power: those elected from the constituencies reserved for scheduled caste women; those unexpected candidates whose candidature is made possible only when general ward becomes reservation wards; those who are unable to even voice their opinion in a panchayat where the president is a former teacher or the grandson of the erstwhile *janmi*. A Dalit woman, whom this author met in connection with a study on decentralization of power, remarked that she had not been able to do anything for her ward in any of the panchayat committees. She further disclosed that no sooner had she begun voicing her opinions than she was neglected by all the members including women representatives. Here one could recall the incident where an Adivasi woman representative from Idukki district was insulted as one who ate bird's eggs. The source of the problem is revealed when one realizes that every panchayat committee is a miniature Kerala that revels in caste and gender hierarchies. One need not go further than this to witness the romantic dream of female bonding fading away and becoming cankerous.

Until a constituency becomes reserved for scheduled caste woman, a Dalit woman is absent from the developmental history of the panchayat. Hitherto no Dalit woman has found a space in the social analysis of the public sphere. Our society demands an immediate recognition that there exist differences among women. This does not imply that other woman representatives do not experience discrimination. On the contrary, there exists a situation outside which helps them survive. Within the scope offered by this structure, the Adivasi woman does not exist as a gendered category, which points to the a-genderization of the Adivasi community.

The above-mentioned scenario is what leads to a critique of the woman's reservation bill which treats all women as a homogeneous entity. One does not reject the concept of reservation for women, rather what is questioned is the way in which it is conceived at present. As long as there exists a simple logic which equates woman with upper caste, it is evident that this bill will not help Dalit, Adivasi women. The deep-rooted casteist consciousness of the average Indian will consider it quietly natural. Unless the Bill ensures separate reservation for Dalit Adivasi Women it will be a mere farce. We will have to wait much longer to listen to different women and their problems in assemblies and parliament.

—*Translated by P.V. Anil Kumar*

Glossary

adiyan	: self-reflexive term denoting low-caste submission.
Abhimanyu	: a character from *Mahabharata*, Arjuna's son.
Adi Cheramars	: argued to be the descendents of the Chera dynasty.
ana	: a coin now in disuse 4 anas = 25 paise.
Aryabharat	: the area of India dominated by the Aryans.
Chakravyuha	: Army arranged in circular form.
chandu	: colour to mark the forehead.
chenda	: a drum suspended with straps from the neck and beaten with a stick and thimbled fingers.
Chengannuramma	: the presiding female deity of the Chengannur temple, the goddess.
Chentamizhu	: classic form of pure Tamil as different from the colloquial varieties like Kadumthamizhu, Karimthamizhu, the standard language during Chera–Chola–Pandya reign (9th–13th centuries AD).
Chera	: one of the three major Tamil kingdoms (Chera, Chola, and Pandya). Cheras are said to have ruled over Kerala for centuries.
chunkam	: toll.
Dharmashastras	: the sacred law books of Hindus.
Dheevaran	: a person of the *Dheevara* community customarily associated with fishing.
edathi	: elder sister or sister-in-law.
illam	: a Brahmin house. It has mythical associations with *yakshis* and other supernatural beings.
Kaala	: messenger of Death.
Kakkan/Kakathi	: men and women of Kurava sub-caste.
kalam	: ceremonial drawing on the ground made with coloured powders and over which rituals are performed.
Kali	: the fierce aspect of Devi, the Divine feminine.

Kaniyan	: a person belonging to the *Kaniyan* community, known for skill in astrology, traditional medicine, etc.
kanji	: rice gruel popular in Kerala.
Kannaki	: a legendary Tamil woman and central character of the Tamil epic *Silapathikaram*, who is now worshipped as a goddess of chastity.
Karkadakam	: last month in the Kollam era (Malayalam calendar) from July to August. It is also known as the Ramayanam month when elder members of Hindu families read aloud from the Ramayana.
karyasthan	: the manager of a wealthy household and property.
kaalakoodam	: in Hindu mythology the deadly poison that God Shiva is believed to have swallowed to save the world.
kollan	: community of blacksmiths.
koothu	: a classical solo theatre-art form.
kovilakams	: term for upper-caste feudal house holds. These were also centres of knowledge and art as they were patrons of art and artists.
koyithamburan	: upper-caste aristocrat.
kuruthi	: blood sacrifice.
maadambi	: a feudal lord.
Maanatthe Vellitheru and *Chandralekha*	: films dealing with unnatural, unrealistic plot, characters, and experiences.
maash	: anglicized Malayalam for master; a common form of address for teachers in Kerala.
Mahar	: the largest low-caste group in the Indian state of Maharashtra.
Mammad	: a local version of the name Muhammad.
Manipravalam	: literary style used in ancient and medieval liturgical texts composition combining phrases in Malayalam and Sanskrit in an aesthetic pleasing manner.
Mappilappattu	: a popular song genre associated with the *Mappila* (Muslim) community of Malabar.
Marmam	: as per ancient medicinal system, vital/mystic points in the human body; touching a marma point in the body is said to change the body's

		biochemistry and can unfold radical alchemical changes in one's make-up.
Maveli/Mahabali	:	the legendary king of Kerala, noted for his benign rule and generosity, whose return from the netherworld to visit his subjects every year is celebrated as Onam.
Mulleli thylam	:	a specific herbal preparation to be rubbed on the body for rejuvenation.
mundu	:	a waist-cloth reaching down to the ankles. A shorter version of the same around the shoulder at times (melmundu).
muram, vatti	:	containers, sieves, etc. made of bamboo.
muthalali	:	commonly used for a rich man or an employer.
Muthan kavu	:	small shrine to Muthan, the deity of paraya community.
nam, nom	:	self-reflexive pronouns used by namboodiris and royal class.
neerattu	:	the elaborate bathing ritual of the royal class.
Niranamkrithikal	:	poetical works (1350–1450 AD) of Madhava Panikkar, Sankara Panikkar, and Rama Panikkar, of Niranam village.
njattu song	:	songs sung during paddy planting
naazhika	:	a measure of time (equal to 24 minutes).
Onam	:	the harvest festival of Kerala which usually falls in September.
ottamthullal	:	a popular solo performing art, introduced by Kunchan Nambiar in the 18th century, as an alternative art form to Chakyarkoothu, a show that satirize prevalent socio-political equations and prejudices of the region.
paala	:	a tall tree with a wide canopy, commonly found in Kerala
Paanan pattu	:	popular songs of the *Paanan* community.
Paanan, Pulaya	:	different sub-sects of low castes in Kerala.
padinjatta	:	a hall/space on the west-side of a house.
pallikuruppu	:	the royal sleeping routine.
panam	:	a unit of currency in Travancore. A silver coin of panam = 16 kaasu. Kaasu is the smallest unit of money.

panchayat	: a local self-governing body.
pappadavadas	: a simple snack made from rice flour and gram flour; which was common in tea shops of Kerala.
Parayan pattu	: ritualistic songs of the *Paraya* community.
Party	: refers to the Communist Party.
podi parayas	: a section of parayas. Usually, they are classified according to their jobs.
palam	: ten tholas—one thola is a weight of a silver rupee about 12 g.
paranki	: Portuguese.
pudava	: wedding garment given by the groom to the bride, one of the tokens of marriage among upper-caste Hindus.
Pulaya	: one of the lower castes.
Pulaya/Paraya	: lower castes.
Pulayan pattu	: ritualistic songs of the *Pulaya* community.
Puranas	: literally, 'stories of old'. Religious works of Hinduism containing legendary and mythological versions of creation, history, and destruction of the universe with its divine, human and subhuman.
raan	: customary expression of lower-caste compliance.
saadhu	: a renunciate.
saamanthar	: feudal lords under the jurisdiction of a royal king.
savarnas	: those who fall within the varna system consisting of four major castes. Untouchables fall outside this system and are termed outcastes, avarnas.
Sheelavathi	: a woman celebrated in Indian mythology as a symbol of chastity.
thamber	: a percussion instrument.
thampuran	: upper-caste aristocrat.
thampuratti	: term used in the past to address a feudal/upper-caste woman
Thiruvonam	: the penultimate day during the Onam (harvest) festival.
Thullal	: a traditional folk dance.
Vamana	: The fifth incarnation of Mahavishnu, as a dwarf. To recover the universe from Mahabali, a ruler famed for his generosity, Vishnu gets the boon

he asks for: as much land as he could cover in three steps. Vishnu changes into a gigantic figure, covers the heavens and earth in two strides and places his third step on Mahabali's head, pushing him to the nether world.

vayapirapithi and therrani : contracts of slave bondage.

Vedan pattu : popular songs of the *Vedan* community.

Vedas : the sacred scriptures of Hinduism composed in Sanskrit and regarded as divine revelation comprising the four Vedas—Rig, Sama, Yajur, and Atharva—the Brahmanas or priestly treatises, the Aranyakas or 'forest' books, and the Upanishads, philosophical or mystical treatises.

Zamorin : *Samorin* or *Saamoothiri*; title of the erstwhile rulers (12th–18th centuries AD) of north Kerala, with Kozhikode (Calicut) as capital.

Note on Authors

POIKAYIL APPACHAN (1879–1939), also known as Poikayil Sree Kumara Gurudevan/Poikayil Yohannan, was born at Eraviperoor, Pathanamthitta district. His parents who belonged to the Paraya community were slaves at Sankaramangalam, a prominent Christian household at Eraviperoor. After completing his primary education, Poikayil tended cattle and worked in the fields. At 17 he sought baptism and joined the Mar Thoma Church, but soon realized that the Bible was not a way of salvation for Dalits. He even set a copy of the Bible on fire. He was an eloquent writer and a prolific orator and poet. *Ratnamanikal* is a compilation of his poems. Poikayil is the founding father of Prathyaksha Raksha Daiva Sabha (PRDS), following which he came to be known as Sree Kumara Gurudevan.

RAGHAVAN ATHOLI (1957–), the gifted artist who juggles with various mediums of expression is the most prolific among contemporary Dalit writers in Malayalam and is a poet, sculptor, painter, cartoonist, novelist, and activist, associated with the rise of the Dalit movement in Malayalam literature. Since his first collection of poems in 1996, he has published another five volumes. His novel *Choraparisam* (2006) won him the prestigious Basheer Award. He has also received accolades for his works in sculpture from the Kerala Lalithakala Akademi Award in 2004 and the Kerala International Arts Festival Award in 2003. A great influence on contemporary Dalit poets, he was a member of the Lalithakala Akademi and has a collection of sketches and cartoons. His poems have been translated into many languages. His poetry collections are: *Kandathi* (1996), *Mozhimattam* (1998), *Kalladuppukal* (2003), *Mounasilakalude Pranayakurippukal* (2004), *Kanalormakal* (2007), *Kathunna Mazhakal* (2007), *Chavumazhakal* (2008). His novels are: *Choraparisam, Mankolangal,* and *Kaliyattam* (2006).

C. AYYAPPAN (1949–2011) who retired as the Principal of Malappuram Government College, challenged the existing notions of aesthetics and created his own landscapes through short stories. He occupies a distinctive space in Dalit literature and believes that the hegemony of the upper caste dismantles the aspirations of Dalits. His stories depict the realities of Dalit life, its dilemma, and agony. His books are: *Uchayurakkathile Swapnangal* (1987), *Njandukal*, and C. *Ayyappante Kathakal* (2008). He is the recipient of the Sahitya Akademi Award in 2007.

K.K. BABURAJ (1961–) is a pioneering Dalit cultural critic, who used the framework of postmodernism to understand hegemonic politics, culture, and power relations. His works critically approach the colonialism of the East and the West as well as subaltern and Marxist readings. Baburaj is currently working at Mahatma Gandhi University, Kottayam. His prominent works are: *Paul M. Sweesi: Samrajyathinteyum Fascisathinteyum Mukhangal, Mattarujeevitham Saadhyamaanu, Yudhathinte Mukham* (a translation), and *Viswasavum Janathayum* (ed.).

T.H.P. CHENTHARASSERI (1928–) from Pattom, Thiruvananthapuram, is the pen name of T. Heera Prasad, a well-known historian. He pioneered the documenting of Dalit history, at a time when subaltern historiography was in its infancy. His first book *Kerala Charithrathinte Ariyapedatha Edukal* was published in 1970; it challenged the Brahminical myth of the Parasurama story and placed the Dalit community as the focal point of Kerala history. His other works on historiography are: *Kerala Charithra Dhara* (1978), *Cheranadu Charithra Sakalangal* (1980), *Kerala Charithrathinoru Mukavura* (1987), *Ilamkulavum Charithravum* (1988), and *Aadi Indiyarude Charithram* (1998). His magnum opus is in the field of biography. He wrote biographies of Ayyankali, Pampady John Joseph, Poikayil Sree Kumara Gurudevan, et al. His books in English are: *Ayyankali: The First Dalit Leader* (1996), *History of Indigenous Indian* (1998), *Dr Ambedkar on some Aspects of the History of India* (2000), which won the Ambedkar International Literary Award in 2000.

PAUL CHIRAKKARODE (1939–2008), born to a Dalit preacher at Maramon village near Thiruvalla, began his career as an advocate and later entered mainstream politics. A well-known social activist and the founder of the Dalit Christian movement in Kerala, he is a prolific writer and has a huge corpus of books to his credit; *Dalit and the Left* and *The Subaltern Uprisings* are his books in English. This most respected Dalit writer's prominent works are: *Mathilukal, Nizhal, Velicham, Ekanthathayude Dweep, Udatham, Ooshara Bhumi, Pulayathara, Nyasanam, Parudeesa* (novels); *Olichu Pokunna Mankoonakal, Nananja Bhoomi* (short stories); *Tagore, David Livingstone, Ambedkar* (biographies); *Dalit Christians, Dalit Kavitha, Dalit Sahityam* (critical studies); and *Poona Pact* (translation).

K.K.S. DAS (1946–) from Kottayam reveals strong socio-political concerns in his poetry and has even been jailed for protesting for freedom of artistic expression. A writer since 1967, he first worked as a teacher. He was a member of the Director Board of Kerala Bhasha Institute and Resident Editor of *Seediyan*. He has published several collections of poetry, a few of them being *Malanadinte Mattoli* (1967), *Karumadi Nritham* (1975), and *Noottandukalkku Marupadi* (2002). His other works are: *Dalit Deshiyatha* (2002), *Yuddavum Aagolavalkaranavum* (2002), *Marxisavum Ambedkar Chinthayum* (2010), and *Dalit Janathayude Swathantryam* (2010).

K.K. GOVINDAN (1921–77), an acclaimed poet and social worker, was the founder of the Ambedkar Study Circle and the Kerala Hindu Mission. He was from Kumbazha, Pathanamthitta district. His prominent works are: *Duravasthayile Prameyam* (literary criticism), *Apprasather, Ayitham, Ethiruppu, Arukolakkandam* (poems), *Ente Samudayam* (short stories).

ELIKULAM JAYAKUMAR (1963–) who works at Mahatma Gandhi University, is from Kottayam. He is the recipient of the 1999 Bharathiya Sahitya Akademi's Ambedkar Fellowship. His major contribution is the biography of Kallara Sukumaran which serves as a historical document. *Globalization and Dalits* (essays) and *Teacher Ammayude Banu* (a novel for children) are his other works.

S. JOSEPH (1965–), a poet with four acclaimed collections of poems to his credit, is from Pathanamthitta. His poetry has been translated into Swedish, English, Hindi, Tamil, Kannada, and Bengali. His poems are also included in the syllabi of various universities in Kerala. He is the recipient of the Kanakasree Award from the Kerala Sahitya Akademi. His second and third books were on the shortlist of the best Malayalam books of the year. His most recent volume *Uppante Kooval Varakkunnu* (2009) won the Thiruvananthapuram Book Fair Award for one of the ten best books of the year 2009. He has also published articles on painting and poetry in noted journals. His collections of poems are: *Karutha Kallu* (2000), *Meenkaran* (2003), *Identity Card* (2005), and *Uppante Kooval Varakkunnu* (2009). He has published a novel for children: *Pulariyile Moonu Thengukal* (2006) and is presently working as assistant professor of Malayalam at Maharaja's College, Ernakulam.

S. KALESH (1983–) is from Kunnamthanam, Pathanamthitta district. He graduated in mathematics from Mar Thoma College, Thiruvalla and postgraduated from School of Technology and Applied Sciences, Mahatma Gandhi University and took a Diploma in Journalism from Press Academy, bagging the Best Journalism Student Award. He has been writing poetry from 1999 and has published in leading journals and periodicals. The awards that came his way are: Prize for Versification in 2003 Youth Festival of Mahatma Gandhi University, Ankanam Kavitha Puraskaram in 2004, Madhyamam/Velicham Kavitha Puraskaram in 2005, and Atlas Kairali TV Kavitha Award for two consecutive years in 2005 and 2006. He is at present working as a journalist in Cochin. His first book of poetry is *Hairpin Bend* (2011).

SUNNY KAVIKKAD (1962–) from Madhuraveli, Kottayam district, is an activist and poet. *Padiyirangunnu* is his first publication of 26 poems, followed by *Baliyadukalude Velipadukal*. He has also published two novels *Nilathezhuthukal* and *Viswasathinte Porulukal*.

SUNNY M. KAPIKKAD (1964–) a postgraduate in philosophy from Kakkara, Kottayam district, is a reputed social thinker, Dalit activist-writer, and editor. He co-edited *Seediyan* and wrote important articles. He has published books like *Haindava Fasisathinte Vipal Soochanakal*, *Deshiya Pourathwam Oru Dalit Vimarshanam*, and contributed articles such as *Dalit Rashtriyathinte Jaiva Parinamangal*. He works in the Life Insurance Corporation of India, Aattingal branch.

K.K. KOCHU (1949–) from Kallara in Kottayam district started his career in the Kerala State Road Transport Corporation (KSRTC) but left to become the pioneer editor of the first Malayalam Dalit magazine *Seediyan*. A well-known social activist and writer, as well as a social critic, he wrote a number of articles in leading Malayalam periodicals. His book *Vayanayude Dalit Padam* explores the politics of language and how hegemonic societies used language as a tool to subjugate marginalized communities. His major works are: *Kalapavum Samskaravum*, *Ambedkar Jeevithavum Dauthyavum* (ed.), and *Vaayanayude Dalit Paadangal*. A book in the making is *A Critique of Kerala History: The Dalit Perspective*. This ex-Naxalite leader is a strong and eloquent presence in the socio-cultural debates of Kerala representing an alternative Dalit perspective. He makes meaningful and creative interventions in Kerala's Dalit/Aadivasi land rights struggles and other socio-political issues.

TAHA MADAYI (1973–) is a freelance journalist/writer and biographer from Kannur district. He began contributing to *Balapankthi* of *Mathrubhumi* weekly and has gone on to author many articles on significant topics, which appeared in leading Malayalam journals. He was instrumental in making visible Dalits and other marginalized groups through the literary genre of life-writing and has also published his interviews with many celebrities. He has made six documentary films and short films. He has presented cultural programmes both on Akashavani and TV. His major works are: *Deshame Deshame Ivarude Jeevitha Varthamanam Kelkku, Nagna Jeevithangal, Jeevitham/Mamukkoya–Kozhikode, Daivathinum Kadalinum Madhye, Asokachottile Kunjunni, Zackaria Vaathil Thurakkunnu, Adikaram Anuragam Aatmarahasyangal, Abuvinte Lokam, Shareeram Chila Pularkala Swapnangal, Jeevitham Padunna Gramaphone,* and *Priayappetta Sambhashanangal.* He wrote the biographies of Kallen Pokkudan, Fabi Basheer, Dr B. Abdulla, et al., and edited the books *Namboothiri, Shaishavam,* and *Kathakalathisadaram.* His latest work is on the poet A. Ayyappan: *Kanneerinte Kanakku Pusthakam* (2011). His book *Mamukkoya* (2007) won him the Best Book Award at the International Book Fair in Thiruvananthapuram, as also the Malayala Manorama Editor's Choice Award and *Basheerinte Ediye* in their respective years of publication (2009).

G. SASI MADHURAVELI (1959–2002) from Kottayam district started writing in the 1980s. His work, a milestone in the progression of the new genre of Dalit poetry, tackled among other things the controversial topic of the conversion of Dalits. His poems were published in periodicals like *Adhasthita Navothana Munnani Bulletin,* and *Yukthirekha, Samakaleena Kavitha.* In 2002, he committed suicide in a bout of depression. In 2001, his poems were published in a collection entitled *Balikkakka.*

M.K. MADHUKUMAR (1966–) from Kumbanad in Pathanamthitta district holds a diploma in Civil Engineering and works as assistant engineer in Kerala State Electricity Board at the Research and Dam Safety wing of the Idukki Hydroelectric Project, Idukki. He has published *Palakkunnante Yathra, Pothenkeri Gramathinte*

Kadhayakoramukhan, Viswasikal Yathra Cheyyumbol, all collections of short stories.

M.B. MANOJ (1972–) has a doctoral degree from Mahatma Gandhi University. He is from Idukki district and works as a Guest Lecturer in Malayalam at Mahatma Gandhi University, Kottayam. He has to his credit three collections of poetry: *Ente Kootare Ithu Mookamanu, Koothanthathayude Ezhupathu Varshangal,* and *Kaanunnilloraksharavum.* He is the co-editor of *Writing in the Dark,* an anthology of Dalit poetry writings. He has also brought out studies on literary criticism such as *Dalit Padanangal* (2008) and a collection of essays *Aadarsham, Adrushyam, Ezhuthu, Avastha* (2008). He is a recipient of the Konatu Publication Award and AKPCTA Poetry Award (2001), Caravan Cultural Award (2005), Kanakasree Award from Sahitya Akademi (2010) for his collection of poems *Kaanunnilloraksharavum.*

SANAL MOHAN (1961–), an academic and writer, he is from Parakkappara, Kannur district. At present he is an associate professor at the School of Social Sciences, Mahatma Gandhi University, Kottayam. He schooled in St. Thomas Upper Primary and High School, in Karikottakari and graduated from Nirmalagiri College, Koothuparamba. His postgraduation and M.Phil. are from the Department of History, University of Calicut and Ph.D. from Mahatma Gandhi University, Kottayam. He has several significant articles to his credit in the *Journal of South Asian Studies and South Asia Research.* He is a fellow of the Centre for Studies in Social Sciences, Kolkota; Charles Wallace India Fellow in History; fellow of School of Orient and African Studies, University of London; fellow of NASSEY University, New Zealand (Social Anthropology); Fellow (Colonial and Post-Colonial Studies/RDI Visiting Fellow Amory University, Atlanta, USA. He has published *History in the Vernacular* (2008) and *Modernity of Slavery: Struggles Against Caste Inequality in Colonial India* (2011).

KAVIYOOR MURALI (1931–2001) from Thiruvalla, Pathanamthitta district was a committed Dalit scholar, activist, and folklorist who dedicated his life to Dalit causes. A Communist Party member, he started his career as a teacher in 1957 and later joined the Public Works Department from where he retired. He was the first writer to initiate research in Dalit history and writings. He started his career as a writer in 1946. His literary pursuits were a fight against the hegemonic notions of literature and he provided an alternative perspective to Kerala's literary history. He was a recipient of the Bharathiya Dalit Sahitya Academy fellowship. His literary contributions include several poems, 16 plays among which *Mathilkettu* won the SC/ST Development Department Award. His contributions to the field of Dalit language and history are invaluable. He compiled a Dalit dictionary, which was published posthumously. *Dalit Sahityam* (2001) is a comprehensive history of Malayalam Dalit literature. Notable amongst his works are: *Vayalchullikal, Darsanam, Dalitharkkezhuthiya Suvisesham* (poems), *Puranannooru: Oru Padanam, Dalit Bhasha* (a study), *Dalit Sahityam* (a study), *Munisanka* (autobiography), *Velultha* (poems unpublished), *Sugandhi* (novel unpublished), *Njekkuvilakku* (essays unpublished).

BINU M. PALLIPAD (1974–) from Haripad, has been writing poems since 1991 and publishing regularly in Malayalam periodicals and journals. He is a gifted flutist who was part of an all India tour accompanying Baul singers from West Bengal and is currently working in Thekkady. His first publication of poems is *Palette* (2009). He has also translated an *Anthology of Tamil Poems* by N. D. Rajkumar into Malayalam.

PRADEEPAN PAMPIRIKUNNU (1969–) is Reader in Malayalam at the Koyilandi Centre of Sree Sankaracharya Sanskrit University. His doctoral degree is in Dalit reading of Kerala culture and literature. An active Dalit critic and writer, he has published widely in journals and periodicals. His publications are *Dalit Padanam Swathwam, Samskaram Saahityam* (2007), *Dalit Paathakal, Keralam Naalvazhikal,* and *Indian Soundarya Sasthra Vimarsham*. Awards like the N. V. Smaraka Vaijnanika Award (2010), and the Sukumar Azhikode Endowment have come his way.

VELAYUDHAN PANIKKASSERI (1934–) worked as the Librarian of Engandiyoor Local Library from 1956 to 1991. He has nearly 20 books to his credit. Panikkasseri is a well-known historian. His notable works are: *Keralam 600 Kollam Munpu, Keralam Pathinanchum Pathinarum Noottandukalil, Sancharikalulm Charithrakaranmarum,* and *Ayyankalimuthal V. T. Vare*.

KALLEN POKKUDAN (1937–), whom comrade A. K. Gopalan referred to as 'Harijan Cub', was the third son of Aringalayam Parotty and Kallen Vellachi. He was born in Ezhom Panchayat. A class two dropout, he joined the Communist Party at 18 and was jailed for his involvement in peasant strikes. In the 1970s, he gradually withdrew from active party politics and involved himself in environmental issues to which he became deeply committed. He planted thousands of mangroves in the coastal belt. He was awarded the 2001 P. V. Thampi Environment Award, Bhoomi Mitra Puraskara of Aluva Paristithi Sangham, special award from World Vision School of Moral Education, and Kerala Government's Vanamithra Puraskaram of 2006. His autobiography *Kandal Kadukalkkidayile Ente Jeevitham* is an in-depth representation of Dalit life experiences.

P.K. PRAKASH (1974–) from Piravam is a postgraduate and M.Phil. in Malayalam Literature who sells lottery tickets in Ernakulam. He completed his education from Government UP School, Kakkad; Government High School, Piravam; Maharaja's College, Ernakulam; and University College, Thiruvananthapuram. Prakash has written a few short stories which were published in the magazine *Soochakam*.

SIVADAS PURAMERI (1966–) from Purameri, Kozhikode district teaches in the Government High School. His first collection of poems *Chornnolikkunna Muri* won him the Professor Joseph Mundsseri Award in 2004. He also got the N. N. Kakkad Smaraka Sangham Award and Adyapaka Kala Sahitya Samithi State Poetry Award. His second collection of poems *Chila Tharam Viralukal* was published in 2007. Through his poetry Purameri resists both selective memory and amnesia about the past.

REKHA RAJ (1978–) from Athirampuzha, Kottayam district is presently working as the State Co-ordinator of the Centre for Advocacy and Research at Cochin, an organization working on Urban Poverty issues. She has degrees in Philosophy and researches at the School of International Relations and Politics, Mahatma Gandhi University, on the topic Politics of Gender and Dalit Identity: Representation of Dalit Women in Contemporary Kerala Discourses. Occasionally she writes jointly with M. R. Renukumar.

D. RAJAN (1932–90) is the pen name of Ebenezer David from Kattakada, Thiruvananthapuram district. An orator with a deep knowledge of philosophy, he graduated as a private candidate and worked as a primary school teacher. Rajan who began writing in the 1950s shot into prominence, but for unknown reasons disappeared from the literary scene after some time. He wrote short stories and a novel *Mukkani* before he passed away.

K.T. REJIKUMAR (1973–) from Kottayam is doing his doctoral degree at the School of International Relations, Mahatma Gandhi University, Kottayam on Human Rights in Iran and is Guest Faculty as well. He has many published articles in leading journals and edited books. His works are *Sree Kumara Guru Charithrarekhayil* and *Adima Vyapara Nirodhana Charithravum Pradhanyavum*.

M.R. RENUKUMAR (1969–) is a poet and prize-winning artist from Kottayam, and has three collections of poems *Keninilangalil, Veshakkaya,* and *Pachhakuppi* (2011). He publishes literary and cultural articles about Dalits in Kerala. He both illustrates and writes stories, particularly for children. He has published an anthology of stories for children entitled *Naalam Classile Varaal* (2008) and a biographical sketch of Poikayil Yohannan for children and also translated a graphic novel *Bhimayana: Experiences of Untouchability* into Malayalam. He is currently engaged in translating a biography of Ambedkar into Malayalam. With MA and M.Phil. degrees in Economics, Renukumar works as a Senior Grade Auditor in Local Funds Audit Department. He was 'Kalaprathiba' of Mahatma Gandhi University in 1994. His *Keninilangalil* won the Kaavyavedi Award in 2006 and *Veshakkaya,* State Bank of Travancore Puraskar in 2009. *Naalam Classile Varaal* bagged the Balasahitya Award for the Best Children's Literature (2010). Occasionally, he co-publishes with Rekha Raj.

A. SANTHAKUMAR (1965–) is a full-time theatre artist from Kozhikode. He has 36 plays to his credit, most of which are about people from the fringes of society, and he was an elected Panchayat member. He is the recipient of several awards: Kerala Sahitya Akademi Award for his play *Perumkollan* (1999); Kerala Sangeetha Nataka Akademi Award (2000); Nilambur Balan Puraskaram for his contribution to drama (2000); Thoppil Bhasi Award (2002); Best Drama Book Endowment Award by Kerala Sahitya Akademi (2003); Best Children's Drama Award by Kerala Sangeetha Nataka Akademi (2004); Atlas Endowment of Kairali TV (2006); Kerala Sahitya Akademi Award for the play *Maram Peyyunnu* (2010); and P. M. Thaj Deshiya Nataka Rachana Award for *Oru Desam Nuna Parayannu* (2010). His major plays are: *Perumkollan, Otta Rathriyude Kaamukimar, Sowarganuragikalkkuvendi Avasana Chumbanam, Swapnavetta, Maram Peyyunnu,* and *Oru Desam Nuna Parayunnu*.

A. SOMAN (1955–2001) who died young was a lecturer in English at the Government Arts and Science College, Kozhikode, a Dalit culture and art critic, and a Naxalite activist. He authored *A Somante Vimarshana Lekhanangal* and *Chodyangal Idapedalukal* (2002).

LOVELY STEPHEN (1957–) from Kottayam district took her postgraduate degree in Social Work from Loyola College of Social Sciences, Trivandrum, and is currently working at the Kerala State Financial Enterprises Ltd. She is one of the founding members of DWS, a forum for Dalit activists, writers, and intellectuals to debate contemporary issues. She has also worked with the Dynamic Action Group in Thiruvalla as a youth organizer and executive editor of the magazine *Dynamic Action*.

P.A. UTHAMAN (1961–2008) is the pen name of P. A. Purushothaman. He was born at Nedumangadu in Thiruvananthapuram district. He was working in Thiruvalla Travancore Sugars and Chemicals before he joined Kerala State Beverages Corporation. He has to his credit four books and a number of radio plays. His books are: *Sunderapurushanmar, Kavadangalkkarikil, Karutha Kurisu* (short-story collections), and *Chavoli* (novel) which won the Kerala Sahitya Akademi Award posthumously. Yet another novel is the posthumously published *Thuppathuppa* (2011).

T.K.C. VADUTHALA (1921–88) was the pen name of T.K. Chathan from Vaduthala, Ernakulam district. He worked in the All India Radio and Kerala Public Relations District Information Office. He has written and published a number of novels which reflect the inner world of Dalits. His noted works are: *Changalakal Nurungunnu, Nanavulla Mannu*, and *Hrithaya Thudippukal*. He has six anthologies of short stories to his credit. This prolific writer who also served as a member of the Rajya Sabha is historically significant in the trajectory of early Dalit fiction in Malayalam. His stories and novels effectively picturize the angst and trauma of Dalit life.

VIJILA (1981–) from Perambra, Kozhikode district, has degrees from government colleges in Madappally and Perambra. She publishes regularly in journals and magazines. Her first collection of poems *Adukkalayillatha Veedu* appeared in 2006. She is active in progressive Left politics. Her second collection of poems is titled *Amma Oru Kaalpanika Kavithayalla* (2009). She works with Mythri Books, Thiruvananthapuram.

Note on Translators

M.T. ANSARI teaches at the Centre for Comparative Literature at the University of Hyderabad. He edited *Secularism, Islam and Modernity: Selected Essays of Alam Khundmiri* (Sage, 2001) and co-edited *Discourse, Democracy and Difference: Perspectives on Community, Politics and Culture* (Sahitya Akademi, 2010). Apart from a few translations, he also published a book in Malayalam *Malabar History and Literature* (DC Books, 2008).

J. DEVIKA is currently associate professor at the Centre for Development Studies, Thiruvananthapuram, Kerala. She has a doctoral degree in history and is interested in bringing to bear her training as a historian on understanding contemporary shifts in gender, development, politics, and culture in Kerala. She writes in English and Malayalam, translates from Malayalam to English, and blogs on contemporary politics and culture in Kerala on www.kafila.com. Her published translations include *The Autobiography of a Sex Worker* (New Delhi: Westland Books, 2007).

SHIRLY MARY JOSEPH is a free-lance translator (Malayalam–English) and haiku poet. She has translated stories of Paul Chirakkarode, a play by K. J. Baby, and a few articles and children's stories, and collects stories from the oral tradition.

P.V. ANIL KUMAR did his MA in English from Sree Kerala Varma College, Thrissur and M.Phil. from University College, Thiruvananthapuram, and is working toward a Ph.D. in the Department of Studies in English, Thalassery Campus, Kannur University. Currently, he teaches English at Sri C. Achutha Menon Government College, Thrissur.

SAJI MATHEW who holds a doctoral degree in Comparative Literature is an assistant professor in the School of Letters, Mahatma Gandhi University, Kottayam, and is actively involved in literary translation. He has earlier translated into English a novel by the renowned Malayalam writer, Anand under the title, *Vyasa and Vighneswara*. As an academic, he has to his credit a number of presentations and publications in the area of Translation Studies/Theory. His areas of interest include Translation Studies,

Postcolonial Theories, Cultural Studies, and Critical Theology and Religion.

T.C. NARAYAN studied in Madras University and embarked on a successful corporate career in India and abroad. He was a multifaceted sportsman, commentator/contributing producer for All India Radio and visiting lecturer at various corporate and other training institutions. Narayan has published three books. *Ettukettu Stories* (Unisun) describes the lifestyle of a middle-class Kerala family of over seven decades ago. He then translated former President Abdul Kalam's *Mission India* (Penguin) from English to Malayalam. *Lore and Legends of Kerala* (2007, Oxford University Press / Malayala Manorama). He has also translated extended excerpts from *A Midsummer Night's Dream* into Malayalam, used by a travelling RADA performance sponsored by the British Council in 2006.

LEKSHMY RAJEEV *is a poet and journalist working for Niyogi Books as their consultant editor.* Her poems have been published in reputed literary magazines and journals such as *Indian Literature, Deccan Herald Sunday Magazine, Poetry Chain, The Little Magazine*, and websites like www.shakespeares-sonnets.com and www.othervoicespoetry.org. Her trans-lations of Malayalam poetry have appeared in *Samyuktha* (Journal of Women's Studies) and *The Journal of Literature and Aesthetics*; did a monthly column, 'Pebbles' for *Deccan Herald Sunday Magazine*, and was Poetry Editor for the website of The British Council for South Asian Women Writers. She has a volume of poetry out of the Central Sahitya Akademi (2011) entitled *Dusk Diary*. She also writes features in *The Hindu, Indian Express, Sahara Time, Travel X, Kerala Kaumudi*, and *Mathrubhumi*.

E.V. RAMAKRISHNAN is a bilingual writer who has published poetry and criticism in Malayalam and English. He has also translated extensively from Indian languages into English, mostly poetry. Among his works in Malayalam are: *Aksharavum Adhunikatayum* (1994), *Vakkile Samooham* (1997), and *Desheeyatakalum Sahityavum*. In English his prominent works are: *Making It New: Modernism in Malayalam, Marathi and Hindi Poetry, Narrating India: The Novel in Search of the Nation* (ed.), *Terms of Seeing: New and Selected Poems* and *Locating Indian Literature: Texts, Traditions and Translations*. He is a recipient of the Kerala Sahitya Akademi Award for Literary Criticism (1995), K. K. Birla

Foundation Fellowship for Comparative Literature (1997–9), Indian Institute of Advanced Study Fellowship (1992–3), and Fulbright Fellowship (2001). He has been part of the Indian delegation to Moscow in 2010. He is at present Professor and Dean, School of Language, Literature, and Culture Studies at Central University of Gujarat, Gandhinagar.

K. SATCHIDANANDAN who has won 27 literary awards is perhaps the most translated of contemporary Indian poets, with 23 collections in 18 languages including Arabic, French, German, and Italian. His *While I Write: New and Selected Poems* (HarperCollins) was published in 2011. Satchidanandan writes poetry in Malayalam and prose in Malayalam and English and has more than 20 collections of poetry besides several books of travel, plays, and criticism. He has represented India in many Literary Festivals across the world including the Berlin, Sarajevo, Montreal Blue Metrolopis, Jaipur, and Hay, and London, Paris, Frankfurt, and Moscow Book Fairs. He has also been a prolific translator of world poetry into Malayalam (16 collections) and Malayalam poetry into English.

AJAY S. SEKHER is Assistant Professor of English in Government College service, Kerala. His doctoral research deals with the representation of caste and gender margins in postcolonial Indian fiction. Ajay Sekher has published articles and translations on literature and culture in English and Malayalam in leading journals including *The Economic and Political Weekly* (2003 and 2006). He has also taught at Sri Sankaracharya Sanskrit University, Kalady (2004–8) and School of Letters, Mahatma Gandhi University (2008–9). His recent published titles include: *Representing the Margin: Caste and Gender in Indian Fiction* (2008), *Writing in the Dark: A Collection of Malayalam Dalit Poetry* (trans. 2008), *Unknown Subjects: Songs of Poikayil Appachan* (trans. 2007), *Samskaram, Prathinidhanam, Prathirodham: Samskara Rashtreeyathilekkulla Kuripukal* (Malayalam, 2009), *Irutile Kali* (trans. of Morrison's *Playing in the Dark* into Malayalam, 2007), *Neelimayeriya Kannukal* (trans. of Morrison's *Bluest Eye*, 2009), and *Sahodaran Ayyappan: Towards a Democratic Future* (forthcoming).

RAVI SHANKER translates from Malayalam and Tamil and into Malayalam. He has translated works by Dario Fo, Paulo Friere, Freidrich Durrenmatt, Bertolt Brecht, and Badal Sircar into Malayalam as theatre projects and published works. He has written a play *Mritabharatam* in Malayalam. English translations include *Harum Scarum Saar and Other Stories* by Bama (from Tamil) and *Mother Forest: The Unfinished Story of C. K. Janu* by Bhaskaran (from Malayalam) both for Women Unlimited and *Waking is Another Dream*, an anthology of Sri Lankan Tamil poetry (along with Meena Kandasamy). He prepared English subtitles for two Malayalam feature films (*Shayanam* and *Ramanam*) and a Tamil feature film (*Sengadal*).

K.M. SHERRIF translator and translation scholar, writes in Malayalam and English and translates into and between Malayalam, English, Hindi, Gujarati, and Tamil. Among his publications are *Ekalavyas with Thumbs*, the first selection of Gujarati Dalit Writing in English translation and *Kunhupaathumma's Tryst with Destiny*, the first study in English of Vaikom Muhammed Basheer's fiction. He is one of the editors for the Malayalam division of the National Translation Mission and a subject expert in English for the Kerala State Council of Educational Research and Training. Sherrif lives in Kozhikode and teaches English at the University of Calicut.

P. SHYMA is currently a research scholar at the Center for Comparative Literature, University of Hyderabad, working on Malayalam Cinema and its popular spaces. She has an M.Phil. degree and is interested in questions of culture, translation and minorities. Her article "Contesting the Modern: Sreenivasan and ChintavishtayayaShyamala" was published in *Cinemas of South India: Culture, Resistance and Ideology* (OUP, 2010)

ABHIRAMI SRIRAM has degrees in English from Jawaharlal Nehru University and University of Hyderabad. She is an editor with Orient BlackSwan, Chennai.

VALSON THAMPU is the Principal, St Stephen's College, Delhi. A theologian, writer, and peace-activist, he has written extensively on spirituality and religion, politics, and socio-cultural issues. His translated works are K. P. Appan's *Bible: Velichathinte Kavacham* as *Bible: The Armour of Light* (1996) and Sarah Joseph's *Othappu: The Scent of the Other Side* (OUP, 2009) which won a National Award for Translation in 2010 and the same author's *Aathi* (*Gift in Green*, HarperCollins, 2011).

CATHERINE THANKAMMA is a writer and translator. Her Ph.D. was on theatre and social activism. She is the translator of Narayan's *Kocharethi* (The Araya Woman), published by OUP (2011).

A.J. THOMAS writes poetry and fiction in English and translates poetry, fiction and drama from Malayalam into English; writes features and reviews on literary and cultural topics; has several books to his credit. He is a recipient of Katha Award, AKMG Prize, and Hutch Crossword Award. Formerly Editor of Indian Literature, the bimonthly English journal of Sahitya Akademi (National Academy of Letters, India), a spell of teaching English in Garyounis University, Benghazi, Libya, he is serving presently as Guest Editor of the same journal. Anthology appearances include: *The Literary Review: (USA)-Indian Poetry, The HarperCollins Book of English Poetry* by Indians (forthcoming), *Open Space*, Marginalized: India Poetry in English (Rodopi, The Netherlands) etc.

SUSHILA THOMAS teaches English in Naipunnya School of Management, Chertala, Alleppey district, a self financing college, affiliated to the University of Kerala. Her special interests are women's writing and translation studies.

SHREEKUMAR VARMA is the author of the novels, *Lament of Mohini* and *Maria's Room*, and books for children: *The Royal Rebel: Pazhassi Raja, Devil's Garden*, and *The Magic Store of Nu-Cham-Vu* (shortlisted, Crossword Award 2009). His plays include *Bow of Rama, Platform, Midnight Hotel*, and *Five*. His short stories and poetry have appeared in several anthologies. He is the grandson of the late H. H. Sethu Lakshmi Bayi, Regent Maharani of Travancore. He is also a columnist and teacher.

Copyright Statement

Every attempt has been made to trace the copyright holders and obtain reproduction rights. In case of any omissions, please contact Oxford University Press India, so that necessary acknowledgements and corrections could be made in subsequent editions of this book.

The volume editors and the publisher would like to thank the following people and organizations for their permission to reproduce material previously published elsewhere:

Poetry

POIKAYIL APPACHAN, 'Songs', Section (1), (8), and (9) from *Poikayil Appachante Pattukal* (1905–59), edited by V.V. Swamy and E.V. Anil, Sahodaran Publishers, Kottayam, 2006.

K.K. GOVINDAN, 'Killing Field', *Writing in the Dark*, Vikas Adhyayan Kendra, Mumbai, April 2008.

KAVIYOOR MURALI, 'The Gospel for Dalits' (*Dalitharkkezhuthiya Suvisesheam*), Current Books, Kottayam, 1997. Reprinted here with permission from Kaviyoor Murali.

K.K.S. DAS, 'My Soil' ('Ente Mannu'), 'The Black Dance' ('Karumaadi Nritham'), from *Bhashaposhini Dalit Pathippu*, August 1997, Vol. 21, No. 3; *Dalit Kavitha: Dalit Ezhuthukarude Rachanakal*, Kottayam, Dalit Sahitya Vedi, 1996; *Writing in the Dark*, Vikas Adhyayan Kendra, Mumbai, April 2008. Reprinted here with permission from K.K.S. Das.

RAGHAVAN ATHOLI, 'Justice Cooked' ('Neethi Vevichu'), 'Where Hunger is Sold' (Vishappu Vilkunnidam'), from *Chaavumazhakal* (poems) D.C. Books, Kottayam, 2008; *Writing in the Dark*, Vikas Adhyayan Kendra, Mumbai, April 2008. Reprinted here with permission from Raghavan Atholi.

SUNNY KAVIKKAD, 'An Uncharted Map' ('Kanakkukalillatha Bhoopadam'), from *Bhashaposhini Dalit Pathippu*, August 1997, Vol. 21, No. 3. Reprinted here with permission from Sunny Kavikkadu.

G. SASI MADHURAVELI, 'With Love' ('Pranayapoorvam'), 'Mother' ('Amma'), from *Balikkakka* (poems), Samanuaya Books, Kottayam, 2001. Reprinted here with permission from G. Sasi Maduraveli.

S. JOSEPH, 'Group Photo' ('Group Photo'), 'Some Dark Spaces' ('Chila Irunda Idangal'), from *Uppante Kooval Varakkunnu*, D.C. Books, Kottayam, August 2009. Reprinted here with permission from S. Joseph.

SIVADAS PURAMERI, 'Some Kinds of Fingers' ('Chilatharam Viralukal'), from *Chilatharam Viralukal: Kavithakal*, Sign Books, Trivandrum, 2007; 'A Leaky Room' ('Chornolikkunna Muri'), from *Chornalikunna Muri*, Current Books, Thrissur, August 2001. Reprinted here with permission from Sivadas Purameri.

M.R. RENUKUMAR, 'The Silent Beast' ('Mindaprani') and 'The Poison Fruit' ('Vishakkaya'), from *Vishakkaya*, D.C. Books, Kottayam, 2007. Reprinted here with permission from M.R. Renukumar.

M.B. MANOJ, 'Mothers' ('Ammamar'), from *Kanunneeloraksharavum*, D.C. Books, Kottayam, 2007; 'O Ant, O Paddystalk' ('Erumbe Kathare'), from *Chengara Aikyadardya Pusthakom*, edited by T. Mohammed, Solidarity Youth Movement, Kozhikode 2009. Reprinted here with permission from M.B. Manoj.

VIJILA, 'A Place for Me' ('Idam'), from *Adukkalayillatha Veedu*, Indian Truth, Kozhikode, 2006; 'I Can't Grow My Nails' ('Enikku Nakham Neettan Kazhiyilla') and 'Autobiography of a Bitch' ('Oru Pennpattiyude Atmakatha'), from *Amma Oru Kaalpanika Kavithayalla* (poems), Mythri Books, Trivandrum, 2009. Reprinted here with permission from Vijila.

BINU M. PALLIPPAD, 'Six Philosophers Unite to Expel Amavasi from the Play' ('Aaru Darshanikar Chernnu Amaavasiye Natakathilninnu Purathakkunnu'), from *Pachakuthira*, February 2010. Reprinted here with permission from Binu M. Pallippad.

S. KALESH, 'Hairpin Bend', 'Siren', 'Not Because She Felt Like Weeping' ('Karachil Vannittonnum Ayirikilla'), from *Chengara Aikyradardya Pusthakom*, edited by T. Mohammed, Solidarity Youth Movement, Kozhikode, 2009. Reprinted here with permission from S. Kalesh.

Short Fiction

T.K.C. VADUTHALA, 'Changranthi Ada', *Chankraanthiadayum Mattu Pradhana Kathakalum: Navodhana Kathakal*, edited by K.C. Ravikumar, D.C. Books, 2003. Reprinted here with permission from T.K.C. Vaduthala.

PAUL CHIRAKKARODE, 'Nostalgia' ('Grihathurathvam'), *Bhashaposhini Dalit Pathippu*, August 1997. Reprinted here with permission from Paul Chirakkarode.

C. AYYAPPAN, 'Madness' ('Branthu'), from *Njandukal*, D.C. Books, Kottayam, 2003. Reprinted here with permission from C. Ayyappan.

P.A. UTHAMAN, 'The Story of a Sickle' (Oru Pullaruppothiyude Katha'), *Karuthakurisu*, Rainbow Book Publishers, Chengannur, 2006. Reprinted here with permission from P.A. Uthaman.

P.K. PRAKASH, 'Luminous White' ('Veluppu'), *Soochakam Monthly*, Vol. 1, No. 4, December 2001. Reprinted here with permission from P.K. Prakash.

M.K. MADHUKUMAR, 'Palakunnen's Journey', ('Palakunnente Yaatra'), *Soochakam Monthly*, Dalit Aatmiya Pathippu, February 2002. Reprinted here with permission from M.K. Madhukumar.

Excerpts from Novels

T.K.C. VADUTHALA, 'When Shackles Break' (*Changalakal Nurungunnu*), Sahitya Pravarthaka Co-operative Society, Kottayam NBS. Reprinted here with permission from T.K.C. Vaduthala.

D. RAJAN, 'The Festival of Muthan Kavu' (*Mukkani*), Mangala Press, Ernakulam, 1987. Reprinted here with permission from D. Rajan.

PAUL CHIRAKKARODE, 'The Pulaya Ghetto', Pulayathara Sree Narasimha Vilasam Book Depot, Thuravoor. Reprinted here with permission from Paul Chirakkarode.

P.A. UTHAMAN, 'The Death Wail' (*Chavoli*), D.C. Books, Kottayam, 2007. Reprinted here with permission from P.A. Uthaman.

RAGHAVAN ATHOLI, 'Legacy of Blood' (*Choraparisham*), Current Books, Thrissur, 2007. Reprinted here with permission from Raghavan Atholi.

Drama

A. SANTHAKUMAR, 'Dreamhunt' ('Swapnavetta'), from *Karkkadakam* (One-Act Plays), Samudra Publishers, Calicut, October 2000. Reprinted here with permission from A. Santhakumar.

LIFE WRITINGS

Autobiography

KALLEN POKKUDAN, 'Selections from My Life' ('Ente Jeevitham') Kandalkkadukalkkidayil, Sreejith Pokkudan, Biography, forthcoming, typed script Ayitham. Kandal kadum parisithithiyum. Reprinted here with permission from Kallen Pokkudan.

Biography

VELAYUDHAN PANIKKASSERI, 'Excerpts from Ayyankali', from *Ayyankali Muthal V.T. Vare*, Current Books, Kottayam, 2003. Reprinted here with permission from Velayudhan Panikaseri.

K.T. REJIKUMAR, 'Poikayil Sreekumara Guru—A Historical Record', *Poikayil Sreekumara Guru—Charithraruparekhayil Sahodaran Prasidhyam*, Kottayam, 2005. Reprinted here with permission from K.T. Rejikumar.

T.H.P. CHENTHARASSERI, 'Pampadi John Joseph' Backward People Development Corporation, Thiruvilla, 1989. Reprinted here with permission from T.H.P. Chentharaseri.

ELIKULAM JAYAKUMAR, 'Kallara Sukumaran', Ambedkar Publications, Ambedkar Bhavan, Peerumedu, October 2000, Cr S. Jayasree Parackal, Elikulam. Reprinted here with permission from Elikulam Jayakumar.

TAHA MADAYI, 'Adiyar Teacher', from *Desame Desame Evarude Jeevitha Varthamanam Kelkku: Biographical Sketches*, DC Books, Kottayam, 2007. Reprinted here with permission from Taha Madayi.

Critical Interventions

KAVIYOOR MURALI, 'The Uncompromising Dalit Language' ('Sandhi Cheyyatha Dalit Bhasha'), from *Dalit Bhasha* (patanam), Current Books, Kottayam, 1997. Reprinted here with permission from Kaviyoor Murali.

K.K. KOCHU, 'Language and People'('Bhashayum Jannathayum') from *Vayangude Dalit Padam* (essays), Poorna Publications, Calicut, 2005. Reprinted here with permission from K.K. Kochu.

A. SOMAN, 'When the Aristocrats Return' ('Thampurakal Thiruchu Varumpol'), 1998.

SUNNY M. KAPIKKAD, 'Dalit Presence in Malayalam Literature' ('Malayala Sahityathile Dalit Saannidhyam'), from *Bhashaposhini Dalit Pathippu*, August 1997, Vol. 21, No. 3.

SANAL MOHAN, 'Caste and Accumulation of Capital' ('Jaathiyum Mooladhana Roopikaranavum'), from *Dalit Varthamanam*, ed. Rajesh Chirappad, Mythri Books, Trivandrum, 2008. Reprinted here with permission from Sanal Mohan.

K.K. BABURAJ, 'Identity, Alienation, Expression: Dalit Writing in Kerala', in *Mattoru Jeevitham Sadhyamanu*, Subject and Language Press, Kottayam, 2007. Reprinted here with permission from K.K. Baburaj.

PRADEEPAN PAMPIRIKUNNU, 'What Did Literary History Say to You?' ('Sahitya Charithrangal Ningalodu Samsarichethenthu?', from *Maadhyamam Weekly*, 22 February 2002. Reprinted here with permission from Pradeepan Pampirikunnu.

LOVELY STEPHEN, 'Issue of Self-liberation' ('Swayam Vimochanathinte Prashnam'). Reprinted here with permission from Lovely Stephen.

REKHA RAJ, 'Dalit Women and Politics' ('Dalith Sthreekalum Rashtriy Adhikaravum'). Reprinted here with permission from Rekha Raj.